The Orphic Hymns

TRANSLATION, INTRODUCTION, AND NOTES BY

Apostolos N. Athanassakis and Benjamin M. Wolkow

JOHNS HOPKINS UNIVERSITY PRESS   BALTIMORE

Johns Hopkins University Press
2715 North Charles Street
Baltimore, Maryland 21218-4363
www.press.jhu.edu

Library of Congress Cataloging-in-Publication Data

Orphic hymns. English.
The Orphic hymns / translation, introduction, and notes by Apostolos N.
Athanassakis and Benjamin M. Wolkow.
pages. cm.
Includes bibliographical references and index.
ISBN 978-1-4214-0881-1 (hdbk. : alk. paper) — ISBN 978-1-4214-0882-8 (pbk. :
alk. paper) — ISBN 978-1-4214-0886-6 (electronic) — ISBN 1-4214-0881-3
(hdbk. : alk. paper) — ISBN 1-4214-0882-1 (pbk. : alk. paper) —
ISBN 1-4214-0886-4 (electronic)
1. Orphic hymns. I. Athanassakis, Apostolos N. II. Wolkow, Benjamin M.
III. Title.
PA4259.E5 2013
292.3'8—dc23   2012027077

A catalog record for this book is available from the British Library.

*Special discounts are available for bulk purchases of this book. For more informa-
tion, please contact Special Sales at 410-516-6936 or specialsales@press.jhu.edu.*

Johns Hopkins University Press uses environmentally friendly book
materials, including recycled text paper that is composed of at least 30 percent
post-consumer waste, whenever possible.

CONTENTS

PREFACE

 N 1977, Scholars Press (Atlanta, Georgia) published the first edition of *Orphic Hymns: Text, Translation and Notes* by Apostolos N. Athanassakis for the Society of Biblical Literature's Texts and Translations, Graeco-Roman Religion Series. The text used for that edition, as for the present one, is that by Wilhelm Quandt. Occasionally Gabriella Ricciardelli's more recent text was also consulted for the present edition. The translation from the first edition has been revisited and rejuvenated. In all cases which involve change the purpose has been to attain a greater flow, especially such as is appropriate to a sacred text consisting of lengthy lists of epithets. The introduction is more comprehensive and the notes offer the reader much more information. It is hoped that the indices will be a welcome addition.

   Professor Athanassakis wishes to express his warmest thanks to Miss Allison Emily Page for her patient assistance in the preparation of substantial portions of the book. He has over the years received a great deal of inspiration from the works of Juha Pentikäinen, who introduced him to the study of the *Kalevala* as well as of bear rituals among the Sami people of the subarctic expanses.

   Dr. Wolkow would like to thank the Classics departments at Duke University, Loyola University Chicago, and the University of Georgia at Athens, and in particular Diskin Clay, Erika Hermanowicz, and Charles Platter. Parts of the introduction and of the notes to hymn 34 were originally presented at a talk he delivered at the University of Georgia entitled "Play It Again, Sun: Cosmic Music and the *Orphic Hymns*," and he is grateful for the warm reception and incisive feedback from the participants that day. He further wishes to acknowledge the influence of former professors Borimir Jordan, Robert Renehan, and, of course, Apostolos Athanassakis, who graciously invited him to take part in the revision of the original edition of the *Hymns*. Finally, he dedicates his contributions to the present volume to his mythology students, both past and future.

The authors are very appreciative of the Johns Hopkins University Press, above all our former and current editors, Michael Lonegro and Matthew McAdam, respectively, for their many indulgences as the project began to take on a life of its own. Professor Louis Karchin, Professor of Music at New York University, has put a few of the hymns to music. Dancers of classical ballet, persons interested in spirituality, and students from as far as China have expressed further interest in the *Orphic Hymns*. All this has helped us sustain our enthusiasm for this rare poetic composition of late antiquity.

INTRODUCTION

A NTIQITY is virtually silent on the *Orphic Hymns*. The oldest reference to them is found in a scholium on Hesiod's *Theogony* by Ioannes Galenos (first half of the twelfth century AD). Galenos refers to them three times in the same scholium but says nothing about their authorship or literary value.

The first manuscript of the *Hymns* to reach the West was the one carried to Venice by Giovanni Aurispa in 1423. It seems that another manuscript was taken to Italy by Franciscus Philadelphus four years later in 1427. Both of these manuscripts, and perhaps four others, have been lost. The loss of the manuscript brought to Venice by Aurispa is especially regrettable since it may have served as the archetype of all surviving codices. Of these we have thirty-six, twenty-five on paper and eleven on skin. Some of these codices contain only a portion of the *Hymns*. The same codices frequently contain the Homeric hymns, Hesiodea, the Orphic *Argonautika*, and the hymns of Proclus and Kallimakhos. As for the date of these codices, it seems safe to infer that they were all copied between 1450 and 1550.

We have reason to believe that the codex Aurispa brought with him from Constantinople in 1423 stirred up considerable excitement among the learned. On the other hand, it may not have been until the arrival in Venice of the Greek sage Georgios Gemistos (usually surnamed Plethon) sometime in the middle of the fifteenth century that the Italians really took notice of the *Orphic Hymns*. The editio princeps was printed in Florence in 1500. It also contains the Orphic *Argonautica* and some of the hymns of Proclus. By the year 1600 there were five more editions, one of which was Aldine's, published in 1517. From the editions that followed in subsequent centuries the one that excels all others—perhaps to this day—is Gottfried Hermann's 1805 work. Abel's edition in 1885 has been received with adverse criticism. Wilhelm Quandt had finished his edition by 1941, but the vicissitudes of the war forced most scholars to wait until 1955 to reap the benefits of his labors from its reprinted and somewhat augmented version.

A date of composition cannot be assigned to the *Hymns* with any certainty. A few ancient sources make direct or oblique references to Orphic hymns, but they need not refer to our *Hymns*. It is much more reasonable to assume that the expression "Hymns of Orpheus" (e.g., Plato *Laws* 829d–e, Pausanias 9.30.12) does not refer to a specific collection such as the one at our disposal but rather to Orphic poetry—perhaps even of the oral variety—that was attributed to the founder of Orphism. In the first oration against Aristogeiton, Pseudo-Demosthenes tells us that "Orpheus says that she [Dike] sits beside the throne of Zeus and watches over all human matters" (25.11). The similarity between this statement and lines 2–3 in the hymn to Dike (hymn 62) has been noticed, but it would be unwise to build a hypothesis of composition on what must have become a common metaphor.[1]

But the *Orphic Hymns* still may have existed quite early and gone unnoticed. After all, antiquity treated the much older Homeric hymns with astonishing indifference. Those scholars who place the composition of the *Orphic Hymns* within the first four centuries of our era are probably closer to the truth. The relative purity of the language and the nearly flawless hexameter would argue for the earlier part of this period. So would also the remarkable absence of anything faintly Christian. There is a syncretism, but the syncretism is that of unmistakably pagan elements. The content of the *Hymns* themselves yields nothing certain. However, the hymn to Apollon (hymn 34) contains some specific musical technical terms, and the collocation of ideas in lines 16–23 strongly suggests that the composer was at least vaguely familiar with Ptolemy's *Harmonics*.[2] This would provide a terminus post quem of about 200 AD. It is true that we have scant evidence for the existence of Orphic cults in the later Roman imperial period. On the other hand, the predilection of the Severan dynasty (193 to 235 AD) for Eastern institutions and ideas favored a movement for religious reform and a tolerance that eventually culminated in the resuscitation and flourishing of many mystic, especially Dionysian, cults. It may have been exactly in this sort of climate and at such a time that underground remnants of Orphism surfaced again to reassert the tenacity of the legendary divine musician of Thrace. Perhaps then a date in the middle of the third century AD is as good a guess as any.

The place in which the *Hymns* were composed and originally used is a mystery. The appearance in the *Hymns* of divinities hardly known or totally unknown to mainland Greece should turn our attention eastward to Asia Minor, where, in fact, the names of some of these less known Asiatic gods have been consistently turning up in inscriptions. The three most telling names are Mise, Hipta, and Melinoe, all three previously known only from the *Hymns* until the soil of western Anatolia revealed their existence in inscriptions. Otto Kern in 1911 was the first to suggest that Pergamum was the birthplace of the *Hymns* and that they were used in mystic Dionysian ceremonies in the *temenos* of Demeter in the city. His suggestion has found both sympathizers and critics among scholars. Until epigraphic and other evidence points to some other place we might consider Kern's theory a distinct possibility.

:::

The *Orphic Hymns* constitute a distinct collection, and they should be seen as one part of a vast ancient literature that modern scholars label "Orphic." However, the term "Orphic" is somewhat misleading. It implies something unified, stable, and definable—something like a movement, a genre, a type of phenomenon. But in actuality "Orphic" is a sort of catch-all term that is used to designate anything and everything directly or indirectly connected to Orpheus. And who this figure was leads to even more ambiguity. We do not know if he ever existed. Traditionally he was from the wilds of Thrace, a foreigner to the Greeks, and a bard of great renown, sometimes thought to be even earlier than Homer and Hesiod. He was so proficient with his stringed instrument, the lyre, that he could sway inanimate objects and even bring the lord and lady of the dead to tears. In addition to his amazing musical talents, he knew of secret rites, usually those of Dionysos, and particularly those dealing with the salvation of the soul after death, and these he taught to his fellow man in the form of mysteries. Indeed, Orpheus himself descended to the land of death in order to win back his beloved Eurydike, who had died before her time. His tragic failure has become one of the most haunting legacies bequeathed to us by the poets of old. There were in fact a number of poems in circulation attributed to Orpheus in the ancient world. Some seem to have been quite old, perhaps even pre-Classical, but others were composed at a later time and claimed to be his. These poems have come down to us in fragments, quoted or alluded to in an astonishing variety of authors from all periods, in both prose and poetry and in both Greek and Latin. The fragments are assiduously collected in Bernabé's Teubner edition. While geared to scholars, even readers with little or no knowledge of ancient languages will find it a useful resource. Bernabé gathers the primary sources, and, with a little tenacity in learning the abbreviations for author and work, one can easily track down a suitable English translation for most of them.

Two notable Orphic documents may be mentioned here. The first one is an extremely important papyrus text that was discovered in Macedonia in 1962, known as the Derveni Papyrus and datable to the second half of the fourth century BC. It is in a lacunose state, but there is ample enough material to determine that the author was writing a philosophical interpretation of some theogonic poem he ascribes to Orpheus.[3] Another is a group known as the Bacchic gold tablets. There are thirty-nine of these, dating from 400 BC to 200 AD, found from Rome to Asia Minor, from Macedonia to Krete. They are inscriptions on thin gold leaf that were found in graves. Some just have a name, presumably of the person buried, who was an initiate in the mysteries. Some contain instructions for the soul on what to do once it arrives at the underworld in order to secure its special dispensation, its reward for being initiated in the mysteries while living.[4]

One important fact that clearly emerges from this "Orphic" literature is that there had developed what we may call an "Orphic" mythology, one that appropriated much from the "official" mythologies in Homer and Hesiod but extended them in idiosyncratic ways. Cosmogony/theogony was a widely disseminated type, although there were numerous variations. Three versions were preserved by the Neoplatonist Damascius, who attributed one to the Peripatetic Eudemos and another to a certain Hieronymos and/or Hellanikos and who cited a third from a poem he called the *Orphic Rhapsodies* (probably the same as the one that appears elsewhere under the title of *Sacred Discourses in Twenty-Four Rhapsodies*).[5] Despite these many and convoluted accounts, certain details are found again and again in our sources with enough consistency that we can at times with some confidence designate something as "Orphic" or at least influenced by "Orphic" literature. Our collection is "Orphic" in this sense.

:::

There is little to force us to the assumption of a single authorship for all the *Hymns*. Indeed, we can scarcely assume that the collection was composed at once. The opening to Mousaios, for example, has come under suspicion.[6] However, the *Hymns* do give the impression of being the work of a religious antiquary who had ready access to some sort of concordance from which he marshaled forth hosts of epithets that he then linked together in hexameters. This is more or less the view of Christian Lobeck, a view that is bound to be shared by those who consider the *Hymns* literary rather than religious documents. Albrecht Dieterich and Kern, and later William Guthrie, have taken exception to this opinion. It is reasonable to think that when in the third century AD many Dionysian cults were revived and made to serve as a convenient umbrella for the resurrection of Orphic elements, revered literary sources and earlier ritual practices, such as the Eleusinian mysteries, were tapped for the creation of appropriate cult literature. Every religion known to man is an amalgamation of various religious movements. Here we must mention the concept of the *bricoleur* suggested by Fritz Graf and Sarah Johnston in discussing how the peculiar Orphic mythology might have been developed.[7]

The *Hymns* stand as a particular example of a very old genre that survived throughout antiquity. A hymn is essentially a poem sung in praise of a god, often with a request or prayer. The word "hymn" can be used as a generic term, or to designate a specific genre, such as Pindar's hymns. Over time, a wide variety developed. A hymn might contain narrative, long or short, such as some of the Homeric hymns. A hymn might have cultic function, such as the Kretan hymn found at Palaikastro that invokes Zeus as the greatest *kouros* (fourth century BC, possibly older). A hymn can be purely lyrical, such as those of Mesomedes (mid-second century AD), some of whose works survive with musical notation. We find hymns as dedications, inscribed on pillars or walls, such as the four hymns by Isidoros of the Fayum (88–80 BC). Some scraps of poetry found in the magical papyri, often metrically faulty, have been titled "hymns" by scholars, but one should regard the reconstructed versions by the editor of the papyri, Karl Preisendanz, with caution. Philosophers wrote hymns, too, such as the Stoic Kleanthes' *Hymn to Zeus* (early- to mid-third century BC) and the surviving group by the Neoplatonist Proclus (fifth century AD). Prose was also a vehicle for hymns. The story of Atlantis that Kritias tells is prefaced with a thanks to Sokrates and also noted as a kind of hymn in honor of Athene, whose festival, the Panathenaia, was taking place (Plato *Timaios* 21a). A number of prose hymns were written by Aelius Aristides (mid-second century AD). Hymns can also be embedded in other works. In Apuleius' *Metamorphoses*, Lucius has had it with being a literal ass, and, after bathing himself seven times in a river (seven being a holy number according to Pythagoras), he invokes Isis the moon goddess in hymnic style (11.2). Finally, Ovid, as one would expect, plays with the genre when he has his lovesick Apollon call out to the fleeing Daphne the identity of her pursuer in terms that are typical of the genre: a list of favorite cult sites and the wide powers of the divinity addressed (*Metamorphoses* 1.515–524). The joke is that it is the god himself, not the petitioner, who utters the hymn; the inversion is both a mocking and serious testament to the power of love.[8]

Our composer has freely drawn on this venerable tradition. In addition to literature and religion, philosophy, too, has made its mark, though it is difficult to adduce parallels with certainty. Stoicism seems to have been particularly influential. Such hymns as those to Ether, the Stars, Physis, Boreas, Zephyros, Notos, being personifications of natural phenomena, may point to Stoic influence. So may the invocation of Pronoia (Providence) in the proemic piece (line 30). The prominence of the fiery element as found, e.g., in hymns 5.4 and 66.4–5 would further appear to reflect Stoic belief. Yet it could be argued for some of these (and others) that the deciding influence was from the Pre-Socratics (e.g., Empedokles, Herakleitos), Pythagoreanism, and even Neoplatonism or Neopythagoreanism. There is so much fusion of different philosophical ideas in this collection that the only thing that can be said of them in this regard is that they represent a confluence and a monument to the syncretism that characterized religion in general during the Hellenistic and especially Imperial era. Their composer was not interested in creating a religious or philosophical system. The initiates wanted to protect their lives and save their souls. And to this end they needed the good will of every god and every *daimōn*. The texts that they used in their rites are interesting not so much as poetry but as repositories of religious ideas, frequently borrowed from a wide range of older literature and expressed by a means peculiar to a category of the hymnic genre. Careful linguistic study of the provenance of many of the epithets in the hymns—especially the hapax legomena—may help us answer some of the vexing questions that surround them.

:::

Like all religions, Orphism had its profound religious beliefs and taboos. The animal sacrifice has a very special place in Greek religion. Those who participate are witnesses to the proper execution of the ritual that involves the sacrificial meal, always performed as an affirmation of shared religious beliefs. It is no accident that Orphism preached respect for animal life and abstention from eating the flesh of animals. Belief in the transmigration of souls, originally a Pythagorean one, made this prohibition necessary. For the Orphics, purification from guilt and pollution was a spiritual necessity, especially since they believed that punishment for wrongs committed in this world was inevitable. If it did not take place in a man's lifetime, it would certainly happen in the subsequent one. The things from which an Orphic had to abstain threatened the purity of his soul with *miasma,* pollution. Purification, *katharsis,* did not simply free the soul from impurity but also protected a person from punishment and gave him the hope of eternal life in Elysium. Those who reached the underworld and its various punishments, all borrowed from Greek mythology, stayed there. They were then the unredeemed, doomed to be eternally deprived of the transmigration of their soul and thus the chance for redemption.[9]

The supreme god of Orphism was Dionysos, and at the center of this religious faith was a cosmogony different from the one we learn from Hesiod's *Theogony.* Orphism preached the simple idea that the world was born from an egg. This primordial egg hatched out the first god, Eros, who was later named Protogonos and Phanes and who was said to be both male and female. He then created the world. The Hesiodic succession of Sky, Kronos, and Zeus was retained. Appended to this was the story of the death of Dionysos at the hands of the Titans, who tore him to pieces and devoured him, and Dionysos' eventual rebirth.[10] This significant theme was reenacted by the ecstatic worshippers of Dionysos. Central to Orphism is the idea that the body is evil and the soul is divine. In fact, the body is a tomb which serves as a prison for the spiritual entity we call the soul. The material part of man, the body, is the evil inheritance of the Titans. The spiritual part, the soul, comes from Dionysos, an immortal god and the son of Zeus. It is obvious that the Homeric concept of the living body as the man himself and of the soul as a pale lifeless shadow of him is completely inverted in Orphism.

The relation of Orpheus to Dionysus is peculiar. Both are connected with Thrace. Dionysos is a god of transitions.[11] Orpheus obviously could cross the boundaries of culture into nature and back. He descended into the underworld to recover his beloved Eurydike and came back alive. The meaning of this myth is twofold. Heavenly song can conquer death and so can devotion to the beloved. But Eurydike, "wide justice," remains in the world below, desired but tantalizingly beyond the reach of the living. The mythic prophet Orpheus dies a strange death; he is torn to pieces by Thracian maenads. This death is analogous to the one Dionysos himself suffered. Clearly the practice of Dionysian orgies, of tearing wild beasts into pieces and devouring their limbs, is a ritual connected with the tragic dismemberment of Orpheus. Maenadic women also in a state of ecstatic frenzy killed Pentheus, king of Thebes. In so many ways, Pentheus in the story that is so powerfully told by Euripides in the *Bacchae* is the surrogate victim. Pentheus dies so that Dionysus may live on forever.

Bits and pieces of Orphism are evident throughout the collection, but there is very little about Orphic theogony, anthropogony, or eschatology. To be sure Protogonos is equated with Phanes and is addressed as "born of the egg, delighting in his golden wings" (hymn 6.2). Orphic anthropogony is alluded to in the hymn to the Titans (hymn 37.4–6): "From you are descended all toiling mortals, / the brood of the sea and of the land, then the brood of the birds, / of all generations of the world born of you." Kronos and Time (Greek *khronos*) are characteristically equated at hymn 13.5 where Kronos is called "begetter of time." And certainly the phrase "dreadful Necessity governs all things" (hymn 3.11) must have been pregnant with meaning for the initiate, since Necessity mated with Time to give birth to Ether, Khaos, and Erebos. There is no hint anywhere of animal sacrifices and of meat eating, even if Dionysos himself is addressed as "ōmadios" ("taker of raw flesh"). This we may interpret as a concession to the non-Orphic side of the god and as part of the comprehensiveness of poems that are essentially conjuring formulae. Interestingly enough, it seems to be the persistent Orphic aversion to the crime of *ōmophagia* (eating of raw flesh and thus also the dismemberment of Dionysos) that accounts for its suppression in the hymn to the Titans (hymn 37). Also Orphic, but not uniquely Orphic, is the sentiment expressed in the varieties of the concluding formula that the addressee grant a good end to a life, since a good life on earth attended by the proper rites of initiation and purification constitutes some sort of guarantee of rewards, or at least of escape from punishment in the afterlife. The idea held by the Orphics that the body was a prison for the soul is expressed in the very last hymn (hymn 87.3–4).[12] Referring as it does to a very central and basic belief, it serves as an unmistakably Orphic capstone of an edifice to which other religions and philosophical systems made generous contributions.

:::

The question of Orphic rituals is a tantalizing one. Poems such as the *Rhapsodies*, *Argonautika*, and *Lithika* were written in late antiquity. Falsely attributed to Orpheus, they are a fantasy literature whose connection with Orphism ranges from non-existent to tenuous. For Pindar, glorious Orpheus is the father of songs (*Pythian Odes* 4.176–177). Immortality is conferred by lofty song. No Orphic ritual can emerge from the musings of this most aristocratic Greek poet. The fascination with the Bacchic gold tablets is justifiably enormous. Yet these fabulous fragments do not amount to a text that can help us reconstruct even one Orphic ritual. Immortality of the soul is the key Orphic belief in them. This central Orphic belief, I think, is the dominant theme of the Homeric *Hymn to Demeter*, composed sometime in the seventh century BC, whose origins specialists in Greek religion trace to an agricultural cult, specifically a fertility ritual. Caution must be exercised here. Syncretism and fusion must not be forgotten. Demeter dips Demophoön into fire to grant him immortality. Demeter's abducted daughter, Persephone, and her journey to Hades and back into the upper world and into life is a great allegory for death and resurrection and hence a great allegory for immortality. There is frequent mention of ritual in connection with Orphism. Ancient references to Orphism and the Orphics are not very helpful in this regard. The beautiful Orphic cosmogony in the *Birds* of Aristophanes (685–704) teaches us ideas about the origin of the world. There is nothing in it as to what one should or should not do. There are many references to Orpheus and his followers in Plato, especially in the *Republic*. They are mostly philosophical speculations about aspects of human eschatology. Orphism inspired Pythagoras to create a rich type of theology that was founded on practice. Various details of the way his followers lived have more to do with a holistic way of life and less with the performance of certain rituals.

The cult of Dionysos was the most widespread in the Hellenized world. Religious associations that honored both Orpheus and Dionysos seem to have existed everywhere, and some rituals were called both Orphic and Dionysian. It seems quite clear from the collection itself that the *Hymns* were used by such a religious association (*thiasos*) of people who called themselves *mustai*, *mustipoloi*, or *orgiophantai* (mystic initiates) and who through prayer (*eukhē*), libation (*loibē*), sacrifice (*thusia*), and, presumably, secret ceremonies (*orgia, teletai*) invoked a series of divinities and asked for their presence or for the gift of some blessing, such as wealth, peace, health, and not infrequently for a blameless end to a good life. These associations had a definite hierarchy. One of the most prominent officials was the *boukolos*, the oxherd. This title occurs only twice in the *Orphic Hymns*: at hymn 1.10 and hymn 31.7. It is reasonable to assume that the underlying idea was that of the mediator who would help the initiates into a Dionysian transformation. And it is equally reasonable to assume that a newly founded *thiasos* commissioned one or more able poets to provide them with religious poetry that should be as authentic and comprehensive as possible.

Most of the *Hymns* are addressed to divinities and concepts of the Hellenistic pantheon and its train of lesser divine or semi-divine figures. Such personified abstractions as Dike, Justice, and Nomos are so old and so common to various schools of Greek philosophical and religious thought as not to be especially Orphic. The only hymn to a god of Near Eastern origin is the one to Adonis. Three hymns are dedicated to Anatolian goddesses (Mise, Hipta, Melinoe), and the Anatolian moon god Men is mentioned in the opening address to Mousaios. The Orphic sympathies of the collection are nowhere more evident than in the number and fervor of individual pieces addressed to Dionysos. There are seven such hymns (possibly nine, if Mise and Korybas are viewed as alternate manifestations of Dionysos), while Zeus has only three that are specifically addressed to him. Dionysos is also frequently invoked or alluded to in many other hymns, and his characteristic epithets seem to have been so infectious and to have assumed such universal significance as to seriously have encroached on the territory of other deities (see further hymn 30). This is as it should be, since Dionysos is the chief Orphic god.

The *Hymns* were devotional. Perfumes are frequently mentioned at the beginning of an individual hymn. Sometimes incense is mentioned specifically. Storax was imported from Phoenicia, while incense and myrrh came from the Arabian Peninsula. There seems to have been a certain protocol, and a preference for this or that kind of aromatic substance. Incense for Sun, frankincense for Nike, Apollon, Artemis,

Dionysos Liknites, and several other divinities. Myrrh was offered to Protogonos, Poseidon, Nereus, and Leto; storax to Prothyraia, Kronos, Zeus, Proteus, Dionysos, Demeter, Chthonic Hermes, etc. Crocus was offered to Ether, opium to Sleep, and simply perfumes for Moon, Physis, Rhea, Athene, etc. As has been observed it is not easy to see the connection between specific aromatic substances and ritualistic practices. The variety might be attributed to the preference of persons who contributed the specific perfume or other material. Perhaps also the season of the year played a role. The distribution of perfumes and aromatic substances as they appear in our *Hymns* is such as to make it impossible for us to offer a rational explanation of any systematic organization.

It makes sense to think that the time of chanting these beautiful hymns was evening. For the initiates the day's labor was done and their worries could be set aside for the replenishment of their souls and for a respite from the mundane realities of the world. The *Hymns* are redolent with elements of mysticism. Indeed, the most pervasive characteristic of the *Hymns,* the ubiquitous epithet, might be, in part, an indication of a link between these hymns and the various remains of magic literature from the Hellenistic and Roman periods. Both direct a propitiatory address to a deity, accompanied by as comprehensive a list of its powers and properties as possible. The difference is that where the initiate seeks to persuade and cajole, the sorcerer seeks to bind and compel. There is no indication of accompanying music in the *Hymns;* however, it would be a mistake to latch onto this omission and think there was no music. First of all, the hymns themselves chanted properly constituted music. Perhaps that was enough for the initiates. Percussion instruments are mentioned, but their appearance might be due to their traditional associations. It is not easy to settle this question. Indic, Iranian, and Muslim cult music should not be excluded from consideration. After all, all these traditions use song as a bridge by which to unite heaven and earth. It should also be recalled that Orpheus was famous as a poet and a singer in addition to being renowned for his role as legendary founder of mystic rites.

We cannot recover the sounds and we do not know exactly what the mood was when the *Hymns* were sung. It might not be too much to suggest that people gathered in places that were sacred to them and that they did so as the softer colors of the evening were settling in on them. Candles provided gentle light. Wisps of incense smoke rose into the air. The magic of song, devotional, undulant, filled all of the sacred space and provoked the human heart to seek union with the divine.

We know the past only through the present. My [A.N.A.] reconstruction of an Orphic evening somewhere in Asia Minor is based on my experiences in the very mystical services of the Orthodox Church. There is no effort here to show an absolutely direct connection between the music of the Orthodox Church at present and the music of the *Orphic Hymns.* However, burning incense, keeping time with the swing of the censer, allowing sacred abandon to take over, and training the human voice to sink and then rise to God cannot have changed much throughout the ages, especially within a culture dominated by the same language and by the poetics of the same tradition.

:::

On the whole, the style of the *Hymns* is homogenous and consistent. At the beginning of each hymn, the invocation, sometimes several divinities are summoned. Usually the name of the divinity or divinities is followed by an imperative, e.g., "Come! Hear!" Variations are to be found in the end of the prayer that asks for blessing, peace, prosperity, and wealth. There appears to be an order to the arrangement of most of the hymns. There are many male/female pairings throughout.[13] The opening ones focus on the gods of the early generations and the theme of birth. Physis, Pan, and Herakles form a triad that sums up the creation of the physical world. Kronos and Rhea lead to Zeus. This begins a series of hymns where the traditional four elements of fire, air, water, and earth provide a coherent structure (hymns 15–27). Everything leads to the first hymn to Dionysos (hymn 30), his "birth" in a sense, which is strengthened by the appearance of divinities connected with the Orphic myth of his birth, death, and rebirth (hymns 31–38). A block of four hymns treats Eleusinian themes (hymns 40–43), and then comes the central cluster of hymns treating Dionysian cult (hymns 44–54). Aphrodite seems to preside over another series (hymns 55–68). A number of minor divinities, mostly in pairs and all of cultic importance, continue to another grouping of hymns associated with the elements (hymns 79–84). The three brothers Sleep, Dream, and Death end the collection. For details, see the introductions to the various individual hymns. The ring composition between birth at the beginning and death at the end is significant, and, if the *Hymns* were performed throughout the night, the dawning of a new day would have symbolically reflected the initiates' hopes for a new life, one that promised the reward of eternal sunshine in the afterlife.

The *Hymns* are catalogues of religious epithets; such catalogues are intended to evoke the many powers of various divinities that are significant to a particular type of religious ideology and practice. The question is: what sources of ancient literature could have inspired and instructed the writers of the *Hymns*? We have already indicated magical incantations. Hesiod's catalogues of the daughters of Nereus and of the daughters of Okeanos are religious documents (*Theogony* 240–264 and 346–363). Homer's catalogue of the Nereids (*Iliad* 18.39–49) is a poetic construct, whose origin is religious. Hesiod's catalogues come from an old religious tradition. A deity must be invoked by words that refer to its attributes. In all likelihood the names of the daughters of Nereus and of the daughters of Okeanos are in fact epithets of the sea, at times older than even Hesiod, epithets that point to a Mother of the Waters. The sea has countless potencies, countless faces. The sea is both a great blessing and a treacherous element that is fraught with peril. The fact that great numbers of feminine divinities, essentially Daughters of the Sea, so frequently rise out of the sea is indicative of a deeply entrenched and old religious feeling that the sea is feminine and maternal, a huge counterpart to the masculine sky. Zeus is the Indo-European sky god. When people pray to him they also pray to the sky. In a tradition that predates the arrival of the Greeks in Greece, the sea and its in-dwelling divinities must have received more attention. The new religion that emerged introduced a male god whose dominion became preeminent. The lists of the daughters of Nereus and of Okeanos are prayer lists that come from an older religious order. Every one of these names has a meaning. The following example is taken from Hesiod's *Theogony*:

> Proto, Eukrante, Amphitrite, and Sao,
> Eudora, Thetis, Galene, and Glauke,
> Kymothoe, Speio, Thoe, and lovely Halia,
> Pasithea, Erato, and Eunike of the rosy arms. (243–46)

In an entirely literal translation:

> First One, Mingling Gently, Water-Girt, and Savior,
> Of the Good Gifts, Nurturing, Calm, and Grayish-Blue,
> Of the Rushing Waves, Of the Numberless Caves, Swift, and lovely Sea,
> Seen By All, Lovely, and Fair Victory of the rosy arms.

The first few lines from the hymn to Nereus offers a good example for comparison (hymn 23.1–4):

> The sea's foundations are your realm,
>   the abode of blue-black darkness,
> you exult in the beauty
>   of your fifty daughters
> as they dance amid the waves.
>   O Nereus, god of great renown,
> O foundation of the sea, O end of the earth.

Even a casual look at these texts shows that they are religious texts that have one main thing in common: they are strings of nouns or epithets addressed to a divinity. A first approach to them leaves the reader puzzled as to their aesthetic, that is to say their poetic value, as well as to their effectiveness. However, here is a suggestion to readers of the Hesiodic catalogues as well as of the *Orphic Hymns*. They are asked to raise their voices as they read to a pleasant and imposing pitch as well as a clear and rhythmically punctuated vocalization of the lines. The tone of voice should strive to approximate dignified chant. Examples are to be found in many cultures. If all this is done, the religious character of the catalogues comes alive. They are no longer boring, and their invocational nature becomes entirely clear.

Every Greek is aware that the Virgin Mary is addressed by various names that have become sacred names. When I [A.N.A.] was working on the Hesiodic and Homeric lists, I decided to find out just how many names were used to address the Virgin Mary in the Hellenic world. I walked into a fine bookshop in Athens, and to my astonishment I discovered four beautiful volumes devoted to an explanation of the nearly five hundred names by which the Virgin Mary is addressed. This rich tradition may indeed ultimately go back even to pre-Hellenic times. The idea suggested here is that the veneration of the Virgin Mary has inherited aspects of the veneration of the sea and its divinities in prehistoric time. Here is just a sample of names which refer to the Virgin Mary: She of the Shoreline, She of the Sea Calm, the Far Heard One, She of the Seas, She of the Lakes, She of the Harbors, She of the Caves, She of the Rivers, She of Good Sailing. It should not be too difficult for anyone to hear in this sample echoes from Hesiod's catalogues of the Nereids. The astonishing number of epithets to the Virgin Mary in the Hellenic lands should not be regarded as some sort of random religious occurrence. Whether the attributes of a divinity are described by epithets, nouns, or periphrastic expressions makes no substantial difference. Relevant here from the Judaic tradition is Exodus 34:6–7 in which God Himself speaks of his own attributes. Muslims believe in one God whose divine qualities are known to them by ninety-nine (some say more) different names.[14] Numbers 12–19 in Siddiqi read as follows: The Rightful / The Fashioner of Forms / The Ever-Forgiving / The All-Compelling Subduer / The Bestower / The Ever-Providing / The Opener / The Victory-Giver / The All-Knowing. However, these sacred names appear throughout the Koran and in this respect they do not resemble the Hesiodic catalogues or the *Orphic Hymns*. It is not so much the semantic content as the tone and cumulative effect of this religious utterance that opens possibilities of comparison with the *Hymns*. The emotionally powerful, indeed ecstatic and repetitive, invocation of Allah by the Whirling Dervishes of the Mevlevi Order dominates the performance of their rituals. The ninety-nine names of Allah are recited in their daily prayers and meditations. Such practices cannot be so very different from the concept and practice of unceasing prayer, such as the Jesus Prayer, so central to the monastic life of Mount Athos. The religious life of the Whirling Dervishes owes its origins to Rumi, a Persian poet who was also an Islamic jurist and theologian. His spiritual teachings took root in Konya, Turkey, not too far from ancient Pergamum, the city that may have produced the *Orphic Hymns*. If we call all this a chain of similar religious phenomena, even a coincidental one, we may come closer to understanding the power of clustering epithets for the creation of an emotional and physical crescendo that might raise our human spirit and help us approach the divine.

There are lines in the *Orphic Hymns* that remind one of the Vedic hymns. For example, from one to Soma: "King Soma, be gracious to us for welfare; / we are thy devotees: know that. / There arise might and wrath O Indu: / abandon us not according to the desire of our foe."[15] Is this not in both spirit and formulation similar to the way practically all the hymns of our collection end? Consider also: "So, O Agni, be easy of access to us / as a father to his son; abide with us / for our well-being."[16] Winthrop Sargeant in his translation of the *Bhagavad gita* has an impressive list of epithets used in this great poetic monument. Here is only a handful from his list: The Bristling-haired One, the Imperishable One, the Immeasurable One, Incomparable Glory, Conqueror of Wealth, the Blameless One.[17] Among the Finnic peoples—the Saami—almost throughout the entire sub-Arctic zone the bear is a very sacred animal, rich in lore and ritual. The primordial bear, more often Father Bear, but then also Mother Bear in various creation stories, is of celestial origin. I [A.N.A.] feel very fortunate that in 1999 I became friends with Juha Pentikäinen, a great Finnish scholar who introduced me not only to a new perspective of the *Kalevala* but also to rare information on the centrality and importance of the bear in the religion and social life of the Finnic peoples. Several years later in 2006, I attended a conference titled "In the Footsteps of the Bear" in Pori, Finland. The proceedings of the conference were published in Pori in 2006 under the title *In the Footsteps of the Bear*.[18] It was in Pori that I learned from Juha and some of his eminent international colleagues that nearly five hundred names are used in the vast sub-Arctic zone to address "the golden king of the forest." Here are some examples: Forest Gold (or simply Darling), Forest Beauty, Graceful Mistress of the Forest.

The *Orphic Hymns* name specific pagan divinities, yet they appeal to universal spiritual powers. Some of them, like the hymns to Dream, Death, and Sleep, are in essence prayers that could be offered to God regardless of specific faith. All this makes excellent sense. The years between 300 and 500 AD were years of transition. It is very naïve to think that the Christian faith simply walked into towns, villages, and hamlets to be triumphantly received. It is much likelier that the new faith made accommodations with places and associations that cultivated the spiritual values. The new faith lacked the language of expressing the new spiritual values. The old faith, especially as expressed in documents like the *Hymns*, possessed a liturgical language ready to be used. Echoes of the compositional mode of the *Hymns*, especially of the effect of clustering epithets, can occasionally be heard in the great devotional and, at the same time invocational, Hymns of the Orthodox Church, such as the *Akathistos Hymnos*: "Spotless, pollutionless, incorruptible, untouched, pure Virgin, Despoina, Bride of God."

The *Orphic Hymns*, as well as similar hymns, have neither plot nor action. They are not at all like the major Homeric hymns in that they do not appeal to any emotion. None of our hymns shows even a trace of humor, rhetorical conceit, or for that matter a desire to delight or shock the initiates. Clearly, elevation of mood and the powerful affirmation of a meaningful and bonding presence are elements that run through the recitation of mighty words and sacred sounds flowing into the eager ears and souls of the faithful. Even the puns serve this purpose. Names chanted or better yet sung or even simply recited in a particular sacred tone have power. Each epithet reverberates into the mind of the celebrant and spins out its own plot and its own action. As one epithet follows another, chains of meaning and sound acquire a power that may exceed that of a highly structured narrative. One name is one thing. Two names are more than two things. The *Orphic Hymns* are beautiful poetry of another kind, a transcendental kind, which must be understood in the context of its own conventions.

THE ORPHIC HYMNS

Orpheus to Mousaios

Friend, use it to good fortune.

Learn now, Mousaios,
    a mystical and most holy rite,
a prayer which surely
    excels all others.
3   Kind Zeus and Earth,
    heavenly and pure flames of Sun,
sacred light of Moon,
    and of all the Stars;
Poseidon, too,
    dark-maned holder of the earth,
6   pure Persephone,
    Demeter of the splendid fruit,
Artemis, arrow-pouring maiden,
    kindly Phoibos,
dwelling on the sacred ground of Delphoi,
    and Dionysos, the dancer,
9   whose honors among the blessed gods
    are the highest;
strong-spirited Ares,
    holy and mighty Hephaistos,
then the goddess foam-born,
    to whose lot fell sublime gifts,
12   and you, divinity excellent,
    king of the underworld.
I call on Hebe, and Eileithyia,
    and the noble ardor of Herakles,
I call upon the great blessings
    of Justice and Piety,
15   I call upon the glorious Nymphs
    and upon Pan the greatest,
I call upon Hera,
    buxom wife of aegis-bearing Zeus.
And I call upon lovely Mnemosyne,
    I call upon the holy Muses,
18   all nine, and then I call upon the Graces,
    the Seasons, and the Year,
upon fair-tressed Leto,
    and upon divine and revered Dione.

I invoke the armed Kouretes,
   the Korybantes, and the Kabeiroi,
21 the great Saviors,
    Zeus' ageless scions,
I invoke the Idaian gods, and Hermes,
   messenger and herald.
Of those in the sky,
   I invoke Themis, diviner of men,
24 and then I invoke Night, oldest of all,
    and I do invoke light-bringing Day.
Faith, Dike, I invoke,
   I invoke blameless Thesmodoteira,
and Rhea, and Kronos,
   and dark-veiled Tethys,
27 the great Okeanos,
    and all of his daughters.
I invoke the might preeminent
   of Atlas and Aion,
of Time the ever-flowing,
   and of the splendid water of the Styx.
30 I call on all these gentle gods,
    and I call on Pronoia,
and on the holy Daimon,
   I also call on Daimon baneful to mortals,
then I invoke divinities dwelling
   in the sky, in the air, in the water,
33 on earth, under the earth,
    and in the fiery element.
Ino, Leukothea,
   Palaimon, giver of bliss,
sweet-speaking Nike,
   queenly Adrasteia,
36 I call upon the great king Asklepios,
    who grants soothing,
upon the battle-stirring maiden Pallas,
   and upon all the winds,
I call upon Thunder, and upon the parts
   of the four-pillared cosmos.
39 I invoke the Mother of the immortals,
    Attis and Men,
I invoke the goddess Ourania,

and the immortal and holy Adonis,
Beginning and End, too,
    which to all is most important,
42 and I ask them to come
    in a spirit of joyous mercy
to this holy rite,
    to this reverent libation.

1. To Hekate

Lovely Hekate of the roads
    and of the crossroads I invoke.
In heaven, on earth,
    then in the sea, saffron-cloaked,
3 tomb spirit reveling
    in the souls of the dead,
daughter of Perses, haunting deserted places,
    delighting in deer,
nocturnal, dog-loving,
    monstrous queen,
6 devouring wild beasts,
    ungirt and repulsive.
Herder of bulls,
    queen and mistress of the whole world,
leader, nymph,
    mountain-roaming nurturer of youths,
9 maiden, I beseech you to come
    to these holy rites,
ever with joyous heart,
    ever favoring the oxherd.

2. To Prothyraia

incense—storax

Hear me, O revered goddess,
    O many-named divinity,
O sight sweet to women in labor,
    you offer them aid in travail.
3 You save women, and you alone

love children,
O kindly goddess
of swift birth, ever helpful to young women,
O Prothyraia.
You hold the keys,
6   you are accessible to all, O mistress,
gracious and fond of nurture,
you have power in every house,
and you delight in festivities.
You loosen girdles, and though invisible
you are seen in every deed,
9   you share pain,
you rejoice in every birth,
O Eileithyia, you free from pain
those in terrible distress.
Upon you alone pregnant women call,
O comforter of souls,
12   and in you alone there is
relief from pains of labor.
Artemis, Eileithyia,
reverend Prothyraia,
hear, O blessed one,
help me and grant offspring;
15   save me, savior of all,
for it is in your nature to do so.

3. To Night

incense—firebrands

I shall sing of Night,
mother of gods and men;
we call Night Kypris,
she gave birth to all.
3   Hear, O blessed goddess,
jet-black and starlit,
for you delight in the quiet
and slumber-filled serenity.
Cheerful and delightful, lover
of the nightlong revel, mother of dreams,
6   you free us from cares,

you offer us welcome respite from toil.
Giver of sleep, beloved of all,
    you gleam in the darkness as you drive your steeds.
Ever incomplete, terrestrial,
    and then again celestial,
9   you circle around in pursuit
    of sprightly phantoms,
you force light into the nether world,
    and then again you flee
into Hades, for dreadful Necessity
    governs all things.
12   But now, O blessed one—beatific,
    desired by all—I call on you
to grant a kind ear
    to my voice of supplication,
and to come, benevolent,
    to disperse fears that glisten in the night.

4. To Sky

incense—frankincense

Sky, father of all,
    eternal cosmic element,
primeval beginning of all,
    end of all,
3   lord of the universe,
    moving about the earth like a sphere.
You are home of the blessed gods,
    your motion is a roaring whirl,
you envelop all,
    celestial and terrestrial guard.
6   Physis' invincible drive
    lies in your breast.
Dark-blue, indomitable,
    shimmering, variform,
all-seeing father of Kronos,
    blessed and most sublime divinity,
9   hearken, bring a life of holiness
    to the new initiates.

5. To Ether

incense—crocus

Yours are Zeus' lofty dwelling,
    endless power, too;
of the stars, of the sun,
    and of the moon you claim a share.
3   O tamer of all, O fire-breather,
    O life's spark for every creature,
sublime Ether,
    best cosmic element,
radiant, luminous,
    starlit offspring,
6   I call upon you and I beseech you
    to be temperate and clear.

6. To Protogonos

incense—myrrh

Upon two-natured Protogonos,
    great and ether-tossed, I call;
born of the egg,
    delighting in his golden wings,
3   the begetter of blessed gods and mortal men;
    he bellows like a bull.
Erikepaios, seed unforgettable,
    attended by many rites,
ineffable, hidden, brilliant scion,
    forever in whirring motion,
6   you scattered the dark mist,
    the mist that lay before your eyes.
Flapping your wings, you whirled about
    throughout this world,
you brought pure light.
    For this I call you Phanes,
9   yes, I call you Lord Priapos,
    I call you bright-eyed Antauges.
O blessed one of the many counsels
    and of the many seeds, come joyfully

to the celebrants of this holy rite,
  of this very intricate rite.

7. To the Stars

incense—aromatic herbs

I call forth the sacred light
  of the heavenly Stars,
with devotional prayers
  I summon the holy *daimones*.
3   Heavenly Stars,
  dear children of black Night,
round your thrones you move in circles,
  you spin in circular ways,
O brilliant and fiery
  begetters of all,
6   you do reveal fate,
  everyone's fate,
you determine the divine path
  for mortals.
Wandering in midair, you gaze
  upon the seven luminous orbits.
9   In heaven and on earth, ever indestructible
  on your blazing trail,
you shine upon the darkness
  of the cloak night wears.
Coruscating and gleaming,
  kingly and nocturnal,
12   visit the learned contests
  of this sacred rite,
finish a noble race
  for works of renown.

8. To the Sun

incense—pounded frankincense

Hear me, O blessed one,
  eternal eye that sees all,
Titan radiant as gold,

Hyperion, celestial light,
3   self-born, untiring,
    sweet sight to living creatures.
On the right you beget dawn,
    on the left you beget night,
you temper the seasons
    as you ride your dancing horses,
6   you rush, you rush very swiftly,
    O fiery and bright-faced charioteer,
you press on your course
    in endless whirl.
Harsh to the impious,
    you teach good to the pious
9   as you hold the golden lyre,
    the harmony of cosmic motion,
as you command noble deeds,
    as you nurture the seasons.
Piping lord of the world,
    fiery circle of motion,
12   life-bringing, coruscating,
    life-giving, fruit-bearing, Paian,
eternal and pure father of time,
    O immortal Zeus,
you are the clear, you are the brilliant,
    you are the all-encompassing cosmic eye,
15   both when you set and when you shine
    your lovely and radiant light.
A paragon of justice,
    O water-loving lord of the cosmos,
you guard pledges and ever the highest,
    you do help all.
18   Eye of justice and light of life,
    O charioteer,
your screaming whip
    drives the four-horse chariot on.
Hear my words and show
    life's sweetness to the initiates.

9. To Selene

incense—aromatic herbs

Hear me, O divine queen,
    O light-bringing and splendid Selene,
O bull-horned Moon,
    crossing the air as you race with night.
3   Nocturnal, torch-bearing,
    maiden of beautiful stars, O Moon,
waxing and waning,
    feminine and masculine,
luminous, lover of horses,
    mother of time, bearer of fruit,
6   amber-colored, moody,
    shining in the night,
all-seeing and vigilant,
    surrounded by beautiful stars,
you delight in the quiet
    and in the richness of the night,
9   you grant fulfillment and favor
    as, like a jewel, you shine in the night.
Long-cloaked marshal of the stars,
    wise maiden whose motion is circular,
come, O blessed and gentle lady,
    lady of the stars, through your own light
12   shine and save, O maiden,
    your new initiates.

10. To Physis

incense—aromatic herbs

O Physis,
    resourceful mother of all,
industrious and rich divinity,
    oldest of all, queen,
3   all-taming and indomitable,
    O lustrous ruler,
ever-honored mistress of all,
    highest goddess,
imperishable, first-born,

fabled glorifier of men,
6 nocturnal, radiant with constellations,
      light-bringing, irrepressible,
   you move swiftly,
      your steps are noiseless,
   O pure marshal of the gods,
      O end that has no end.
9 All partake of you,
      you alone partake of no one.
   Self-fathered, hence fatherless,
      virtue itself, joyous, great,
   you are accessible, O nurse of flowers,
      you lovingly mingle and twine,
12 you lead and rule,
      you bring life and nourishment to all.
   Self-sufficient,
      many-named persuasion of the Graces,
   Dike herself, queen of heaven,
      queen of the earth and of the sea,
15 bitter to the vulgar,
      sweet to those who obey you,
   wise in all, giver of all,
      nurturing queen of all,
   abundant nourishment is yours
      as you dissolve whatever ripens,
18 father and mother of all,
      nurturer and nurse,
   giver of swift birth, O blessed one,
      giver of wealth of seeds
   and of the fever of seasons.
      A rich and mighty divinity,
21 you give shape and form to all things.
      Eternal, setting all in motion,
   skilled and discreet,
      you are ever turning the swift stream
   into an unceasing eddy,
      flowing in all things,
24 circular and ever changing form,
      fair-throned and precious,
   you alone accomplish your designs,
      mighty mistress of booming thunder,

you rule over those who hold the scepter,
    O loud-roaring divinity,
27 fearless, all-taming,
    destined fate, fire-breathing,
you are life everlasting,
    you are immortal providence.
You are all things to all,
    because you alone do.
30 You are the all,
    you alone do,
you bring peace and health,
    you bring growth to all.

11. To Pan

incense—et varia

I call upon Pan, the pastoral god,
    I call upon the universe,
upon the sky, the sea, and the land,
    queen of all,
3 I also call upon immortal fire;
    all these are Pan's realm.
Come, O blessed and frolicsome one,
    O restless companion of the Seasons!
Goat-limbed, reveling,
    lover of frenzy, star-haunting,
6 weaver of playful song,
    song of cosmic harmony,
you induce fantasies of dread
    into the minds of mortals,
you delight in gushing springs,
    surrounded by goatherds and oxherds,
9 you dance with the nymphs,
    you sharp-eyed hunter, lover of Echo.
Present in all growth, begetter of all,
    many-named divinity,
light-bringing lord of the cosmos,
    fructifying Paian,
12 cave-loving and wrathful,
    veritable Zeus with horns,

   the earth's endless plain
      is supported by you,
   and the deep-flowing water
      of the weariless sea yields to you.
15   Okeanos who girds the earth
      with his eddying stream gives way to you,
   and so does the air we breathe,
      the air that kindles all life,
   and above us the sublime eye
      of weightless fire;
18   at your behest
      all these are kept wide apart.
   Your providence alters
      the natures of all,
   on the boundless earth you offer
      nourishment to mankind.
21   Come, frenzy-loving, spirit-possessed,
      come to these sacred libations,
   come and bring my life
      to a good end.
   Send your madness, O Pan,
      to the ends of the earth.

12. To Herakles

incense—frankincense

   Herakles, stout-hearted and mighty,
      powerful Titan,
   strong-handed, indomitable,
      doer of valiant deeds,
3   shape-shifter,
      O gentle and endless father of time,
   ineffable, lord of all,
      many pray to you,
   all-conquering and mighty
      archer and seer,
6   omnivorous begetter of all,
      peak of all, helper to all,
   for the sake of men
      you subdued and tamed savage races.

Peace was your desire;
    she brings dazzling honors and nurtures youths.
9 Self-grown, weariless,
    bravest child of the earth,
O illustrious Paion,
    your primordial scales gleam.
Round your head
    dawn and dark night cling,
12 and your twelve deeds of valor
    stretch from east to west.
Immortal, world-wise,
    boundless and irrepressible,
come, O blessed one,
    bringing all charms against disease,
15 with club in hand
    drive evil bane away,
with your poisonous darts
    do ward off cruel death.

13. To Kronos

incense—storax

Everlasting father
    of blessed gods and men,
resourceful, pure and mighty,
    O powerful Titan,
3 you consume all things
    and replenish them, too.
Unbreakable is the hold you have
    on the boundless cosmos,
O Kronos, begetter of time,
    Kronos of the shifting stories,
6 child of Earth,
    child of starry Sky.
In you there is birth and decline,
    O revered and prudent lord of Rhea,
you are the progenitor,
    you dwell in every part of the world.
9 I am a suppliant, hear my voice,
    O wily and brave one,

and to a good life
    bring a blameless end.

14. To Rhea

incense—aromatic herbs

Mighty Rhea,
    daughter of many-faced Protogonos,
your sacred chariot is drawn
    by bull-slayers,

3   you dance to the sound of drums and cymbals,
    O frenzy-loving maiden,
O mother of Zeus,
    aegis-bearing lord of Olympos.
Illustrious and honored,
    Kronos' blessed consort,

6   you delight in the mountains
    and in the horrid shrieks of mortals.
Strong-spirited Rhea, queen of queens,
    lover of the battle din,
liar, savior, redeemer,
    first by birth, mother of gods

9   and of mortals,
    from you come the earth,
and the wide sky above,
    and the sea and the winds.
Ethereal and restless, come,
    O blessed goddess,

12   O gentle-minded savior,
    come, bring peace and wealth
and abundance of possessions,
    and do send death and the filth of pollution
to the ends of the earth.

15. To Zeus

incense—storax

Much-honored Zeus, great god,
    indestructible Zeus,

we lay before you in prayer
    redeeming testimony.
3   O king, you have brought to light
    divine works—
earth, goddess and mother,
    the hills swept by the shrill winds,
the sea and the host of the stars,
    marshaled by the sky.
6   Kronian Zeus, strong-spirited god,
    the thunderbolt is your scepter,
father of all,
    beginning and end of all,
earth-shaker, increaser
    and purifier, all-shaker,
9   god of thunder and lightning,
    Zeus the sower.
Hear me, god of many faces,
    grant me unblemished health,
please grant me divine peace and riches,
    please grant me glory without blame.

16. To Hera

incense—aromatic herbs

You lodge yourself in dark hollows,
    and your form is airy,
O Hera, blessed queen of all,
    consort of Zeus.
3   The soft breezes you send to mortals
    nourish the soul,
O mother of rains, mother of the winds,
    you give birth to all.
Life does not exist without you,
    growth does not exist without you.
6   You are in everything,
    even in the air we venerate,
you are queen,
    and you are mistress.
You toss and turn
    when the rushing wind tosses and turns.

9   O blessed goddess,
         many-named queen of all,
     may you come with kindness
         on your joyous face.

17. To Poseidon

incense—myrrh

Hearken, dark-maned Poseidon,
    holder of the earth,
horse god, you hold
    the bronze trident in your hand,
3   you dwell in the foundations
    of the full-bosomed sea.
Shaker of the earth,
    deep-roaring ruler of the waters,
the waves are your blossoms, O gracious one,
    as you urge horses and chariots on,
6   rushing on the sea,
    splashing through the rippling brine.
The unfathomable sea
    fell to your lot, the third portion.
Waves and their wild dwellers please you,
    O spirit of the deep.
9   May you save the foundations of the earth
    and ships moving at full tilt,
bringing peace, health,
    and blameless prosperity.

18. To Plouton

You dwell below the earth,
    O strong-spirited one,
a meadow in Tartaros,
    thick-shaded and dark.
3   Sceptered Chthonic Zeus,
    please accept this sacrifice,
O Plouton, holder of the keys
    to the whole earth.

To mankind you give
    the wealth of the year's fruits,
6   yours is the third portion,
        earth, queen of all,
seat of the gods,
    mighty lap of mortals.
Your throne rests
    on a dark realm,
9   the realm of distant, of untiring,
        of windless, and of impassive Hades;
it does rest on gloomy Acheron,
    the river who girds the roots of the earth.
All-receiver, master of death,
    master of mortals, host of many,
12   Euboulos, you once took as your bride
        pure Demeter's daughter:
you tore her away from the meadow,
    and through the sea
you carried her to an Attic cave
    upon your steeds—
15   it was the district of Eleusis,
        where the gates to Hades are.
You alone were born to judge
    deeds obscure and conspicuous.
Holiest and illustrious ruler of all,
    frenzied god,
18   you delight in the respect
        and in the reverence of your worshippers.
I summon you, come with favor,
    come with joy to the initiates.

19. To Zeus the Thunderbolt

incense—storax

Father Zeus, sublime is the course
    of the blazing cosmos you drive on,
ethereal and lofty
    the flash of your lightning
3   as you shake the seat of the gods
        with a god's thunderbolts.

The fire of your lightning
   emblazons the rain clouds,
you bring storms and hurricanes,
   you bring mighty gales,
6   you hurl roaring thunder,
   a shower of arrows.
Horrific might and strength
   sets all aflame,
dreadful missile
   makes hearts pound and hair bristle.
9   Holy and invincible,
   it comes with a sudden crash,
an endless spiral of noise,
   omnivorous in its drive,
unbreakable and threatening,
   ineluctable, too, the gale's
12   sharp and smoke-filled shafts
   swoop down
with a flash dreaded
   by land and sea.
Wild beasts cringe
   when they hear the noise,
15   faces reflect the brilliance
   of thunder roaring
in the celestial hollows.
   You tear the robe
that cloaks heaven,
   you hurl the fiery thunderbolt.
18   O blessed one . . .
   the anger of the sea waves,
the anger of the mountain peaks—
   we all know your power.
Enjoy this libation and give all things
   pleasing to the heart:
21   a life of prosperity,
   queenly health,
divine peace that nurtures youths,
   crowned with honors,
a life ever blooming
   with cheerful thoughts.

20. To Astrapaios Zeus

incense—powdered frankincense

I call upon great and pure,
    upon resounding and illustrious,
upon ethereal and blazing Zeus,
    whose racing fire shines through the air.
3   Your light flashes through the clouds
    with an ear-splitting clap.
O horrid, O wrathful and pure,
    O invincible god,
lord of lightning, I call upon you,
    O begetter of all, O great king,
6   to be kind and to bring
    a sweet end to my life.

21. To the Clouds

incense—myrrh

Airy Clouds, you nourish fruits
    and rove the sky,
you bring rain as you are driven
    everywhere by the wind.
3   Filled with blazing thunder,
    filled with water, you resound
with awesome crashes
    in the air-filled vault of heaven
as you are repelled
    by the attack of raging winds.
6   To you I offer my prayers:
    your dewy cloaks, blown by fair breezes,
send fruit-nourishing rains
    to mother Earth.

22. To the Sea

incense—pounded frankincense

I call upon gray-eyed Tethys,
    bride of Okeanos,

dark-veiled queen
    whose waves dance
3   as they are blown onto the land
      by the sweet breezes.
You break your tall waves
    upon the rocky beaches,
you are calmed by races
    that are gentle and smooth,
6   you delight in ships,
      your waters feed wild beasts.
Mother of Kypris,
    mother of dark clouds,
mother of every spring
    round which nymphs swarm,
9   hear me, O holy one,
      please help,
send a fair tail wind to ships,
    O blessed one.

23. To Nereus

incense—myrrh

The sea's foundations are your realm,
    the abode of blue-black darkness,
you exult in the beauty
    of your fifty daughters
3   as they dance amid the waves.
      O Nereus, god of great renown,
O foundation of the sea, O end of the earth,
    O beginning of all,
Demeter's sacred throne trembles
    when you hold prisoner
6   the gusty winds driven
      to your gloomy depths.
O blessed one,
    ward off earthquakes and send
to the initiates peace and prosperity
    and gentle-handed health.

24. To the Nereids

incense—aromatic herbs

O lovely-faced and pure nymphs,
    daughters of Nereus, lord of the deep,
at the bottom of the sea
    you frolic and dance,
3   fifty maidens revel in the waves,
    maidens riding on the backs of Tritons,
delighting in animal shapes,
    bodies nurtured by the sea,
and in the other dwellers
    of Triton's billowy kingdom.
6   Your home is the water,
    you leap and whirl round the waves
like glistening dolphins
    roving the roaring seas.
I call upon you to bring
    much prosperity to the initiates,
9   for you were first
    to show the holy rite
of sacred Bacchos
    and of pure Persephone,
you and mother Kalliope
    and Apollon the lord.

25. To Proteus

incense—storax

I call upon Proteus,
    key-holding master of the sea,
first-born, who showed
    the beginnings of all nature,
3   changing matter
    into a great variety of forms.
Honored by all, he is wise,
    and he knows what is now,
what was before,
    and what will be in the future.

6   He has all at his disposal,
      transformed far beyond
  all other immortals
      who dwell on snowy Olympos
  and fly through the air
      and over land and sea,
9   for Physis was the first to place
      everything in Proteus.
  Father, attended by holy providence,
      visit the mystic initiates,
  and bring a good end to a life
      of industry and prosperity.

26. To Earth

incense, any grain save beans, and aromatic herbs

  Divine Earth, mother of men
      and of the blessed gods,
  you nourish all, you give all,
      you bring all to fruition, you destroy all.
3   When the season is fair, you teem
      with fruit and growing blossoms,
  O multi-formed maiden,
      seat of the immortal cosmos,
  in the pains of labor
      you bring forth all fruit.
6   Eternal, revered,
      deep-bosomed and blessed,
  your joy is the sweet breath of grass,
      O goddess bedecked with flowers,
  yours is the joy of the rain,
      the intricate realm of the stars
9   revolves in endless
      and awesome flow.
  O blessed goddess,
      may you multiply the delicious fruits,
  and may you and the beautiful Seasons
      grant me kindly favor.

27. To the Mother of the Gods

incense—et varia

Divine are your honors, O mother
    of the gods and nurturer of all.
Yoke your swift chariot
    drawn by bull-slaying lions,
3   and join our prayers, O mighty goddess.
      You bring things to pass,
O many-named and revered one,
    you are queen of the sky;
in the cosmos yours is the throne,
    the throne in the middle,
6   because the earth is yours,
      and you give gentle nourishment to mortals.
Of you were born
    gods and men,
you hold sway
    over the rivers and over all the sea.
9   Hestia is one of your names,
      they call you giver of prosperity,
because you bestow on men
    all manner of blessings.
Come to this rite,
    queen whom the drum delights,
12   all-taming savior of Phrygia,
      consort of Kronos,
honored child of Sky,
    frenzy-loving nurturer of life,
joyously and graciously
    visit our deeds of piety.

28. To Hermes

incense—frankincense

Hear me, Hermes,
    messenger of Zeus, son of Maia,
almighty in heart, lord of the deceased,
    judge of contests,
3   gentle and clever, O Argeiphontes,

you are the guide
of the flying sandals,
a man-loving prophet to mortals.
A vigorous god, you delight
in exercise and in deceit.
6   Interpreter of all you are
and a profiteer who frees us of cares,
who holds in his hands
the blameless tool of peace.
Lord of Korykos, blessed,
helpful, and skilled in words,
9   you assist in work and you are
a friend of mortals in need.
You wield the dreaded, the respected
weapon of speech.
Hear my prayer and grant
a good end to a life of industry,
12   gracious talk,
and mindfulness.

29. Hymn to Persephone

Persephone, blessed daughter
of great Zeus, sole offspring
of Demeter, come and accept
this gracious sacrifice.
3   Much-honored spouse of Plouton,
discreet and life-giving,
you command the gates of Hades
in the bowels of the earth,
lovely-tressed Praxidike,
pure bloom of Deo,
6   mother of the Erinyes,
queen of the nether world,
secretly sired by Zeus
in clandestine union.
Mother of loud-roaring,
many-shaped Eubouleus,
9   radiant and luminous,
playmate of the Seasons,

revered and almighty,
    maiden rich in fruits,
brilliant and horned,
    only-beloved of mortals,
12 in spring you take your joy
    in the meadow of breezes,
you show your holy figure
    in branches teeming with grass-green fruits,
in autumn you were made
    a kidnapper's bride.
15 You alone are life and death
    to toiling mortals,
O Persephone, you nourish all,
    always, and kill them, too.
Hearken, O blessed goddess,
    send forth the fruits of the earth
18 as you blossom in peace,
    and in gentle-handed health
bring a blessed life
    and a splendid old age to him who is sailing
to your realm, O queen,
    and to mighty Plouton's kingdom.

30. To Dionysos

incense—storax

I call upon loud-roaring,
    reveling Dionysos,
primeval, two-natured,
    thrice-born Bacchic lord,
3 savage, ineffable, secretive,
    two-horned and two-shaped,
ivy-covered, bull-faced,
    warlike, howling, pure.
You take raw flesh in triennial feasts,
    wrapped in foliage, decked with grape clusters,
6 resourceful Eubouleus,
    immortal god sired by Zeus
when he mated with Persephone
    in unspeakable union.

Hearken to my voice, O blessed one,
    you and your fair-girdled nurses,
9   breathe on me in a spirit
      of perfect kindness.

31. Hymn to the Kouretes

Leaping Kouretes,
    stepping to the sound of arms,
howling mountain men
    whose feet pound the ground,
3   discordant is the lyre you strike
      as you pace, light of foot,
O renowned marshals,
    O arm-carrying guards,
priests in the train of a mother
    struck with mountain frenzy.
6   Kindly visit the people
    who praise you with words,
with joyous heart
    be gracious to the oxherd.

32. To Athene

incense—aromatic herbs

Reverend Pallas,
    great Zeus bore you by himself,
noble and blessed goddess,
    brave in the din of war.
3   Renowned and cave-haunting,
    spoken of and then ineffable,
your domain is
    on wind-swept hilltops,
shaded mountains,
    dells that charm your heart.
6   Arms please you, and you strike men's souls
    with frenzy,
O vigorous maiden,
    O horrid-tempered one,

slayer of Gorgo, O blessed mother of the arts,
   you shun the bed of love,
9   you bring madness to the wicked,
     you bring prudence to the virtuous, O impetuous one.
Male and female,
   shrewd begetter of war,
she-dragon of the many shapes,
   frenzy-loving, illustrious,
12   destroyer of the Phlegraian Giants,
     driver of horses,
victorious Tritogeneia,
   O goddess, you free us from suffering,
day and night,
   ever into the small hours.
15   Hear my prayer and give me
     a full measure of peace,
of riches, and of health,
   accompanied by happy seasons,
O gray-eyed and inventive queen,
   to whom many offer their prayers.

33. To Nike

incense—powdered frankincense

I call upon mighty Nike,
   beloved of mortals;
she alone frees man
   from the eagerness for contest,
3   from dissent,
     when men face each other in battle.
In war you are the judge
   of deeds deserving prizes;
sweet is the boast
   you grant after the onslaught.
6   Nike, mistress of all,
     on your good name depends noble glory,
glory that comes from the strife
   and teems with festivities.
O blessed and beloved one,
   come with joy in your eyes,

9   come for works of renown,
        bring me noble glory.

34. To Apollon

incense—powdered frankincense

Come, O blessed Paian, O slayer of Tityos,
    O Phoibos, O Lykoreus,
giver of riches, illustrious dweller of Memphis,
    O god to whom we cry "Ië,"
3   O Titan and Pythian god,
        yours are
    the golden lyre, the seeds, and the plows.
        Grynean, Sminthian, slayer of Python,
    Delphic diviner, wild, light-bringing,
        lovable god you are, O glorious youth.
6   You shoot your arrows from afar,
        you lead the Muses into dance,
    O holy one, you are Bacchos,
        Didymeus, Loxias, too,
    lord of Delos, you are the eye that sees all,
        you bring light to mortals,
9   your hair is golden,
        your oracular utterance is clear.
    Hear me with kindly heart
        as I pray for people.
    You gaze upon all
        the ethereal vastness,
12   upon the rich earth you look
        through the twilight.
    In the quiet darkness
        of a night lit with stars
    you see earth's roots below,
        you hold the bounds
15   of the whole world;
        the beginning and the end to come are yours.
    You make everything bloom
        with your versatile lyre,
    you harmonize the poles,
        now reaching the highest pitch,

18 now the lowest,
        now again with a Doric mode,
    harmoniously balancing the poles,
        you keep the living races distinct.
    You have infused harmony
        into the lot of all men,
21 giving them an equal measure
        of winter and summer:
    the lowest notes you strike in the winter,
        the highest notes you make distinct in the summer,
    your mode is Doric
        for spring's lovely and blooming season.
24 This is why mortals call you
        lord and Pan,
    the two-horned god
        who sends the whistling winds;
    it is for this you have
        the master seal of the entire cosmos.
27 O blessed one, hear the suppliant voice
        of the initiates and save them.

35. To Leto

incense—myrrh

    Dark-veiled Leto, revered goddess,
        mother of twins,
    great-souled daughter of Koios,
        queen to whom many pray,
3   to your lot fell the birth pains
        for Zeus' fair children,
    you bore Phoibos
        and arrow-pouring Artemis,
    her on Ortygia,
        him on rocky Delos.
6   Hear, lady goddess,
        come with favor in your heart
    to bring a sweet end
        to this all-holy rite.

36. To Artemis

incense—powdered frankincense

Hear me, O queen,
    Zeus' daughter of many names,
Titanic and Bacchic,
    revered, renowned archer,
3   torch-bearing goddess bringing light to all,
    Diktynna, helper at childbirth,
you help women in labor,
    though you know not what labor is.
O frenzy-loving huntress,
    you loosen girdles and drive distress away;
6   swift arrow-pouring goddess of the outdoors,
    you roam in the night.
Fame-bringing and affable,
    redeeming and masculine in appearance,
Orthia, goddess of swift birth,
    you are a nurturer of mortal youths,
9   immortal and yet of this earth,
    you slay wild beasts, O blessed one,
your realm is in the mountain forest,
    you hunt deer.
O revered and mighty queen of all,
    fair-blossomed, eternal,
12   sylvan, dog-loving,
    many-shaped lady of Kydonia,
come, dear goddess,
    as savior to all the initiates,
accessible to all, bringing forth
    the beautiful fruit of the earth,
15   lovely peace,
    and fair-tressed health.
May you dispatch diseases and pain
    to the peaks of the mountains.

37. To the Titans

incense—frankincense

Titans, glorious children
    of Sky and Earth,
ancestors of our fathers,
    you dwell down below
3   in Tartarean homes,
    in the bowels of the earth.
From you are descended
    all toiling mortals,
the brood of the sea and of the land,
    then the brood of the birds,
6   of all generations
    of the world born of you.
I call upon you
    to banish harsh anger
if some earthly forefather of mine
    stormed your homes.

38. To the Kouretes

incense—frankincense

Bronze-beating Kouretes,
    the weapons of Ares are yours.
Dwellers of heaven, of earth and sea,
    thrice-blessed ones,
3   life-giving breezes,
    glorious saviors of the world,
you dwell in the sacred land
    of Samothrace,
you ward off dangers
    for mortals roaming the seas,
6   you were first to set up
    sacred rites for mortals.
O immortal Kouretes,
    the weapons of Ares are yours.
You rule Okeanos,
    you rule the sea and the forests,

9   the earth resounds with the pounding
      of your nimble feet,
and with the glories in your gleaming armor.
      All wild beasts cringe
at your onrush,
      the din and the shouts rise heavenward,
12   the dust from your feet,
      as you march briskly,
reaches the clouds;
      every flower is in bloom.
Immortal gods, you nurture,
      you also destroy
15   when you fret angrily
      over mankind,
you ruin livelihoods and possessions,
      you ruin men themselves.
. . . the great deep-eddying
      sea groans,
18   lofty trees are uprooted,
      they fall upon the earth,
the noisy tremor of the leaves
      echoes in the sky.
Kouretes, Korybantes,
      mighty lords,
21   masters of Samothrace,
      true Dioskouroi,
ever-blowing breezes,
      soul-nurturing and airy,
you're called celestial twins
      on Olympos.
24   Gentle saviors, you bring
      fair breezes and clear weather,
nurturers of seasons and of fruits,
      breathe upon us, O lords.

39. To Korybas

incense—frankincense

I call upon the greatest king
      of eternal earth,

blessed Korybas, the warlike,
    the one of the forbidding countenance,
3 the nocturnal Koures
    who saves us from dreadful fear.
Korybas, you save us from fantasies
    as you wander in deserted places.
Many are the shapes, O lord,
    of your twofold divinity;
6 your blood is tainted
    with the murder of twin brothers.
You follow Deo's thinking,
    you changed your holy form
into the shape of a savage,
    dark dragon.
9 O blessed one, hear our voices,
    banish harsh anger,
free from fantasies
    souls stunned by compulsions.

40. To Eleusinian Demeter

incense—storax

Deo, divine mother of all,
    goddess of many names,
revered Demeter, nurturer of youths,
    giver of prosperity and wealth,
3 you nourish the ears of corn,
    O giver of all,
you delight in peace
    and in toilsome labor.
Present at sowing, heaping, and threshing,
    O spirit of the unripe fruit,
6 you dwell
    in the sacred valley of Eleusis.
Charming and lovely,
    you give sustenance to all mortals;
you were the first to yoke
    the ploughing ox,
9 the first to send up from below a rich,
    a lovely harvest for mortals.

You are growth and blooming,
    O illustrious companion of Bromios,
torch-bearing and pure,
    you delight in the summer's yield.
12   From beneath the earth you appear,
    gentle to all,
O holy and youth-nurturing lover
    of children and of fair offspring.
You yoke your chariot
    to bridled dragons,
15   round your throne
    you whirl and howl in ecstasy.
You are an only daughter, but you have many children
    and many powers over mortals;
the variety of flowers reflect
    your myriad faces and your sacred blossoms.
18   Come, O blessed and pure one,
    come with the fruits of summer,
bring peace,
    bring the welcome rule of law,
bring riches, too, and prosperity,
    and bring health that governs all.

41. To Mother Antaia

incense—aromatic herbs

Queen Antaia,
    goddess and many-named mother
of immortal gods
    and of mortal men,
3   weary from searching,
    weary from wandering far and wide,
you once ended your fast
    in the valley of Eleusis,
you came to Hades
    for noble Persephone.
6   Your guide was
    the innocent child of Dysaules,
who brought the news
    of pure Chthonic Zeus' holy union;

you bore divine Euboulos
    by yielding to human need.
9   O goddess, O queen to whom many pray,
        I beseech you
to come graciously
    to your pious initiate.

42. To Mise

incense—storax

I call upon law-giving Dionysos,
    who carried the fennel stalk,
unforgettable and many-named
    seed of Eubouleus,
3   I call upon the sacred and holy,
        upon the ineffable queen Mise,
whose twofold nature is male and female.
        Redeeming Iacchos, lord, I summon you,
whether you delight in Eleusis
    in your fragrant temple,
6   or with Mother you partake
        of mystic rites in Phrygia,
or you rejoice in Kypros
    with fair-wreathed Kythereia,
or yet you exult in fields
    wheat-bearing and hallowed
9   along Egypt's river
        with your divine mother,
the revered and black-robed Isis,
        as your train of nurses tends to your needs.
Lady, kindheartedly come
    to the noble contests of our initiation.

43. To the Seasons

incense—aromatic herbs

Seasons, daughters of Themis,
    daughters of Lord Zeus,
Eunomia and Dike

and thrice-blessed Eirene,
3   pure spirits of spring,
         of blossoming meadows,
you are found in every color, in all scents
         wafted by the breezes.
Ever-blooming, revolving, and sweet-faced,
         O Seasons,
6   you cloak yourselves with the dew
         of luxuriant flowers.
At play you are companions
         of holy Persephone, when the Fates
and the Graces in circling dances
         come forth to the light,
9   pleasing Zeus
         and their mother, giver of fruits.
Come to the new initiates
         and their holy and reverent rites,
bring perfect seasons
         for the growth of goodly fruit.

44. To Semele

incense—storax

I call upon the daughter of Kadmos,
         queen of all,
fair Semele of the lovely tresses,
         of the full bosom,
3   mother of thyrsos-bearing,
         joyous Dionysos.
She was driven to great pain
         by the blazing thunderbolt,
which, through the counsels of Kronian Zeus,
         the immortal god, burned her.
6   Noble Persephone
         granted her honors
among mortal men,
         honors given every third year.
For all mortal men reenact your travail
         for your son Bacchos:

9   the sacred ritual of the table,
        the ritual of the holy mysteries.

45. Hymn to Dionysos Bassareus and Triennial

Come blessed Dionysos,
    bull-faced god conceived in fire,
Bassareus and Bacchos,
    many-named master of all.
3   You delight in bloody swords,
        you delight in the holy Maenads,
as you howl throughout Olympos,
    all-roaring and frenzied Bacchos.
Armed with the thyrsos, wrathful in the extreme,
    you are honored
6   by all gods and all men
        who dwell upon the earth.
Come, blessed and leaping god,
    bring abundant joy to all.

46. To Liknites

incense—powdered frankincense

I summon to these prayers
    Dionysos Liknites,
born at Nysa, blossoming,
    beloved and kindly Bacchos,
3   nursling of the Nymphs
        and of fair-wreathed Aphrodite.
The forests once felt your feet
    quiver in the dance
as frenzy drove you and the graceful Nymphs
    on and on.
6   The counsels of Zeus brought you
        to noble Persephone,
who reared you to be loved
    by the deathless gods.
Kindheartedly come, O blessed one,
    accept the gift of this sacrifice.

47. To Perikionios

incense—aromatic herbs

I call upon Bacchos Perikionios,
    giver of wine;
he enveloped
    all of Kadmos' house,
3   with his might he harnessed,
    he calmed the heaving earth,
when the blazing thunderbolt,
    when the raging gale
stirred all the land,
    as everyone's bonds sprang loose.
6   Blessed reveler,
    come with joyful heart.

48. To Sabazios

incense—aromatic herbs

Hear me, father Sabazios,
    son of Kronos, illustrious god,
you sewed into your thigh
    Bacchic Dionysos,
3   the roaring Eiraphiotes,
    that he might come whole
to noble Tmolos
    by the side of fair-cheeked Hipta.
O blessed ruler of Phrygia,
    supreme king of all,
6   come kindheartedly to the aid
    of the initiates.

49. To Hipta

incense—storax

I call upon Hipta, nurse of Bacchos,
    maiden possessed,
in mystic rites she takes part,
    she exults in the worship of pure Sabos

3   and in the dances
         of roaring Iacchos.
     O queen and chthonic mother,
         hear my prayer,
     whether you are on Ida,
         Phrygia's sacred mountain,
6   or you take your pleasure on Tmolos,
         fair seat of the Lydians,
     come to these rites
         with joy on your holy face.

50. To Lysios Lenaios

     Hear, O blessed son of Zeus and of two mothers,
         Bacchos of the vintage,
     unforgettable seed,
         many-named and redeeming *daimōn,*
3   holy offspring of the gods,
         reveling Bacchos, born of secrecy,
     plump giver of many joys,
         of fruits which grow well.
     Mighty and many-shaped god,
         you burst forth from the earth to reach the wine press,
6   to become a healer for men's pain,
         O sacred blossom!
     A sorrow-hating joy to mortals,
         O lovely-haired . . . ,
     a redeemer and a reveler you are,
         your thyrsos drives to frenzy,
9   you are kind-hearted to all
         gods and mortals who see your light.
     I call upon you now,
         come, O sweet bringer of fruit.

51. To the Nymphs

incense—aromatic herbs

     O Nymphs, daughters
         of great-hearted Okeanos,

you dwell inside
    the earth's damp caves;
3   you are as secret as your paths, O joyous,
       O chthonic nurses of Bacchos.
You nurture fruits, you haunt meadows,
    O sprightly and pure
travelers of the winding roads,
    who delight in caves and grottos.
6   Swift, light-footed, and clothed in dew,
      you frequent springs,
visible and invisible,
    in ravines and among flowers
you shout and frisk with Pan
    upon mountainsides,
9   gliding down on rocks,
      you hum with clear voice.
O mountain-haunting maidens of the fields,
    of gushing springs and of woodlands,
sweet-smelling virgins,
    clothed in white, fresh as the breeze,
12   herds of goats, pastures, splendid fruit,
      you protect; wild animals love you.
Though you are tender, cold delights you;
    you feed many, you help them grow,
Hamadryad maidens,
    playful, water-loving.
15   Spring is your joy, O Nysian and frenzied,
      O healing ones,
in the company of Bacchos and Deo,
    you bring grace to mortals.
Come to this blessed sacrifice
    with joyful heart,
18   pour streams of pure rain
    during the grain-giving seasons.

52. To the God of Triennial Feasts

incense—aromatic herbs

I call upon you, blessed, many-named,
    frenzied Bacchos,

bull-horned, Nysian, Lysios,
    Lenaios, conceived in fire.
3   Nourished in the thigh, Liknites,
      you lead torch-lit processions,
you lead them in the night, O filleted,
    O thyrsos-shaking Eubouleus.
Your nature three-fold, your rites ineffable,
    O secret offspring of Zeus,
6   primeval, Erikepaios,
      father and son of the gods,
you take raw flesh, and sceptered you lead us
    into the madness of revel and dance,
into the frenzy of triennial feasts
    that bestow calm on us.
9   You burst forth from the earth in a blaze . . . ,
    O son of two mothers,
horned and clad in fawn skin, you roam the mountains,
    O lord worshipped in annual feasts.
Paian of the golden spear,
    nursling, decked with grapes,
12   Bassaros, exulting in ivy,
      followed by many maidens . . . ,
joyous and all-abounding, come,
    O blessed one, to the initiates.

53. To the God of Annual Feasts

incense—all other things, save frankincense—a libation of milk, too

I call upon Bacchos, the god we worship annually,
    chthonic Dionysos,
together with the fair-tressed Nymphs
    he is roused.
3   In the sacred halls of Persephone
      he slumbers and puts to sleep
pure
    Bacchic time, every third year.
When he himself stirs up
    the triennial revel again,
6   he sings a hymn
      together with his fair-girdled nurses.

As the seasons revolve,
    he puts to sleep and wakes up the years.
O blessed and fruit-giving Bacchos,
    O horned spirit of the unripe fruit,

9   come to this most sacred rite
    with a glow of joy on your face,
come teeming with fruit
    that is holy and perfect.

54. To Silenos Satyros and the Bacchae

incense—powdered frankincense

Hear me, foster father
    of Bacchos, father and nurturer,
best of the Silenoi,
    honored by all the gods,

3   honored by mortal men
    in the same triennial feasts.
Pure and prized marshal
    of the pastoral band,
wakeful reveler and companion
    of the fair-girt nurses,

6   leader of the ivy-crowned
    Naiads and of the Bacchantes,
take all the Satyrs,
    half-men, half-beast,
come howling
    to the Bacchic lord.

9   The Bacchantes escort
    the holy Lenaian procession
in sacred litanies
    revealing torch-lit rites,
shouting, thyrsos-loving,
    finding calm in the revels.

55. To Aphrodite

Heavenly, smiling Aphrodite,
    praised in many hymns,

sea-born revered goddess of generation,
   you like the night-long revel,
3   you couple lovers at night,
   O scheming mother of Necessity.
Everything comes from you:
   you have yoked the world,
you control all three realms,
   you give birth to all,
6   to everything in heaven,
   to everything upon the fruitful earth,
to everything in the depths of the sea,
   O venerable companion of Bacchos.
You delight in festivities,
   O bride-like mother of the Erotes,
9   O Persuasion, whose joy is in the bed of love,
   secretive giver of grace,
visible and invisible,
   lovely-tressed daughter of a noble father,
bridal feast companion of the gods,
   sceptered, she-wolf,
12   beloved and man-loving,
   giver of birth and life.
Your maddening love-charms
   yoke mortals,
they yoke the many races of beasts
   to unbridled passion.
15   Come, O goddess born in Kypros:
   you may be on Olympos,
O queen, exulting
   in the beauty of your face,
you may be in Syria,
   country of fine frankincense,
18   you may be driving
   your golden chariot in the plain,
you may lord it over
   Egypt's fertile river bed.
Come, whether you ride your swan-drawn chariot
   over the sea's billows,
21   joining the creatures of the deep
   as they dance in circles,
or on land in the company

of the dark-faced nymphs
    as light-footed they frisk
over the sandy beaches.

24   Come lady, even if you are
    in Kypros that cherishes you,
where fair maidens and chaste brides
    throughout the year sing of you,
O blessed one,
    as they sing of immortal, pure Adonis.

27   Come, O beautiful,
    O comely goddess,
I summon you with holy words,
    I summon you with a pious soul.

56. To Adonis

incense—aromatic herbs

Hear my prayer, O best,
    O many-named god.
Fine-haired, solitary,
    ever bursting with lovely song,

3   Eubouleus, many-shaped,
    noble nurturer of all,
male and female in one . . .
    unwithering bloom, O Adonis,
you vanish and then shine again
    in the fair season's turn.

6   Two-horned spirit of growth,
    much loved and wept for,
fair one, joyful hunter,
    god of the luxuriant mane,
desire is in you, O sweet blossom,
    O son of Aphrodite and Eros,

9   born on the bed
    of lovely-tressed Persephone.
You dwell deep
    in murky Tartaros,
then again toward Olympos
    you carry your blossoming body.

12   Come, O blessed one, bring
     earth's fruits to the initiates.

57. To Chthonic Hermes

incense—storax

You dwell on the road all must take,
    the road of no return, by the Kokytos,
you guide the souls
    of mortals to the nether gloom.
3   Hermes, offspring of Dionysos
    who revels in the dance,
and of Aphrodite, the Paphian maiden
    of the fluttering eyelids,
you haunt the sacred house of Persephone
    as guide throughout the earth of ill-fated souls,
6   the souls you bring to their destined harbor
    when their time has come;
you charm them with your sacred wand,
    you give them sleep
from which you rouse them again.
    It is to you indeed
9   that Persephone gave the high office
    throughout broad Tartaros
to lead the way
    for the everlasting souls of men.
O blessed one, grant a good end
    for the labors of the initiates.

58. To Eros

incense—aromatic herbs

I call upon you, great, pure,
    lovely and sweet Eros,
winged archer who runs
    swiftly on a path of fire,
3   who plays together with gods
    and mortal men.

Inventive, two-natured,
    you are master of all:
of the sky's ether, of the sea and the land,
    of the all-begetting winds,
6   which for mortals the goddess
        of grass and grain nurtures,
    of all that lies in Tartaros,
        of all that lies in the roaring sea;
    you alone govern
        the course of all these.
9   O blessed one, come to the initiates
        with pure thought,
    banish from them
        vile impulses.

59. To the Fates

incense—aromatic herbs

Boundless Fates,
    dear children of dark Night,
hear my prayer,
    O many-named
3   dwellers on the lake of heaven,
        where the frozen water is broken
    by night's warmth
        in the shady hollow of a sleek cave;
    from there you fly to the vast earth,
        home of mortals, from there,
6   clothed in purple, you march
        toward men,
    whose noble aims
        match their vain hopes,
    in the realm of the dead,
        where glory drives her chariot on
9   all over the earth
        beyond the ends of Justice,
    of anxious hope, of primeval law,
        of the measureless principle of order.
    In life Fate alone watches;

the other immortals
12   who dwell on the peaks
          of snowy Olympos do not,
      except for Zeus' perfect eye.
          Fate and Zeus' mind
      know all things
          for all time.
15   I pray to you to come,
          gently and kindly,
      Atropos, Lakhesis, Klotho,
          offspring of noble stock.
      Airy, invisible, inexorable,
          ever indestructible,
18   you give all and take all,
          being to men the same as necessity.
      Fates, hear my prayers,
          receive my libations,
      come gently to the initiates,
          free them from pain.

60. To the Graces

incense—storax

Hear me, O illustrious,
    O renowned Graces,
daughters of Zeus
    and full-bosomed Eunomia,
3   Aglaia, Thalia,
        blessed Euphrosyne,
    lovely, wise, and pure
        mothers of joy,
    many-shaped, ever-blooming,
        beloved of mortals.
6   We pray that each in her turn
        with a flower's beauty on her face, enchanting,
    come, ever gentle, to the initiates
        to bring them prosperity.

61. Hymn to Nemesis

Nemesis, I call upon you,
    O goddess, O great queen,
your all-seeing eye looks upon
    the lives of man's many races.
3   Eternal and revered,
    you alone rejoice in the just,
you change and vary,
    you shift your word.
All who bear the yoke
    of mortality fear you,
6   you care about the thoughts of all;
    the arrogant soul,
the reckless one,
    finds no escape.
You see all, you hear all,
    you arbitrate all.
9   O sublime deity,
    in whom dwells justice for men,
come, blessed and pure one,
    ever helpful to the initiates,
grant nobility of mind,
    put an end to repulsive thoughts,
12   thoughts unholy,
    fickle and haughty.

62. To Dike

incense—frankincense

I sing of the all-seeing eye
    of comely and radiant Dike,
who is seated upon the sacred throne
    of lord Zeus.
3   From heaven you watch the lives
    of the many human races,
you crush the unjust
    with just retribution,
matching things lawless
    through the truth of equality.

6 For whenever base opinions
        prevail in difficult verdicts,
   because men wish more
        than is fair,
   you intervene and rouse
        justice against her foes.
9 An enemy of the unjust,
        you are a gentle goddess to the just.
   O goddess, come evenhanded
        to thoughts that are noble,
   until that fated day
        descends on my life.

63. To Justice

incense—frankincense

O paragon of justice to mortals,
        blessed and beloved one,
   you take equal pleasure
        in all men who are just.
3 Honored by all and blissful,
        O bold, O lofty Justice,
   you are pure of thought,
        you reward propriety,
   your own conscience is unbreakable
        for you break all
6 who do not submit to your yoke,
        but . . .
   in their greed upset
        the balance of your mighty scales.
   Dauntless, charming,
        a lover of revel loved by all,
9 you rejoice in peace, you strive
        for a life that is stable.
   You loath unfairness,
        but fairness delights you;
   in you knowledge of virtue
        reaches its noble goal.
12 Hear, O goddess,
        rightly shatter wicked men,

so that mortals who eat
    of the fruits of this earth
and also all living creatures
    nursed in the bosom
15 of Earth, the divine mother,
    nursed in the bosom of sea-dwelling Zeus,
may follow a path
    both balanced and noble.

64. Hymn to Nomos

Upon the holy lord
    of men and gods I call,
heavenly Nomos, who arranges
    the stars and sets a fair limit
3 between the earth and the waters of the sea;
    it is his laws
that ever preserve nature's balance,
    obedient and steady.
Journeying on the heavens,
    he brings the laws from above,
6 with a roar he drives out
    malicious envy.
Nomos summons
    a good end to mortal life,
he alone steers the course
    of everything that breathes,
9 ever the steadfast companion
    of righteous thought.
Primeval and wise, in peace he shares
    the same house with all who abide by the law,
bringing harsh vengeance
    upon the lawless.
12 O blessed bringer of prosperity,
    beloved of all and honored,
with kindness of heart send forth
    memory of you, O mighty one.

65. To Ares

incense—frankincense

Unbreakable, strong-spirited,
    mighty, powerful *daimōn,*
delighting in arms, indomitable,
    man-slaying, wall-battering,
3 lord Ares, yours is the din of arms.
    Ever bespattered with blood,
you find joy in killing
    in the fray of battle, O horrid one,
your desire is for the rude clash
    of swords and spears.
6 Stay the rage, stay the strife,
    relax pain's grip on my soul,
yield to the wish of Kypris,
    yield to the revels of Lyaios,
exchange the might of arms
    for the works of Deo,
9 yearning for youth-nurturing peace,
    bliss-bringing peace.

66. To Hephaistos

incense—powdered frankincense

Hephaistos, powerful and strong-spirited,
    unwearying fire,
shining in the gleam of flames,
    a god bringing light to mortals,
3 mighty-handed,
    eternal artisan,
worker, part of the cosmos,
    blameless element,
most sublime, all-eating,
    all-taming, all-haunting—
6 ether, sun, stars,
    moon, pure light:
all these parts of Hephaistos
    are revealed to mortals.
All homes, all cities,

all nations are yours.
9   O mighty giver of many blessings,
           you dwell in human bodies.
       Hear me, lord, as I summon you
           to this holy libation,
       that you may always come
           gentle to joyful deeds,
12   end the savage rage
           of untiring fire
       as nature itself
           burns in our own bodies.

67. To Asklepios

incense—frankincense

Asklepios, lord Paian,
    healer of all,
you charm away the pains
    of men who suffer.
3   Come, mighty and soothing,
         bring health,
     put an end to sickness,
         then to the harsh fate of death.
     O blessed spirit of joyful growth,
         O helper, you ward off evil,
6   honored and mighty son
         of Phoibos Apollon.
     Enemy of disease,
         consort of Hygieia the blameless,
     come as savior, O blessed one,
         bring life to a good end.

68. To Hygeia

incense—frankincense

Charming queen of all,
    lovely and blooming,
blessed Hygeia, mother of all,
    bringer of bliss, hear me.

3   Through you vanish
           the illnesses that afflict man,
     through you every house
           blossoms to the fullness of joy.
     The arts thrive when the world
           desires you, O queen,
6   loathed by Hades,
           the destroyer of souls.
     Apart from you all is
           without profit for men:
     wealth, the sweet giver of abundance
           for those who feast, fails,
9   and man never reaches
           the many pains of old age.
     Goddess, come, ever-helpful
           to the initiates,
     keep away the evil distress
           of unbearable diseases.

69. To the Erinyes

incense—storax—powdered frankincense

     Hear, Tisiphone, Allekto,
           noble Megaira,
     revered goddesses
           whose Bacchic cries resound.
3   Nocturnal and clandestine,
           you live deep down
     in the dank cave
           by the sacred water of the Styx.
     Men's unholy designs
           do incur your anger;
6   rabid and arrogant, you howl
           over Necessity's dictates,
     clothed in animal skins,
           you cause the deep pains of retribution.
     O dreaded maidens of the thousand faces,
           your realm is in Hades,
9   phantoms airy, invisible,
           swift as thought you are.

The speedy flames of the sun
   and the moon's glow
cannot arouse life's delights
   without your aid,
12 neither can the excellence of wisdom,
   as well as the virtue and the joy
in bold enterprise
   and in the sleekness of fair youth.
Upon the races of all men
   that remain countless,
15 you gaze as the eye of Dike,
   ever in charge of justice.
O snake-haired and many-shaped
   goddesses of fate,
change my thoughts of life
   into gentle and soft ones.

70. To the Eumenides

incense—aromatic herbs

Hear me and be gracious,
   O renowned Eumenides,
O pure daughters
   of the great Chthonic Zeus
3 and of lovely Persephone,
   fair-tressed maiden.
Over the lives of impious mortals
   you keep a careful eye,
in charge of Necessity,
   you punish the unjust.
6 Black-skinned queens,
   your awesome eyes flash forth
flesh-eating
   darts of light.
Everlasting, repugnant,
   frightful, sovereign,
9 paralyzing the limbs with madness,
   hideous, nocturnal, fateful,
snake-haired, terrible
   maidens of the night,

it is you I summon
    to bring me holiness of mind.

71. To Melinoe

incense—aromatic herbs

I call upon Melinoe,
    saffron-cloaked nymph of the earth,
whom revered Persephone bore
    by the mouth of the Kokytos river
3   upon the sacred bed
    of Kronian Zeus.
In the guise of Plouton Zeus tricked
    Persephone and through wily plots bedded her;
a two-bodied specter sprang forth
    from Persephone's fury.
6   This specter drives mortals to madness
    with her airy apparitions
as she appears in weird shapes
    and strange forms,
now plain to the eye, now shadowy,
    now shining in the darkness—
9   all this in unnerving attacks
    in the gloom of night.
O goddess, O queen
    of those below, I beseech you
to banish the soul's frenzy
    to the ends of the earth,
12   show to the initiates
    a kindly and holy face.

72. To Tyche

incense—frankincense

I summon you here through prayer,
    Tyche, noble ruler,
gentle goddess of the roads,
    for wealth and possessions,

3   I summon you as Artemis the guide,
         renowned and sprung from the loins
     of Eubouleus,
         your wish is irresistible.
     Funereal and delusive,
         you are the theme of men's songs.
6   In you lies the great variety
         of men's livelihood:
     to some you grant a wealth
         of blessings and possessions,
     to others you bring evil poverty
         if you harbor anger against them.
9   O goddess, I beseech you,
         come in kindness to my life,
     grant me happiness,
         grant me abundant wealth.

73. To Daimon

incense—frankincense

     I call upon Daimon,
         the grand and the dreaded leader,
     gentle Zeus, who gives birth to all,
         who gives livelihood to mortals.
3   Great Zeus, wide roving,
         avenger, king of all,
     giver of wealth when you enter the house
         in the abundance of your powers,
     you refresh the life of mortals
         worn out with toil,
6   you possess the keys to joy
         and sorrow as well.
     So, O pure and blessed one,
         drive painful cares away,
     cares that dispatch ruin to all that live
         throughout the whole earth,
9   and bring a glorious end to my life,
         a sweet and noble one.

74. To Leukothea

incense—aromatic herbs

I call upon Leukothea,
    daughter of Kadmos, revered goddess,
mighty nurturer
    of fair-wreathed Dionysos.
3   Hearken, O goddess,
    O mistress of the deep-bosomed sea,
you delight in waves,
    you are the greatest savior to mortals,
on you depends the unsteady heave
    of seafaring ships,
6   you alone save men
    from wretched death at sea,
men to whom you swiftly come
    as welcome savior.
O divine lady,
    come to the aid
9   of well-benched ships,
    do kindly save them,
bring upon the sea
    a fair tail wind to the initiates.

75. To Palaimon

incense—powdered frankincense

Comrade of joyous Dionysos
    in the revel of the dance,
you dwell in the sea's
    pure, restless depths.
3   I call upon you, O Palaimon,
    to come to these sacred rites
with kindness in your heart,
    with joy on your youthful face,
come to save your initiates
    on land and on sea.
6   When storms come upon ships
    that ever rove the seas,
you alone appear incarnate

to save men,
    to stay the harsh anger
        over the briny swell.

76. To the Muses

incense—frankincense

Daughters of Mnemosyne,
    daughters of thundering Zeus,
Pierian Muses,
    renowned and illustrious,
3   many-shaped and beloved
        of the mortals you visit,
you give birth to unblemished virtue
    in every discipline,
you nourish the soul,
    you set thought aright
6   as you become leaders,
        as you become mistresses of the mind's power.
Sacred and mystic rites
    you taught to mortals,
Kleio, Euterpe,
    Thaleia, Melpomene,
9   Terpsichore, Erato,
        Polymnia, Ourania,
mother Kalliope,
    mighty goddess Hagne.
Do come to the initiates, O goddesses,
    in your manifold holiness,
12   do bring glory and emulation
        that is lovely and sung by many.

77. To Mnemosyne

incense—frankincense

I call upon queen Mnemosyne,
    Zeus' consort,
who gave birth to the holy,
    the sacred, the clear-voiced Muses.

3   Evil oblivion that harms the mind
    is alien to her
who gives coherence
    to the mind and soul of mortals.
She increases men's power,
    their ability to think,
6   sweet and vigilant,
    she reminds us of all
the thoughts we store
    forever in our breasts,
never straying and ever rousing
    the mind to action.
9   O blessed goddess,
    for the initiates stir the memory
of the sacred rite,
    ward off oblivion from them.

78. To Dawn

incense—powdered frankincense

Hear, O goddess, you bring
    the light of day to mortals,
resplendent Dawn, you blush
    throughout the world,
3   messenger of the great,
    the illustrious Titan.
Murky, dark,
    journeying night
you send below the earth
    when you arrive;
6   mortal men you lead to work
    as you tend to their lives.
The race of mortal men
    delights in you,
no one escapes your sight
    as you look down from on high,
9   when from your eyelids
    you shake off sweet sleep,
when there is joy
    for every mortal,

for every reptile,
    for animals,
12 for birds,
        for the broods the sea contains.
    All blessings that come from work
        are your gift.
    Goddess, blessed and pure, give
        more sacred light to the initiates.

79. To Themis

incense—frankincense

I call upon pure Themis,
    daughter of noble Sky
and Earth, Themis the young,
    the lovely-faced maiden,
3   the first to show mortals
        the holy oracle
    as prophetess of the gods
        in her Delphic hideaway
    on Pythian ground
        where Python was king.
6   You taught lord Phoibos
        the art of giving laws.
    Amid reverence and honor
        you shine in the night,
    for you were first
        to teach men holy worship,
9   howling to Bacchos
        in nights of revelry;
    from you come the honors
        of the gods, the honors of the holy mysteries.
    O blessed maiden,
        come in a joyous, in a kindly spirit
12 to your very sacred,
        to your mystical rites.

80. To Boreas

incense—frankincense

Freezing Boreas, your wintry breezes
   make the world's
lofty air quiver,
   come from snowy Thrace!
3   Dissolve the rebellious alliance
   of clouds and moist air,
turn the water
   to rushing drops of rain,
bring fair weather everywhere,
   brighten Ether's face
6   as the sun's rays
   shine upon the earth.

81. To Zephyros

incense—frankincense

Western breezes born of the open sea,
   ethereal wonders,
as you blow gently
   your whisper brings rest from toil.
3   Vernal, meadow-haunting,
   you are loved by harbors
because to ships you bring
   a gentle passage, soft light wind.
Come in a generous spirit,
   blow in unblemished ways,
6   O airy, O invisible,
   O light-winged ones.

82. To Notos

incense—frankincense

Quickly leaping
   through the moist air
as both of your swift wings vibrate,
   O father of rain, come,

3   riding the southern clouds.
    Zeus did grant you
this lofty prerogative:
    to send the rain-giving clouds
from sky to earth.
    For this we pray to you, O blessed one,
6   take delight in our sacrifice,
    do send fruit-nourishing rains to mother Earth.

83. To Okeanos

incense—aromatic herbs

I summon Okeanos,
    ageless, eternal father,
begetter of immortal gods,
    begetter of mortal men.
3   Your waves, O Okeanos,
    gird the boundaries of the earth.
From you come all the seas,
    from you come all the rivers,
from you come the pure, the flowing waters
    of earth's springs.
6   Hear me, O blessed god,
    O highest, O divine purifier,
where you end the earth ends,
    the pole begins where ships glide on,
come, grant favor,
    grant grace to the initiates.

84. To Hestia

incense—aromatic herbs

Queen Hestia,
    daughter of mighty Kronos,
mistress of ever-burning fire,
    you dwell in the center of the house.
3   May you raise the holy initiates
    in these sacred rites,
may you grant them unwithering youth,

wealth as well, prudence and purity.
Home of the blessed gods,
   men's mighty buttress,
6   eternal, many-shaped,
   beloved, grass-yellow,
smile, O blessed one,
   kindly accept these offerings,
waft upon us prosperity,
   breathe upon us gentle-handed health.

85. To Sleep

incense with opium poppy

Sleep, you are lord of all,
   lord of blessed gods and of mortal men,
of every living thing
   the broad earth nurtures,
3   for you alone are master of all,
   you do visit all,
binding their bodies
   with fetters unforged.
You free us of cares, you offer
   sweet respite from toil,
6   you grant holy solace
   to our every sorrow,
you save souls by easing them
   into the thought of Death,
since to Death and Oblivion
   you are a true brother.
9   But, O blessed one, I beseech you
   to come sweet-tempered,
to be a kindly savior of the initiates,
   that they may serve the gods.

86. To Dream

incense—aromatic herbs

I call upon you, blessed,
   long-winged, baneful Dream,

messenger of things to come,
    greatest prophet to mortals.
3   In the quiet of sweet sleep
        you come silent,
you speak to the soul,
    you rouse men's minds,
in their sleep you whisper
    the will of the gods;
6   silent you come to show
        the future to silent souls
that walk the noble path
    of devotion to the gods.
Good always wins the race
    in people's minds,
9   good leads their lives
        to pleasures anticipated,
to a respite from suffering,
    that god himself may reveal
the firmament of the divine lords
    . . . through vows and sacrifices.
12   The end to which the pious come
        is always so sweeter,
but to the impious never
    does a dreamy phantom,
a prophet of evil deeds,
    reveal future need
15   so that they may find the cure
        from pain to come.
But, O blessed one, I beg you,
    show me the behests of the gods,
in all things bring me close
    to the path that is straight,
18   do not through weird apparitions
    show me evil signs.

87. To Death

incense—powdered frankincense

Hear me, you who steer
    the path of all mortals

and give sacred time to all
    from whom you are distant.
3   Your sleep tears the soul
    free from the body's hold,
whenever you undo
    nature's powerful bonds,
bringing the long slumber,
    the endless one, to the living.
6   Common to all,
    you are unjust to some,
when you bring swift end to youthful life
    at its peak.
In you alone is executed
    the verdict common to all,
9   for to entreaties and to prayers
    you alone are deaf.
O blessed one,
    with pious vows, with sacrifices,
I beg you, I pray to you,
    grant me long life,
12 that old age might be
    a noble prize among men.

Abbreviations

OHx.y(-z)   *Orphic Hymns*, hymn number **x**, line(s) **y(-z)**. An **n** appended refers to the relevant note; an **i** appended refers to the introduction to the relevant hymn. References combined are indicated by a + sign. The opening address of Orpheus to Mousaios is indicated by the letter **O**.

   PGM   *Papyri graecae magicae* (Betz 1986)

   PMG   *Poetae melici graeci* (Page 1962)

  PMGF   *Poetarum melicorum graecorum fragmenta* (Davies 1991)

  SVF **x.y**   *Stoicorum veterorum fragmenta* (von Arnim 1903–1921), volume **x**, fragment **y**

Introduction

1. Cf. Hesiod *Works and Days* 259 and Sophokles *Oedipus at Kolonos* 1382.
2. See *OH* 34.16–23n.
3. For details, see Betegh 2004 and Kouremenos/Parássoglou/Tsantsanoglou 2006.
4. For details, see Graf/Johnston 2007.
5. For a summary of these (and other) Orphic theogonies, see Betegh 2004, pp. 140–152, and, for a reconstructed diachronic evolution, see West 1983.
6. See *OH* Oi.
7. See Graf /Johnston 2007, pp. 70–80 and passim.
8. For a detailed treatment of the genre, see Furley/Bremer 2001.
9. Cf. Euripides *Hippolytos* 954, Aristophanes *Frogs* 1032, Plato *Republic* 364e, Plato *Cratylus* 402b, Plato *Philebus* 66c, and Aristotle *De anima* 410b.
10. See *OH* 37i.
11. See *OH* 30i.

12. See also *OH* 87.3–4n.

13. See *OH* 14.8–9n.

14. For a convenient list, see Siddiqi 1990.

15. Macdonell 1917, no. 8.

16. Macdonell 1917, no. 9.

17. Sergeant 2009, p. 37.

18. For a very thorough treatment of the names of the bear in the Finnic lands, see Pentikäinen 2007, esp. pp. 94–117.

Orpheus to Mousaios

The opening poem of the collection portrays the fiction of Orpheus instructing Mousaios in a rite. A loose parallel may be adduced in the case of Hesiod, who tells us of his transformation from shepherd to poet in the beginning of the *Theogony* (1–114); note in particular how the Muses there are initially described singing a hymn to a list of divinities (11–21), similar to what we find in this poem. Inclusivity is a characteristic of Greek polytheism, and it can be dangerous to omit the wrong divinity. This is a recurring theme in myth (e.g., the Kalydonian Boar because Artemis was neglected, the infidelity of Helen and her sister Klytemnestra because Aphrodite was neglected, the apple in the Judgment of Paris because Strife was snubbed).

For Orpheus, see the introduction to the translation. Mousaios was also a semi-legendary figure of questionable antiquity who was thought to be both a poet (his name means "of the Muse") and a founder of religious rites. He was considered to be the father of Eumolpos, the eponymous ancestor of the Eumolpids, one of the two hereditary families entrusted to administrating the Eleusinian Mysteries (see *OH* 40i). Mousaios seems to have been originally independent of Orpheus but later was made his son and/or disciple. The address "friend" here suggests at least the latter. For more on Mousaios, see West 1983, pp. 39–44.

There is a question whether this poem belongs with our collection or was added at some later date after the *Hymns* had been made part of a greater compilation of ancient hymns. It will become immediately apparent that the order of divinities in this poem does not, for the most part, match the order of the hymns to individual deities. Furthermore, some personalities, such as Hebe, are mentioned only in this poem, while others who have a hymn devoted to them in the collection, such as Hestia, do not appear here. West argues that this opening address to Mousaios was not part of the original collection but instead might have been the *Thuēpolikon* (*Sacrifice* or *Mystic Rites*) mentioned among the works of Orpheus in the Souda, a tenth-century AD Byzantine lexicon/encyclopedia (West 1968, pp. 288–289). However, the arguments against originality are certainly not insurmountable. For example, given how interconnected various hymns are (through language and motif), the opening may have been felt comprehensive enough despite the discrepancy between the divinities invoked in it and those that receive hymns in the rest of the collection. Another possibility is that the poem was an independent entity that our composer somewhat inartfully grafted onto his efforts. The opening and closing lines could easily have been altered from, and/or added to, the original. Indeed, the original might even have been the inspiration for creating a series of hymns dedicated to individual entities, and the collection could then be viewed as an (imperfect) expansion of it, adapted to the exigencies of the particular ritual in which it was performed.

It should also be pointed out that the fiction presented here of the master Orpheus passing on wisdom to his disciple Mousaios would have had great significance for the initiates.

Beyond the fancy that attributing the rite to the august figure Orpheus lends the whole affair an aura of prestige and legitimacy, in the performance of this poem it is not only Mousaios who is the beneficiary of Orpheus' special knowledge but also the initiates themselves. The poem could represent the foundational act of the ritual and have been felt to provide the raison d'être for the cult's existence. There might be an element of play-acting here, of taking on another role, something that is prevalent in Dionysian worship (see *OH* 30i). One wonders if it was not the group but a figure of authority (the "oxherd"?) who opened the ceremony by chanting these verses in the guise of Orpheus. We find the theme of foundation of rites appearing intermittently throughout the collection; see *OH* 76.7n. It is perhaps significant that many such instances involve groups, which might also be serving to break down the divide of mythic past and present reality.

For the divinities mentioned in this poem who have their own hymn(s), the reader is referred to the appropriate introduction and notes for more information.

3–5: The use of elements as an ordering technique found elsewhere in the collection (see *OH* 15i and *OH* 79i) seems to be used here as well, with Zeus representing air, Earth herself, the celestial bodies fire, and Poseidon water. The same grouping, albeit in a different order, appears in lines 32–33. See also note to line 38. For Zeus as the first god mentioned, see note to line 41.

11: Aphrodite, the coy goddess, is coyly alluded here. Her position after Hephaistos might be due to the fact that she is sometimes his wife in mythology (see *OH* 66i).

12: Hades is meant. He is often addressed by such circumlocutions since it was considered ill-omened to mention him by name (see also *OH* 18.3n and *OH* 69i).

13 Hebe: Her name means "youth." She is the daughter of Zeus and Hera. In traditional myth she was the cup-bearer of the gods, until Zeus abducted Ganymede and installed him in her place. Later she became the wife of the deified Herakles; see *OH* 12i.

14 Justice and Piety: *OH* 63 is addressed to the personified Justice. For her relationship to Piety, see the introduction to that hymn.

18 Year: Proclus cites some lines from a poem he attributes to Orpheus where in the version of Aphrodite's birth from the castration of Kronos, it is Year that gives birth to her after she had been surrounded by foam; Proclus elsewhere states that "the theurgists" worshipped Year, as well as Time, Day, Night, and Month (*Orphic fragment* 189). Aelian reports that in Gadeira (modern day Cádiz), the inhabitants had an altar for Year and Month (*Orphic fragment* 19). See also *OH* 12.3n.

19 Dione: In Homer, she is the mother of Aphrodite and consoles her after she is wounded by Diomedes (*Iliad* 5.370–417). She assists in the birth of Apollon (Homeric *Hymn to Apollon* 3.93), which may explain her place after Leto here. For Hesiod, she is an Okeanid (*Theogony* 353) and one of the divinities praised by the Muses in song as they head out to Olympos from Helikon (*Theogony* 17). Apollodoros, in contrast to Hesiod, makes her a Titan (1.1.2) and the mother of Aphrodite (1.3.1; see also *OH* 55i). The *Rhapsodies* also made Dione a Titan (*Orphic fragment* 179; see also *OH* 4i).

20–22: A number of similar divinities are clustered together here. While the Kouretes and Korybantes are separate entities, they often are confounded with one another, as at *OH* 38.20–21, where they are also identified as the gods of the Samothracian mystery cult and Zeus' sons Kastor and Polydeukes, the Dioskouroi (see *OH* 27i and *OH* 38.20–21n). Here the Kabeiroi, called saviors and the sons of Zeus, apparently are being identified with the Dioskouroi. However, they usually are separate as well, the gods of a mystery cult at Lemnos and Thebes that was connected with blacksmiths (see Burkert 1985, pp. 281–282, *OH* 39i and *OH* 66i). Interestingly enough, the Kabeiroi seem to have been worshipped on Samothrace, too (Herodotos 2.51.2; but see Burkert 1985, p. 283), which might have influenced the composer of this hymn. The Dioskouroi, Kouretes, and Kabeiroi are all possible identities of the mysterious "Boy Lords" worshipped in a mystery cult at Amphissa (Pausanias 10.38.7). The Idaian gods are a reference to the Idaian Dactyls, for whom see *OH* 12i. They, too, had a connection with Samothrace (see Graf/Johnston 2007, p. 170), which further suggests that the Kabeiroi here are being associated with that island.

24 Day: Hesiod makes Day the child of Night and Erebos (*Theogony* 124). See also note to line 18 and *OH* 3i.

25 Faith: We find Faith personified first in Theognis, who says that only Hope remains among men, but Faith, Prudence, and the Graces have fled to Olympos (1135–1138). This is a pastiche of Hesiod's tale of Pandora and the jar and the departure of Shame and Nemesis from the earth (*Works and Days* 90–99 and 197–201). Faith occasionally is worshipped in cult, most notably for our collection at Pergamon, where she shared an altar with Concord (see Nilsson 1961, p. 357).

25 Thesmodoteira: The name means "she that gives laws." Demeter was known as Thesmophoria ("she that bears laws"), and it is possible that this Thesmodoteira is either another identity of Demeter or a goddess who has been detached from Demeter and given a life of her own.

28–29: According to Hesiod, Atlas is a Titan who supports the sky on his shoulders, both out of "harsh necessity" and because this burden had been imposed upon him by Zeus (*Theogony* 517–520). This idea was taken up in Orphic mythology and justified by Atlas' participation in the murder of Dionysos (*Orphic fragment* 319). Homer, however, has him in the sea supporting both the earth and the sky (*Odyssey* 1.52–54), perhaps reminiscent of the Hittite Ullikummis. Aion (Eon, Eternity) is closely related to Time; Euripides makes Aion the son of Time, perhaps married to Fate (*Herakleidai* 900). He was a late-comer to cult; for an exhaustive review of the sources, see Nock 1934, pp. 83–98 (with discussion of this line on pp. 88–89), and Nilsson 1961, pp. 498–505. Time is an important figure in some Orphic cosmogonies. He is counted among the first entities in creation, and the one responsible for the birth of Protogonos (see *OH* 6i+6.1n).

29 Styx: One of the rivers of the underworld; see *OH* 69.4n.

30 Pronoia: See the introduction to the translation.

32–33: The serial listing of the sky, earth, and sea—with some variations—is a recurring theme in the collection; see *OH* 10.14–16n.

35 Adrasteia: See *OH* 61i.

38 Thunder: Interestingly enough, we have a hymn for Zeus the Thunderbolt and one for Zeus of the Lightning, but not one for the third of the group, Zeus of the Thunder; conversely, only Thunder is mentioned here, not Lightning or Thunderbolt; see further *OH* 20i.

38 four-pillared cosmos: The four pillars should probably be understood as the four elements; see note to lines 3–5.

39: For Attis, see *OH* 27i. Men is a moon god of Asia Minor; see *OH* 9.4n.

40 Ourania: We find this as an epithet to Aphrodite, and, since Adonis is immediately mentioned next (thus following the order of their hymns in our collection), it would seem likely that Ourania here refers to Aphrodite (see *OH* 55i+1n), despite the fact that this goddess has already been invoked at line 11 (albeit not by name). Ourania is also traditionally one of the names of the Muses, and she is mentioned at *OH* 76.9.

41 Beginning and End: These appear to be nothing more than abstractions of philosophical terms. A papyrus fragment containing a commentary on a poem of Alkman that is no longer extant reveals a cosmogony that started from undifferentiated matter that was given form through Poros (Way) and Tekmor (End, Limit), which the commentator interprets as signifying the beginning and end of things (*PMGF* 5 fr. 2 col. iii; translation and discussion in Kirk, Raven, and Schofield 1983, pp. 47–49). In all three extant versions of an Orphic hymn to Zeus, the god is described as being the first and last (see *OH* 15.3–5n), and in *OH* 15.7 he is called "the beginning and end of all" (and see note; however, the Greek word for "end" there is different than the one found here). It is perhaps no surprise, then, that Zeus begins the list of deities in this poem. He may even be understood as Beginning and End here, which would neatly close the long list of divinities in this poem by ring composition. Note, too, that the word "rite" (Greek "thuēpoliē") appears in the first and last line.

1. To Hekate

Hekate is a murky goddess on the fringes of Greek religion, and it is very possible that she was originally a native goddess of the Karians, a people in Asia Minor. Her earliest mention is in Hesiod's *Theogony*, a relatively long digression of such effusive praise that it is often referred to as a "hymn to Hekate" (411–452). Hesiod asserts that Zeus did not strip her of the honors she held before the defeat of the Titans, among whom she numbers. The poet then goes on to list the wide-ranging powers of the goddess and whom she can help or hinder as she pleases: kings, men speaking in assemblies, soldiers in battle, athletes at competitions, horsemen, sailors (along with Poseidon), and fishermen. Along with Hermes, she can bring fertility or sterility to flocks, and her role in nurturing youths closes out this astounding list of domains. Hesiod also stresses the fact that she is an only child. This picture of Hekate is unique in extant literature. Later on she was frequently identified with Artemis and Moon; see *OH* 9i and *OH* 36i. Hesiod perhaps is already moving in this direction, as he calls her a "nurturer of youths," an epithet usually applied to Artemis (cf. *OH* 36.8). Moreover, in Hesiod's genealogies, Hekate is first cousin to Artemis and Apollon, since their mothers, Asteria and Leto respectively, are sisters (*Theogony* 404–409). The connection with Moon is already suggested in another early poem, the Homeric *Hymn to Demeter*. After Persephone had been snatched by Hades, Hekate approaches Demeter and informs her that she heard the screams of the abducted girl but did not see the perpetrator (2.51–61). This information is supplied by Sun (2.62–90). Hekate is described as "carrying a light in her hands" (2.52), and, as the female counterpart to Sun in their role as witnesses, seems to be imagined as the moon goddess in these lines; see *OH* 2i and *OH* 9.3+n. Note, too, that the name of her mother in Hesiod's genealogy, Asteria, means "starry."

Thus in early Greek literature Hekate had definite celestial connections. But her association in Hesiod with fertility hints at chthonic relations, as does her connection in the story of the abduction of Persephone. When mother and daughter are reunited in the Homeric *Hymn to Demeter,* Hekate joins in their celebration and becomes Persephone's "attendant and follower" (2.438–440). She is therefore connected with the world of the dead, and it is this attribute that comes to dominate her aspect in later times. In the magical papyri, she is also explicitly equated with Persephone, along with other entities such as the Fates (*PGM* 4.2714–2783 and 2785–2870). No longer is she a (potentially) beneficial deity that might deign to grant a person blessings; instead she has become a sinister and dangerous, sometimes demonic, creature of the night (compare lines 5–6 of this hymn). Madness (cf. *OH* 71i), suffering, and death are her gifts, and she is often described in bestial terms. Curse tablets, too, invoke this dread goddess for their efficacy.

However, Hekate also received more formal worship in antiquity, both civic and private. She was a goddess of crossroads (see line 1), and such places could receive offerings and contain an image of the goddess. Sacrifices to her were notorious for their use of dog meat as offerings (cf. line 5). Hekate was involved in mystery cults, and of particular interest to this hymn is that Pausanias reports of mystery rites performed in honor of Hekate on Aigina, rites that Orpheus himself was said to have introduced (2.30.2). For more information on the worship of Hekate, see Larson 2007, pp. 165–167.

1 of the roads and of the crossroads: The Greek word used here for "of the roads," "enodia," was also the name of a local goddess at Thessaly, a land that in antiquity was notorious for its connection with witches and witchcraft. For a particularly gruesome literary representation of such, see Lucan *Civil War* 6.413–830, especially 434–506. The crossroads are understood here to be the confluence of three roads. This number is of particular significance for Hekate, who is often described and depicted as triple-faced and/or triple-bodied.

2 in heaven, on earth, then in the sea: Hekate has a share in these same three realms in Hesiod's praise of the goddess. Her widespread powers are further invoked in line 7. The collocation of heaven, earth, and sea appears throughout the collection; see *OH* 10.14–16+n.

2 saffron-cloaked: The same epithet is used of Melinoe, who might be another manifestation of Moon; see *OH* 71i+1n.

3 reveling: Hekate is described in terms of a wild Bacchant, a female worshipper of Dionysos; see *OH* 52i. The appellation "mountain-roaming" in line 8 has similar associations. Note also the Dionysian imagery implicit in the "herder of bulls" in line 7. Other goddesses described as maenads, or at least in maenadic terms, are the Nereids (*OH* 24.3+9–11n), Artemis (*OH* 36.2n), Demeter (*OH* 40.15+n), the Nymphs (*OH* 51.15–16+n), and the Erinyes (*OH* 69.2+n). Palaimon is also imagined as part of a Dionysian *thiasos* (see *OH* 75.1+n).

4 daughter of Perses: The hymn follows Hesiod's genealogy, but we find others in the sources. The poet Bacchylides, drawing on Hekate's chthonic pedigree, makes her the daughter of Night (fragment 1b). Kallimakhos is said to have called her a daughter of Demeter and Zeus, as do some Orphic sources (*Orphic fragment* 400), and a sister of Persephone, whom she seeks in the underworld after her abduction by Hades (*Orphic fragment* 466). Zeus is also her father according to Mousaios, but Asteria, as in Hesiod, is the mother, before she marries Perses (fragment 87).

8 nurturer of youths: As mentioned in the introduction to this hymn, this was a common epithet for Artemis. The identification is also suggested in line 4, "delighting in deer," as this animal often is connected with Artemis in her role as "Mistress of Animals"; see *OH* 36i.

10 oxherd: This refers to some official of the cult. The figure is found in other Dionysian mystery cults as well; for example, see Alexander 1933 for a summary of a second century AD Greek inscription found near Tusculum that lists a number of initiates and their titles and Morand 2001, 249–282, for a detailed study.

2. To Prothyraia

"Prothyraia" literally means "at the door" or "at the door-way." There is no goddess proper with this name. The word is a cult title shared by Eileithyia, Artemis, and even Hekate. Our hymn identifies her primarily as Eileithyia, the goddess of childbirth, who assists women in labor and who is invoked for a smooth delivery. Giving birth was fraught with danger in antiquity both for the woman and the child; compare Medeia's famous assertion that she would rather stand in battle three times than to give birth once (Euripides *Medeia* 250–251). Artemis was also connected with childbirth (see *OH* 36.8), and this hymn explicitly equates all three goddesses at line 13. The chorus in Aeschylus' *Suppliant Women* prays to Artemis-Hekate as the goddess who protects women in childbirth (674–677). Moon, who is often identified with Artemis and Hekate, is called Eileithyia by Nonnus (*Dionysiaca* 38.150).

In myth and literature, Eileithyia is limited to her role in helping childbirth, most famously in the Homeric *Hymn to Apollon* (3.97–116). Hera, angry at Leto for having been impregnated by Zeus and about to give birth to Apollon, prevents Eileithyia from hearing about Leto, who is suffering greatly on the island of Delos, since she cannot give birth until Eileithyia comes. The other goddesses send Iris with a bribe to coax Eileithyia from Olympos. As soon as the goddess sets foot on the island, Leto goes into labor. In Ovid's account of the birth of Herakles (*Metamorphoses* 9.273–323), Eileithyia (spelled Ilithyia and also called by her Roman name, Lucina) sits by an altar outside the door of the house of the pregnant woman. She bunches her knees against her chest, holds them together in an embrace with her fingers locked, and chants magic spells. This is a case of sympathetic magic, where the goddess' position represents the blocking of the infant's passage out of the womb. Galanthis, a serving girl, is able to trick the goddess into releasing her knees, thus breaking the spell and allowing Herakles to be born. Ovid's story is quite intriguing, since the goddess is sitting outside the doorway and employing magic. It is quite possible that the poet has in mind the epithet "prothyraia," and the use of magic suggests associations with Hekate as well as Moon.

Hera herself has connections with the timing of giving birth, too. In Homer's brief account of the birth of Herakles (*Iliad* 19.114–119), Hera is the one who delays the birth of the hero by holding back the "Eileithyias" (the plural is also found at *Iliad* 11.269–270), while causing another birth, that of Eurystheus, to occur prematurely. Traditionally, Eileithyia is the daughter of Hera and Zeus, and the sibling of Hebe and Ares (Hesiod *Theogony* 921–923); note that the opening address to Mousaios mentions Eileithyia between Hebe and Herakles (an eventual wife/husband pair) at line 13. Pausanias also reports that the Kretans considered the goddess a daughter of Hera (1.18.5). Krete, in fact, boasts of a very early worship of Eileithyia. Homer mentions a cave of Eileithyia at Amnisos, near Knossos (*Odyssey* 19.188), and this has been corroborated with a listing in a Linear B tablet from Knossos, which calls for an offering of honey for Eileithyia at Amnisos, as well as the archaeological record, which spans from Neolithic to Roman times.

But Pausanias in the same passage mentions another account of Eileithyia, reporting the view that the goddess came to Delos from those famous mythological people from the far north, the Hyperboreans, in order to assist Leto in giving birth, presumably to Apollon and Artemis. The cult of Eileithyia was established on the island and thence spread to the rest of Greece. Pausanias also notes that the Delians sacrificed to Eileithyia and sang a hymn composed by Olen, a legendary poet and prophet—a figure very similar to Orpheus. Pausanias mentions the hymn of Olen in two other passages that suggest that this goddess might have been associated with an older cosmic power. At 9.27.2, Pausanias tells us that in Olen's hymn Eileithyia is the mother of Eros. Elsewhere, Pausanias remarks that Olen called her "the good spinner" and surmises that Olen identified her with fate (8.21.3). We find a similar connection elsewhere. Both Pindar (*Olympian Odes* 6.41–42 and *Nemean Odes* 7.1–4) and Plato (*Symposium* 206d2) represent Eileithyia working in tandem with the Fates at birth. A story of Herakles' birth similar to Ovid's by the Greek poet Nikandros, summarized at Antoninus Liberalis 29, has the Fates assisting Eileithyia in preventing the birth; the serving girl who tricks the goddess is transformed by the Fates and receives some honor from Hekate and Herakles. Thus Eileithyia seems to have been imagined at times in the form of a personal Tyche or the individual Good Daimon (see *OH* 72i and *OH* 73i).

The position of the hymn in our collection is pregnant with symbolism. There is an emphasis on "birth" in the opening hymns, which are balanced by the last hymn dedicated to Death (see also *OH* 87i). Thus the collection is framed by both life and death, set in motion by the first hymn which addresses Hekate as "queen and mistress of the whole world" (*OH* 1.7). Prothyriaia/Eileithyia, as already mentioned, is sometimes identified with Hekate, so the transition is an easy one. Both Hekate and Eileithyia are portrayed in their iconography as bearing torches. This might have significance for the actual rite for which our hymns were composed, which probably began after nightfall (see the introduction to the translation and *OH* 3i). The initiates could very well have been carrying torches as the hymns were performed. Graf suggests that this hymn was sung as the initiates proceeded indoors to wherever the ritual was enacted (Graf/Johnston 2007, p. 155).

3. To Night

Night (Greek Nux) is personified in Hesiod. She is born from Khaos along with her brother Erebos, with whom she mates and bears Ether and Day (*Theogony* 123–125; see also *OH* 5i). Night produces by means of parthenogenesis a brood of personified abstractions, notably for our collection Death, Sleep, and the race of Dreams (*Theogony* 211–225; cf. lines 5–7 of this hymn and *OH* 85i). Hesiod also mentions Night in connection with the geography of the underworld. She owns a house, where her children Sleep and Death also live. Day lives there, too, but is never there at the same time at Night; they only greet each other as one leaves and the other returns from the world above (*Theogony* 744–761; cf. lines 10–11 and see also *OH* 78.4–5+n). Night perhaps should be seen as belonging to a pre-Olympian generation of divinities in Homer. In the *Iliad*, as Hera tries to cajole Sleep into inducing Zeus to slumber, Sleep maintains his readiness to bring his gift to all gods, even Okeanos, the father of the gods (14.246, and see *OH* 83i), but recalls the catastrophe barely averted the last time he put Zeus to sleep against his will. At that time, he escaped the anger of Zeus by the intervention of Night (implied to be Sleep's mother?), who is described as having power over immortals and mortals and whom Zeus is hesitant to displease (14.256–261). It is not clear what place Night has in Homer's cosmology, but the respect and fear Zeus shows and feels toward her suggests that Homer considered her to be an old and powerful figure.

This is the role she has in various Orphic theogonies, where she is considered to be among the earliest divinities. In light of the Homeric passage, it is first interesting to note that Night gives Zeus oracular advice, e.g., on how to reconstitute the world (*Orphic fragment 241*; cf. also 113 and 237). In the *Rhapsodies* there are up to three individual Nights (see West 1983, p. 70, and Betegh 2003, pp. 141–142). The first one existed before Protogonos (*Orphic fragment 112–113*). Another Night is the daughter of Protogonos (*Orphic fragment 148*), who later abdicates his throne to her in the symbolic passing of his scepter (*Orphic fragment 168–171*; see also *OH* 6i and *OH* 10.26+n; cf. *Iliad* 2.100–108 for similar symbolism). She (or a third Night?) also appears as Protogonos' lover and gives birth to Sky and Earth (*Orphic fragment 149*; see also *OH* 4i). In other theogonies similar to those ascribed to Orpheus, Night is one of the oldest, if not the oldest, beings. Mousaios puts her among Tartaros and Aer (fragment 81), while Epimenides places her alongside Aer as the two primeval beings (fragment 46). Aristotle notes that even "the ancient poets" do not claim that the primeval beings (mentioned are Night, Sky, Khaos, and Okeanos) "are king or rule," but rather Zeus (*Metaphysics* 1091b4–6). He does not name names, but it is possible that for Okeanos he had Homer in mind, and for Khaos Hesiod. Night and Sky do not correspond to any known theogony, but, the fact that our collection has a hymn to Night as "mother of gods and men" followed by a hymn to Sky who is called "father of all," suggests that perhaps there was such an Orphic theogony, now lost to us, circulating in antiquity and well known by Aristotle's time; see *OH* 4i and also *OH* O.24, where Night is called "oldest of all."

In terms of cultic worship, there are very few instances. Pausanias mentions an oracle of Night on the acropolis of Megara, along with a temple to Dionysos, a temple to Zeus, and a sanctuary to Aphrodite (1.40.6). Note that Night has oracular powers in the Orphic poems, as mentioned already. In Pergamon, where there was a mystery cult to Demeter, religious officials dedicated a number of altars to various gods and goddesses; one official, a *hymnetria* (a female singer of hymns), is attested to have dedicated an altar to Night, Rites, and Happenstance (see Nilsson 1961, p. 355). The connection between night and rites probably is indicative of the setting of the ritual. Likewise, the early placement of our hymn as well as the appeal at the end for Night to make an appearance before the initiates suggest that the rites for which the collection was written probably began after sunset and proceeded throughout the night (see also *OH* 54.5+n, *OH* 78i, *OH* 86i, and the introduction to the translation).

1 **mother of gods and men**: This is answered by "father of all" in the first line of the following hymn to Sky. See also *OH* 10.1n.

2 **Kypris**: Another name of Aphrodite, used also at *OH* 22.7 and *OH* 65.7. It is appropriate here of Night, who is given generative powers; cf. *OH* 55.2 where Aphrodite is called "revered goddess of generation" and someone who "like[s] the night-long revel." Among the progeny of Night reported by Hesiod (*Theogony* 224), we find Deception (Greek Apatē) and Sexual Passion (Greek Philotēs), both representing characteristics normally associated with Aphrodite; see also *OH* 55i and *OH* 59i. Just as Night, so too is Aphrodite called the "mother of gods and men" in the magical papyri (*PGM* 4.2916), and she "give[s] birth to all" at *OH* 55.5 (cf. also lines 3 and 12 of that hymn).

4 **delight in the quiet**: So too Moon at *OH* 9.8. Moon is also called "mother of gods and men" in the magical papyri (*PGM* 4.2832–2833) and, in fact, even addressed as Night (*PGM* 4.2857), among a host of other names.

6: These functions are normally handled by Sleep; see *OH* 85.8n.

8–11: These lines have many echoes in the following hymn: both divinities are described as terrestrial (as part of their nature), both move in a circle, both are constrained by Necessity; see *OH* 4.3n. Night can be considered both terrestrial and celestial because, as alluded to in lines 10–11 and just as Hesiod describes (see the introduction to this hymn), she alternates her time in the worlds above and below with Day, and vice versa; see also *OH* 4.5n and *OH* 7.9n. Orpheus' address to Mousaios mentions Night and Day together (*OH* O.24). That she is always incomplete suggests the continuity of Night and Day's alternation: Night is always changing (cf. also *OH* 4.7n and *OH* 10.21–24n).

4. To Sky

Sky (Greek Ouranos) is one of the chief primeval figures in Greek mythology. As a sky god, he is eventually supplanted by his grandson Zeus. In Hesiod's *Theogony*, Sky is son and husband of Earth (126–153), and Kronos is their son who, in fact, conspired with Earth to castrate his father (154–210). The marriage between Sky and Earth fits the common mythological motif of the marriage between Father Sky and Mother Earth (see also *OH* 15i). Their children are the (cosmic) Kyklopes, the Hundred-Handers, and the Titans. Orphic theogony seems to have integrated, or at least borrowed liberally, from the Hesiodic account that had become almost canonical. In the *Rhapsodies*, Night and Protogonos produce Sky and Earth, who thereupon marry and produce children, including the Fates, Kyklopes, and Hundred-Handers; the Titans, of whom there are fourteen instead of the Hesiodic twelve (added are Phorkys and Dione; for the latter, see *OH* O.19+n), are born from Earth without the knowledge of Sky. Night raises this brood, and all of the Titans except Okeanos take part in the castration of Sky. As with Hesiod, the Giants and Aphrodite are born from this act (*Orphic fragment* 149 and 174–189; for Aphrodite Ourania, see *OH* O.40n and *OH* 55i+1n). In another version, Sky and Earth are born from the two halves of the egg out of which Protogonos is hatched; see *OH* 6.2n. Sky appears on the Bacchic gold tablets as well. In no less than twelve the initiate claims to be born of Earth and "starry Sky" (nos. 1, 2, 8, 10–14, 16, 18, 25, 29) and in three of these to be of the "heavenly race" as well (nos. 2, 8, 29; for interpretation, see Graf/Johnston 2007, pp. 111–116). This probably is intended to link the initiate, as a human being, with the Titans, whose destruction by Zeus engendered the human race (see *OH* 37i). A further connection between Sky qua "heaven" and human beings might be in the notion that the soul, as the sky, is composed of fire; for this idea, cf. *OH* 5.3 and see *OH* 66.9n.

Our hymn does not give much information about Sky's mythology, although there would be little need since the initiates would know the story, whatever versions they had at their disposal. Instead, Sky is treated here more as the vague personification of a celestial phenomenon. This is not surprising, as Sky in myth is a rather colorless figure whose function seems more to give the later gods an ancient pedigree than to serve as a concrete expression of religious sentiment. Indeed, this might explain why the hymn to Sky appears in this position in the collection and before the one to Ether and Protogonos, both of whom come into existence before Sky. The hymn to Night opens with reference to her role as "mother of gods and men" (*OH* 3.1), while Sky is called "father of all" right at the start. There are other connections between these two hymns that further reinforce their pairing (see notes passim). It is also suggestive that he is not linked with Earth, as one would expect. Might, then, Sky be invoked as representative of the masculine power of generation, being the oldest such being, paired with Night as the feminine power of generation, also in turn being the oldest of her kind? It would fit the pattern of hymns arranged in male/female pairings, a structural technique found throughout the collection (see *OH* 14.8–9n). Furthermore, Sky is said to succeed Night in a brief notice found in a commentary on Aristotle's *Metaphysics* by Alexander of Aphrodisias, where the order of generation is given as Khaos, Okeanos, Night, Sky, and Zeus, king of the immortal gods (*Orphic fragment* 370). It is possible that our composer was aware of this or a similar cosmogony and was perhaps influenced by such to give Night a male analogue (see also *OH* 3i). Sky, then, could be the son and/or junior partner of Night. Be that as it may, the fact remains that this hymn to Sky breaks the sequence Night-Ether-Protogonos that one might have expected based on our extant sources (see further *OH* 5i).

1 father of all: This continues the theme of birth found in the early hymns; cf. the first line of the previous hymn to Night, "mother of gods and men," and "the begetter of blessed gods and mortal men" used of Protogonos at *OH* 6.3.

2 beginning of all, end of all: Zeus is also so addressed in the *Hymns*; see *OH* 15.7+n.

3 lord of the universe, moving about the earth like a sphere: This suggests a geocentric view of the universe, as, for example, Ptolemy maintained (see *OH* 34.16–23n), as opposed to the heliocentric hypothesis of Aristarkhos of Samos (third century BC), which might have been known to our composer. "Moving about the earth" is also found at Kleanthes *Hymn to Zeus* 7, in the same exact position of the hexameter line, used of the universe (*kosmos*) that dutifully obeys Zeus' rule. Diogenes Laertius reports that Pythagoras was the first to call the sky "universe" (8.48). Night in the previous hymn also moves in circular fashion (see *OH* 3.9+8–11n). See further *OH* 7.8+n, *OH* 27.9n, and *OH* 40.15+n.

4 home of the blessed gods: Sky is "the firm seat of all the blessed gods" already in Hesiod (*Theogony* 128); compare also *OH* 5.1+n. Hestia, too, is called the same thing (*OH* 84.5).

4 your motion is a roaring whirl: Sun is similarly described; see *OH* 8.7+n. The word translated as "roaring" is "rhombos," which more properly designates either the bull-roarer or kettle-drums, both of which were used in ecstatic and mystery cults, particularly ones tied to Dionysos and the various Eastern mother goddesses; see *OH* 27.11n and *OH* 31.2, where the Kouretes are literally called "rhombosters" ("rhombētai"). It is quite possible that in the performative context of our hymns such an instrument would have been used and perhaps even supplemented the singing of lines such as this one that indicate either the instrument itself or the sound it makes. The *rhombos* is also one of the toys that the Titans used to lure the child Dionysos to his death (*Orphic fragment* 306 and 578).

5 celestial and terrestrial guard: Sky participates in both parts of the cosmos (see note to line 3); so, too, does Night (see *OH* 3.8+8–11n). Sky, insofar as he is identified with the sky, naturally becomes viewed as a being who sees all that passes under him, just like Sun and Zeus (see line 8 and *OH* 8.1n). Orpheus is said to have called Sky both the "watcher and guardian of all things" (*Orphic fragment* 151), and his name was at times thought to derive from the Greek word "ouros," meaning "watcher"; Plato *Cratylus* 396b–c gives an alternate etymology from a phrase in Greek meaning "I look at the things above."

6 Physis' invincible drive: The invincible drive is Necessity; see *OH* 55.3n. For the personified Physis, see *OH* 10i.

7 shimmering, variform: There is a play on words in the Greek ("pan*aiole*," "*aiolomorphe*"). The reference here is probably to the changing nature of the sky due to meteorological phenomena; cf. *OH* 3.8–11n.

8 all-seeing: A number of celestial divinities possess this attribute; see *OH* 8.1n.

5. To Ether

The upper atmosphere tended in antiquity to be divided into two levels: the lower, misty air that we breathe and the higher, and hence purer, stratum of ether. This conception is already found in Homer; at *Iliad* 14.286–288, Sleep climbs up the largest fir tree on Mount Ida, which is said to "reach the ether through the air." Ether is usually considered to be composed of fire or to be fire itself. Hesiod tells us (*Theogony* 124–125) that Ether and Day were born from Erebos and Night (it is interesting to note that two dark entities produce two bright ones, as light follows day in Genesis). Ether is one of the primordial beings in Orphic cosmogony (*Orphic fragment* 78 and 111). Along with Khaos and Erebos, he was born from the serpentine Time. The cosmic egg out of which Protogonos hatched is said to be either made out of, or placed in, Ether by Time (see *OH* 6i+1n), and thus Ether is considered his father (*Orphic fragment* 124–125). This probably explains why the hymn to Protogonos immediately follows, intervening between this hymn and those to the other celestial entities: the Stars, Sun, and Moon. However, as with Sky, Ether is presented less as an anthropomorphic deity and more as a cosmic principle in the form of the highest and purest expression of fire. Both deities are connected, with Sky presented as an embodiment of physical space and Ether as physical substance constitutive of that space. This may have facilitated Sky's placement in the collection; see *OH* 4i.

1 Zeus' lofty dwelling: Zeus is often imagined as inhabiting the ether (e.g., *Iliad* 4.166, Hesiod *Works and Days* 18, and *Orphic fragment* 852). It is an appropriate location for a sky god, and, as ether is connected with fire, for a god who wields the fiery lightning bolt; see *OH* 19i. Note that Hestia is called "home of the blessed gods" (*OH* 84.5), and she, too, is strongly connected with fire. Sky, who is closely associated with the ether, is also the "home of the blessed gods" (see *OH* 4.4+n).

2: The stars, sun, and moon all are located in the upper air, and so Ether may rightly be said to "claim a share." But since Ether is a bright, primordial being that appears before the others in cosmological speculation, he might be thought to "claim a share" in the sense that he was the first to perform the functions of the younger beings; children abrogating their parents' prerogatives is a recurring theme in mythological thought. Note that the Stoics held that the sun, stars, and even the moon were formed from the ether (see, e.g., Long and Sedley 1987, fragment 47D and Plutarch *De facie quae in orbe lunae apparet* 928c–d, where this view is rejected). Even more pertinent here is that all celestial phenomena—ether, sun, stars, moon—are said to be "parts of Hephaistos" at *OH* 66.6–7, who is conceived as a quasi-personified form of the element fire. The order "stars—sun—moon" in this line mirrors the order of their respective hymns and is probably intentional.

3 life's spark for every creature: For the soul as composed out of the element fire, see *OH* 66.9+n.

4 best cosmic element: Empedokles' theory of the four elements (or, as he called them, "roots") that constitute the physical world was accepted—with some variations and elab-

orations—throughout antiquity. They are earth, water, air, and fire; these manifest themselves in larger physical bodies, i.e., the earth proper, sea, lower air, and ether, whose fiery
and luminous qualities are mentioned in the surrounding lines of this hymn; see also *OH*
11.2–3+n and 13–17. For the use of the four elements as a structural motif in the collection,
see *OH* 15i. That Ether (i.e., fire) is the "best" of the four may be a reflection of Pythagorean
and/or Stoic doctrine, which regarded fire as the element at the head of the creation of the
universe and into which all physical bodies eventually disintegrate. Hephaistos qua fire is
called the "blameless element / most sublime" (*OH* 66.4–5+n).

6 temperate and clear: Ether is here being treated as a weather phenomenon, not as a cosmic
force, almost loosely being identified with the sky. We find a similar conception at the end
of the hymn to Boreas, the north wind, where there is also a request for fair weather and
mention is made of Ether and the sun's rays (*OH* 80.5–6+n). Sun is called "the clear" (*OH*
8.14) with the same connotation of favorable weather, and the Kouretes are asked to bring
"clear weather" in their second hymn (*OH* 38.24–25).

6. To Protogonos

Protogonos (First-born, Primeval) is the name/epithet of one of the most important figures
in Orphic cosmological speculation. This being has many appellations: Phanes (Bright One),
Metis (Counsel, Resourcefulness, Wisdom), Eubouleus (He of Good Counsel), Antauges
(The One Reflecting Light), Eros, among others. He shares with Dionysos the names Eubouleus, Erikepaios, and Bromios and is indeed identified at times with Dionysos himself
(see *OH* 52.6+n) as well as Zeus. For convenience and consistency, we shall refer to this god
as Protogonos. In the cosmogonies found in the *Rhapsodies* and in Hieronymos' account,
Protogonos is born from an egg that Time has a role in creating (see note to line 1) and is a
teratomorphic creature. He is portrayed with golden wings, and he seems to have been described in the *Rhapsodies* as having four (pairs of) eyes, four heads (ram, bull, lion, serpent;
cf. Euripides *Bacchae* 1017–1019 and *OH* 50.5n), and four (pairs of) horns, while in Hieronymos' cosmogony he has bulls' heads growing from his sides and a serpent's head that nonetheless resembles all kinds of beastly shapes (*Orphic fragment* 80 and 129–136). Protogonos is
the first "king" of the universe (*Orphic fragment* 165–167; cf. 86), who later passes this title on
to his daughter/lover Night (see *OH* 3i). We find Protogonos described as creating the various attributes of the (material) universe and the gods themselves (*Orphic fragment* 144–164;
see also line 3 and note); it is no accident that the following hymns in our collection are
addressed to the Stars, Sun, Moon, and Physis. Moreover, Ether plays a role in the birth of
this god (see *OH* 5i), and the placement of the hymn to Ether before this one is probably a
reflection of this genealogy. Protogonos is the first name in one of the Bacchic gold tablets
(no. 4). This tablet is very strange: it is in the form of a prayer addressed to a number of divinities (including Phanes, who is listed some distance apart from Protogonos) with nonsensical
groups of letters sprinkled throughout. A relief from Modena (second century AD) depicts a
figure that appears to have some connection with Protogonos (see West 1983, pp. 253–255).

1 two-natured: This probably refers to Protogonos' androgyny. The same word is used of
Dionysos (*OH* 30.2), Mise (*OH* 42.4), and Eros (*OH* 58.4); Mise is also explicitly called
both male and female. See also *OH* 9.4n.

1 **ether-tossed**: In the *Rhapsodies*, Time places the egg from which Protogonos is born in Ether (*Orphic fragment* 114); in Hieronymos' version, Time fashions the egg out of its children Ether, Khaos, and Erebos (*Orphic fragment* 78–79).

2: In the theogony attributed to Hieronymos, the bottom half of the egg becomes Earth, the upper part Sky, and betwixt them is the "two-bodied" Phanes; see *Orphic fragment* 80 and compare the two egg halves on the relief from Modena. The separation of the sky and the earth is a very old motif found in Sumerian, Babylonian, Egyptian, and Hittite cosmologies. The chorus of birds in Aristophanes' *Birds* give an account of the creation of the world which includes an egg out of which golden-winged Eros is hatched (685–704). Eros, traditionally represented as winged (as in *OH* 58.2), is another name for Protogonos, as mentioned in the introduction to this hymn. Similarly, an invocation to Eros in the magical papyri lists a number of attributes that suggest an affinity with this Orphic divinity: golden-winged, first-born, invisible, and yet light-producing (*PGM* 4.1748–1810). It is not clear, however, if Aristophanes is drawing from an Orphic source. Protogonos' birth from the egg is not attested until later, so this could have been influenced by Aristophanes or perhaps it comes from a common third source (which need not originally have been Orphic). We should also keep in mind that Aristophanes is more interested in eliciting a chuckle rather than dutifully reporting actual cult practice and that what he presents is being filtered through the fun-house mirror of comedy. It is reflecting something, but what that "something" might be is difficult to determine without sufficient *comparanda*.

3 **begetter of blessed gods and mortal men**: An attribute he shares with Zeus, who in the *Rhapsodies* is said to have swallowed Protogonos under the direction of Night and from this act reenacted the creation originally performed by Protogonos (see *OH* 15.3–5n). Okeanos is also similarly addressed in the collection (*OH* 83.2), and Pan, who is sometimes identified with Protogonos, is the "begetter of all" (*OH* 11.10). Also in the *Rhapsodies*, Protogonos is said to carry "the famous seed of the gods" (*Orphic fragment* 140), and this is probably what "of the many seeds" (line 10) is intended (in part) to indicate (note, too, that Physis is a "giver of wealth of seeds"; see *OH* 10.19). Protogonos is strictly speaking not the first being in the various Orphic theogonies, but he is "first-born" in the sense of being the first to come into existence by a kind of procreation (via the egg) and/or the first god to procreate in the narrow sense of sexual intercourse (albeit with him/her/itself). This ambiguity is underlined by the direct juxtaposition of "begetter" and "seed" in the Greek text as well as by the different connotations of "seed" in the Greek language that this hymn exploits. The "seed unforgettable" in line 4, as the singular implies, refers to Protogonos himself (see also *OH* 50.2+n), while the "many seeds" in line 10 represents his cosmic generative powers. A similar oxymoron is found in line 5, "ineffable, hidden, brilliant scion" (see also note to line 8). Dionysos/Erikepaios is addressed as "father and son of the gods" in *OH* 52.6.

3 **bellows like a bull**: As mentioned in the introduction to this hymn, the head(s) of a bull are part of the physical makeup of this composite being; cf. *Orphic fragment* 130: "discharging bulls' bellows and those of a fierce lion." This animal is particularly connected with Dionysos, who can take the form of a bull or otherwise shares the features of a bull; see *OH* 30.3–4n.

4 **Erikepaios**: This non-Greek name also appears in *OH* 52.6 as an alternate name to Dionysos; note, too, that the word translated there as "primeval" could also be understood as

the proper name Protogonos (and see note to line 3 "begetter of blessed gods and mortal men" above). The late author Malalas says that the name means "giver of life" (*Orphic fragment* 97). An alternate version of the name, Irikepaios, appears in a fragmentary papyrus from the middle of the third century BC (the Gurôb Papyrus), where it is invoked along with Eubouleus, Pallas, and perhaps Protogonos and Demeter and where it might be another name for Dionysos; see the translation in Graf/Johnston 2007, pp. 188–189. The line "attended by many rites" has been taken by scholars as evidence for the widespread appearance of this god in actual Orphic practice. An altar from the second century AD at Hierokaisareia in Lydia was dedicated by a hierophant to "Dionysos Erikepaios."

5–7 in whirring motion. . . you whirled about throughout this world: The verb that appears in this hymn as "whirled" ("dinētheis") is found in an interesting fragment preserved by Macrobius where the name Dionysos is fancifully derived from it (*Orphic fragment* 540). In this fragment, Time reveals to the gods a being known by the names Eros, Phanes, Dionysos, Eubouleus, and Antauges (also mentioned in line 9 of our hymn). For Eubouleus, see *OH* 41.8n. As for the "whirring motion" of line 5, a similar description of movement is found for Sun and others in the *Hymns*; see *OH* 8.7n.

8: Another oxymoron (see note to line 3). Despite being invisible to the naked eye (cf. line 5), Protogonos is the source of light and thus seems to take on a function similar to Sun. Macrobius explicitly says that Orpheus called Phanes "Sun" (*Orphic fragment* 540). Although he has wings, he is also imagined to drive a chariot, much like Sun (*Orphic fragment* 172–173), while Sun is occasionally described as winged in poetry (see West 1983, p. 215). The name Phanes in antiquity was connected with light, as here, or sometimes with the verb "phainō," which in its active sense means to "show, reveal" (Protogonos brings light to the universe for the first time; thus the hidden, unrevealed being in turn "reveals" it) and its passive sense to "appear" (Protogonos is "first-born," being the first living thing to appear; cf. *Orphic fragment* 126).

9 Priapos: A curious reference. Priapos is connected with Dionysos in cult. According to Athenaios, the people of Lampsakos even considered Priapos to be another name for Dionysos (1.30b–c); however, Pausanias reports that they considered him to be the son of Dionysos and Aphrodite (9.31.2). Inasmuch as Eros, a son of Aphrodite in myth, is sometimes identified with Protogonos, this might have facilitated an identification between Priapos and Protogonos, if Pausanias is correct. Then, too, Priapos is a god with definite fertility connections, particularly sexual, and is usually portrayed as ithyphallic (e.g., Boardman 1975, pl. 335.1). Such an association also overlaps with Protogonos as a creator; see the note to line 3. Furthermore, Priapos is a rustic entity, who protects flocks and gardens, and is sometimes found in Dionysos' retinue. Thus in his functions, he bears a close affinity to Pan, another divinity that is sometimes equated with Protogonos, and this is another possible avenue by which Priapos could have been eventually connected with Protogonos; see also *OH* 11.10–12n.

10 many counsels: The Greek word "polumēti" puns on Metis, yet another name for Protogonos (see the introduction to this hymn).

7. To the Stars

The stars did not receive cult honors in Greek religion, although some mystery cults, notably Mithraism, did call on the stars as divine beings as our hymn does. Constellations were identified with various objects and personages already in Homer, and they were employed to mark weather phenomena for agricultural and nautical endeavors; see Hesiod's *Works and Days* and, for a more self-consciously literary treatment, Aratos' *Phainomena*. In later antiquity the importance of the stars extended to astrology, particularly in connection with the destiny of individuals; cf. the similar role of Tyche (*OH* 72i). Heroes such as Herakles could be considered to have been turned into stars upon their death. In classical times, there was popular belief that all people became a star after their death (see Aristophanes *Peace* 832–841). This belief lived on, but another conception, opposite to this one, developed in later antiquity. Each star corresponded to a living person—a case of natural sympathy akin to the connection between Hamadryads and their trees (see *OH* 51.14+n)—and a shooting star implied that someone on earth had died (see Pliny the Elder *Natural History* 2.6). This belief was doubtlessly connected with the idea of the stars as responsible for individual destiny. The one constant in these various views is the conviction that celestial phenomena are somehow connected with terrestrial affairs. Our hymn shares this view but also treats the stars as minor divinities aloof from the humans whose fate they map out in their nightly wanderings.

This hymn forms with the following two to Sun and Moon a triplet of ones dedicated to celestial phenomena. They probably owe their position in the collection to their early appearance in ancient cosmogonies; see further *OH* 6i.

2 holy *daimones*: Mythological figures are often connected with constellations, usually as a result of transformation; for example, see the story of Callisto and Arcas in Ovid *Metamorphoses* 2.401–507. Important gods were assigned to the planets, but lesser ones to the stars. For example, the seven stars of the Pleiades were identified with the seven daughters of Atlas, one of whom, Maia, was the mother of Hermes. The association of specific deities with specific celestial bodies easily slides into a vague notion that the stars are simply generic minor divinities, as is the case in our hymn.

3 children of black Night: A genealogy based on observation. Hesiod on the other hand says Dawn is the mother of the winds, the Morning Star, and—curiously—all the stars (see *OH* 78i). West suggests that Hesiod started with the Morning Star being a child of Dawn, which does conform to observation, and then brought all the other stars into this relation "by association" (West 1971, pp. 270–271). It is possible that Night is made their mother here because of the Stars' chthonic nature (see line 9 and note), perhaps even to strengthen it. In Orphic cosmogony, the stars, as well as the other celestial bodies, are created by Protogonos (*Orphic fragment* 153, and see *OH* 6i) and then recreated by Zeus (see *OH* 15.3–5n). Note that the Fates are the daughters of Night, too (*OH* 59.1).

8: This line, as well as the circular movement mentioned in line 4, refers to the place of the stars in the cosmos according to geocentric astronomical teachings; see *OH* 4.3n. The seven luminous orbits are the movements of the five planets (Mercury, Venus, Mars, Jupiter, Saturn), the sun, and the moon. They were conceived to be attached to spherical rings and to rotate in perfect circles around the spherical earth. The stars in this system usually were not thought to move but were understood to be affixed to the outmost, inert sphere (for Plato, though, they moved, albeit in the opposite direction from the rest of the celestial bodies; see *OH* 8.9n). The Homeric *Hymn to Ares* also alludes to the seven orbits and, at least in part, addresses the planet as well as the god. This information suggests that it is a late hymn that had been added to the Homeric collection (see *OH* 65i).

9 in heaven and on earth: As with Night (*OH* 3.8+8–11n), their mother, and Sky (*OH* 4.5+n), so, too, are the Stars connected both to the celestial and earthly realms. Their chthonic nature might also be a result of their connection with the dead. Sometimes the soul is imagined as returning to the stars (see Cicero *De respublica* 6.18), and we have already noted the old folk belief that stars are born when people die (see the introduction to this hymn and further *OH* 15i and *OH* 59.3–4n).

12–13: These lines give us clues as to the content of the ritual in which our collection was employed, but not enough specific details for any certain inferences. The "learned contests" might indicate a competition that was held among initiates or that served as part of the rite for those about to be initiated. That they are "learned" suggests they were intellectual and treated points of cultic lore. Perhaps they were in the form of a catechism. The Stars, like other addressees in the collection, are invited to join the festivities; however, what is unusual in this case is that it is not just their presence but their direct participation that is desired. The word "race," like the Greek word it translates, "dromos," may signify a competition or the mere act of motion. The word "dromos" appears in the second part of a compound in line 9, where it has the latter connotation ("puridromoi," meaning "blazing trail"). It is often used to describe celestial motion, and here it is "noble" because it is part of the cosmic order, which has an ethical dimension (see *OH* 8.16n). Thus the stars' natural course coheres with the movements of the ritual, and so the participants of the ritual might have felt that they themselves also became participants in the cosmic order. Another possible interpretation is that the context suggests an agonistic interpretation of "race" but it is difficult to see against whom the Stars would be racing. In Alkman's *Parthenion* (*PMGF* 1) the group of young girls, whose performance of the poem is an act of worship in a state cult, at one point say they are "fighting" the star cluster of the Pleiades; one interpretation of these hotly-debated lines is that the girls, perhaps with (mock?) consternation, are worried that they will not finish their nightly ritual before the Pleiades set and dawn appears. Our participants were almost certainly engaged in a nightly ritual, too (see *OH* 3i), but there is nothing in our hymn to suggest that they are competing with the Stars; indeed, the Stars are invited to join the proceedings. Perhaps the Stars are summoned to help the initiates complete their rite before the arrival of dawn (see *OH* 78i). In this case, the "works of renown" would denote the ritual itself. The same phrase appears again of Nike, who is asked to come to the initiates "for works of renown" (*OH* 33.9+i), and Mise is also asked at the end of her hymn to attend the contests of the ritual (*OH* 42.11+n); see also *OH* 28.2n, *OH* 30i, *OH* 76.12+n, and *OH* 87.12n.

8. To the Sun

The veneration of the sun in ancient times involves complexities. The only major cult center was on the island Rhodes, but scholars suspect that this cult was not of great antiquity. Pindar celebrates the island with three myths, including Sun's love of the island; they produced seven sons, the ancestors of the island's inhabitants, and their grandchildren became the eponymous founders of the three main cities on the island (*Olympian Odes* 7.20–80). These cities combined to found the federal city Rhodes in 408 BC, which instituted a festival, the Halieia, that included athletic and musical contests. In 282 BC the inhabitants contracted the Colossus of Rhodes to be built, an enormous bronze statue of the personified sun and one of the so-called seven wonders of the ancient world. Rhodes, though, seems to be the main exception that proves the rule; references in Herodotos (1.131), Aristophanes (*Peace* 406–413), and Plato (*Cratylus* 397c) suggest that cultic worship of the sun and moon was considered to be a characteristic of non-Greek cultures. Nevertheless, the sun did figure prominently as an oath deity, as we see already in Homer (e.g., *Iliad* 3.103–104, invoked along with Earth and Zeus). And there is evidence of more humble devotion. Children would clap their hands and call for the sun to come out when a cloud obscured it (Aristophanes fragment 404). One might greet the sun and moon with a prayer or some other ritual action (e.g., Plato *Laws* 887d–e). Such an act is reported to have appeared in a lost play by Aeschylus, *Bassarai* or *Bassarides* (*The Thracian Bacchantes*). According to the summaries of this play we find in later sources, Orpheus, after his experience in the underworld, neglected his previous worship of his father, Dionysos, and instead began to venerate the sun, whom he called Apollon; he would climb Mount Pangaion ("pangaion" means "all-earth") to offer a prayer to the rising sun; Dionysos in anger incited the Thracian Bacchantes at the end of one of their nocturnal revels to tear Orpheus apart limb-by-limb (see *Orphic fragment* 536). The equivalence of Apollon-Sun seems to have been first made by philosophers in the fifth century BC (Parmenides and Empedokles); a fragment of Sophokles also suggests this (see note to line 13 "Zeus"). In the ideal city-state depicted in the *Laws*, Plato makes the highest magistrates priests of both Apollon and Sun. The identification of these two divinities also occurs in the Orphic corpus (*Orphic fragment* 102, 323, 413). A vase from Olbia, which may have Orphic connections, contains this inscription: "Life Life Apollon Apollon Sun Sun Cosmos Cosmos Light Light" (*Orphic fragment* 537; see also Graf/Johnston 2007, p. 188). It is unclear when this equivalence was first attributed to Orpheus, but Aeschylus' play suggests at least the earlier part of the fifth century. This raises the interesting question of whether the philosophers might have adopted the identification from an Orphic cult or vice versa. Also connected with the name Orpheus is a hymn to Sun (*Orphic fragment* 538–545) in which this divinity is equated with Zeus, Hades, Dionysos, Eubouleus, Phanes, and Antauges (see *OH* 6i, and note to line 9 below). The extensive identification speaks of Hellenistic provenance or later. Sun as a distinct being does not play a large role in mythology. Probably the most important and famous story is that of his son Phaethon, who asked for, and was given, leave to drive Sun's chariot; but the lad was unable to maintain control over the team and was killed by Zeus' thunderbolt as the chariot careened to the earth, threatening a catastrophic conflagration (Ovid *Metamorphoses* 1.746–2.400). More relevant to our collection is his interaction with Demeter in identifying Hades as the abductor of Persephone; see note to line 1.

As with Sky, Ether, and Moon, the mythology and the cultic aspects of Sun are absent from the hymn. It is Sun's place in the cosmic order—including its ethical dimension—that is emphasized, and here the philosophical tradition has made its mark. Many of the ideas can be traced back to the Pre-Socratics; see the notes passim. But above all it is the traditional imagery that dominates by its repetition: the all-seeing eye and the golden, life-nourishing light driven by the swift four-horse chariot. Compare this hymn with the Homeric *Hymn to the Sun*, as well as Mesomedes' and Proclus' hymns to Sun. He is also invoked in the magical papyri (see in particular *PGM* 1.297–327, 341–347; 3.187–262; 4.436–461, 930–1114, 1928–2005; 8.74–81). See also *OH* 34i.

1 **eternal eye that sees all**: Sun, in his capacity as a celestial god, is often portrayed as perceiving all events that take place on earth. We list a few of the more famous examples. It is Sun who finds out about the affair between Ares and Aphrodite, Hephaistos' wife, and who informs the lame god of this indignity (*Odyssey* 8.270–272 and 302). In the Homeric *Hymn to Demeter*, Sun, along with Hekate (probably in her capacity as moon-goddess), perceives Hades' abduction of Persephone (2.24–27 and 62–90; see *OH* 9.3n and *OH* 41i). Finally, the fettered Prometheus calls to witness a host of natural phenomena and concludes by invoking the "all-seeing orb of the sun" at Aeschylus *Prometheus Bound* 88–92. The idea of Sun as witness is surely related to his role in oaths; see the introduction to this hymn and note to line 17. Other divinities described as all-seeing in the collection are Sky (*OH* 4.8), Moon (*OH* 9.7), Apollon (*OH* 34.8 and 11), Zeus (*OH* 59.13), Nemesis (*OH* 61.2 and 8), Dike (*OH* 62.1), and the Erinyes (*OH* 69.15, connected with Dike). The latter three also connect perspicuous vision with justice (see note to line 16 below). The sun is referred to as "the sublime eye of weightless fire" at *OH* 11.17.

2 **Hyperion**: This is actually the name of Sun's traditional father, one of the original twelve Titans. For Hesiod's genealogy, see *OH* 9i.

3 **self-born, untiring**: The idea that the sun reforms each day goes back to the philosopher Xenophanes (Kirk, Raven, and Schofield 1983, no. 175) and perhaps Herakleitos (Kirk, Raven, and Schofield 1983, no. 225; see also Kirk, Raven, and Schofield's commentary on both fragments). It is also found in the magical papyri. The phoinix, a legendary bird that was supposed to recreate itself from the ashes of his father, was sometimes thought to radiate fire, and Herodotos (2.73) reports that it brings the corpse of his father to the temple of Sun in Heliopolis, Egypt. That the sun is born again anew every day is probably a reasonable, if fantastical, extension of the observation that fire alone of the elements is capable of self-generation (see Theophrastos *On Fire* 1). The sun is already called "untiring" in Homer (*Iliad* 18.239, 484). Compare the opening of Mimnermos fragment 12.1–3: "For Sun has obtained by lot a labor for all his days, / and there is never any respite / for his horses or himself." The Greek words translated here as "self-born" and "untiring" are also used of Herakles in *OH* 12.9.

7 **endless whirl**: The same motion is ascribed to Sky (see *OH* 4.4+n) and Zeus the Thunderbolt (*OH* 19.10); compare the motion of Protogonos, who is sometimes identified with the sun (see *OH* 6.5–7+n), and likewise Physis (*OH* 10.21–24n).

9: The idea that heavenly bodies produce musical notes in their revolutions and that together they form a harmony goes back to the Pythagoreans, perhaps even Pythagoras himself. Their views are probably what Aristotle describes in *De caelo* 290b21–29. In book ten of the *Republic*, Plato describes a system where there rotate on the Spindle of Necessity eight whorls, on which the earth, sun, moon, planets, and stars move; also on each whorl sits a Siren who utters a pure note of a certain pitch, and they together produce a harmony; the three Fates sing along of the past, present, and future (616b–617d). See also *OH* 7.8n. A late source reports that some believed the seven notes on Orpheus' lyre were tuned to the rotations of seven celestial bodies; for an account of how this developed and its probable Pythagorean origins, see West 1983, pp. 29–32, and *OH* 11i. Such an image could very well have influenced our hymn, even though Sun should be producing one of the notes, not playing the lyre that produces the whole harmony. The lyre is typically associated with Apollon; but since the sun is associated with this god (see the introduction to this hymn, and note to line 12 below), it would be natural to transfer this attribute to him, and, in fact, the hymn to Apollon gives a fuller description of the cosmic lyre (*OH* 34.16–23+n). The Stoic Kleanthes is reported to have called the sun "plektron" (literally, "instrument for striking," a musical technical term for "pick," whence English "plectrum" via Latin), whose rays strike the universe and produce a "course in tune" (Clement of Alexandria *Stromateis* 5.8.48.1); Thom 2005 suggests this idea had been taken over from the late fifth- or early fourth-century poet Skythinos of Teos (p. 78 n. 188). Insofar as Sun is equated with Zeus in this hymn (see line 13 and note), Sun's prominence in producing the full harmony, not merely being part of it, is also understandable.

10 **as you nurture the seasons**: The same idea recurs in connection with the Kouretes, albeit for a different reason; see *OH* 38.25.

11 **piping lord of the world**: Sun has already been described as holding the lyre, and now we find that he is a piper as well. The whistling sound this instrument makes is consistent with the type of sound implied by the rushing chariot (line 6) and the "screaming whip" (line 19). The playing of pipes is usually associated with Pan, and there are points of contact between this god and Sun in the collection. Pan's music is described as an accompaniment to the cosmic harmony (*OH* 11.6), and he is also called "light-bringing lord of the cosmos" (*OH* 11.11). Furthermore, Pan is a "companion of the Seasons" (*OH* 11.4), a "begetter of all" (*OH* 11.10), a "veritable Zeus with horns" (*OH* 11.12), and he brings "nourishment to mankind" (*OH* 11.20; cf. line 12 of this hymn). Apollon may be added to this pair, for he is called Pan in the context of his divine music that regulates the seasons (*OH* 34.24), and Pan, in turn, is called Paian (*OH* 11.11), as Sun in the next line. Thus, these three divinities are brought into relation with one another as beings who maintain the cosmic order.

12 **Paian**: For this name/title of Apollon, see *OH* 34.1n; for Apollon's identification with the sun, see the introduction to this hymn. There are a number of overlapping attributes between this hymn and the one to Apollon (*OH* 34).

13 **father of time**: Moon is called "the mother of time"; see *OH* 9.5+n. Herakles is also called "father of time"; see *OH* 12.3+n.

13 **Zeus**: There are a number of attributes that Zeus and Sun share that would suggest such a correspondence: both are sky gods, both are associated with fire and light, both are believed to see all things, both are concerned with justice, and both were invoked in oaths (often together). A late source cites the following fragment from Sophokles (fragment 752): "O Sun, may you take pity on me / you whom the wise [*sophoi*] call the begetter of the gods / and father of all." The source introduces this quote with the following: "those who believe that the sun is Zeus say that Sophokles also calls the sun Zeus." Since we do not know the original context, we cannot be sure whether Sophokles actually intended to make this connection. The idea that Zeus is the father of all things is a commonplace in Greek literature; in Orphic cosmogony, this is taken literally (see *OH* 15.3–5n). The sun's role in producing life on earth could easily have suggested an identification with Zeus.

16 **a paragon of justice**: Sun's role in oaths naturally connects this divinity with justice. In a discussion of the etymology for "dikaion," a word meaning "justice," Sokrates says that he heard from many men that justice is the element that moves through (*diaion*) all things, which is the cause of generation, and that this is also why it is connected with the irregular root of Zeus ("dia"); upon further inquiry as to the nature of justice, one man claims it is the sun, since the sun governs all things, another man says it is the essence of heat that

resides in fire, and yet another man holds, after Anaxagoras, that it is Mind (Plato *Cratylus* 412c–413d). Plato's authorities might very well be the ones who are called "the wise" in Sophokles fragment 752 (see note to line 13 "Zeus"), and Kahn 1979, p. 156, conjectures that Plato's source might be Herakleitos or his followers. The idea that the physical nature of the cosmos also consists of an ethical dimension—a type of universal that is the standard to which the human sphere ought to attain—is found in some of the early hymns (see also note to line 1, *OH* 7.12–13n and *OH* 10.14–16n) and is picked up again later on (see *OH* 64i).

16 water-loving lord of the cosmos: Sun might be said to love the water due to the fact that it signals the end of his laborious journey for the day. In mythology, Sun is sometimes portrayed as riding a cup at night on Okeanos in his return east to rise again the next day. It is interesting to note that some of the Pre-Socratics (Anaximenes, Xenophanes, Herakleitos: see Kirk, Raven, and Schofield 1983, nos. 148–149, 175–179, 225, and their comments) and Stoics believed that the sun was created or maintained by evaporation from bodies of water on the earth (see, e.g., Plutarch *De stoicorum repugnantiis* 1053a, *De Iside et Osiride* 367e).

17 guard pledges: This alludes to Sun's role as an oath god; see the introduction to this hymn and note to line 1.

19 four-horse chariot: Sun is often conceived as a charioteer in Greco-Roman literature and art. Festus, a second-century AD writer, in a note discussing various horse sacrifices mentions one at Rhodes, where a four-horse chariot is driven into the sea; he tells us that this symbolized the course of the sun as it traveled around the world; see Burkert 1985, p. 175.

9. To Selene

Selene, whom we are calling Moon for consistency (see note to lines 1–2 below) had very little role in Greek cult, even less than that of Sun, who at least had a major cult center at Rhodes. Her importance in religion is due largely to her identification with Artemis and Hekate. In later times, she was adopted into pre-existing cults, along with other figures (e.g., Sun). Moon appears in magical texts, as well as a curse tablet from Megara, but even in these cases she is not quite divorced from the other goddesses who are identified with her. In our collection she is closely linked with the Stars and Sun, both of whose hymns precede this one, and the obscure figure Melinoe might well be a specific manifestation of Hekate as moon goddess (see *OH* 71i). Moon also does not have much of a presence in myth. She is perhaps best known for her love affair with Endymion; the story is first attested for Sappho (no text survives) and in modern times is most famously retold in Keat's eponymous poem. In Hesiod's *Theogony*, she is the daughter of the Titans Hyperion and Theia and the sister of Sun and Dawn (371–374). In later times, she is sometimes said to be the daughter of Sun, this genealogy perhaps reflecting a belief that the moon reflected the light of the sun (already postulated by Anaxagoras; see Kirk, Raven, and Schofield 1983, nos. 500, 502), the inferior status of the secondary light being expressed in genealogical terms. It is interesting to note that a number of words describing the light of the moon in this hymn (and in the magical papyri) are ones that more typically describe the sun's light. *Orphic fragment* 155 explicitly calls the moon "another earth" (see note to lines 1–2); for the moon's chthonic associations, see *OH* 59.3–4n. We also find Mousaios addressed as the offspring of Moon (Mousaios fragments 11T–14T); the same relationship was claimed by the Kretan shaman Epimenides (fragment 33) and the oracle-monger Alexander of Abonoteikhos, who slapped a human face on a snake and called it Asklepios (second century AD; Lucian devotes an entire essay, *Alexander, or the False Seer* to vilify the man). Some accounts hold that the Nemean Lion came from the moon.

As is the case with Sun in the previous hymn, Moon appears all but devoid of her religious and mythical heritage. The focus is almost exclusively on the moon as an astronomical phenomenon; in particular, the play of light and darkness seems to have captured the imagination of the author. This hymn should be compared with the short Homeric *Hymn to the Moon*. For Moon's role in magic, of particular interest are a series of prayers and invocations to Moon/Hekate (*PGM* 4.2241–2358, 2441–2784). Theokritos' second idyll is a literary account of love magic in which Moon is invoked. Lucian parodies the idea of the moon as another world in his *True History* 1.9–27. See also *OH* 1i, *OH* 36i, and *OH* 71i.

1–2 Selene, / . . . Moon: The hymn in quick succession invokes the moon under the two names by which she was known. "Selēnē" is derived from the Greek noun "selas," "light, brightness, gleam" (compare Latin "luna," "moon," from "lux," "light"; see also *OH* 71i), and might have developed as a euphemism for the moon proper (Greek "mēnē"). If this is correct, the demonic Hekate/Moon found in the magical papyri would have quite an ancient pedigree. *Orphic fragment* 155, describing the creation of the world by Protogonos (or its recreation by Zeus), also uses both names in close proximity: "And he conceived another earth, boundless, which Selene / the immortals call, but those upon the earth Mene; / it has many mountains, many cities, many houses." The idea that gods and mortals call the same thing by different names appears elsewhere in epic poetry (e.g., the river Skamandros, *Iliad* 20.74) and this also happens among different mortals (e.g., in the case of Hektor's child, *Iliad* 6.402–403). The preference in our collection for "mēnē" instead of "selēnē" might be due to the Orphic fragment, where the former is the term that mortal men use.

3 torch-bearing: Both Artemis and Demeter are called "torch-bearing" in their hymns (*OH* 36.3+n and *OH* 40.11+n); the same epithet is used of Hekate/Artemis/Moon in the magical papyri (*PGM* 4.2559, 2718). The torch is one of the standard attributes of Hekate. She, along with Sun, perceived Hades' abduction of Persephone. This pairing implies Hekate's capacity as a moon goddess; indeed, the Greek word used of the light of her torch is *selas* (Homeric *Hymn to Demeter* 2.52 see the note to lines 1–2 above and *OH* 1i). Torches are also standard in processions (see *OH* 40.11n) and the iconography of maenads (see *OH* 52i).

4 feminine and masculine: A number of divinities are described as androgynous in the collection: Physis (*OH* 10.18), Athene (*OH* 32.10), Mise (*OH* 42.4), and Adonis (*OH* 56.4). The goddess Artemis is also called masculine at *OH* 36.7. Protogonos is "two-natured" (*OH* 6.1), and this probably refers to this being's androgynous nature; see also *Orphic fragment* 80, 121, and 134. One might also compare two versions of an Orphic hymn to Zeus, where the god, invoked as the embodiment of the cosmos, is depicted by a number of complementary characteristics, including masculine and feminine features, and in particular is asserted to be the sun and the moon (*Orphic fragment* 31.4, 6; 243.3, 16). Likewise, Dionysos and Eros are also "two-natured" (*OH* 30.2 and *OH* 58.4) which probably indicates dual gender. In the magical papyri, we find Moon invoked thus: "I summon you, triple-faced goddess, Moon, lovely light, Hermes and Hekate together, an androgynous shoot" (*PGM* 4.2608–2610). The dual gender of Moon is curious, particularly since she is described as "mother of time" in line 5, while Sun, who is not depicted as androgynous, is called the "father of time" (*OH* 8.13). The masculine side of the moon might be an oblique reference to the non-Greek moon-god Men (pronounced "main"), whose worship was widespread in Asia Minor and who is mentioned in Orpheus' address to Mousaios at *OH* 0.39, admittedly, however, far removed from the Moon's presence in line 4.

5 mother of time: Sun is called "father of time" in his hymn (*OH* 8.13). The ancients in general employed a lunisolar calendar. The months were calculated by the phases of the moon; indeed the words "moon" and "month" are cognate; compare also Greek "mēnē" ("moon") and "meis, mēnos" ("month, moon") as well as Latin "mensis" ("month"). However, in terms of a recurring pattern, a strictly lunar calendar quickly falls out of step with the seasons, which are tied to the earth's circuit around the sun, so that the same month that occurs in winter will occur in summer within a generation. The ancients were well aware of this difficulty and so employed various means to keep the solar year in tune with the lunar months. For detailed information on Greco-Roman calendars, see Samuel 1972; for a more concise account on time reckoning, whose scope extends beyond ancient Mediterranean cultures, see Holford-Strevens 2005. The Demiurge in Plato's *Timaeus* creates the sun, moon, the planets, and the stars to fix and measure time (38b–39e). *Orphic fragment* 156, in the context of the (re)creation of the cosmos, says that the moon was given a month-long orbit analogous to the year-long one of the sun.

6 amber-colored: See *OH* 71i.

7 all-seeing: Similar to Sun, Moon is able to see all things from her vantage point in the celestial sphere; see *OH* 8.1n.

10 long-cloaked marshal of the stars: The moon, as the most conspicuous heavenly body in the night sky, can naturally be conceived as the leader of the lesser lights. At the start of the "Prayer to Moon" in the magical papyri, Moon is addressed as one "who in the triple shapes of the triple Graces, dances with the stars in festive revel" (*PGM* 4.2793–2795).

12: Light in Greek literature often connotes deliverance from some trouble. This line seems to indicate that the rites performed with this collection took place at night (see *OH* 3i).

10. To Physis

Physis (Nature) was conceived by the Greeks since early times as the loosely personified sum total of the creative powers or creative genius of the cosmos at work. The word is derived from the Greek verb "phuō" which means "I grow, I am (by nature)" (a word, incidentally, cognate with English "be"). The notion, in both of its senses, was important from the earliest schools of philosophy. Indeed, there are a number of ancient philosophical treatises entitled "Peri phuseōs" ("On Nature"; cf. Lucretius' Latin poem *De rerum natura*, "On the Nature of Things"). Our hymn conceives of Physis in such vague terms as to render it very difficult to point to a definite connection with any particular philosophical school. There do seem to be a number of resonances with the Zeus in the Stoic philosopher Kleanthes' *Hymn to Zeus*, where the god is addressed as the "originator of nature [*phuseōs*]" (line 2). He is also "many-named" and "master of all" (line 1 ~ *OH* 10.4 and 13), "ruler" (2 ~ *OH* 10.3), mingled with celestial bodies (12–13; cf. *OH* 10.6), has powers over the earth, heaven, and sea (15–16; cf. *OH* 10.14), and is a "giver of all" (32 ~ *OH* 10.16), among other verbal overlaps. A familiarity with this work is likely. Interestingly enough, the so-called Pythagorean *Golden Verses*, a collection of moral precepts of unknown date but certainly well known by late antiquity, cast Physis in the role of a priestess in a mystery cult revealing secrets to the initiates: "But take courage, for mortals have a divine origin, / to whom Physis displays and shows each sacred object" (63–64, translation by Thom 1995). The language here is suspiciously Orphic, as Thom discusses in his commentary on these lines (pp. 205–212). An earlier pair of verses (52–53), which looks at the universality of nature (here probably not personified), also admits of potential Stoic, Pythagorean, or even Orphic provenance (see Thom 1995, pp. 190–191). Mesomedes composed a hymn to Physis, identifying this divinity with Sun towards the end. He apostrophizes Physis with "O you who kindle the whole world with your brilliant rays" (15–16) and calls Physis "Aion" (a figure sometimes equated with Sun in the magical papyri; see *OH* O.28–29n), "Paian" (= Apollon), and "Titan" (referring to Sun or his father, Hyperion; cf. *OH* 8.2, and for this relationship, see Hesiod *Theogony* 134). As in the *Golden Verses*, the language of mystery cults also appears in this hymn, as the poet calls on Sun-Physis to grant blessings "to your Bacchant" (19–20). Further points of contact are mentioned in the notes passim. The personified Physis also appears in the magical papyri in a number of associations. She is mentioned immediately following Aion in a long list of invocations (*PGM* 1.310), and possibly equated with Sun himself (*PGM* 4.939, but there is textual corruption). It is perhaps not too much of a surprise to find her identified with Aphrodite, given that goddess' strong connection with generative powers (*PGM* 4.2917). This is perhaps comparable to the address as the "persuasion of the Graces" in line 13, as both the Graces and the personified Persuasion are traditionally connected with Aphrodite (see *OH* 55.9n and *OH* 60i). Also due to the association with fertility is the equation of Physis with Moon-Artemis-Hekate (*PGM* 4.2832). The Physis of the magical papyri shares some of the epithets used of this goddess in our hymn.

Our composer, then, has apparently appropriated an idea found in a number of congenial contexts and adapted it to one suitable for the purposes of the collection. Physis is here presented as the mysterious and ineffable power that infuses all of creation. The position of the hymn is significant in this respect. There are many verbal reminiscences with the earlier hymns, and the birth motif makes yet another appearance. Given that Hekate and Moon are often fused together as one entity, they can be seen as functioning in the collection as a type of ring composition that bookends the hymns to the cosmic powers, who are primarily presented in abstract terms. The hymn to Physis, along with that of Pan, might very well have been intended as a summary of this earliest stage of personified abstractions, which afterward gives way to more anthropomorphic figures, starting with the twelfth hymn to Herakles. Note, too, that the hymns to Physis and Pan are also verbally connected through the frequent use of the Greek word "pan" ("all") in this hymn, either as an independent word or as part of compound.

1 **mother of all**: This is also used of Physis twice in the magical papyri: once in her identification with Aphrodite (*PGM* 4.2916–2917), the other time with Moon-Hekate-Artemis (*PGM* 4.2832–2833). An obscure poem from later antiquity on the powers of plants calls *physis* (probably not to be personified) by the same epithet. We find this and similar descriptive phrases applied throughout the collection to various fertility figures: Night (*OH* 3.1), Rhea (*OH* 14.8–9), Demeter (*OH* 40.1), Mother Antaia (*OH* 41.1–2), and Hygeia (*OH* 68.2). In particular, Earth can also have the same epithet used here (see Aeschylus *Prometheus Bound* 90 and *Orphic fragment* 243.27), and she is addressed as "mother of men and of the blessed gods" in her hymn (see *OH* 26.1+n).

2 **oldest of all**: Mesomedes calls her the "oldest mother of the cosmos" in line 2 of his hymn.

6–7: A similar sequence is found in line 3 of Mesomedes' hymn: "[you who are] night, light, and silence." Given the reference to mystic initiates in the following line of his hymn, Mesomedes might be alluding to nocturnal ritual.

9: There are many instances of contradictory, or at least paradoxical, formulations throughout this hymn and, indeed, the collection as a whole. See lines 3, 6 (dark/bright), 8, 10, 17 (life/death), and 18. The idea of causing a quality without possessing that quality itself is already found in Aristotle's notion of the "unmoved mover" (and note that Mesomedes calls Physis a "first principle" in line 1 of his hymn); see also line 21 of this hymn, where Physis is said to "[set] all in motion."

10 self-fathered: Physis is called "self-growing" (the Greek *autophuē* is a pun on *phusis*) in the magical papyri (*PGM* 1.310).

14–16: Physis is not just a concretization of the powers of generation but also is responsible for the underlying ethical dimension of the world. She is Dike (meaning "right") personified (compare *OH* 62 and *OH* 63), and "virtue" (Greek "aretē") in line 10 might also be intended as a personification. See further *OH* 8.16n. Many divinities are connected with the realms of heaven, earth, and sea in this collection. Some, like Physis, are described as having dominion over them: Kybele (*OH* 27.4–8), Aphrodite (*OH* 55.4–7), and her son Eros (*OH* 58.5–7). Aphrodite is also said to be the source of these three spheres, as are Rhea (*OH* 14.9–10) and Zeus (*OH* 15.3–5), whose descent as the thunderbolt also affects the same areas (*OH* 19.12–19). Pan (*OH* 11.13–18) and Nomos (*OH* 64.2–4) keep everything in its place. Some divinities are described as dwelling in these locations: Hekate (*OH* 1.2), Pan (*OH* 11.2–3, where fire, probably a metonomy for ether, is also included), Proteus (*OH* 25.6–9, where he is the locus of creation by Physis), and the Kouretes (*OH* 38.2). In the opening address to Mousaios, Orpheus at one point invokes all the gods of the sky, air, water, earth, underworld, and ether (*OH* O.32–33). In a related vein, the animals that inhabit the land, air, and sea are listed at *OH* 37.5 and *OH* 78.11–12. This motif is related to that of the four elements (see in particular *OH* 11.2–3n). Heaven, earth, and sea figure prominently in various stories of creation. In particular, note the song of Orpheus at Apollonios of Rhodes *Argonautika* 1.493–502, and compare the song of Silenos at Vergil *Eclogues* 6.31ff., where, before his song begins, Silenos is compared favorably to Apollon and Orpheus. See also *OH* 34.11–15+n.

18 father and mother of all: The earlier hymns to Night and Sky (*OH* 3 and *OH* 4) form a generative pair. Sun and Moon, as father and mother of time (*OH* 8.13 and *OH* 9.5), are similarly related, while Moon herself is both masculine and feminine (see *OH* 9.4+n). Mesomedes addresses Physis in line 2 of his hymn as the "oldest mother" but his later identification of the goddess with Sun-Aion-Apollon (15–20) suggests that he also saw this first principle (see line 1 of his hymn) as androgynous.

19 swift birth: Prothyraia-Eileithyia in *OH* 2.4 and Artemis in *OH* 36.8 are also called goddesses "of swift birth."

19 giver of wealth of seeds: The same Greek epithet is used of Protogonos (*OH* 6.10, where it is translated as "of many seeds"); see also *OH* 6.3n.

21–24: Possibly a reference to the river Okeanos, whom Homer calls the "begetter of all" (see *OH* 83i). Physis, like this river and other personified celestial phenomena (Sky in *OH* 4.4, the Stars in *OH* 7.4, Moon in *OH* 9.10; see further *OH* 8.7n), is also conceived as moving in a circle (also compare Kleanthes *Hymn to Zeus* 7). She is constantly changing her form in the sense that she produces an astonishing variety of living beings (cf. *OH* 3.8–11n).

26 **those who hold the scepter**: Mortal kings are the ones who usually hold the scepter. In the *Rhapsodies*, we find mention of a six-part scepter (*Orphic fragment* 166), which seems to refer to the sequence of six rulers of the cosmos (Protogonos, Night, Sky, Kronos, Zeus, and Dionysos), while Night is explicitly said to hold the scepter she obtained from Protogonos (*Orphic fragment* 168 and 170, and see *OH* 3i and *OH* 15.6+n).

27 **all-taming, . . . fire-breathing**: The same epithets are used of Ether at *OH* 5.3. The association with fire is perhaps related to the identification of Physis with Sun in other sources (see the introduction to this hymn) and, along with the following line ("you are life everlasting"), perhaps also is to be connected with the idea that the soul is composed of fire (also *OH* 5.3; see further *OH* 66.9+n).

11. To Pan

Pan is a divinity with an interesting history. He originally appears to have been a woodland god in Arkadia, one who roamed the mountains, hunted small game, and frolicked in song and dance with nymphs. He is traditionally represented as a bearded man with horns on his head, whose upper body is human and whose lower parts are capriform. Later considered to be the quintessential symbol of paganism, his features were adopted in representations of the Christian devil. Pan was worshipped in Arkadia with the traditional accoutrements of Greek religion (see, e.g., Pausanias 8.37.10), but outside of this area he was typically venerated in sacred caves or grottos. Herodotos (6.105) narrates a tale from the Persian invasion of Attika: the Athenians sent an accomplished runner, Pheidippides, to the Spartans in order to solicit their help, and, while he was passing through a mountain in Arkadia, the god appeared to him and asked why the Athenians did no honor to him, although he had helped them in the past and would do so again in the future. After the battle of Marathon, the Athenians decided to make good their past neglect by dedicating a cave on the northwest slope of the Akropolis to Pan. One feature of their worship of Pan was a torch-race, and it is interesting that one of the sanctuaries of Pan in Arkadia had a racetrack, according to Pausanias (8.38.5).

Pan was often invoked along with Hermes and the nymphs. Indeed, like Hermes, he can multiply flocks and bring good fortune to those he chooses. An example of this may be seen in one of the caves of the ancient marble quarry on Paros; there at the entrance one finds a Hellenistic frieze depicting Pan and the nymphs. A further connection with Hermes is found in many of the versions of Pan's genealogy. He is usually represented as the son of Hermes, often through a nymph, as in the Homeric *Hymn to Pan*, where the mother is the daughter of Dryops. We also find Penelope, the wife of Odysseus, claimed to be the mother, with Hermes, Apollon, or even all the suitors as the father. The Arkadian connection is also seen in variations that make Zeus the father and Kallisto, a nymph and mother of Arkas, the eponymous hero of Arkadia, the mother. Other parentages are considered below.

Pan was connected with sudden bouts of fear or madness (whence English "panic"), already in the Classical period (e.g., Euripides *Medeia* 1172). The Homeric *Hymn to Pan* alludes to this attribute in the birth of Pan. When the mother and nurse see the baby born with a beard and goat features, they run away screaming, while the father, Hermes, happily scoops up the infant in his arms and brings him to Olympos; all the gods delight in the baby, Dionysos most of all (19.27–47; see also *OH* 14i and *OH* 46.7n). Pan's madness could overtake men and beasts in the lonely places of mountains, and sometimes the explanation is put forth that this was due to a sudden gust of wind from the instrument of Pan, the panpipes, constructed out of a number of reeds bound together and stopped with wax (see below and the notes to lines 7 and 9). In literature and iconography Pan is often portrayed carrying this instrument. It was also supposed that "panic" was a frenzy occasioned by being directly possessed by the god; see *OH* 52.7–8n and cf. *OH* 30i+4n.

It is perhaps this notion of madness and possession that brought Pan into the orbit of ecstatic and mystery cults. As already mentioned, he is particularly tied to Dionysos in the Homeric *Hymn to Pan*, and he is often found in the Dionysian *thiasos*. Both divinities also share a connection with pastoral settings and nymphs. Pindar brings Pan together with Mother: he puts him in her retinue (*Pythian Odes* 3.77–79) and calls him the "attendant" (fragment 95) and "dog" (fragment 96) of the goddess. Pan is associated with other divinities connected with madness. The nurse in Euripides' *Hippolytos* asks Phaedra if she is possessed by Pan, Hekate, the Korybantes, or Kybele, the mountain mother (141–144); see also *OH* 27.8n. Madness and frenzy play a role in our hymn and elsewhere in the collection with similar entities; see *OH* 27.13n and *OH* 71.11n. One obscure genealogy of Pan makes him the son of Ether and a nymph named Oinoe. Given the role of Ether in Orphic mythology, it is tempting to see an Orphic source for this notice. Mysterious, too, is the story of the death of Pan, told by Plutarch at *De defectu oraculorum* 419b–e. As a ship was heading up the coast of Epiros in northwest Greece at the time of the Emperor Tiberius, a voice from an island called out to the Egyptian helmsman Thamous, who ignored the voice twice but responded after a third time. The voice bade him to announce to the land by Lake Palodes that "Pan the Great has died." Thamous does so, and even before he finishes his words, groaning and shouts of amazement were heard from somewhere on land.

Possibly also in the context of mystery cults there developed the notion of the "cosmic" Pan as found in our hymn. It was sometimes claimed that he did not have any parents but was "without a father" or "autochthonic" and "earth-born." One obscure writer calls Pan "celestial." Of particular interest is a recurring notion that the physical constitution of Pan symbolizes the entire universe. The horns on his head represent both the rays of the sun and the horns of the moon. His ruddy complexion is the ether. The leopard or fawn skin he wears (a typical article of clothing for a follower of Dionysos), being spotted, refers to the stars in the sky. His hairy lower shanks correspond to the trees and shrubbery that clothe the earth, and his hard goat hooves suggest the stability of solid ground (cf. also *OH* 10.14–16n and *OH* 15.3–5n). Two other notable attributes are mentioned by Servius in his commentary on Vergil's *Eclogues* 2.31. He says that the shepherd's crook that Pan holds, because it is curved back, points to the recurring year and that the panpipes he holds are made up of seven reeds, corresponding to the seven notes of the cosmic harmony. In this context Servius refers to Vergil *Aeneid* 6.645, where Orpheus (the "Thracian priest") is depicted in the Elysian Fields, playing his seven-stringed lyre. Note, too, that Sun in his hymn is represented as playing the cosmic harmony by the lyre and by piping (*OH* 8.11+n). It is unclear where Servius is drawing this connection between the music of "cosmic" Pan and Orpheus, although it is likely he has the poem entitled *Lyre* in mind, which was attributed to Orpheus (*Orphic fragment* 417–420; see also West 1983, pp. 29–32). It is also suggestive that in the Orphic theogony reported by Hieronymos, Protogonos was called Zeus, who, as master of the entire cosmos, was also known as Pan (*Orphic fragment* 86; see also note to lines 10–12). In this context, note that Silenos, a figure with much affinity with Pan, sings a song of creation at Vergil *Eclogues* 6.31ff. (see *OH* 10.14–16n).

This identification of Pan and Zeus helps explain why Pan became a god whose domain extends over all creation. The Greek word for "all, whole, entire" is "pan," and we find such etymologizing explanations mentioned elsewhere in the context of "cosmic" Pan (cf. *OH* 25i). This seems to be a later development, though, and other explanations of this god's name were offered earlier. In the Homeric *Hymn to Pan*, it is explained he was called Pan because "all" the gods took delight in him (19.47). Writers who make "all" the suitors of Penelope the father of this god offer a more salacious hypothesis. The root "pa" seen in the Greek "*pasomai" ("I will acquire") and Latin "pascor" ("I feed, graze on") is a more likely ancestor to the name Pan. He is the god who nourishes the flocks and can increase their number.

This hymn, like Pan himself, is a hybrid mix, combining a charming rustic materialism with the sublime power that permeates all creation. Similar to Physis in the previous hymn, Pan is connected with growth and nourishment of life (note the appearance of the birthing motif again). Indeed, the epithet "begetter of all" ("pantophuēs") in line 10 combines words that are cognate with both divinities. And also like the previous hymn, this one serves as a summary of the cosmic powers already honored (see also *OH* 10i). Thus Pan functions as a transition to the more anthropomorphic figure of Herakles of the next hymn.

One detail that perhaps is not directly relevant to this hymn but deserves mention is that Herodotos in his digression treating Egypt in book two of his *Histories* mentions that the Greek divinities Dionysos, Herakles, and Pan have a different chronology from their Egyptian counterparts (2.145). For the Greeks, the order of birth is Dionysos, Herakles, Pan (Herodotos making him the son of Penelope and Hermes, and thus born after the Trojan War), while the Egyptians place their Pan among the eight primeval gods (the Ogdoad), Herakles among the subsequent dynasty of the twelve gods, and Dionysos in a third dynasty. While admittedly there is little Egyptian influence on our collection, it is certainly possible that a distant source for the "Titan" Herakles in the subsequent hymn was influenced by the same account related by Herodotos (or even by Herodotos' account itself).

2–3: The sky, sea, land, and fire (probably the ether is meant) correspond to the four elements: air, water, earth, and fire (see lines 13–18, *OH* 5.4n and *OH* 14.9–10n). A similar broad range of domains is found in many hymns in the collection; see *OH* 10.14–16n.

5 reveling: The word has distinct Bacchic connotations, and Pan has a special relation to Dionysos; see the introduction to this hymn and *OH* 52i.

7 fantasies of dread: A reference to Pan's madness, which he is asked to banish at the end of the hymn. A number of divinities in the collection have similar powers; see *OH* 71.11n.

9 dance with the Nymphs, . . . lover of Echo: Pan is often found carousing with nymphs, and there are a number of similarities between this hymn and the one to the Nymphs (*OH* 51). The two are mentioned in the same line of Orpheus' address to Mousaios (*OH* O.15). Despite Pan's proud assertion of bachelorhood in Lucian's humorous portrayal of the god (*Dialogue of the Gods* 22), in mythical tradition he is involved in a number of failed relationships. The most famous one is with the nymph Syrinx, memorably told by Ovid (*Metamorphoses* 1.689–712). She rejects Pan's advances and, as she flees from him, is turned into a clump of reeds. When Pan reaches to grasp her, he finds instead the bunch of reeds in his hands. He sighs, and his breath goes through the reeds and produces sweet music. Thus did Pan invent the panpipes (Greek "surinx"), a common attribute of his evermore. Another nymph, named Pitys, rejected Pan and she was turned into a pine tree (Greek "pitus"). Our hymn directly refers to Echo, who is usually associated with Narcissus. However, she is sometimes an amorous interest of Pan, and, like Syrinx and Pitys, rejects his advances. In Longus' novel *Daphnis and Chloe* (3.23), Daphnis explains to his lover Chloe the origin of the "echo." The nymph Echo was taught by the Muses in every sort of singing and musical instruments. Pan, in anger over her skills and at the fact that she fled from him, sent his madness to the shepherds and goatherds, who promptly tore Echo apart. As a favor to the Muses, Earth echoes back sounds just as the nymph was able to do when alive. This story has interesting parallels to that of Orpheus, famed for his music and, in some accounts, torn to shreds by maenads maddened by Dionysos, either because Orpheus had stopped venerating the god or because the nymphs themselves were enraged that Orpheus had sworn off women after the death of Eurydike; see also *OH* 87.9n. For the ripping apart of an animal as part of maenadic ritual (*sparagmos*), see *OH* 52i. Pan is sometimes considered to be the source of echoes himself. It is not always easy to determine whether a writer has in mind "echo" or "Echo" in connection with Pan (see, for example, Homeric *Hymn to Pan* 19.21). For Pan and nymphs in cult, see *OH* 51i.

10–12 many-named divinity. . . veritable Zeus with horns: Pan is called "many-named" and then in quick succession we have a number of identifications. Zeus is directly mentioned, and Pan's role as "begetter of all" fits in well with Zeus' role as father of gods and men in the tradition. As noted in the introduction to this hymn, Zeus is called Pan in *Orphic fragment* 86. Another fragment calls Zeus "the god of all and the mixer of all" (*Orphic fragment* 414); the Greek words for "mixer" and "horned" are the same ("kerastēs"), except they are accented differently. There may be a word-play here, and the second line of this fragment adds "whistling with winds and air-mingled sounds" (the Greek for "whistling is "surizōn," cognate with "surinx"). Given Pan's connection with a wind instrument, and the sounds in the mountain that cause his special kind of fear, it is possible that the author of this fragment intended an allusion to Pan. Another fragment from the same poem lists a number of gods and their domains, ending with the observation "all these things are one" (*Orphic fragment* 413.12). The reference to Paian is a bit vague. Normally, Paian is another name for Apollon (*OH* 34.1+n), but it is also attributed to Sun (*OH* 8.12), Dionysos (*OH* 52.11), and Apollon's son Asklepios (*OH* 67.1). But as Sun is also called "fruit-bearing, Paian" (the Greek there is the same as in this hymn) and is also a piper (*OH* 8.11+n), the immediate identification here is most likely that between Sun and Pan. That leaves "light-bringing lord of the cosmos." This could describe Sun, but a better candidate is perhaps Protogonos, who is a "begetter of blessed gods and mortal men" (*OH* 6.3) and also brings light to all (*OH* 6.8). It is very interesting in connection with Protogonos that our composer in the next line addresses him as Priapos, a rustic divinity similar to Pan (*OH* 6.9+n), and also that when Zeus is called Pan in *Orphic fragment* 86, he has earlier been identified with Protogonos, suggesting that all three were considered different names for the same deity. As mentioned in the introduction to this hymn, Pan's presence seems to be meant as a more concrete realization of the abstract entities addressed in the earlier hymns and a transitional figure to more anthropomorphic ones.

17: For the idea of the all-seeing eye of Sun, see *OH* 8.1+n.

19 your providence alters the natures of all: Interestingly enough, the lovers who reject Pan often undergo transformation (see note to line 9). Compare, too, *OH* 10.21.

12. To Herakles

Herakles is the most storied of all the legendary Greek heroes. His popularity and the sheer bulk of his adventures, probably the result of accretions over a long period of time, have effaced the true origins of this figure (for his possible Eastern connections, see Levy 1934). He is already mentioned a few times in the *Iliad* and *Odyssey*, and a poem attributed to Hesiod, the *Shield*, focuses on his battle against the bandit Kyknos. For a summary of Herakles' life, see Apollodoros 2.4.8–2.7.8. There is also a Homeric hymn in his honor. In the tradition, we find this larger-than-life hero represented in many different ways. He is the great slayer of the monsters in the wild, thus opening the world for the expansion of civilization. He can be seen as a paragon of virtue, as in the parable of the Sophist Prodikos, preserved by Xenophon, where the young Herakles chooses the Hesiodic rough road of Virtue over the easy path of Vice (Xenophon *Memorabilia* 2.21–34). For the Stoics, Herakles symbolized the endurance needed to face adversity with equanimity and the ability to persevere and ultimately prevail.

The connection of Herakles with Dionysian cult is not easy to explain, but there are a number of factors that, when taken together, help illuminate his position in our collection. Herakles dies when he puts on a poisoned robe given to him by his jealous wife Deianira, who had been tricked into thinking it was a love charm. After Herakles builds his own pyre and immolates himself, he is translated to Olympos, where he becomes a god and takes Hebe (meaning "youth"), a daughter of Zeus and Hera, as his wife. In Homer, Odysseus encounters the shade of Herakles in the land of the dead, although the divine part of Herakles is said to be a god on Olympos (*Odyssey* 11.601–614). Herodotos reports that the Greeks worshipped Herakles both as a hero and as a god (2.44), and Pindar calls Herakles a "hero-god" (*Nemean Odes* 3.23). The golden apples of the Hesperides, which Herakles fetches in his eleventh labor, are sometimes interpreted as symbols of immortality (as are the labors as a whole), and even Hebe herself, the goddess of youth, might be understood to signify eternal life. This special status of Herakles is connected with his leading a virtuous life, and this pattern of achieving divine status after death, particularly tied to one's virtue or goodness, is one of the concerns found in the Bacchic gold leaves (Graf/Johnston 2007, pp. 94–136; see also note to line 16. In fact, we find Herakles being initiated in mystery cults, such as the Eleusinian Mysteries (Xenophon *Hellenika* 6.3.6; see also Boardman 1989, pl. 392). Both he and Dionysos seem to have been worshipped together at Thasos, one of the oldest cult centers for Herakles (see Larson 2007, pp. 185–186). A cup painting shows the two of them together in a symposiastic setting, attended by satyrs (Boardman 1975, pl. 376; cf. also Boardman 1989, pl. 131). Herakles is often depicted as wearing the skin of the Nemean Lion, and Dionysos often wears the skin of an exotic animal (leopard, panther) in his iconography. Both have Theban connections, both are sons of Zeus by mortal women, and both are struck by their father's lightning bolt (Dionysos, albeit indirectly, is struck while in Semele's womb; Herakles, in some versions, has his pyre ignited by Zeus' lightning). Herakles also has fertility associations (see Levy 1934, pp. 43–45).

Finally, there are a few indirect ways Herakles might have been brought into connection with Orpheus. Both are numbered among the Argonauts, and both return alive from a journey to the underworld. The legendary poet and musician Linos taught music to Herakles, who eventually killed his teacher in a paroxysm of rage; Linos is variously related to Orpheus in the tradition as brother, grandfather, teacher, or disciple. Lastly, there is a connection with the Idaian Dactyls from Krete. These were famous magicians and metalworkers who were also priests of mystery cults; in some cases, they are considered the teachers of Orpheus (see

Graf/Johnston 2007, pp. 170–172). Pausanias calls one of the Dactyls Herakles (9.19.5, 9.27.8), adducing elsewhere as an authority the legendary poet Onomakritos (8.31.3). Pausanias also says that the men of Elis reported to him that this Herakles was the first to hold an athletic contest at Olympia during the time when Kronos was the ruler of the cosmos (5.7.6–7), while other authors make Herakles the founder of the Olympian Games. Indeed, his twelve labors feature on the metopes of the temple of Zeus at Olympia (early- to mid-fifth century). In this context it should be noted that Herodotos was already aware of a multitude of Herakleis (2.43).

The curious fact that this hymn to Herakles immediately precedes the one to Kronos is probably to be understood along these lines. Despite the nominal association with the hero who was the son of Zeus, Herakles seems to have been conflated with an older generation of divinities in Orphic mythology. In one Orphic theogony Herakles was another name for Time (see note to line 3). Our hymn, which calls Herakles a Titan (line 1), seems also to associate him with Sun (see note to line 10). He is here an anthropomorphized cosmic force, the last in a series that starts from an abstraction (Physis) and continues through a hybrid creature (Pan). He thus bears a close resemblance to the Herakles supposed to have been invoked by Pythagoras (alongside Zeus and the Dioskouroi) as the "force of nature" in libations before a meal (Iamblichus *Life of Pythagoras* 155).

1 mighty, powerful Titan: Kronos is similarly addressed in the following hymn (*OH* 13.2). It is possible that "child of the earth" in line 9 (also used of Kronos at *OH* 13.6) is meant to reinforce Herakles' connection with the Titans.

3 father of time: In the Orphic theogony attributed to Hieronymos, Herakles is sometimes another name for Time (*Orphic fragment* 76 and 79; note, too, the "primordial scales" in line 10, a characteristic of the Orphic Time). An obscure arithmological treatise that has come down to us among the writings of the Neoplatonist Iamblichus (mid-third / fourth century AD), *The Theology of Arithmetic*, lists the significance of the numbers one through ten. For the "tetrad" (number four), we find, "And again, they call the tetrad 'Heracles' with regard to the same notion of the year, as giving rise to duration, since eternity, time, critical time and passing time are four, as moreover are year, month, night and day, and morning, midday, evening and night" (translation by Waterfield 1988, p. 62). Sun is also called "father of time" (*OH* 8.13), and there are other parallels connecting both figures, e.g., both are addressed as Titan, both are "self-born" and "untiring" (*OH* 8.3), and both are invoked by alternate forms of a name usually associated with Apollon (Paian and Paion). In the *Dionysiaca* of Nonnus, a hymn to Sun begins "star-cloaked Herakles, lord of fire, marshal of the universe" (40.369). At lines 11–12 in our hymn, dawn and dusk are worn on Herakles' head, and the twelve labors are said to "stretch from east to west," the same path Sun takes on his daily journey. Sun is connected with Herakles in myth as well, as the former lent the latter his cup, in which he rides on the river Okeanos (which flows counterclockwise) during his return journey from west to east (see Stesikhoros *PMGF* S17; Boardman 1975, pl. 300). Herakles had gone west to retrieve the cattle of Geryon, and the suggestion of a cycle in Herakles' wanderings (east-west-east) might have facilitated a connection with the sun's circuit in antiquity. The twelve labors of Herakles could also be seen as representing the twelve months of the year (see Morand 2001, p. 84). Thus in these two lines, the idea of four time periods, as mentioned in the *Theology of Arithemetic* ("year, month, night and day"), might be intended; see also *OH* O.18n.

5 all-conquering: The Greek word is "pankrates." This was the name of a god in Athens who was represented as a mature, bearded man accompanied by a younger, unbearded man. This younger man is sometimes called Pankrates Herakles in dedications, and he bears the traditional Heraklean attributes of lion skin and club (see Mikalson 1998, p. 144 n. 20).

5 archer and seer: Both of these are also attributes of Apollon; see note to line 10.

6: This line is noticeable for its collocation of words meaning "all" (including "omnivorous"), which is "pan" in ancient Greek, and thus evocative of the preceding hymn. For other cases where we find Pan and Herakles in proximity, see *OH* 11i and the note to line 10 below.

10 Paion: An alternate name of Apollon (see *OH* 34.1n), also spelled "Paian," it is used of a number of other personalities in the collection, almost all of whom share affinities with Herakles in this hymn. His association with Sun is discussed in the note to line 3 above. Pan is called Paian in the previous hymn, which bears other similarities with this one (see also note to line 6 above). Paian is also used of Asklepios at *OH* 67.1, and elsewhere we find Herakles associated with this god as well. Aristides (see *OH* 86i) relates a story told to him by a stranger, who claimed that in a dream he had sung a hymn to Herakles composed by Aristides that began "ie Paian Herakles Asklepios!" (*Orations* 40.12). It is therefore notable that Herakles is asked to bring "all charms against disease" in line 14. In fact at Athens, he was invoked to keep plagues away (Larson 2007, p. 185; see p. 220 n. 7 for references). One of Herakles' adventures was the killing of the eagle that had been devouring Prometheus' liver, and Hesiod metaphorically calls the eagle a "disease" (*Theogony* 523–534). Both Herakles and Asklepios are culture heroes, and this would naturally facilitate a closer relation between them; see also *OH* 67i.

15 club in hand: This is one of the most common iconographic attributes of Herakles. He also often wears the skin of the Nemean Lion like a cowl.

16: The last three labors of Herakles (cattle of Geryon, apples of the Hesperides, Kerberos) are instances that fit the wide-spread mythological pattern of the hero overcoming death. During his last labor, he sometimes is credited with freeing Theseus from the underworld, where he had been trapped for his role in assisting Peirithoös' attempt to abduct Persephone. Herakles actually wrestles Death (Greek Thanatos) in order to win back the soul of the departed Alkestis (see Euripides' play of the same name). Herakles as a liberator from death (the threat of death, the mundane existence of the soul in the underworld) fits in well with the concerns of the initiates in Dionysian mystery cults (and see the introduction to this hymn). The "poisonous darts" refers to the arrows that Herakles dipped in the poisonous blood of the slain Hydra.

13. To Kronos

Kronos is traditionally the youngest of the Titans, one of three broods born to Earth and Sky. He is the one who castrates his father and consequently frees the other Titans who had been blocked from exiting the womb of Earth. The other two fraternal groups, the Hundred-Handers and the Kyklopes, he deigns not to liberate. Earth and Sky get their revenge when they advise Kronos' wife Rhea on how to put an end to her husband's ingestion of their children. This involves the trick of substituting a stone for the newly born Zeus, who eventually overthrows his father. Kronos and most of the other Titans attempt to overpower the upstart Zeus and his brethren in the long, pitched battle known as the Titanomachy, but Zeus is able to prevail and imprisons the enemy Titans in Tartaros, a particularly murky area in the underworld. For details, see Hesiod *Theogony* 132–210, 453–506, and 617–731. In general, Orphic theogony appears to have appropriated many of these traditional elements, although in one account Zeus tricks Kronos by getting him drunk with honey (wine having not yet been invented, doubtlessly due to the fact that Dionysos had not yet been born) and castrating him in turn (see *Orphic fragment* 220, 222, and 225; see also *PGM* 4.3100). Kronos, along with the Titans, is also responsible for the brutal murder of Dionysos in Orphic lore, and it is the destruction of the Titans by Zeus that leads to the birth of the human race (see note to line 1 below).

While Kronos is cast in the role as adversary to the gods, there is an alternate, positive strand in his mythology. In Hesiod's myth of the five races of man, the first and best, the Golden race, enjoys a paradisiacal existence under Kronos' rule (*Works and Days* 109–126). A similar kind of lifestyle is enjoyed by certain select members of humanity after death in the Elysian Fields or on the Isle of the Blest. In Homer, it is relatives of Zeus that qualify for such an honorific dispensation (e.g., Menelaos, as a son-in-law of Zeus, at *Odyssey* 4.561–569). In Hesiod it is an unspecified number of men of the Heroic race that are awarded a carefree life (one similar to that of the Golden race) after death (*Works and Days* 166–173; compare the more agonistic Norse notion of Valhalla). Pindar designates the Isle of the Blest as a place for "those who have endured / three times in either realm / to keep their souls untainted / by any injustice" (*Olympian Odes* 2.68–70, translation by Nisetich 1980) and explicitly says that these souls will "travel / Zeus' road to the tower of Kronos," (*ibid.*, 70–71) located on the islands where the dead bask in leisure (72–80). For the idea of "ethical selection" after death and the promise of blessings in the afterlife for Orphic initiates, see Graf/Johnston 2007, pp. 100–105 and 115–116. At a festival called the Kronia, celebrated in Athens and elsewhere in Greece, the slaves would join their masters at the feast and, according to one source, were served by them (cf. the Roman Saturnalia). The effacement of social class probably has its roots in the idea of a "golden age," when there was no need to toil on the land and hence no slavery (Burkert 1985, pp. 231–232). Kronos shared a temple with Rhea and Earth at Athens (Pausanias 1.18.7).

Our hymn seems little concerned with the mythological Kronos, either in his positive or negative aspects. He is addressed as an august ancient divinity, and in particular his association with Time, an integral deity in the Orphic theogonies, is stressed (see note on line 3). In the previous hymn Herakles is identified with Time and is called a Titan (lines 3 and 1, respectively, and see notes). This hymn neatly transitions to the all-important Olympian gods through the illustrious pair of Kronos and Rhea, the parents of Zeus (for similar pairings, see *OH* 14.8–9n).

1 father of blessed gods and men: As Time (see note to line 3), he is indeed the father of gods and men, since he sired the primeval elements, Khaos, Erebos, and Ether. This line, though, admits of other interpretations. The "blessed gods" could be a specific reference to the Olympian gods, of whom Kronos, either directly or indirectly, may rightly be called the "father." He also may be considered as father of men in the sense that he is the most prominent of the Titans, out of whom man was born in Orphic myth (see *OH* 37i), or to the extent that he might be identified with Prometheus (see note to line 7), who very often is credited with the creation of man (e.g., Aristophanes *Birds* 686, Plato *Protagoras* 320d; cf. the creation of Pandora by Hephaistos, a god with some similarities to Prometheus, at Hesiod *Works and Days* 60–63 and 70–71; see also *OH* 66i). Note that in the spell "Oracle of Kronos" found in the magical papyri, Kronos is credited with creating "the entire inhabited world" (*PGM* 4.3099). See also "progenitor" in line 8. The birthing theme found in the previous hymns continues. In the following hymn, Kronos' wife Rhea is called "mother of gods / and of mortals" (*OH* 14.8–9).

3 **you consume all things and replenish them**: The identification of Kronos with Time (Greek Khronos) is a later development, but one that was easily made. The idea of consuming and replenishing perhaps hints at the swallowing and subsequent regurgitation of his children and thus might have facilitated equating Kronos to Time. Note, too, that his son Zeus swallows and then "recreates" the entire world in the theogony found in the *Rhapsodies* (*Orphic fragment* 241). Kronos is the source of our "Father Time," whose sickle, incidentally, has its origins as the device used to castrate Sky. Further references to Kronos as Time in our hymn can be found in lines 5 and 7.

4: The "unbreakable chains" of Kronos are proverbial. Plato portrays them as being inferior to the "bonds of virtue" by which Hades keeps the virtuous dead in his kingdom (*Cratylus* 404a). In the magical papyri, they turn up in a binding spell (*PGM* 4.2326) as an attribute of Moon, along with a scepter that has writing on it authored by Kronos (*PGM* 4.2841), and in the spell called the Oracle of Kronos (*PGM* 4.3086–3124).

6 **child of Earth, child of starry Sky**: A similar formulation is found in Hesiod *Theogony* 106 for all the gods born of Earth and Sky. The Titans as a group are called the "glorious children of Sky and Earth" in their hymn (*OH* 37.1). Many of the Bacchic gold tablets instruct the initiate to claim that he or she is a child of Earth and starry Sky and of a heavenly race; see *OH* 4i and compare the claim made by the initiate to Persephone and the other underworld gods that he or she is from the same race (see Graf/Johnston 2007, nos. 5, 6, and 7, as well their discussion on pp. 111–114).

7 **revered and prudent lord of Rhea**: Rhea is both sister and wife to Kronos; see the following hymn. The word translated as "prudent" is "promētheu," which some have translated as "Prometheus," thus positing an equivalence between these two proverbially clever Titans. The craftiness and intelligence of Kronos is emphasized in this hymn: he is "resourceful" (line 2), "of the shifting stories" (line 5), and "wily" (line 9). A further reason why these two figures are blended might be their involvement in the creation of man (see note to line 1).

14. To Rhea

Rhea is a Titan, daughter of Earth and Sky, and the sister of Kronos, whom she married after he successfully rebelled against Sky. Her place in mythology was essentially limited to her importance as the mother of Zeus and in particular her role in the succession myth between her son and husband/brother (see *OH* 13i). However, she accrued more prominence when she was later identified with Kybele, the great Phrygian mountain mother of the gods, who was also known as Mother (Greek Mētēr), and Mother of the Gods. This is one of many equivalences that was made between a Greek goddess of fertility and the Phrygian goddess. The lyric poet Melanippides (ca. mid-fifth century BC) equated Demeter and Mother (*PMG* 764), while the lyric poet Telestes (late fifth century BC) also added Rhea to the equation (*PMG* 809). Such identifications apparently had already been made in early Orphic thought, for the author of the Derveni papyrus quotes the following from a poem he attributes to Orpheus, "Earth, Meter, Rhea, Hera, Demeter, Hestia, and Deio" (for this last name, see *OH* 40.1n), while also giving some etymologizing explanations for the various appellations (*Orphic fragment* 398, and see Betegh 2004, pp. 189–190). In our collection, there is some overlap between this hymn and the one addressed to the Mother of the Gods (*OH* 27); compare also the ones to Earth (*OH* 26) and Eleusinian Demeter (*OH* 40). We find some correspondences as well with the Homeric *Hymn to the Mother of the Gods* and, to a lesser extent, the Homeric *Hymn to Earth, Mother of All*. In Orphic mythology, Zeus, in the form of a snake, mates with his mother, Rhea, who had also changed herself into a snake to escape the advances of her son, which leads to the birth of Persephone (*Orphic fragment* 87). Here we find a blending of Demeter, Persephone's traditional mother, and Rhea (see also *OH* 29i). The monstrous appearance of Persephone frightened Rhea so much that she refused to offer her breast to the child (*Orphic fragment* 88), a motif also found in the Homeric *Hymn to Pan* (see *OH* 11i). Rhea is the one who puts the pieces of her grandson Dionysos back together after he is murdered by the Titans (for references and further discussion, see Graf/Johnston 2007, pp. 75–77).

The position of this hymn emphasizes Rhea's prestige as the wife of Kronos and the mother of Zeus, her customary associations in Greek mythology. However, the content of the hymn itself vacillates between stressing this side of the goddess and her identification with Kybele; see notes passim.

1 daughter of many-faced Protogonos: This is true, insofar as Rhea is considered the same as Earth, for in one version of the Orphic myth of creation, Protogonos and Night give birth to Earth and Sky (*Orphic fragment* 149). Strictly speaking, though, she is their granddaughter.

2 bull-slayers: This is a kenning for lions, animals typically associated with Kybele. See further *OH* 27.2+n.

3 you dance to the sound of drums and cymbals, O frenzy-loving maiden: Percussive instruments are characteristic of the ecstatic elements of Kybele's cult; see *OH* 27.11n. Euripides explicitly associates this with Rhea in the *Bacchae*. The chorus of Bacchantes first sings of the dance of the Kouretes to the drums and *auloi* as they protected the infant Zeus, which is presented as the invention of the custom. Next, the chorus tells us, the drum was passed down to Rhea, from whom the maddened satyrs stole it. Finally, it reached the hands of the Kouretes for use in Dionysian ritual (120–134). The Phrygian drum of Rhea is mentioned earlier in the play by the chorus (58–59). For the role of madness in this cult, see line 6 below and *OH* 27.13n, which supplies further references to the theme of insanity that runs throughout the *Hymns*. Rhea's connection to the ecstatic Kouretes and the Kretan cave cult of Zeus probably facilitated her identification with the Phrygian goddess, who was associated with a similar band of ecstatic youths, the Korybantes (see *OH* 27i and *OH* 31i). Wild dancing is also typical of maenadic worship; see *OH* 52i.

6 horrid shrieks of mortals: The conjunction of this phrase with "in the mountains" probably means these shrieks are those of the worshippers of Dionysos, possessed by the god and in a state of ecstasy. They can be "horrid," because of the terrible things that these raving adherents sometimes effect; an example is their tearing apart of Pentheus, which Euripides grippingly portrays in the *Bacchae*. Likewise, this phrase might refer to madness in general (see note to line 3). To be sure, ecstasy and madness are concepts that the Greeks did not consider completely distinct from one another, and we, too, need not be detained by a pedantic precision; see further *OH* 30i.

8 liar, savior, redeemer: Quandt has postulated that "liar" refers to Rhea's deception of her husband at the birth of Zeus, and he draws attention to Pausanias, who describes Kronos as being deceived by his sister-wife (9.41.6). She thus can also be considered "savior" and "redeemer" of the child, just as she sometimes is of Dionysos in Orphic mythology (see the introduction to this hymn). There may also be an oblique reference to this tale in Apollodoros who says that after Dionysos had been driven insane by Hera, he came to Mount Kybela in Phrygia where he was purified by Rhea and taught initiatory rites (3.5.1; see also Graf/Johnston 2007, pp. 146–147, and *OH* 27.13n). However, soteriological and redemptive powers turn up throughout the collection among other divinities, often near the close of the hymn when the addressee is enjoined to appear.

8–9 mother of gods / and of mortals: This is paralleled by Kronos being called "father of blessed gods and men" (*OH* 13.1+n). Kybele is also expressly attributed as such (*OH* 27.7); see also *OH* 26.1+n. There are other mother goddesses in the collection (see *OH* 10.1n), as well as a number of explicit male/female pairings: Night/Sky (*OH* 3/4), Zeus/Hera (*OH* 15/16), Nereus/Nereids (*OH* 23/24), Persephone/Dionysos (*OH* 29/30), Sabazios/Hipta (*OH* 48/49), Aphrodite/Adonis (*OH* 55/56), Asklepios/Hygeia (*OH* 67/68), Tyche/Daimon (*OH* 72/73), and Leukothea/Palaimon (*OH* 74/75); see also *OH* 61i, *OH* 69i, and *OH* 76i.

9–10 earth, /... sky ... sea ... winds: These lines elevate Rhea to the status of the primeval womb of creation; compare the Homeric *Hymn to Earth, Mother of All*: "Her beauty nurtures all creatures that walk upon the land, / and all that move in the deep or fly in the air" (30.3–4). Insofar as the sky is connected with ether, and hence fire, these four physical items are symbolic of the four elements that constitute the physical world (see *OH* 11.2–3n). A similar range of natural features (albeit without the symbolism of the four elements) appears in Apollonios of Rhodes *Argonautika* 1.1098–1099, when the seer Mopsos advises Jason to propitiate Mother of the Gods, "for on her the winds and sea and earth's foundations / all depend, and the snowy bastion of Olympos" (translation by Green 1997). See also *OH* 27, addressed to the same Mother of the Gods, the "queen of the sky" (line 4), to whom the earth belongs (line 6) and who "hold[s] sway over the rivers and over all the sea" (line 8). In the Epidaurian hymn to Mother of the Gods, she asks for half of heaven, earth, and sea, apparently in recompense for the abduction of her daughter (19–24; see also *OH* 27i). For other mentions of the earth, sea, and sky in the collection, see *OH* 10.14–16n. The mention of the winds last neatly transitions to the attributes "ethereal" and "restless" in the next line.

15. To Zeus

Zeus is the chief deity of the Greek pantheon, and his role in myth and cult is as wide-ranging as his power. A large portion of Hesiod's *Theogony* treats his ascendancy to ruler of the universe. He is hidden away on Krete as a babe, frees his siblings who had been swallowed by his father, Kronos, at birth, and then leads a successful rebellion against him and most of his father's brethren, the Titans (see *OH* 13i). Hesiod then gives a brief portrayal of his victory over a second threat, the monstrous Typhon (820–880; see Apollodoros 1.6.3 for a fuller account). After dividing the universe among himself and his brothers (see *OH* 17.7n), Zeus takes on a series of wives, who give birth to a number of important divinities and heroes (886–926). Of his countless affairs in mythology, the two most significant ones to Orphism are his union with his mother Rhea, which produces Persephone (this is specific to Orphism; see *OH* 14i and *OH* 29i), and his relations with Semele, which produces Dionysos (see *OH* 44i).

In cult, Zeus was worshipped in diverse ways, from a personal, household deity that brought good fortune (cf. line 11 below and *OH* 19.20; see also *OH* 73i) to a Panhellenic god who symbolized a common Greek culture (e.g., at Olympia and the Olympian Games). As a weather god, he is often called on to bring life-nourishing rain to the crops; he thus has fertility associations. In *Iliad* 14.346–351, when Zeus embraces Hera before they make love on Mount Ida, the earth itself blossoms into a breath-taking array of flowers and they draw a golden cloud around them that sheds dew; this scene seems to be reminiscent of a very old myth of the union of Father Sky and Mother Earth as the source of life itself (see also *OH* 4i). An inscription found at Palaikastro, Krete, preserves a hymn that invokes him as the "greatest *kouros* [youth]" and prays that he "leap into" the flocks, fields, and homes as a spur to growth (see also *OH* 31i). The fertility aspect of Zeus may even endow this celestial god with a chthonic character (cf. *OH* 7.9n), and he sometimes is depicted in the form of a snake. Note, too, that when Zeus impregnates Rhea/Demeter, both are in the form of a snake. Another important aspect of Zeus in Greek religion is his role in maintaining social institutions. He is one of the gods who protects the sanctity of oaths (like Sun; see *OH* 8i). Both guest and host are under his guardianship, as well as suppliants and beggars. In general, justice and order, the underlying principles of human community, are his responsibility. This is symbolized in myth, where Dike is his daughter and Themis his first wife (see *OH* 43i, *OH* 62i, and *OH* 79i). For more on his role in Greek religion and cult, see Burkert 1985, pp. 125–131, and Larson 2007, pp. 15–28.

It is interesting that in this hymn there is scarcely any attention paid to his mythological exploits or his role in human affairs. He is above all presented as a cosmic god, the creator of the universe and universal order, all-powerful and majestic. The same is true of the other two hymns addressed to him as "Thunderbolt" and Astrapaios, respectively (*OH* 19 and *OH* 20). His placement in this collection serves as a culmination of the cosmogonic arc that defines the previous fourteen hymns, all of which are addressed to primeval beings. There is a gradual movement from abstractions to concrete anthropomorphism (see *OH* 11i, *OH* 12i, and *OH* 13i); it is almost as if the known universe is taking shape before the initiates' eyes. Once the divine pair of Zeus and Hera is reached, the cosmogony proper has come to a close, and the theogony can begin (see also note to lines 3–5). This is further reinforced by the following consideration. The direction of the arrangement of entities up until now has been chronological, but only four of the original six Olympian gods are grouped together here. The hymns to Demeter and Hestia should properly find their place among these. But the dynamic, chronological movement has ended; instead the collection takes a more static, horizontal approach, branching out as it were over the family tree of Zeus (eventually focusing, of course, on Dionysos and Dionysian cult). Furthermore, the constituent elements of the world—fire, air, water, and earth—are singularly emphasized in the hymns to Zeus, Hera, Poseidon, and Plouton, respectively. This sequence is repeated by the following hymns, which adhere to the same order: fire (*OH* 19–20), air (*OH* 21), water (*OH* 22–25), and earth (*OH* 26–27). Demeter, who also is associated with the element earth, is in a sense already present in *OH* 26–27 by dint of her identification with primeval goddesses (Rhea, Kybele). Furthermore, her prominence in the Eleusinian Mysteries makes her hymn more appropriate of the central group that treats figures of Dionysian cult (*OH* 40–54). The domestic associations of Hestia, who could be equated with the element fire, would not easily fit the cosmological context (see further *OH* 84i). This "elemental" placement of hymns also recurs toward the end of the collection (*OH* 79–84), albeit in a different order (see *OH* 79i), and similar groupings are found in the opening address to Mousaios (see *OH* O.3–5+n, and *OH* O.32–33). The order of hymns 15–18 and 19–27 is the same as in the Stoic creation of the elements out of the primeval fire, attributed to Khrysippos, following Zeno (Long and Sedley 1987, fragment 47A; cf. 46C).

There is a very short Homeric hymn addressed to Zeus where he is paired with Themis. Kallimakhos and the Stoic philosopher Kleanthes each wrote a hymn to Zeus, and Aratos opens his *Phainomena* with an invocation to Zeus as the one who set the stars in the sky as signs for mankind (1–18).

3–5: In the first instance, these lines are typical in the way the power of a god is presented by describing his efficacy throughout the range of creation. Kleanthes uses the same technique in his hymn to Zeus (15–16), and we also find it elsewhere in our collection (see *OH* 10.14–16n and in particular *OH* 19.9–19). Nevertheless, there is special point to its appearance here, for it is probably meant literally. In the Orphic cosmogony found in the *Rhapsodies,* Zeus is said to have swallowed Protogonos and with him the entire cosmos and then to have reconstituted them again in a second act of creation; it seems that some version of this account was already present by the Classical period, for the exegete in the Derveni papyrus (fourth century BC) alludes to a similar, if not the same, story (see *Orphic fragment* 12, 14, 31, 237–243, West 1982, pp. 84–93, 218–220, 237–241, and Betegh 2004, pp. 111–122, 125–126, 169–181). Of particular note is the existence of a hymn to Zeus, found in the Pseudo-Aristotle *De mundo* (401a25 = *Orphic fragment* 31) and the *Rhapsodies* (*Orphic fragment* 243), which probably ultimately derive from whatever poem the Derveni author is analyzing (see *Orphic fragment* 14). The one in the *Rhapsodies,* far more extensive than the other two, actually matches physical features with Zeus' body parts; compare the allegorical interpretation of "cosmic Pan" (see *OH* 11i) and in Norse mythology the creation of the world out of the carcass of Ymir by Óðin, Vili, and Vé. The act of swallowing is also reminiscent of Kronos' attempts to thwart any potential threat from his children by swallowing them, and it should be recalled that Zeus swallows Metis when he learns that she is fated to bear a son mightier than he is (Hesiod *Theogony* 886–900). The motif is taken up in the Orphic story but turned on its head. Zeus is not worried about losing his supremacy; rather he is seeking to establish it (see also note to line 7).

6 scepter: Traditionally the symbol of a sovereign's power. The symbolism is also employed in the Orphic succession stories (see *OH* 10.26n).

7 beginning and end of all: We find similar sentiments in all three Orphic hymns to Zeus (see note to lines 3–5); compare also Aratos *Phainomena* 14. By swallowing Protogonos and recreating the world, Zeus in effect becomes the oldest being. Betegh argues that the strange second creation is meant, among other things, to resolve a contradiction that was felt between Zeus' supreme power and the fact that he is not among the oldest, but rather youngest generation of gods; by having Zeus recreate the world, one and the same entity acquires both priority in age and power (Betegh 2004, pp. 172–174). Our collection might also be attempting to come to grips with the problem in another way. This hymn to Zeus appears in its proper chronological sequence, but Zeus is the first god mentioned in Orpheus' address to Mousaios (*OH* O.3, right before Earth). For the personified Beginning and End, see *OH* O.41+n. The same phrase here is used of Sky in his hymn (see *OH* 4.2+n).

8–9: The reference to thunder and lightning, as well as the thunderbolt mentioned in line 6, anticipate *OH* 19 and *OH* 20. The role of Zeus as weather god and Zeus as fertility god is suggested in these lines ("increaser," "sower"). While purity is of great concern in many contexts, it is interesting to note that Zeus was sometimes worshipped under the title Katharsios (Purifier); see *OH* 20i and also *OH* 30.4n.

10–11 health, / . . . peace and riches: While such requests are made throughout the collection, it is nevertheless perhaps significant that Eirene (Peace) is one of the Seasons, daughters of Zeus and Themis (see *OH* 43i). Hygeia, health personified, is the addressee of *OH* 68; she is sometimes invoked with Zeus over libations poured at symposia (see *OH* 68i and *OH* 73i). The collocation of health, peace, and wealth appear frequently in requests: see *OH* 14.12–13 (Rhea), *OH* 17.10 (Poseidon), *OH* 19.21 (Zeus the Thunderbolt), *OH* 23.8 (Nereus), *OH* 32.15–16 (Athene). Note that fertility replaces wealth in *OH* 10.31 (Physis) and *OH* 36.14–15 (Artemis). In *OH* 40 (Eleusinian Demeter), this type of request reaches a crescendo, combining health, peace, wealth, and law, perhaps because of the hymn's prominence in the collection (see *OH* 40i+18–20n).

16. To Hera

Hera is a daughter of Kronos and Rhea, and the sister-wife of Zeus; see, e.g., the Homeric *Hymn to Hera*. She has fertility connections, as can be seen in Homer, who in the *Iliad* portrays her and Zeus making love on top of a mountain, reminiscent of the marriage between Father Sky and Mother Earth (see *OH* 15i). She is identified with a number of earth-mother goddesses, along with Hestia, in an Orphic verse cited in the Derveni papyrus (see *OH* 14i). As with Earth herself, Hera is able to produce children parthenogenetically, such as Typhon (Homeric *Hymn to Apollon* 3.326–352), whose parents, according to Hesiod, are Earth and Tartaros (see *OH* 18.2n). Typhon becomes the arch-enemy of Zeus, and this incident reflects one of the more pervasive themes in mythology, namely, the constant bickering of Hera and Zeus. Occasionally Hera stands up to Zeus directly; Homer, for example, briefly mentions her role with Athene and Poseidon in their attempted coup of Zeus (*Iliad* 1.396–406). More often, however, Hera unleashes her fury on Zeus' lovers and illegitimate children. She is particularly adamant in pursuing Herakles. Dionysos and those around him do not escape her wrath, either. By her machinations Semele is destroyed (see *OH* 44i), Ino suffers (see *OH* 74i), and Dionysos himself, as Herakles and Io, is driven mad (see Euripides *Kyklops* 3, Plato *Laws* 672b, and Apollodoros 3.5.1). In the Orphic myth of Dionysos' death, it is sometimes Hera who spurs the Titans to kill the child (see *OH* 37i and *Orphic fragment* 304). While in the myth known as the "Return of Hephaistos" (see *OH* 66i) Dionysos does appear to help Hera, nonetheless it is also possible that the reconciliation Dionysos indirectly effected by leading Hephaistos back to Olympos also led to a grudging reconciliation between him and his step-mother. Thus two outsiders would be integrated into the divine order together.

Despite Hera's antipathy to Dionysos in myth, we do in fact sometimes find them together in cult. Alkaios refers to a sanctuary dedicated to Zeus, Hera, and Dionysos on Lesbos (fragment 129). At Olympia, where her temple predated the one to Zeus, there was a chorus in honor of Physkoa, a local lover of Dionysos, performed at games held in Hera's honor (Pausanias 5.16.1–8). In general, Hera's role in cult is largely one of maintaining social order. She is usually worshipped as a civic goddess, one who protects and maintains the well-being of the community, particularly in her capacity as the goddess of marriage, one of the most important institutions in the ancient world. For more information on her role in Greek religion, see Burkert 1985, pp. 131–135, and Larson 2007, pp. 29–40. In this hymn, however, her traditional cultic roles are omitted as is her mythological persona. Indeed, she is scarcely conceived as an anthropomorphic goddess but instead closely identified with the air and life-bringing rains. Her fertility associations are thus maintained without the usual concomitant chthonic character. While Zeus is sometimes equated with air (see Betegh 2004, pp. 193–197), it is Hera who more often is considered a manifestation of this element. Plato etymologically relates her name and the word for air (*Cratylus* 404c), and the Stoics also make the identification (see Long and Sedley 1987, fragment 54A, and *OH* 21i). It is possible that such a connection was also attributed to Orpheus; see *Orphic fragment* 202(iv). As already mentioned, Hera is sometimes claimed to be the mother of Typhon. This creature is associated with destructive winds (Hesiod *Theogony* 869–880; see also *OH* 23.5–7n), and perhaps the version that makes Hera his mother was influenced by a play on Hera/air as in Plato. This hymn thus fits in the sequence of gods that are correlated with the four elements, and the hymn to the Clouds (*OH* 21) would be its analogue in the subsequent group that replicates this pattern (see *OH* 15i). It also forms a male/female pair with the previous hymn, a common structural feature of the collection (see *OH* 14.8–9n).

3 soft breezes you send . . . nourish the soul: The word for "soul" in Greek, "psukhē," also has the connotations of "life" in general, and this is probably its sense here as it is at *OH* 38.22 of the Kouretes, who appear to be manifestations of the "soft breezes" (see also *OH* 38.3+n). Furthermore, it is etymologically connected with the verb "psukhō," "I blow," and our composer, who elsewhere displays an ear for such wordplay, likely intends one here as well.

4 mother of rains, mother of the winds: For the connection of rain and wind, see *OH* 21i.

4 you give birth to all: The epithet used here is also given to Hera by Alkaios (fragment 129).

17. To Poseidon

Poseidon is a son of the Titans Kronos and Rhea, and a brother of Zeus and Hades. He is the god of the sea, and sometimes the sea itself, as in the *Lesser Krater*, attributed to Orpheus (*Orphic fragment* 413.7). As our hymn explains, the sea fell to him by lot when the world was divided (line 7 and see note), and all bodies of water fall under his control. Nevertheless, he does infringe a bit on Zeus' power over the storms, and we often find him stirring them up in mythology (e.g., *Odyssey* 5.282–296). Also like Zeus, Poseidon is a father of heroes, Theseus being the most famous example. In some variants Poseidon is even the father of Persephone, mating with Demeter in the form of a horse (see *OH* 69i), which also produces the wonder horse Areion. This points to another important sphere of Poseidon, that of horses (see, e.g., *Iliad* 23.306–308, Sophokles *Oedipus at Kolonos* 712–715, and Aristophanes *Knights* 551–558). A famous equine offspring of his is Pegasos, born to Medousa after she is beheaded by Perseus (Hesiod *Theogony* 278–281). Another important function of Poseidon is his role in causing earthquakes; his common epithet "shaker of the earth" appears in line 4. He was also imagined to hold or embrace the earth, as another common epithet of his, "holder of the earth," attests (see line 1). Both epithets are juxtaposed as a playful oxymoron by Hesiod (*Theogony* 15), and we find each one used in cult. Poseidon was an important deity in bronze-age Pylos (Nestor's father, Neleus, is his son), and of course he was especially worshipped by those communities whose livelihood depended on the sea, such as Korinth. One tradition reported by Pausanias claimed that Poseidon was the god of Delphi along with Earth until he switched places with Apollon, taking this god's old site at Kalaurea (2.33.2, 10.5.6). This is an island off Troizen, where Poseidon was an important divinity, and it was also the birthplace of Theseus. Poseidon contended with Athene for this island, but Zeus awarded it to both of them (Pausanias 2.30.6). They also fought over Athens, but here Athene was victorious; the myth is depicted on the west pediment of the Parthenon. A strange ritual to Poseidon as god of horses is portrayed in the Homeric *Hymn to Apollo* 3.230–238. For more details on his cults, see Burkert 1985, pp. 136–139, and Larson 2007, pp. 57–68. Orphism seems to have adopted the traditional view of this god. Indeed, this hymn is wholly composed of conventional items. It represents the element of water, and it is the third of a series of hymns that links some of the Olympian divinities sprung from Kronos and Rhea with the four elements (see *OH* 15i). *OH* 22–25, dedicated to maritime divinities, are analogously placed.

1: This line is almost identical to the one in the Homeric *Hymn to Poseidon*, except that instead of "hearken" the Homeric hymn reads "hail" (22.6). The opening address to Mousaios also refers to Poseidon as the "dark-maned holder of the earth" (*OH* O.5).

3: For one view of how the Greeks imagined his abode, see the languorous dreamscape of Poseidon's palace depicted by Bacchylides (17.97–129); see also *OH* 24.2–3+n.

5–6: Poseidon's driving his chariot on the sea is a literary trope as old as Homer (*Iliad* 13.23–31).

7: After Zeus becomes king, he divides the world among himself and his two other brothers. They draw lots: Hades wins the underworld, Poseidon the seas, and Zeus the sky (see *Iliad* 15.185–195, Hesiod *Theogony* 881–885, and Apollodoros 1.2.1). This was adopted into Orphic mythology as well (*Orphic fragment* 236). A very similar line appears in line 6 of the following hymn; cf. also *OH* 15i.

9–10: As the "shaker of the earth" (line 4), Poseidon naturally has the power both to cause and prevent earthquakes. Likewise, as the god of the sea he is able to wreck ships or save them (see Hesiod *Works and Days* 665–668, where he shares this power with Zeus). The Kouretes also hold the power to hinder or help sailors (*OH* 38.5, 14–17, 23–25), the latter function easing their identification with the Dioskouroi, who are traditionally worshipped as saviors of sailors (see *OH* 38.21+i). Other gods, too, are invoked in this capacity as well: Tethys (*OH* 22.9–10), Leukothea (*OH* 74.4–9) and Leukothea's son Palaimon (*OH* 75.5–8).

18. To Plouton

Plouton is another name for Hades. His name is connected with "ploutos" ("wealth"), although Ploutos also is the name of a separate divinity (see *OH* 40.16n), one of the many personified divine abstractions found in Greek religious thought. Originally Plouton was a separate god, but he merged with Hades sometime before the fourth century BC and their names became more or less interchangeable. This early merging is probably at the root of the god's dual function as both lord of the dead (Hades) and as provider of the fruits of the earth, including mineral wealth (Plouton). While at first blush it might seem odd for a god to be so intimately connected with both life and death, it should be kept in mind that many divinities hold power over binary opposites. Persephone, too, is a goddess of life and death; see OH 29+i, especially lines 15–16, and OH 30i. Crops and other vegetation come out from below the earth and thus could be interpreted as being caused by Hades and Persephone. There are very few myths associated with Hades-Plouton. The most prominent one is his abduction of Persephone, which is mentioned in lines 12–15 (see OH 41i). This story is part of the foundation myth of the Eleusinian Mysteries (see OH 40i). When Hades receives cult attention, it is almost always in his capacity as a fertility god, and he is usually worshipped alongside his wife Persephone, also called Kore (a word that means "maiden" in Greek). Hades is the son of Kronos and Rhea, and thus brother to Zeus and Poseidon. The placement of this hymn completes the genealogical pattern of Zeus-Poseidon-Hades. Further, with the strong association of Plouton with earth, it also ends the series of the four elements that was initiated with the hymn to Zeus; see OH 15i. The analogous hymns are OH 26–27, and note that OH 29 is a hymn addressed to Persephone.

2 meadow in Tartaros: While the "psukhai" ("spirits, souls") of the dead are portrayed as wandering on asphodel meadows (e.g., *Odyssey* 11.539), Tartaros is usually envisioned as a distinct place, where the Titans and Typhon, after being defeated by Zeus, are imprisoned (Hesiod *Theogony* 717–733 and 868; see also OH 37.3+n). It is in effect the Alcatraz of mythology. Tartaros was originally a vaguely personified primordial being with whom Earth mated to produce Typhon (Hesiod *Theogony* 119 and 820–822; see also OH 16i). Sacred meadows also appear in the Bacchic gold tablets as part of the special dispensation the initiate receives after death (nos. 3, 27; see also OH 29i and OH 87.12n). *Orphic fragment* 340 distinguishes the "beautiful meadow" by the river Acheron (see note to line 10), whither those who did good deeds while alive go after they die, from Tartaros, whither the malefactors go by way of Kokytos (see also OH 71.2n). Another meadow that has chthonic connections is the one where Persephone was picking flowers before being abducted by Hades; it is mentioned in line 13.

3 Chthonic Zeus: A common periphrasis for Hades, who is rarely mentioned by name (see also OH O.12+n). The expression does not imply that Zeus and Plouton are the same person, but rather that Plouton is lord of his own element, the depths of the earth, and by extension of the whole earth (see line 6 and note). Similarly, Poseidon is called "sea-dwelling Zeus" at OH 63.15. Hades is also known as Aidoneus, as well as by a number of epithets that essentially function as titles (such as the list given in lines 11–12). This scruple reflects ancient belief that calling a divinity by name might draw their attention to the one invoking them, and Hades, in his capacity as the lord of death, is a god one normally wishes to avoid as long as possible (cf. OH 87.11–12). Our initiates must nevertheless propitiate him, as he would have the power to keep them from a blessed afterlife (compare lines 17–18).

4 holder of the keys to the whole earth: Hades' portrayal as one who holds the keys to the underworld can represent his power to keep the dead locked up and his ability to prevent them from returning to the land of the living (Pausanias 5.20.3). In this case, however, the keys are more likely intended to be symbolic of the god's power to give or withhold the wealth of the earth, as is made clear by the employment of the name Plouton in this context; see also *OH* 25.1 and *OH* 29.4.

6 yours is the third portion: See *OH* 17.7n.

9 of windless, and of impassive Hades: Just as it is in the use of the word "Tartaros" at line 2 (and see note), a blurring between person and place is seen in the usage of the word "Hades," which designates both the god and the realm he rules (see also line 15). Hades is often described by adjectives and phrases that indicate the lack of something: other typical examples include "tearless" and "without laughter." The underworld is often seen as the inverse of the land of the living. Comparable is Odysseus' sojourn to the land of the dead in book 11 of the *Odyssey.* The *psukhai* cannot speak, until they drink blood, considered by the early Greeks to be one of the vital forces that make life possible (another one being air; see also *OH* 66.9+n). There is also an inversion of social custom here. Normally a host provides for the strangers who come to their door, but in this situation Odysseus, although a visitor, must provide for his hosts—and not the hosts themselves at that, but their subordinates.

10 Acheron: The "river of woe," it is sometimes specially designated as the one which the *psukhai* must cross to reach Hades proper; see also note to line 2.

12 Euboulos: The name means "of good counsel" and is another form of the name Eubouleus; see *OH* 41.8n.

12–15: The beginning part of the abduction of Persephone. "Attic cave" and "Eleusis" are clearly intended to evoke the Eleusinian Mysteries, the most famous mystery cult in antiquity and the one with the most participants (see *OH* 40i).

16 you alone were born to judge: Usually the judges of the dead are prestigious heroes. The most important ones are Minos, king of Krete, his brother Rhadamanthys, and Aiakos, all sons of Zeus (see, e.g., Plato *Gorgias* 523a–524a). Sokrates at his trial even adds Triptolemos, one of the Eleusinian heroes (Plato *Apology* 41a), a detail perhaps embellished to play to the sympathy of his judges, of whom some were doubtlessly initiates in the Eleusinian Mysteries. Of course, Hades and Persephone are often depicted as exercising their executive prerogatives, as numerous figures in mythology appeal to them to allow them return to the land of the living, such as Orpheus himself, when he requested to bring back Eurydike (see also *OH* 87.9n).

19. To Zeus the Thunderbolt

The display of light and sound during a powerful thunderstorm is an awesome sight to behold, even to the modern mind, which of course knows there are rationally grounded scientific principles that explain the meteorological phenomena it perceives. How much more it must have captured the imagination of the ancients when the previously serene skies suddenly and inexplicably exploded in a violent eruption of elemental fury! It is no wonder that a god who wields the thunderbolt would hold a prominent place in any pantheon, and for the Greeks this is in the hands of the chief deity Zeus. In myth, thunder and lightning are supplied to him by his uncles, the Kyklopes, of whom there are three: Brontes (Thunderer), Steropes (Flash), and Arges (Brightness). These Kyklopes gave the thunderbolt to Zeus out of gratitude for his releasing them from the underworld (Hesiod *Theogony* 139–146, 501–506;

Apollodoros 1.1.2 and 1.2.1; *Orphic fragment* 228). They are usually portrayed as smiths (e.g., *Orphic fragment* 269, where they are the teachers of Hephaistos and Athene) and so ought to be distinguished from the unsophisticated rustic race of Kyklopes that Odysseus encounters on his journeys. Zeus uses his great power to defeat the enemies of order and civilization; see, e.g., the similar depictions of his might in the Titanomachy and the defeat of Typhon in Hesiod *Theogony* 687–710 and 839–868. The lightning bolt of Zeus also makes short work of mortals who transgress boundaries and commit hubris, such as Asklepios, the son of Apollon, who effaced the line between life and death by resurrecting men from the dead (see *OH* 67i). The weapon sometimes kills unwillingly: in the story of Dionysos' birth, Semele is destroyed by the thunderbolt of a reluctant Zeus bound by an oath (see *OH* 44i). We find this story adopted into Orphic mythology, which further relates that the Titans are again kerblasted by the lightning of Zeus, this time for their murder of Dionysos (see *OH* 37i). In cult, Zeus is worshipped, as he is addressed here, as Keraunios (Thunderbolt) and also Kataibates (Descender); in fact, both had an altar at Olympia (Pausanias 5.14.7, 10). Those who died by lightning strike were often accorded special honors after death (see *OH* 20i).

Our hymn focuses on the physical manifestation of the thunderbolt itself in a surprisingly vivid and extended description that fills almost the entire hymn. Like a painter, the poet guides our eye from the appearance of the bolt in the sky, through its dizzying descent, and down to its epiphany on the surface world. It thus encompasses the same collocation of realms as found in other hymns in the collection (see *OH* 10.14–16n and in particular *OH* 15.3–5+n) and thus accentuates the cosmological significance of Zeus' power. Another similarity to *OH* 15 is that the element fire is emphasized, as it is in the companion hymn that follows. This hymn begins a series that is arranged on the same principle of the four elements that defined the order of *OH* 15–19 (see *OH* 15i). Kleanthes also praises the power of Zeus' thunderbolt, stressing that it is the tool Zeus employs to steer the world with reason (*Hymn to Zeus* 9–13); compare also the statement that "thunderbolt directs everything," attributed to Herakleitos (Kirk, Raven, and Schofield 1983, no. 220).

16–17: Possibly a vague reference to the birth of Protogonos as reported by the *Rhapsodies*, where the egg out of which he is born is also called a "cloud" and a "bright robe" (*Orphic fragment* 121; see also *OH* 21i).

20. To Astrapaios Zeus

This hymn forms a pair with the previous one to Zeus the Thunderbolt. It is shorter, but they have a number of similarities: stress on fire, atmospheric description, and detail of sound. "Astrapaios" means "of lightning," and, strictly speaking, refers to the gleam of light that accompanies the thunderbolt. The Greeks sharply distinguished between the sound of thunder, the flash of lightning, and the physical bolt itself (see West 1971, p. 207), and so it is perhaps surprising there is no hymn for Zeus of the Thunder included in this sequence. Thunder, however, is personified and mentioned in the opening address to Mousaios (see *OH* O.38+n), and as a physical phenomenon thunder appears in this hymn and the previous one, as well as the first one dedicated to Zeus, either explicitly or implicitly (see *OH* 15.9; *OH* 19.6, 9, 14–15; cf. *OH* 20.3). *OH* 19 and *OH* 20 essentially refer to the same aspect of Zeus, although they do not fully overlap. Zeus as cosmic begetter appears in this hymn (line 5; cf. *OH* 15.3–5). He is not invoked to bring a myriad of blessings, as in the previous hymn (*OH* 19.20–23), but rather to give the initiate a "sweet end to . . . life." It is interesting to note that, while there are a number of hymns in the collection that ask in one way or another for a noble end of life, the only ones where the addressee is asked to bring a sweet one is here and in *OH* 73 to Daimon, who is probably being identified with Zeus (see *OH* 73i; cf. also *OH* 86.12). It may have particular point here since there was special religious significance attached to death by lightning. In fact, some of the Bacchic gold tablets seem to refer to being killed by Zeus' lightning; see nos. 5, 6, 7, and Graf/Johnston 2007, pp. 125–127. Their suggestion—that the initiates are expressing hope of being purified in death and enjoying the same special status in the underworld as the heroes—may be at work in this hymn as well (see further *OH* 87.12n). The idea, of course, is not that the initiates wish to be struck by lightning but that their efforts in following the cult would effectively purify their *psukhē* in preparation for death. Fire often has importance as a purifying agent in Greek religion, and it is significant that Zeus is addressed as "pure" in the opening line of this hymn (see also *OH* 15.8+8–9n). The "sweetness" of the end of life might then be proleptic.

21. To the Clouds

This hymn corresponds to the hymn to Hera; see *OH* 16i. This goddess has a connection with clouds in mythology, which might have strengthened the association in our composer's eyes. When the mortal Ixion makes advances on Hera, Zeus creates a cloud doppelganger of his wife, with whom Ixion then has relations. He is punished in the underworld for this outrage, tied to a flaming wheel that endlessly spins throughout eternity. The cloud, though, becomes pregnant and gives birth to the centaurs (see Apollodoros, epit. 1.20). In this hymn, the Clouds are represented, in a similar way Hera is portrayed in hers, purely as meteorological phenomena that produce rain and are the loci for thunder and lightning. There were a number of explanations for these manifestations of weather in antiquity. Anaximander speculated that they occur when wind breaks through a cloud (Kirk, Raven, and Schofield 1983, nos. 129–131); Anaximenes added that clouds themselves are formed when the air is condensed and that further condensations eventually squeeze out rain (Kirk, Raven, and Schofield 1983, no. 158). Herakleitos contended that thunder comes from the crashing of winds and clouds, lightning from the kindling of the clouds, and rain from their quenching (Diels and Kranz 1951–52, 22A14), while Anaxagoras attributed thunder to the collision of clouds, and lightning to their friction (Diogenes Laertius 2.9). The Sokrates in Aristophanes' *Clouds* explains thunder and rain as the result of clouds, filled with water, colliding and lightning as the result of a dry wind, caught inside a cloud and breaking forth (367–411). These details have probably been cobbled together from Pre-Socratic theories by Aristophanes, if not outright invented, to set up a number of scatological and political jokes. The founder of Stoicism, Zeno, appears to have been unsure whether lightning, thunder, and the thunderbolt itself were the result of the friction or the striking of the clouds occasioned by the wind (*SVF* 1.117). The explanation in our hymn seems closest to Aristophanes', and there are a number of verbal reminiscences of his work that suggest direct influence; compare also Sokrates' "Hymn to the Clouds" at 263–274 of that play. That the Clouds are already "filled with blazing thunder" perhaps alludes to the relationship between Zeus, who is identified with the thunderbolt in *OH* 19, and his wife Hera. The Stoics, when allegorizing Zeus as fire and Hera as air, note that the fire is the superior, active principle, with air being subject to it and passive (see *SVF* 2.1066, 1070, 1075). The Clouds in this hymn do seem quite passive, even impregnated; that they are invoked to send rain at the end (6–7) is not necessarily a contradiction, since this is a conventional formulation. It is repeated verbatim at the end of *OH* 82 (see also *OH* 82.4n). For the belief that the clouds were born from the sea, see *OH* 22.8n. In the Orphic *Rhapsodies,* the egg out of which Protogonos is born is called a "cloud" as well as a "bright robe" (*Orphic fragment* 121; see also *OH* 19.16–17n and West 1983, p. 202).

22. To the Sea

Sea is here identified with the Titaness Tethys, the wife of Okeanos. For their role in traditional and Orphic cosmogony, see *OH* 83i. That she and her husband might have had a more important role in certain Orphic accounts of creation might explain why our composer has opted to identify the sea with her, as opposed to another primeval watery figure such as Pontos. The male/female pattern we see employed as a way to group hymns elsewhere in the collection is not used here (but note that Tethys and Okeanos appear together at *OH* O.26–27). Perhaps the reason is to be found in Okeanos' association with death; see *OH* 83i. Their daughters, the Okeanids, are identified with the Nymphs to whom *OH* 51 is addressed (and also see line 8).

This hymn, along with the next three, form a group that is associated with water and is the third in the series that repeats the pattern of elements found in *OH* 15–18 (see *OH* 15i). It is also interesting to note that this hymn follows the one to the Clouds just as the hymn to Okeanos follows three separate ones to the winds, which receive prominent notice here and in the previous hymn. For the connection between sea, air, and clouds, see note to line 7.

2 dark-veiled: The same epithet is used of Tethys at *OH* O.26.

7 mother of Kypris: Kypris is another name for Aphrodite, who in one version is born out of the sea; see *OH* 3.2n and *OH* 55i.

7 mother of dark clouds: The idea that the clouds and winds are "born" from the sea goes back to the Pre-Socratics. Xenophanes mentions this explicitly (Kirk, Raven, and Schofield 1983, no. 183), and it seems implicit in Anaximander (Kirk, Raven, and Schofield 1983, no. 129). Aristophanes is probably alluding to this doctrine when he makes Okeanos the father of the Clouds (*Clouds* 271 and 277); see also *OH* 82.4n. For the weather phenomena produced by clouds, see *OH* 21i.

8 mother of every spring round which nymphs swarm: Aside from creation myths where Okeanos and Tethys are considered the first (or first progenitors) of all, they are credited with being the parents of smaller bodies of water. Hesiod lists some of the three-thousand rivers (male) and three-thousand springs (female) that are their brood (*Theogony* 337–370). Like other personified water divinities, their human form may be loosely considered separate from the actual physical body of water. In the theogony sung by Orpheus at Apollonios of Rhodes *Argonautika* 1.495–512, the Okeanid Eurynome becomes the consort to Ophion, and this pair of gods precedes Kronos and Rhea as the rulers of Olympos (see also *OH* 83i).

9–10: A common request of sea divinities in our collection; see *OH* 17.9–10n.

23. To Nereus

According to Hesiod, Nereus is the oldest child of Pontos, a male personification of the sea and a child of Earth (*Theogony* 233–236). Hesiod describes this divinity as being particularly honest, gentle, and mindful of lawful things. His main importance in myth, other than being the father of the Nereids (see following hymn) is his identification with "the Old Man of the Sea" (e.g., at Pausanias 3.21.9), a role he shares with other figures, particularly Proteus (see *OH* 25i). He plays no role elsewhere in Orphic cult, and his inclusion here seems to be entirely because of his daughters, with whom he forms another male/female pairing (see *OH* 14.8–9n).

5–7: Like his son-in-law Poseidon, Nereus is connected with earthquakes. "Demeter's sacred throne" is a kenning for the earth. The theme of winds continues from the previous two hymns. Here they are locked up under the earth, and it seems that their violent motion thus constrained is imagined to be the cause of earthquakes. This might be intended as an interesting twist to the story of the bag of winds that Aiolos, warden of the winds, gives to Odysseus (*Odyssey* 10.1–75). All of the winds are contained in the bag except for the gentle west wind Zephyros (see *OH* 81+3–4n) that conveys Odysseus' ship home. However his men, not knowing the bag's contents, but thinking that Odysseus was hiding something good from them, foolishly open the bag, thus letting all the violent winds out (similarly, Pandora; see Wolkow 2007). These promptly blow the ship back to Aiolos, who refuses further assistance to the beleaguered Odysseus. Comparable, too, is the imprisonment of Typhon in Apollodoros' version of his battle with Zeus (1.6.3). This creature has wind associations and, although imprisoned below Mount Etna by Zeus, is the source of its volcanic activity; see also *OH* 16i and cf. *OH* 32.12n.

7–8: The same requests are made of Poseidon at the end of *OH* 17, who also is additionally petitioned to keep ships safe.

24. To the Nereids

The traditional genealogy, retained in this hymn, makes the Nereids daughters of Nereus (which is what their name literally means) and the Okeanid Doris. There are usually fifty of them. Hesiod gives a complete list of their names (*Theogony* 240–264), while Homer only manages thirty-four, including Thetis (*Iliad* 18.39–49), the mother of Akhilleus, who, along with Amphitrite, wife of Poseidon, are the most famous ones. One anonymous poem, however, calls them the daughters of Amphitrite (*PMG* 939.10–11). Their worship was wide-spread and localized (Pausanias 2.1.8), and Sappho invokes them along with Aphrodite to bring her brother back home safe (fragment 5). Thetis is found with her own cults separate from the group (see Burkert 1985, p. 172). Their importance in folk religion is attested by the modern Greek "Neráides," the generic appellation for all female nature spirits, who take their name from them. This hymn continues the theme of water.

2–3: Bacchylides 17.100–108 paints a similar scene; see also *OH* 17.3n and cf. *OH* 75.1–2+1n.

3: The Tritons are a mythological race of mermen, the chief figure of whom is the eponymous Triton, mentioned in line 5.

9–11: "mother Kalliope" is probably meant to evoke the fiction of Orpheus dictating these hymns to Mousaios; see also *OH* 76.7n+i. Apollon's presence might similarly be explained, since he is sometimes considered the father of Orpheus (*Orphic fragment* 895–898; with Kalliope as mother, 896). The connection of the Nereids with the rites of Dionysos is curious. The Nereid Thetis succors Dionysos when he is chased by Lykourgos (*Iliad* 6.130–137), but this probably says more about Thetis as a helpful goddess (she also rescues Hephaistos, as related at *Iliad* 18.394–405) than about any particular connection with Dionysian cult. Ino, who nursed her nephew Dionysos and later became the sea goddess Leukothea (see *OH* 74i), is said to dwell among the Nereids by Pindar (*Olympian Odes* 2.28–30 and *Pythian Odes* 11.2). The Nereids are very similar to the Okeanids, who are identified with the nymphs who nurse Dionysos in *OH* 51.1. Furthermore, the two groups, both of which are composed of a plurality of young female water divinities, are sometimes confused, despite the Nereids' connection with salty water and the Okeanids' with fresh. A further source of confusion is that the Nereids are cousins to the Okeanids, since their mother, Doris, is a daughter of Okeanos, and thus they are half-Okeanid themselves! Interestingly enough, the Hellenistic poet Simias makes the nymphs the daughters of Doris (fragment 13; he probably has the Nereids in mind). As in the case of Sun, Pan, and Apollon, our composer has partially blended three originally separate entities, for which some precedents were found in the earlier tradition. The Nereids' connection with Dionysian cult is explicitly made in line 3, where they are said to "revel in the waves." This carries the connotations of maenadic frenzy (see *OH* 1.3+n and *OH* 52i), and note that the Okeanids are similarly portrayed at *OH* 51.15–16.

25. To Proteus

Like Nereus, Proteus is an "Old Man of the Sea" (see *OH* 23i) and in fact may very well just be another name for Nereus. In this hymn, however, he takes on a more cosmic significance. Our composer plays on the folk etymology of his name ("the first") in lines 2 and 9; Proteus is raised to the level of a primeval being. The same "cosmic etymologizing" from a name also appears in the hymn to Pan (see *OH* 11i), and Proteus is described as having power over a similar range of realms as Pan (see note to line 9 below). Our hymn also connects the shape-shifting abilities of Proteus (see note to lines 4–8) with his new primeval origin. He is able to change his form because he contains all forms in himself (line 9), even as he himself is the one who has apparently created these forms out of undifferentiated matter (lines 2–3). Proteus is thus cast in the role of a demiurgic figure. This is not as strange as it might first appear, since water in both myth and philosophical speculation is often regarded as the origin of the universe, or at least a very early feature of it; see *OH* 83i. Water, being an element that is easily observed to possess no firm structure, is an obvious choice for those seeking a single origin for the concrete pluralities in the empirical world; its character is probably also a reason why mythological beings connected with water are often shape-shifters themselves (see note to lines 4–8). This hymn ends the series of ones addressed to water divinities.

1 key-holding master of the sea: For the symbolism of holding keys, see *OH* 18.4n.

2–3: The epithet "first-born" is quite similar to the name Protogonos, a very important deity in Orphism, who has a central role in the creation of the world (see *OH* 6i). Physis is also said to be "first-born" (*OH* 10.5). The word used here for "matter," "hulē," is a philosophical technical term. Quandt in his edition of the *Orphic Hymns* cites Stoic doctrine that called matter "mutable, changeable, and in flux" (*SVF* 2.305).

4–8: Both Proteus and Nereus are able to change their shape. They are also considered very wise and capable of prophecy, which for the Greeks comprised not just the ability to see the future but also to know of the past and to interpret the present, as lines 4–5 delineate. Shape-shifting and prophecy combine in the one important myth of Proteus (*Odyssey* 4.348–570). When Menelaos is returning from Troy, he becomes stuck on Pharos, an island off Egypt, due to an act of impiety. A daughter of Proteus, Eidothea, takes pity on the men and instructs Menelaos on how to get the information he needs from her father. He and three companions kill seals from Proteus' herd, cover themselves with the skins, and wait for Proteus to take his noonday siesta. Then they jump on him and do not let go, even as he changes his shape into various creatures and elements, until he returns to his original form. After being released, Proteus truthfully explains to them what they must do to appease the gods. He also answers Menelaos' questions about the whereabouts of Lokrian Aias, Agamemnon, and Odysseus. Finally, Proteus reveals to Menelaos that he will not go to the underworld when he dies but rather to the Elysian Fields. Vergil models his account of Aristaeus and his bees on this story. After his bees suddenly die, Aristaeus' mother directs him to wrestle Proteus in order to find out why, and he learns that it is due to the anger of Orpheus at Aristaeus' role in the death of Eurydike (*Georgics* 4.387–527). Nereus is also involved in wrestling and prophecy. During Herakles' quest for the Apples of the Hesperides, he first needs to secure information from Nereus vital to his success; they wrestle and Herakles must keep hold of Nereus as he constantly alters his form until the old man yields and gives up the information (see Apollodoros 2.5.11). Of course, the ability to transform is not always connected with prophecy. Peleus must hold onto the Nereid Thetis, who keeps changing her shape, until she agrees to marry him (see Apollodoros 3.13.5), and Herakles again wrestles a shape-shifting god, this time the river Achelous, for the hand of Deianira (Ovid *Metamorphoses* 9.1–88).

9: For Physis, see *OH* 10i. She is said to preside over the heaven, earth, and sea in her hymn (see *OH* 10.14–16+n).

26. To Earth

Earth (Greek Gaia or Gē), is the quasi-personified figure of the productive powers of the land, the land itself, and often of procreation in general. She is, to an extent, a generic mother goddess, and thus shares many affinities with her more particular incarnations, such as Rhea (*OH* 14), Mother of the Gods (*OH* 27), and Eleusinian Demeter (*OH* 40), as well as with certain closely related male fertility gods, such as the Kouretes (*OH* 31 and *OH* 38). For her identification with other fertility goddesses in Orphic mythology, see *OH* 14i. She plays a central role in Hesiod's cosmogony and theogony. Born after Khaos, she parthenogenetically gives birth to a number of similarly quasi-personifications of physical features: Sky, Pontos ("sea," but a different word than the one personified as the addressee of *OH* 22), and the mountains. She then mates with Sky in the usual way to produce the Kyklopes, the Hundred-Handers, and the Titans (*Theogony* 116–118; 126–153). In the succession myths that follow, she connives with her youngest son, Kronos, to put an end to the oppressive behavior of her son-husband (154–175) and, in turn, now with Sky, helps Rhea end Kronos' swallowing of their children (453–500). However, she helps her grandson Zeus avoid the danger of being overcome by his progeny with Metis; instead, Metis is swallowed by Zeus, and Athene is later born from his head (886–900; 924–926). See further the note to line 2 below. Earth herself received worship in Greek religious practice; for details, see Larson 2007, pp. 157–158. We also find her connected with the pre-Apollo Delphic oracle (see *OH* 79.3–6n).

This hymn is the first in the last group of a series (*OH* 19–27) arranged by physical element, here earth, which mirrors the same order in the hymns to Zeus, Hera, Poseidon, and Plouton-Hades (*OH* 15–18); see *OH* 15i.

1 **mother of men and of the blessed gods**: Compare Homeric *Hymn to the Mother of the Gods* 14.1 and Homeric *Hymn to Earth, Mother of All* 30.1, 17; see also *OH* 10.1+n, *OH* 14.8–9+n, and *OH* 27.7+n. Earth, like Physis, is portrayed more as a natural force than a personified entity, and there are close affinities between their hymns in the collection.

2 **you bring all to fruition, you destroy all**: Life and death, although opposites, were nevertheless conceived as intricately bound polarities, and, as usual in Greek mythic thought, having power over one often implies having power over its contrary. Persephone also holds the power of life and death in her hymn (*OH* 29.15–16+n; see also *OH* 30i). A similar sentiment is found in the Homeric *Hymn to Earth, Mother of All*: ". . . you are the source of fair children and goodly fruit, / and on you it depends to give life to, or take it away from, / mortal men" (30.5–7). Perhaps comparable is a certain ambiguity of Earth in myth, as, for example, found in Hesiod's *Theogony*. The blood that falls from the castrated Sky fecundates Earth, who produces the brutal Giants and the horrid Erinyes but also the lovely Ash Tree Nymphs (183–187). Also, after the defeat of the Titans, Earth mates with Tartaros to produce the scourge of the gods, the monstrous Typhon; yet it was Earth who suggested to the gods that Zeus be made ruler after the defeat of the Titans (820–838; 881–885).

4 **seat of the immortal cosmos**: Hesiod calls Earth "the firm seat of all / the immortals who hold the peaks of snowy Olympos" (*Theogony* 117–118); compare also *OH* 18.6–7. See further *OH* 27.9n.

6 **deep-bosomed**: Compare Hesiod *Theogony* 117, where Earth is called "broad-breasted." This epithet is used twice of the sea in the collection: *OH* 17.3 and *OH* 74.3.

27. To the Mother of the Gods

The Mother of the Gods is the Phrygian goddess Kybele. She was also simply known as Meter (Mother). Her worship wound its way from the Greeks in Asia Minor to the mainland and appears to have gained traction in the sixth century BC. She is an earth fertility goddess, and so quickly became identified with other such figures in Greek mythology and religion: Rhea, Demeter, Earth, Hera—even Aphrodite and Hestia (see *OH* 14i and the note to line 9 below). Likewise, Hipta, a goddess of Asia Minor, might be a local version of Mother; see *OH* 49i. Wild music and dancing, ecstatic possession and ritual madness, and the close connection of her worship with mountains were all characteristic of the cult; see notes to lines 11 and 13. While her worship made some headway into official Greek cult, it was for the most part relegated to marginal members of society. Her wandering beggar-priests, called "mētragurtai" ("collectors for Mother") and "kubēboi," were held in low regard. In terms of myth, insofar as Kybele is identified with Demeter, she is the mother of Persephone and, just like Demeter in the Homeric *Hymn to Demeter*, she keeps away from the gods in anger over her daughter's abduction; see Euripides *Helen* 1301–1368. The story may have been the subject of the Epidaurian hymn to Mother of the Gods (translation with brief discussion in Furley 1995, pp. 43–45). In later antiquity, Agdistis, a doublet for Mother, takes on a younger consort, Attis, whom in her jealousy she drives to such heights of madness that he castrates himself (Pausanias 7.17.10–12). There seems to be no reference to him in this hymn, although the name does appear in Orpheus' address to Mousaios (*OH* O.39). Kybele is connected with the Korybantes, an ecstatic band of warriors who are associated with the Kouretes (see *OH* O.20, *OH* 31.5+n and *OH* 38.20), hence connecting Kybele with Rhea (see *OH* 14.3n) and also, in our collection, Athene (see *OH* 32i). The power of the goddess' madness reaches its gory peak in the self-castration of particularly dedicated male worshippers, known as Galloi, for whom the myth of Attis serves as an etiology. Among the works attributed to Orpheus are *Enthronements of the Mother* (*Orphic fragment* 602–605; cf. line 5 and note to line 9) and *Korybantic Rite* (*Orphic fragment* 610–611), for which see West 1983, p. 27. For more on the cult of Kybele, see Burkert 1985, pp. 177–179, Larson 2007, pp. 170–171, and the detailed monographs of Vermaseren 1977 and Borgeaud 2004. This hymn should be compared to the hymn to Rhea in this collection (*OH* 14) and the Homeric *Hymn to the Mother of the Gods*. It naturally follows the previous one addressed to Earth, and it ends the second sequence of hymns arranged by their association with the four elements; see *OH* 15i.

2 swift chariot drawn by bull-slaying lions: A typical attribute of the goddess, mentioned at *OH* 14.2 as well. Bull-slaying lions also appear at Sophokles *Philoktetes* 400–401, where the goddess is called Earth. The Homeric *Hymn to the Mother of the Gods* 14.4 associates both wolves and lions with the goddess. See also *OH* 36i.

7 of you were born gods and men: See *OH* 26.1n.

8 you hold sway over the rivers and over all the sea: Kybele is also the "queen of the sky" (line 4) and the earth belongs to her as well (line 6), a natural association for a fertility goddess. For the motif of the geographical extent of a divinity's power, see *OH* 14.9–10+n. In particular, she shares such broad authority with Pan (*OH* 11.2–3), a god connected to her through his ability to bestow madness (for this, see *OH* 11i). In the next line, Kybele is identified with Hestia, who is associated with fire (*OH* 84.4n); perhaps, then, the related theme of the four elements is also relevant here (see *OH* 10.14–16n).

9 Hestia . . . giver of prosperity: Kybele's throne is described as being located in the center of the cosmos (line 5), thus corresponding to the central position of the hearth in the home; see *OH* 84i+2n and cf. *OH* 40.15+n. Compare also the previous hymn where Earth is the "seat of the immortal cosmos" (*OH* 26.4) around which "the intricate realm of the stars / revolves in endless and awesome flow" (*OH* 26.8–9). This is reflecting a geocentric, not a heliocentric or pyrocentric, view of the cosmos; see *OH* 4.3n and Burkert 1972, p. 317. Euripides in a lost play equated the Earth with Hestia (fragment 944). As with Kybele in this hymn, so too is Hestia called on at the end of her hymn to grant prosperity.

11 whom the drum delights: Drums and other percussive instruments such as cymbals, clappers, and castanets are frequently found in the iconography of Kybele and Dionysos (see further *OH* 30.1n). Along with the *aulos*, they play an important role in the wild, frenzy-inducing music that constitutes their rites (see also note to line 13 below). These instruments are mentioned in the Homeric *Hymn to the Mother of the Gods* 14.3. See also *OH* 4.4+n. Music and madness is a recurring theme in our collection: see *OH* 11i, *OH* 14.3+n, and *OH* 31.3+n. It is particularly tied to maenadism; see further *OH* 52.7–8n. In a fragment from a dithyramb, Pindar imagines ecstatic worship of Dionysos celebrated by the gods: Kybele leads off with the beating of drums amid castanets, torches, and the wild shrieks of Naiads (water nymphs); Ares is present, and Athene, too, with the hissing of the countless serpents on her shield; finally Artemis arrives, having yoked lions, as a Bacchant (fragment 70b.6–21). This shows that already by the early fifth century, Dionysos and Kybele were closely related.

12 **all-taming savior of Phrygia, consort of Kronos**: In this line the identities of Kybele and Rhea are fused. For "savior," see *OH* 14.8n.

13 **frenzy-loving**: The goddess raves and is able to send madness to those she chooses. The rituals of Kybele and the Korybantes (possibly separate from Kybele's) were supposed to cure madness, and Dionysos himself had that power; see *OH* 71.11n. Hera, who is sometimes identified with Kybele, has the ability to send madness as well. She drives Herakles insane so that he kills his first wife, Megara, and even more pertinently she employs madness to disrupt the lives of those who help the infant Dionysos (e.g., Ino; see *OH* 74i) and, in some accounts, she drives Dionysos himself to madness (see *OH* 14.8n).

28. To Hermes

Hermes is a god with a wide range of functions, which nevertheless boil down to one essential idea: the ability to negotiate boundaries and bridge gaps. Many modes of travel are available to him, including the ability to fly through the air as well as to skim along the surface of the oceans (as beautifully portrayed at *Odyssey* 5.43–54). He can be a guide to men, directing their travels and even overcoming obstacles that block their path. Thus, for example he is able to bring Priam unharmed through the camp of the Greeks to meet with Akhilleus (*Iliad* 24.322–467). He is even able to traverse that most awesome divide between life and death; it is Hermes who leads the souls of the dead to the underworld. His ability to journey anywhere makes him an ideal messenger, a role he often undertakes in myth on the behalf of Zeus. Naturally, he is the god of heralds and diplomats. An important skill for these professions is that of speaking well, and thus he is also a god of language. Sometimes, though, a herald might find himself in circumstances where it is preferable to smooth over a difficult situation with words, even if the truth might have to suffer a bit. Hermes knows how to deceive with words. Indeed, Hermes knows how to deceive, period; he is a trickster figure of the first order, much like Prometheus and the Norse Loki. He is a god of thieves, but likewise he is the god of merchants who can protect against thieves. As so often, a god is responsible for the positive and the negative in a specific domain (see *OH* 30i). Like other trickster figures, Hermes is also a culture hero, inventing things that do much to further the civilized life. The longer Homeric *Hymn to Hermes* (no. 4) is full of the god's innovations: the lyre, fire sticks, sacrifice, and wondrous shoes that hide his tracks. The introduction of fire and sacrifice is also attributed to Prometheus, who steals fire from the heavens and whose deception of Zeus at Mekone becomes the paradigm for future human sacrifice (Hesiod *Theogony* 535–570 and *Works and Days* 49–53; see also *OH* 40.8–9n). The Homeric hymn, marked by its cleverness and wit, is itself a piece worthy of Hermes himself. It seamlessly and playfully integrates in its narrative many of the gods' prerogatives. His role as a god of minor divination is explained as one of Apollon's gifts to him: Hermes does not receive a share of Delphic honors, but he is permitted to learn about prophecy from the strange bee women who live nearby and who taught Apollon as a child (4.533–566). He also is allowed to keep some of the cows he stole from Apollon, becoming a god of cowherds (4.567–568). This, too, is a mythological etiology that touches on a broader reality. Hermes is the god of all those who look after any herd of animals, such as sheep and goats. Fertility associations are not foreign to this god, who is able to increase the flocks of those he favors (see *OH* 11). When the basis of wealth changed from agricultural to commercial, Hermes remained the god who brought profit. He is also the lucky god, and a piece of good luck was called a "hermaion," literally "a thing of Hermes." The god is often found in pastoral settings, frolicking with nymphs and other creatures of the wild. Yet he is also a god of physical exercise and athletics, particularly of the gymnasia and wrestling grounds, both very "urban" institutions.

Worship of Hermes tended to be domestic and personal; for details, see Burkert 1985, pp. 156–159, and Larson 2007, pp. 144–150. He seems to have had only a small role in Orphism, at least as far as can be deduced from the little said about him in our extant sources. His role as guide of the dead, which one would figure to be of particular interest in Orphic cults, is highlighted in our collection by a separate hymn to Chthonic Hermes, who seems to have become a separate entity (see *OH* 57i). Our hymn here, though, is quite traditional in the various attributes it lists, although it is not by any means comprehensive. There is a particular emphasis on Hermes as the god of language. This is understandable in a body of work whose main interest lies in convincing deities through the use of language to be favorable and propitious. It is notable that the rustic side of the god does not appear at all; this may be taken as circumstantial evidence that the cult for which the *Orphic Hymns* were composed was purely an urban one.

The placement of this hymn is curious at first blush. *OH* 15–27 are structured along the lines of the four elements, and the following hymn to Persephone would seem also to belong to this pattern, in as much as she is associated with earth (cf. *OH* 29.4, 6, 17). We might then expect this hymn to stress the chthonic side to Hermes, which it clearly does not do, despite his being called "lord of the deceased" in line 2; instead, the hymn to Chthonic Hermes has that function. However, as already mentioned, Hermes is a figure who negotiates transitions, and it seems this hymn performs the same duty. It serves as a dramatic pause, setting off the next two hymns to Persephone and Dionysos, who of course are divinities of the utmost importance for the initiates. Their hymns begin the central portion of the collection, focusing on the birth of Dionysos and Dionysian cult.

1 son of Maia: The traditional genealogy of Hermes makes him the son of Zeus and Maia, a daughter of Atlas; for details see both of the Homeric *Hymns to Hermes* (no. 4.1–19 and no. 18). Chthonic Hermes in our collection has a completely different parentage (see *OH* 57.3–5+n).

2 judge of contests: This epithet appears in Greek literature applied to Hermes, the earliest witnesses being a fragment of Simonides (*PMG* 555) and Pindar *Pythian Odes* 2.10. The original context of the Simonides fragment is unknown, but the Pindar citation comes from a victory ode celebrating the victor's winning of a chariot race. The "contests" in our hymn may only be limited to athletic contests, something that is within the domain of Hermes, or refer to any contest in general, given that Hermes is also a god of good fortune. If there were contests involved in the ritual during which our hymns were sung, then the epithet might have a more immediate significance, especially if these contests involved some kind of speech (see *OH* 7.12–13n; for athletic contests as a metaphor, see *OH* 87.12n).

3 **Argeiphontes**: This epithet of Hermes has been understood as "slayer of Argos" in antiquity and in modern times, referring to Hermes' exploit in freeing Io from this multi-eyed giant who guarded her. However, this interpretation has been questioned and "slayer of dogs" has been offered as another possibility. For a technical discussion, see West 1978, pp. 368–369. Both explanations portray Hermes in his guise as the god of thieves, who often need to dispatch guards, whether watchmen or watchdogs.

6 **interpreter of all**: The word "interpreter" in Greek is "hermēneus," and there is an intentional play on the name Hermes (also in *Orphic fragment* 413.1). The word and name do not appear to be etymologically related, however. See also Plato *Cratylus* 407e–408b (and note the pun on Hermogenes' name!).

8 **lord of Korykos**: Korykos is the southern promontory of the Erythraian peninsula in Kilikia. The mountain most frequently connected with Hermes is the one where he was born, Kyllene in Arkadia. That he is the "lord of Korykos" and not "lord of Kyllene" in this hymn may be due to the location of the cult in Asia Minor, where Korykos would have been more familiar than Kyllene (and thus possibly would have been a place of more emotional attachment for the initiates).

10: The ancient Greeks certainly realized that speech could be used for good or ill. The ambiguity can be seen in the portrayal of Odysseus, the skillful speaker par excellence. His gift with language saves him from the Kyklops Polyphemos. But there are also failures, such as his unsuccessful embassies to the Trojans and to Akhilleus, and the speech that wins him the arms of Akhilleus in turn leads to the death of the great warrior Aias. More to the point, it is Hermes who endows Pandora, that bane for mankind, with language, which allows her to wheedle and lie (Hesiod *Works and Days* 77–82).

29. Hymn to Persephone

Persephone was called Phersephone and P(h)ersephoneia by the poets, Pherrephatta by the Athenians, and Proserpina by the Romans. However, she is often merely known as Kore ("maid"). She is the daughter of Zeus and Demeter already in Hesiod (*Theogony* 912–914). Orphism adopts this genealogy but also at times equated Demeter with Rhea, the mother of Zeus (see *OH* 27i); she flees the advances of her son by turning herself into a snake, but he does so as well and eventually mates with her (see also *OH* 40i). The story repeats itself in the case of Persephone. She, too, is pursued by Zeus who again takes the form of a snake (Clement of Alexandria *Protrepticus* 2.16.1). Their offspring is Dionysos, and this might have produced Melinoe as well (see *OH* 71i). The most important myth involving Persephone is her abduction by Hades, the most famous version of which is found in the Homeric *Hymn to Demeter*; for a summary, see *OH* 41i. There was at least one Orphic version as well. She is usually closely associated with her mother in cult, in which fertility and other aspects of a woman's life receive emphasis, particularly marriage. For an overview of important cults, see Larson 2007, pp. 69–85. Her connection with the underworld and Dionysos is particularly important to Orphism. She frequently appears on the Bacchic gold tablets. A few short ones merely convey greetings to her (nos. 15, 17, 31, 37). In others the initiate appeals to her for their reward in the afterlife for which their initiation into the cult had prepared them, and there is sometimes an allusion to the initiate's guilt inherited from his Titan forbears who killed Dionysos, Persephone's son (nos. 5–7, 9, 26a, b; cf. no. 8). In one tablet, the initiate is assured to reach the "holy meadows and groves of Persephone" (no. 3). For an analysis of these tablets, see Graf/Johnston 2007, pp. 66–164; see also *OH* 18.2n and *OH* 87.12n. We also find the chthonic connection of Persephone stressed in the magical papyri through her thorough identification with other goddesses. There she is identified with Moon, Hekate, and Artemis (see further *OH* 1i and *OH* 59.3–4n). In our hymn both sides of Persephone are addressed. She is a fertility goddess, due to her connection both to Demeter and Hades, who, although the lord of the dead, nevertheless has a connection with life in that he can be seen as the one who sends up crops and other growing things from his realm under the earth (see *OH* 18i). His abduction of Persephone and her reunification with Demeter, and the consequent compromise between the two over her, was interpreted by the Greeks as symbolizing the cycle of growth: the seed is sown under the earth, where it lies dormant throughout the winter until its fruit miraculously reappears in the spring (but see Burkert 1985, p. 160, for another interpretation). Yet, through her marriage to Hades, Persephone is the queen of the dead. Their relationship had a rough beginning, and she can even have a sinister side. Odysseus fears that she might send up a ghost or monster to vex him during his visit to the land of the dead (*Odyssey* 11.633–635); see also *OH* 71.4–5+n. It is perhaps for this reason that the poet has omitted the more unsavory details of her birth and abduction (as in the case of her mother in *OH* 40). This hymn together with the following one to Dionysos forms a mother-son pair; for other similar collocations, see *OH* 14.8–9n.

1 sole offspring: As in *Orphic fragment* 294. Demeter also bears this epithet; see *OH* 40.16+n. It is used of Hekate in Hesiod *Theogony* 426, a goddess who sometimes is identified with Persephone. This might be one of the reasons why the source of Apollodoros made Styx, and not Demeter, the mother of Persephone (Apollodoros 1.3.1).

4 the gates of Hades: Compare *OH* 18.4, where Plouton is said to hold the keys to Hades.

5 Praxidike: The name means "exacter of justice." Pausanias tells us that a group of goddesses called Praxidikai were worshipped at Haliartos (9.33.3). The *Orphic Argonautika* mentions the "mysteries of Praxidike" (31) without further elaboration.

6 mother of the Erinyes: In Orphic myth, the Erinyes are the children of Persephone and Hades (sometimes Apollon); see *OH* 70.2–3n. Once in the magical papyri it seems that Persephone is the name of one of the Erinyes; see *OH* 69.1n. In our collection, she is also implied to be the mother of Adonis (see *OH* 56.8–9+n) and Melinoe, although the allusion to the story of the latter's birth is obscure (see *OH* 71.4–5+n).

7–8: Eubouleus ("good counsel") is a name applied to different divinities (see *OH* 41.8n), but here it refers to Dionysos. The epithet "loud roaring" is characteristic of the god. In the next hymn, he is also described as "loud roaring" (*OH* 30.1+n), and he was often called Bromios (Roarer), as in *OH* 40.10. Our composer here euphemistically summarizes the doublet of Persephone and Dionysos' birth in Orphic myth, as he does in the following hymn. No mention is made of snakes or rape.

9–11 radiant and luminous. . . brilliant and horned: When Demeter gives birth to Persephone, the infant has an extra pair of eyes on her forehead and horns, and the mother flees in terror at the sight (see *OH* 14i). This line might be alluding to an identification with Moon, who is often portrayed as bright and horned (*OH* 9.1–2). As mentioned in the introduction to this hymn, Persephone was identified with the moon goddess, and in later antiquity the phases of the moon were associated with her split existence between the land of the living and the land of the dead (see Richardson 1974, p. 285).

9 playmate of the Seasons: In their hymn, the Seasons are described as playmates of Persephone (*OH* 43.7+i).

12–14: The poet subtly glides between Persephone as a person and Persephone as the fruits of the earth itself; the same effect is used with Dionysos and the grape (see *OH* 50.5+n). In the Orphic version of Persephone's abduction, she is weaving a robe of flowers when Hades appears (*Orphic fragment* 288). The pointed contrast between spring and autumn is mirrored in the life-death imagery in lines 15–16.

15–16: As is often the case, a god has control over opposites. Many fertility goddesses double as death goddesses; see *OH* 26.2+n. The Greek in line 16 contains an etymologizing play on words: "*Phersephonē pher*beis . . . kai . . . *phon*eueis" ("Persephone, you nourish . . . and . . . kill"). Hekate is called the "all-nourisher" in the magical papyri (*PGM* 4.2749) shortly after she is addressed as Persephone (4.2747). The Stoic philosopher Kleanthes is reported to have made a similar play on words: he equated *Phersephonē* with warm air ("pneuma") that is carried ("*pheromenon*") through crops and is killed ("*phoneumenon*").

19 a splendid old age to him who is sailing: This refers to the crossing of a river on Charon's ferry in the underworld in order to reach Hades proper. For interpretation of "old age," see *OH* 87.12n.

30. To Dionysos

Dionysos is a very difficult divinity to define—and one suspects that this is exactly how he would want it to be. He is a god of vegetation, particularly of the creeping vine (see lines 4–5). He is a god of liquid fertility: the catalyst that initiates the process of growth, the vital force that sustains it, and the fluid nourishment that flows from it. Semen, blood, water, wine, honey, milk—Dionysos is all of this. His very essence is a fluidity that is at once defined and undefined. At his roots, he is a god of transitions, but in order for there to be a transition, there must be a point A and a point B between which a transition exists. Dionysos swings between these extremes. At any moment, the god can move from one to the next. He is a god of opposites: peaceful and warlike, human and animal, sober and drunk, alive and dead, sacred and profane. Dionysos blurs the lines. There are many Greek gods who oversee conflicting spheres, such as Apollon, the god of medicine and disease. Yet none are so thoroughly defined by the juxtaposition of opposites as Dionysos. The *Hymns* themselves teem with paradox and contradiction. Even more, they seem to embrace it, to actively present the conflict wherever possible. This frequently occurs at the verbal level and expands to include the addressed divinities themselves. Identities are spliced (e.g., the Erinyes and Eumenides); entities are merged (e.g., Okeanids and the Nymphs). The Dionysian spirit lurks behind this, too. A crucial element of his worship is the process which the Greeks called *enthousiasmos*, "the god inside" (whence English "enthusiasm"), the belief that the god enters into the worshippers and possesses them (see further *OH* 50i), which leads to a state of *ekstasis*, "a standing out (of oneself)" (whence English "ecstasy"). To a degree unmatched by other divinities, Dionysos is with his followers (cf. *OH* 32i). The effacing of the distinction between divine and human, the strange encounter where someone at the same time is somehow both himself and not himself, coheres perfectly with the transitional nature of the god himself. In the *Hymns*, religious experience becomes poetic strategy. The various hymns are not merely words to be mechanically recited. It is in their performance that they find their ultimate fulfillment. Through this (and the other ritual acts), the Dionysian spirit was evoked, made manifest, and entered into the very breath of the initiates—an *enthousiasmos* of language that transported the worshippers, however briefly, beyond their quotidian existence and allowed them to touch the divine. This is the key to understanding the whole collection (see also the introduction to the translation). In one respect, then, performing the *Hymns* enables one, in essence, to become the god (see also *OH* 33i and *OH* 52i). The initiation ritual mirrors Dionysos: as the god is ripped apart by the Titans and is born again, so, too, the initiates, blasted by the vagaries of life, are reborn through initiation into something pure and holy. And just as the pieces of the murdered divine child must be gathered and reconstituted anew, so the initiates, in performing the *Hymns* where the details of cultic myth and eschatology are scattered in obscure allusions but subtly linked through a complex web of shared and similar epithets and descriptions, reconstitute the esoteric knowledge that leads to a revelation of the secrets of life and death. The learned contests we find mentioned sporadically in the collection might be understood in this light; see *OH* 7.12–13n. Yet encounter with the divine is fraught with peril. The frenetic invocations of various deities to appear, coupled with the uncertainty as to how they will react to being so summoned, lead to anxieties. Thus the initiates repeatedly call on figures to come kindly disposed and a few times even explicitly request the more dangerous ones to dispel the madness they bring (see *OH* 71.11n).

This hymn is the first of many that address Dionysos. Coming as it does after the hymn to Persephone, who is (one of) his mother(s) (see note to line 2 below), it functions in a sense as the birth of Dionysos, and in many ways it culminates the series of divinities addressed in the previous hymns. His birth is the moment the entire universe has been anticipating. This initial hymn is followed by figures who play a role in the god's early years (see *OH* 32i). Starting with *OH* 40, the collection moves away from cosmology and mythology to a decided emphasis on cultic practice. This reaches its climax through a number of hymns dedicated to different cultic identities of Dionysos (*OH* 45–47 and *OH* 50–53), particularly as the divine child, and ends with a hymn dedicated to the traditional *thiasos* of the god (*OH* 54). Various Dionysian themes are interwoven in this grouping; imagery and concepts merge and blur the identities of the addressees. These hymns occupy the central portion of the collection and most likely the ritual itself.

For more on Dionyos' role in myth and religion, see Burkert 1985, pp. 161–167, and Larson 2007, pp. 126–143; for Dionysos and Orphism, see Graf/Johnston 2007, passim. There are three Homeric hymns dedicated to this god (nos. 1, 7, 26).

1 loud roaring, reveling: Dionysian worship, particularly the ecstatic elements, was marked by noise: voices raised in song, the clatter of percussive elements (see also *OH* 27.11n), the sounds of the victim. The epithet used here is closely related to Bromios (Roarer), another name for Dionysos; see *OH* 40.10+n. Compare "howling" in line 4, and see further *OH* 29.8, *OH* 45.4, *OH* 48.3, and *OH* 49.3. The "Bacchic cries" of the Erinyes are similarly described (*OH* 69.2) as well as the crashing of the rain clouds (*OH* 21.3). For a description of the (maenadic) revel, see *OH* 52i.

2 primeval, two-natured, thrice-born: A numerical sequence. The word translated here as "primeval" is "prōtogonos," also used of Dionysos at *OH* 52.6. It is one of the names of the pivotal Orphic divinity responsible for the creation of the world. The two gods share many features and indeed can be considered the same being (or different manifestations thereof); see *OH* 6i and note to lines 3–4 below. "Two-natured" probably refers to Dionysos' androgyny, a characteristic shared with Protogonos and other divinities in the collection (see *OH* 6.1+n and *OH* 9.4n). It is interesting to note that Apollodoros says that Zeus instructed Ino to raise Dionysos as a girl (3.4.3), and that Mise seems to be interpreted as Dionysos in his feminine manifestation (see *OH* 42i). Another possibility is that "two-natured" reflects the andromorphic and teratomorphic side of the god, but this is probably what "two-shaped" in the following line is meant to indicate. See also *OH* 52.5+n, where the god is said to have a "three-fold" nature. The epithet "thrice-born" also contains some ambiguity. In traditional mythology, Dionysos was born from Semele and from Zeus, insofar as Zeus saved the child after the death of Semele and kept him in his thigh until the child fully gestated (see *OH* 44i; cf. *OH* 45.1 and *OH* 50.3+n). Orphism presented an alternate birth, one where Zeus mated with Persephone in the form of a snake, as briefly mentioned below in lines 6–7 (see also *OH* 29i+7–8n). Also, in Orphic mythology Dionysos is eventually torn apart and killed by the Titans (see *OH* 37i); he is then either reconstituted (by Rhea, Demeter, Apollon, or Zeus; see *Orphic fragment* 59, 322, 325–326) or born again through Semele (see *OH* 44i). Some authors who refer to a "thrice-born" Dionysos count the birth from Semele, Zeus, and the reconstitution of Dionysos after being dismembered by the Titans (see *Orphic fragment* 59). It is difficult to securely affirm that interpretation here, as our poet explicitly considers Dionysos the son of Persephone (but see *OH* 46.6–7+n). The matter is further complicated by the fact that Dionysos is said to have two mothers at *OH* 50.1. This would indicate Persephone and Semele, but it is hard in that case to reconcile the third birth as either Dionysos being born from Zeus' thigh (which would seem to contradict the idea of Persephone as mother) or as the reconstitution of the dismembered Dionysos (which would seem to be how some Orphics worked in Semele as the mother of Dionysos). In other words, the births to which "thrice-born" here refers are problematic, since there are four possible births found in our sources (Semele, Zeus, Persephone, reconstitution), all of which are alluded to at different points throughout the collection. The ambiguity, though, might be intentional (see the introduction to this hymn).

3 ineffable, secretive: Just like the god, so too the cult. It is a typical characteristic of mystery cults that certain aspects of their rites are known only to the privileged few who have undergone initiation; cf. "pure" in line 4. See also *OH* 42.3, *OH* 50.3 and *OH* 52.5.

3–4 two-horned ... / ... bull-faced: The bull is used as a sacrificial animal in Dionysian cult, and Dionysos, the suffering god, is sometimes identified with the victim. Plutarch reports that the women of Elis called on Dionysos to come with the following verses: "Come, o hero Dionysos / to the Eleans' temple / with the Graces / to the pure temple / descend your oxen-foot / o worthy bull / o worthy bull" (*Quaestiones graecae* 299a–b = *PMG* 871). Likewise, Pentheus, under the spell of the god, experiences double vision and perceives him horned like a bull (Euripides *Bacchae* 918–924; cf. also 99–104 and 1017). Protogonos "bellows like a bull" in *OH* 6.3 (and see note to that line). Dionysos is bull-faced again at *OH* 45.1 and is described as horned at *OH* 52.2 and 10, and *OH* 53.8. See also *OH* 50.5+n.

4 warlike: Dionysos occasionally engages in combat. Most famous is his participation in the Gigantomachy (Apollodoros 1.6.2). In Euripides *Bacchae*, the maenads, roused to violence, attack a village and rout its defenders (751–764), and the god is explicitly linked to the panic of war (303–304; cf. *OH* 11i and *OH* 32.6n). Korybas, who seems to be an analogue for Dionysos, is also called "warlike" (*OH* 39.2+n). See further *OH* 45.5+n.

4 pure: Purity is essential in ritual, and, as in line 3, the god and his worshippers share the same quality; see introduction as well as *OH* 15.8+8–9n, *OH* 40.11+n, *OH* 53.4, and *OH* 84.4+n. The idea recurs in the Bacchic gold tablets; see the discussion in Graf/Johnston 2007, pp. 121–131.

5 raw flesh in triennial feasts: An important part of maenadism is the notion of *sparagmos*, the ripping apart of wild animals by the frenzied women, and of *ōmophagia*, the eating of the raw flesh afterward (see *OH* 52i). It is not known whether this was actually practiced in cult or is merely a mythological embellishment. Dionysos is invoked as Omestes (Eater of Raw Flesh) by Alkaios (fragment 129). See also *OH* 52.7, where Dionysos also is said to take raw flesh in the hymn dedicated to him as God of Triennial Feasts.

5 wrapped in foliage, decked with grape clusters: Dionysos appears to be imagined as the grape-vine itself at *OH* 50.5 (and see note to that line).

6 Eubouleus: Dionysos is also called this at *OH* 52.4. The name is also used of Zeus and Adonis in the collection and elsewhere of Protogonos; see *OH* 6i and *OH* 41.8n.

8 fair-girdled nurses: A number of female divinities are called the nurses of Dionysos in the collection: the Nymphs (*OH* 42.10, *OH* 46.3, *OH* 51.3, and *OH* 53.6; in this last they are also called "fair-girdled"), Aphrodite (*OH* 46.3), and Hipta (*OH* 49.1). See further *OH* 46.2–3n and *OH* 51.3n.

31. Hymn to the Kouretes

The Kouretes are a band of armed young men connected with Krete. In myth, they dance about the infant Zeus and clatter their arms in order to muffle the sound of his crying. Hesiod tells the story of how his mother, Rhea, was sent to Krete, but he does not mention the Kouretes (*Theogony* 453–500). The poet, however, is aware of them, for in one of the fragments from the *Catalogue of Women* he mentions them as "sportive, dancing gods" (fragment 123); they are either the siblings or cousins of the satyrs and the mountain nymphs. Already in Hesiod, then, there is some relationship with Dionysian figures. Kallimakhos narrates the story of their dancing around Zeus in his *Hymn to Zeus* 52–54. These various characteristics—percussive sounds, wild dancing, mountain dwelling, and the link with Rhea—facilitated an identification with the Korybantes of Kybele (see *OH* 14.3n and *OH* 27i), and the two names are often interchangeable (e.g., *OH* 38.20 and cf. Kallimakhos *Hymn to Zeus* 46). Our hymn blends Kretan and Phrygian imagery. The Kouretes, whose name translates as "youths," played a role in Kretan cult. A hymn found inscribed at Palaikastro in Krete addresses Zeus as the "greatest *kouros*" and calls on him to usher in fertility for the new year. In particular he is asked to "leap into" the fields, animals, and homes of the town to spark fertility and bring wealth; see also *OH* 45.7n. A fragment from Euripides' *Kretans* hints at an initiatory ritual that is possibly Orphic (fragment 472 = *Orphic fragment* 567). Pythagoras is supposed to have been initiated in their cult at Mount Ida, where he also allegedly saw the tomb of Zeus, who was considered to die and then be reborn each spring. The existence of a religious fraternity that bore the name Kouretes at Ephesos lends special significance to the whole collection (see Burkert 1985, p. 173). The Kouretes also gained prominence within Orphic circles. They guard the infant Dionysos on Krete, just as they guarded the infant Zeus (*Orphic fragment* 297), sometimes with Athene (see *OH* 32i). However, they do not seem to be hiding him but outright guarding him, and, unlike in the case of Zeus, they fail to protect him against the machinations of the Titans. On occasion we find the Kouretes surrounding Dionysos in the material record; for example, they appear on a relief from an altar at Kos, dated to the middle second century BC (see Burkert 1993, pp. 270–271). Some sources have them guarding the infant Persephone/Kore as well (*Orphic fragment* 279). Athene is some-times imagined to be their leader (*Orphic fragment* 267–268), the overlap with dancing in armor a clear point of contact (see Plato *Laws* 796d, where he also mentions the Dioskouroi of Sparta). This helps explain why her hymn immediately follows; see *OH* 32i. The Kouretes are invoked by name in the fragmentary Gurôb Papyrus, shortly after Demeter and Rhea, with whom they might have been explicitly connected as they are in the Orphic fragments. For more information, see West 1983, pp. 166–168, Larson 2007, pp. 24–25, and Graf/Johnston 2007, pp. 82–83. This hymn should be compared to *OH* 38 and *OH* 39.

1–4: In Greek cult, young men sometimes danced in armor, the most famous of which was the *pyrrhikhē*, although this is sometimes used as a quasi-technical term to describe all such dances. A number of origins for the *pyrrhikhē* were proposed by ancient scholars, and the Kouretes are sometimes thought to be its inventors. Interestingly enough, Attic vase paintings sometimes have the very unwarlike satyrs dancing in armor, a curious in-version of roles that may be parody or may hint at a Dionysian connection with the dance (see Ceccarelli 2004, pp. 108–111). Other armed dances were known, too, and they did not always take place in cultic settings. For an example of such entertainment at a symposium performed by a woman, see Xenophon *Symposium* 2.11. Armed young men dancing and singing in cult are also found in Rome, where a group known as the Salii would dance and sing at certain festivals; we find mention of a particular song, the *carmen saliare*, in ancient sources, but what little text has come down to us is very corrupt.

3 **discordant is the lyre you strike**: Harmony, both in music and in its more general applica-tion to anything exhibiting a balanced structure, was an important component of Greek morality, and we find writers, notably Plato, using the idea of harmonious music as a sym-bol of order, civilization, and rationality. Conversely, the lack of harmony often carries the opposite connotations. Thus, the cacophony implied by this line goes hand-in-hand with the wild, "out of control" ecstatic dance movements of the Kouretes and thus prepares for the mention of "mountain frenzy" in line 5 (compare also the "howling" in line 2). See also *OH* 27.11n.

5 **priests in the train of a mother**: Compare *OH* 38.6, where the Kouretes are mentioned as the "first to set up sacred rites for mortals." In both passages, the Kouretes gain significance as the mythical paradigm for the practitioners of the actual ritual for which our collection was composed.

32. To Athene

Athene is one of the chief divinities of the Greek pantheon. Her life begins in impressive fash-ion. Zeus takes as his first wife Metis (Counsel, Resourcefulness, Wisdom) but finds out later that she is destined to give birth to a mighty daughter and a son who will overthrow his father.

Zeus' grandfather, Sky, had tried to forestall a similar fate by pushing his children back into Earth's womb at birth, which did not work. His son, Kronos, took the next step of swallowing his children at birth to avoid a similar fate, but this, too, failed to prevent his demise. Zeus goes even further—he swallows the mother before she is even able to give birth! Eventually, though, he gets a headache. Hephaistos performs exploratory surgery and splits his head open with an axe—then suddenly out pops a goddess, fully armed, shouting a lusty battle cry, and scaring the assembled gods. Thus Athene makes her debut on the cosmic stage; see Hesiod *Theogony* 886–900 and 924–926, Homeric *Hymn to Athene* (no. 28), Pindar *Olympian Odes* 7.35–44, and Apollodoros 1.3.6. The motif was popular in Attic vase painting.

From the very beginning, then, Athene is associated with war. However, she is unlike Ares, the other war god, in that he revels in the blood and gore of fighting, while she, taking after her mother, is more interested in the intellectual aspects of strategy and tactics (see OH 65i). The battle of Herakles and Kyknos, a son of Ares, in Hesiod's *Shield* is, in some ways, a battle by proxy between these two divinities. War is not the only pursuit to which she applies her wisdom. Athene is the goddess of all sorts of handiwork, both in the female domain, such as weaving, and in the male domain, such as carpentry (see note to line 8). She is very much a figure invested in human civilization. Her closeness to the mortal sphere is reflected in her intimate relationship with heroes, as for example when she appears to her favorite Odysseus, a hero after her own mind, on Ithaka (*Odyssey* 13.221–440). She is also particularly connected with Herakles. An instructive contrast to her relation with human beings would be the aloofness of Apollon (see OH 34i), although she falls short of Dionysos' "possessive" nearness (see OH 30i).

It is perhaps not surprising, then, that she was a very popular figure in cult, especially at Athens, the city after which she seems to have been named. Her claim to this polis is told in the story of her competition with Poseidon. They vied for the title of its chief divinity and held a sort of contest. Poseidon caused a salt spring to gush forth on the acropolis, while Athene planted an olive tree. She was chosen because of the utility of her gift (see Herodotos 8.55 and Apollodoros 3.14.1–2). The most important festival in Athens, the Panathenaia, was held every year in her honor, on the occasion of her victory against the giants in the Gigantomachy. Every fourth year the Panathenaia was more elaborately celebrated and included athletic and poetic contests. The cultural hegemony of Athens throughout the centuries ought not to blind us, however, to her extensive worship throughout all of Greece. For example, Kallimakhos' fifth hymn, known as the *Bath of Pallas*, alludes to a rite at Argos during which her cult image, the Palladion, was washed in the river Inakhos and carried with the shield of Diomedes in a procession (1–56). For more information on her role in myth and cult, see Burkert 1985, pp. 139–143, and Larson 2007, pp. 41–57.

Orphism seems to have accepted her traditional birth (see *Orphic fragment* 263–266 and cf. also Mousaios fragment 75), but she is given a special role in accounts of the infant Dionysos' death at the hands of the Titans. She saves the still beating heart of the dismembered child and returns it to Zeus, who later brings about the rebirth of Dionysos (see OH 44i). Such a connection between these divinities may seem odd at first glance, but there are a number of points of contact. Both were prominent at Athens, both were born from the body of Zeus (head, thigh), both are famous for their role in the Gigantomachy (see note to line 12), and both have a connection with vegetation (olive, ivy). Athene, like Dionysos, is sometimes associated with mountains (see note to lines 4–5) and madness (see note to line 6), while both have a touch of the androgynous about them (see note to line 10). Her role in saving his heart might have been influenced by the story of the Athenian king Erikhthonios. He was born when Hephaistos, enamored of Athene, wanted to make love to her. She refuses his advances (cf. line 8), but some of his semen falls on her thigh. Disgusted, she wipes it off with wool, and throws it down upon the earth, which, thus fecundated, becomes pregnant and gives birth to a child. This child Athene hides in a box with a serpent (in some versions the child himself is serpentine) and entrusts the box to the daughters of the Athenian king Kekrops with orders not to open it. Of course they disobey the order, and eventually they are either killed by the snake or, driven mad by Athene, leap from the acropolis to their death (see Euripides *Ion* 20–26 and 267–274, Pausanias 1.18.2, and Apollodoros 3.14.6). Athene's protection of a child, the chthonic character of this child, and the element of madness could easily have suggested to the person who originated the Orphic tale a way to work in Athene. Furthermore, the infant Dionysos is guarded by the Kouretes, whose leader is sometimes said to be Athene (see *OH* 31i). In one sense, then, this virgin goddess has a somewhat analogous relationship to her younger half-brother Dionysos as Artemis does to Apollon, whose birth she assists shortly after her own in some versions of the story (see *OH* 36i). Both goddesses are also virgin goddesses who can offer protection (to young people and warriors), and in our collection both are associated with mountains, are described as masculine, and are said to be fond of madness (see note to lines 4–5 and 10 below). The connection with the Kouretes, mountains, and madness also brings Athene into connection with Kybele, the Phrygian mother goddess (see *OH* 27i) as well as Rhea (see *OH* 14i). Athene, then, is intricately bound up in a web of associations centered around chthonic divinities.

This role of the Kouretes and Athene in the (re)birth of Dionysos in the tradition probably explains why their hymns follow the first one in the collection addressed to him. Apollon also has a part to play in the Titans' attack on Dionysos, and this might well be the reason why the hymns to Apollon and the Titans (*OH* 34 and *OH* 37) occur in this sequence, too. The first hymn to Dionysos functions symbolically as his "birth," and it is not surprising that we find in quick succession a number of divinities (along with related ones subordinated to them) at this point in the collection. The second hymn to the Kouretes and the one to Korybas form a bridge to the one to Eleusinian Demeter (*OH* 38–40; see *OH* 39i), which is the first hymn of the central group that focuses on Dionysos in his cultic aspects (see *OH* 40i).

This hymn to Athene should be compared to the two Homeric hymns in her honor (nos. 11 and 28) and Proclus' *Hymn to Athene Polymetis* (no. 7). The fact that the name Athene never appears in the collection as well as this hymn's lack of attention to Athenian myth suggests that the composer is consciously presenting the goddess as a Panhellenic (or even Panmediterranean) divinity.

1 **Pallas**: A common alternate name of Athene, who is often invoked with both. The ancients interpreted the name to mean "brandisher, shaker (of arms)" or "virgin." Another attempt at etymology was offered in Orphism, where the name was thought to refer to the fact that Athene saved Dionysos' heart while it was still "shaking," i.e., beating (see Clement of Alexandria *Protrepticus* 2.18.1 and West 1983, p. 162). In some accounts, Pallas is the name of a giant that Athene killed in the Gigantomachy and from whom she took the name (see note to line 12 and Burkert 1985, p. 140). This giant is said to be her father in some versions of this story, thus offering a faint reflection of the implicit threat to Zeus that Athene and her unborn brother once posed (compare also her role with Poseidon and Hera in a failed

coup against Zeus at *Iliad* 1.396–406). The name Pallas appears in the Gurôb Papyrus; see Graf/Johnston 2007, pp. 188–189.

4–5 hilltops / . . . mountains: One of Athene's most important cult functions was her role as protector of the polis, and so she was often worshipped on fortifications built on top of hills and mountains used to defend the polis (see Burkert 1985, p. 140, for a list of historical sites). In this context, though, her association with mountains connects her to Dionysos as well as other figures such as the Kouretes (see *OH* 31.2, 5), Artemis (see *OH* 36i), and Kybele (see *OH* 27i).

6 frenzy: The madness here is associated with that of battle (see, e.g., *Odyssey* 22.297–309). In some versions of Athene's birth, the gods standing about Zeus recoil in terror as she leaps out in full panoply, roaring. Ares is connected with battle rage (see *OH* 65.6+7n), and Pan, too, is a source of panic on the battlefield and elsewhere (see *OH* 11i). But madness, as well as loud noise, are also typical characteristics of Dionysos (for noise, see *OH* 30.1n; cf. *OH* 30.4n). Athene is also said to cause madness in the wicked (line 9) and to be "frenzy-loving" (line 11), the latter epithet also being used of Pan (see *OH* 11.5, 21). Similar descriptions are used of other divinities, particularly Kybele, with whom the Korybantes/Kouretes are associated (see *OH* 27.13+n).

8 slayer of Gorgo: The epithet is also applied to Athene at Euripides *Ion* 1478; earlier in the play, the story of Athene's triumph over the giant Gorgo in the Gigantomachy is briefly mentioned (987–997); see also note to line 12. After slaying this monster, Athene strips him of his breastplate, which was adorned with snakes. This is the aegis, a common prop for Athene in both literature and iconography. It is sometimes related to Medousa, whom Perseus slew with the help of Hermes and Athene (Apollodoros 2.4.2). In Pindar fragment 70b.17–18, the hissing snakes of Athene's aegis contribute to the gods' celebration of Dionysian rites (see also *OH* 36.2n).

8 blessed mother of the arts: The intelligence of Athene finds outlet not only in war but in skilled labor: for a list, see Homeric *Hymn to Aphrodite* 5.8–15. Hesiod calls a carpenter the "servant of Athene" (*Works and Days* 430). She is credited with assisting in the building of the Trojan Horse (*Odyssey* 8.492–495) and Jason's ship, the *Argo* (Apollonios of Rhodes *Argonautika* 1.18–20, 526–527, etc.). This goddess is sometimes worshipped under the title of Ergane (Worker), e.g., at Athens (Pausanias 1.24.3). The school of Anaxagoras rationalized Athene as skill (*tekhnē*) personified (see Betegh 2004, p. 286).

9 you bring prudence to the virtuous: Athene was identified with prudence by the Stoics; see West 1983, pp. 242–243.

10 male and female: Similarly in Proclus' *Hymn to Athene Polymetis* 7.3. Athene's close association with heroes, her virginity, and her many pursuits that were typically reserved for men all combined to give the goddess a particularly masculine bent (as she declares herself at Aeschylus *Eumenides* 736–738). Likewise, she can be portrayed as rejecting what was considered to be typically feminine behaviors; see Telestes *PMG* 805 (preserved in Athenaios 14.616f–617a), where it is denied that Athene had rejected playing the pipes because they disfigured her face (and where it is asserted that she gave them to Dionysos as a gift), and also Kallimakhos *Bath of Pallas* 13–32. In this collection, though, she is one among a number of divinities that are addressed as androgynous, including Artemis and Dionysos; see *OH* 9.4n.

10 **shrewd**: The Greek word for "shrewd" is "mētis," a play on the name of Athene's mother; see introduction to this hymn. Note that in Orphism Metis is one of the names applied to Protogonos (see *OH* 6i).

11 **many shapes**: Athene often takes disguises when dealing with mortals, particularly in the *Odyssey*; note especially Odysseus' acknowledgment at 13.313. However, this, too, is a characteristic shared by many of the divinities in the collection.

12 **Phlegraian Giants**: For the battle of the Gigantomachy, see Apollodoros 1.6.1–2 and Proclus *Hymn to Athene Polymetis* 7.4. In addition to Pallas (see note to line 1) and Gorgo (see note to line 8), Athene also kills the giant Enkelados by tossing the island Sicily on him, perhaps reminiscent of how her father defeats Typhon (see *OH* 23.5–7n).

12 **driver of horses**: According to Pindar (*Olympian Odes* 13.63–82), Athene invented the bridle and gave it to Bellerophon so he could tame Pegasos, and in gratitude he established an altar to Athene Hippias (Athene the "horse-rider" or "knight"). There was also an altar to Athene Hippias at Olympia (Pausanias 5.15.6). Appropriately enough, she is Diomedes' charioteer during his battle against Ares (*Iliad* 5.793–863).

13 **victorious Tritogeneia**: The Greek word "nikēphore," "victory-bringing," anticipates the following hymn to Nike (Victory); it was also a cult title of Athene at Pergamon. The name Tritogeneia is obscure. It appears already in Homer as an epithet of the goddess (*Iliad* 4.515). Hesiod (*Theogony* 894–898) seems to interpret it as Athene being "born for three" (for herself, her mother, and her unborn brother). The name was also connected in antiquity with Lake Triton, said to be the location of her birth or where she was raised; both the one in Boiotia and the one in Libya were given this honor (see Aeschylus *Eumenides* 292–294, Pausanias 1.14.6 and 9.33.7).

16 **health**: This is also one of the items Proclus requests of Athene at the close of his *Hymn to Athene Polymetis* 7.43–44. Athene was also worshipped as Health in Athens (see Plutarch *Pericles* 13.8 and *OH* 68i).

33. To Nike

Nike (Victory) is first attested at Hesiod *Theogony* 383–385, where she is said to be the daughter of Styx and Pallas and the sister of Zelos (Rivalry), Kratos (Power), and Bia (Force). She never really evolves beyond her origin as a personified abstraction and consequently plays no role in mythology or Orphic literature. At Athens, a temple to Athene Nike was dedicated near the south entrance of the acropolis. The great statue of Athene by Pheidias in the Parthenon portrayed Athene holding a winged Nike in her right hand (Pausanias 1.24.7). We find a similar motif in another statue by Pheidias, this one of Olympic Zeus at Olympia (Pausanias 5.11.1–10). Nike also had her own altar at Olympia (Pausanias 5.14.8). She was a popular cult figure and frequently represented in art; one of the most famous extant sculptures from the ancient world is the Nike of Samothrace (see further *OH* 38i). The position of the hymn in our collection, following the one to Athene, fits the pattern of inserting subordinate divinities immediately after the governing one. Much of the hymn seems to focus on Nike's role in warfare (lines 3–7), which is certainly consistent with the martial motif found in the preceding hymn to Athene. Yet Nike could also be invoked in other agonistic contexts as well, and note that Nike is asked to appear for "works of renown," just as the Stars are asked to visit in the context of a "race for works of renown" (see *OH* 7.13+12–13n and cf. *OH* 76.12+n). Thus the ritual act the initiates are performing appears to merge with the Homeric idea of winning glory in battle. This notion might have further significance beyond endowing the initiation with a certain prestige. Some of the Bacchic gold tablets suggest that the initiates felt that they would join the heroes of old in a pleasant afterlife or even become a hero themselves (see *OH* 87.12n and Graf/Johnston 2007, pp. 115–116); "works of renown" might be referring to a similar idea here.

34. To Apollon

Apollon is one of the chief divinities of the Greek pantheon. Leto, a daughter of the Titans Phoibe and Koios, is his mother and Zeus his father (Hesiod *Theogony* 404–408, 918–920). Artemis is his sister, sometimes born with him, sometimes born shortly before and assisting Leto in his birth on the island Delos (see *OH* 35.5n). Apollon is a god who presides over many spheres; listings of such are common in literature (e.g., Homeric *Hymn to Apollon* 3.131–132, Plato *Cratylus* 405a, and Kallimakhos *Hymn to Apollon* 42–46). He is perhaps most famous for his role in divination, with Delphi being the most renowned of a plethora of oracles in his name. Both sickness and the healing of sickness fall under his jurisdiction, and Asklepios is often said to be his son (see *OH* 67i). Apollon is also the god of archery. This is sometimes joined with his ability to bring disease, as those whom he hits with his arrows suffer sickness and death (e.g., *Iliad* 1.43–52). Music, dance, and festivities are dear to him. He is the god of the lyre, and the one who protects poets (Hesiod *Theogony* 94–95; Homeric *Hymn to the Muses and Apollon*). It is very possible that his connection with the bow facilitated one with this instrument (or vice versa); compare the vivid simile at *Odyssey* 21.404–411 and see also *OH* 67.2n. Orpheus himself is sometimes said to have been one of his sons (Apollodoros 1.3.2). In myth, he almost always appears as a young man, not quite an adult, who can be somewhat dour and aloof, especially in his relation to human beings (e.g., *Iliad* 21.461–467). Nevertheless, the god does have a sense of humor (as at *Odyssey* 8.333–343), and his worship often involves joyous and extravagant displays of music and pomp. Along with Hermes, he is idealized as a paragon of male beauty (see Kallimakhos *Hymn to Apollon* 36–38). Gold and light are often used to describe him and his implements (cf. the tongue-in-cheek treatment at Kallimakhos *Hymn to Apollon* 32–35). His identification with Sun perhaps begins in the late Archaic or early Classical period and is quite common in Hellenistic times and afterward, as well as in Orphic circles (see *OH* 8i). They were originally distinct entities, though, as can be seen in their different genealogies in Hesiod *Theogony* (371–374 vs. 918–920). Apollon was as popular in cult as he was in myth, and he was worshipped widely throughout the Greek-speaking world. Delphi and Delos were his two main cult centers, but he was also particularly important at Sparta and other Dorian cities. For more information, see Burkert 1985, pp. 143–149, and Larson 2007, pp. 86–100; relevant details are noted passim in the notes below. In Orphism, he sometimes brings to Delphi the remains of his half-brother Dionysos, torn apart by the Titans, and there revives him (see *OH* 46i for this story and Dionysian worship at Delphi). His role in Dionysos' death and rebirth is probably the reason for the position of his hymn in the collection; see *OH* 32i. For his possible parentage of the Eumenides in Orphic mythology, see *OH* 70.2–3n.

The structure of this hymn falls into two main divisions. The first part mentions the various traditional associations of the god in terms of cult centers, attributes, and epithets; it comes to an end in line 10, marked by a direct appeal to the god, an element that usually closes a hymn. The second part picks up on the solar aspects mentioned in the first and gives them a cosmic dimension, culminating in the expanded discourse of universal harmony (lines 16–25). This hymn particularly recalls the earlier ones to Sun (*OH* 8) and Pan (*OH* 11) and to a lesser extent Protogonos (*OH* 6). In some ways it functions in a similar manner to *OH* 15–18 in that it fully anthropomorphizes the fundamental abstract powers that constitute the universe (see *OH* 15i). The palpable two-fold division is curiously reminiscent of that in the longer Homeric *Hymn to Apollon*, which easily falls into a Delian (3.1–178) and a Delphic (3.179–546) section (and many scholars suppose that two originally separate hymns have been imperfectly merged into one). It just may be that our composer took a cue from the Homeric hymn, insofar as he understood it. There is a shorter Homeric *Hymn to Apollon* (no. 21) and another one dedicated to both him and the Muses (no. 25). The reader will find it fruitful to consult Kallimakhos' *Hymn to Apollon* (no. 2), as well as Mesomedes' and Proclus' hymns to Sun. Apollon is also invoked with hymnic language in the magical papyri, sometimes with Daphne, one of his mythological lovers (found in the following spells: *PGM* 1.262–347; 2.1–64 and 64–184; 3.187–262; 6.1–47); compare also the invocations of Sun therein (for further references, see *OH* 8i).

1 Paian: Paian seems originally to have been a completely separate divinity from Apollon, but he eventually becomes subsumed under this god. Nevertheless, Paian occasionally remains clearly distinguished, such as in the magical papyri (*PGM* 1.296–297). He gives his name to the "paian," a particular type of song that has strong associations with healing (*Iliad* 1.472–474; and cf. *Iliad* 5.899–904, where the god Paieon heals Ares) and victory (*Iliad* 22.391–394). For an exhaustive overview of both god and song, see Rutherford 2001. The cry "Iē" often accompanies an invocation of Paian (see line 2); for a fanciful etymology, see Kallimakhos *Hymn to Apollon* 97–104. In our collection, the name Paian is also used of Sun (*OH* 8.12), Pan (*OH* 11.11), Dionysos (*OH* 52.11), and Apollon's son Asklepios (*OH* 67.1); the alternate spelling Paion is used of Herakles (*OH* 12.10).

1 slayer of Tityos: This was a giant who tried to rape Leto during her wanderings after she had given birth to Apollon and Artemis. He was shot dead by the baby Apollon (and sometimes by his twin sister Artemis as well) from the arms of his mother. For such a monstrous act, he was punished in a way similar to Prometheus, by having his ever-regenerating liver continually eaten by vultures in the underworld. For the story, see *Odyssey* 11.576–581 and Apollodoros 1.4.1–2. Artemis is also called "slayer of Tityos" in Kallimakhos *Hymn to Artemis* 110.

1 Phoibos . . . Lykoreus: Phoibos (Bright One) is a common epithet of Apollon, found throughout the collection (*OH* O.7, *OH* 35.4, *OH* 67.6, *OH* 79.6). Lykoreus means "the one of Lykoreia," which is the name of the summit of Mount Parnassos at Delphi or a village thereupon; see Strabo 9.3.3 and Pausanias 10.6.2–3. The collocation of Phoibos and Lykoreus is also found at Kallimakhos *Hymn to Apollon* 19 and Apollonios of Rhodes *Argonautika* 4.1490.

2 dweller of Memphis: Apollon is routinely identified with the Egyptian Horus (Herodotos 2.156.5; Plutarch *De Iside et Osiride* 356a and 375f; *PGM* 4.455, 988–989, and 1985). Apollon/Horus does not seem to be particularly connected with Memphis, but perhaps our composer is positing a connection (or confusing him) with Hephaistos/Sun, who was (Herodotos 2.153.1, and see Vanderlip 1972, p. 29 n. 8).

3 Titan: Technically speaking, Apollon is the grandson of a Titan, not a Titan himself; cf. *OH* 36.2. However, Sun is also invoked as Titan in *OH* 8.2, and most likely Apollon is being addressed here in his role as sun god. He is also called Titan at *PGM* 2.86.

3 Pythian god: Pytho was another name used for Delphi or its environs. It is here that Apollon slew a dragon that resided there and that was, in some versions, guarding the oracle held by Earth (for this oracle, see *OH* 79.3–6n and 5n). This story is one of the many variations of a hero slaying a dragon (see Fontenrose 1959 and Watkins 1995). After the monster was killed, Apollon crowed over the corpse that it rot on the spot, and Sun obliged (note the close connection—and distinction—here of Apollon and Sun, perhaps significant in light of their later identification). This was said to be the origin of the name Python, coming from the Greek verb "puthō" ("I rot"); hence the appellation "slayer of Python" in line 4. See Homeric *Hymn to Apollon* 3.300–374 for the canonical account. The story also served as the foundational myth for the Pythian Games, one of the great Panhellenic events of ancient times, second in prestige only to the Olympian Games. There were musical contests as well as athletic ones, and Sakadas, a three-time champion in the competition for instrumental music on the *auloi,* is credited with the creation of the Pythian *nome,* a piece that used music to symbolically describe Apollon's victory over the serpent and that quickly became a standard piece in the aulete's repertoire; for more details, see West 1992, pp. 212–214.

4 Grynean, Sminthian: Gryneion was an Aeolic city near Kyme where a temple and an oracle to Apollon existed. "Sminthian" is a cult epithet, already found in Homer (*Iliad* 1.39). It is usually connected with a Greek word for mouse, and hence could also be translated as "Mouser." This connects Apollon with agriculture, as mice are often a pestilence in the fields as well as the granary.

6 you lead the Muses into dance: Apollon is traditionally the leader of the Muses, and together they entertain the gods (e.g., *Iliad* 1.601–604 and Homeric *Hymn to Apollon* 3.186–206), providing a divine paradigm to be emulated in the human realm. See also *OH* 43i. The Homeric *Hymn to the Muses and Apollon* (no. 25) is probably a hymnic variation on Hesiod *Theogony* 94–97 and 104.

7 Bacchos, Didymeus, Loxias: If "Bacchos" is the correct reading of "Bakkhie," Apollon is being identified with his half-brother. Note that Dionysos is called Paian (*OH* 52.11) and that both gods are "wild" or "savage" (Apollon at line 5 and Dionysos at *OH* 30.3). For the Delphic connection between the two, see *OH* 46i. Apollon is called "ivy-tressed" in the magical papyri (*PGM* 2.99). In Neoplatonic theology, both gods together with Sun form a triad (*Orphic fragment* 305(ii), 311(x), and 322(v); van der Berg 2001, pp. 63 and 170), and in Proclus' hymn to Sun, both Paian/Apollon and Dionysos are his children (1.21–24). One could, however, read "Bakkhie" as "Bacchic" instead, and the evidence cited above could certainly also be used to support this interpretation. Perhaps also relevant is that the Egyptian god Osiris, who was identified with Dionysos, had a brother and a son named Horus, both of whom were identified with Apollon (Herodotos 2.156.5; Plutarch *De Iside et Osiride* 355e–356a). A couple of the manuscripts of the *Orphic Hymns,* though, have "Brankhie." This would refer to Brankhos, who was a lover of Apollon, and became a seer at Didyma (Kallimakhos fragment 229, in Nisetich 2001, pp. 127–129), a town near Miletos that in historic times was famous for its temple to Apollon and oracle (Herodotos 1.42). Brankhos is also credited with delivering Miletos from a plague (Kallimakhos fragment 194.28–31, in

Nisetich 2001, p. 105). The juxtaposition with "Didymeus" in our hymn perhaps speaks for reading "Brankhie." Loxias is a common epithet of Apollon. It means "the oblique one," referring to the riddling and enigmatic character for which Apollon's oracles are (in)famous (cf. Herakleitos in Kirk, Raven, and Schofield 1983, no. 244; for a concrete example, see the famous misinterpretation by Kroisos at Herodotos 1.53 and 1.90–91).

8 the eye that sees all: Here Apollon is clearly identified with Sun; see *OH* 8.1+n. The eye in this line is a terrestrial one, looking down on human activity. Compare with the "gaze" in line 11, which begins the second section, where Apollon's eye encompasses the entire cosmos. When Orpheus invokes Apollon at the beginning of the *Rhapsodies*, he addresses him as the "eye that sees all" (*Orphic fragment* 102; see also West 1983, p. 6).

11–15: The classic tri-partite view of the world, already in Hesiod, is present here: sky-earth-underworld. The expanse of Apollon's gaze is comparable to the power of other divinities described elsewhere in the collection; see *OH* 10.14–16n. There may also be an implied transition day-twilight-night, with the "day" component being understood from the identification Apollon/Sun and his position in the ether.

16–23: The theme of cosmic harmony has already appeared at *OH* 8.9, 11, and *OH* 11.6, but here gets its most detailed treatment, being explicitly connected to the seasons (already anticipated at *OH* 8.9 and perhaps *OH* 11.4). See *OH* 8.9n and 11n, as well as *OH* 11i. The musical ideas expressed in this hymn seem to have been drawn from Claudius Ptolemaeus (called Ptolemy in modern times), the famous astronomer who was active at Alexandria in the second century AD. At *Harmonics* 3.12 he writes: "In connection with these movements, the Dorian tonos, being the most central of the tonoi, we must compare to the middle crossings in latitude, those positioned towards the equinox, as it were, in each sphere. . . . Those tonoi which on account of their higher melody are higher than the Dorian are arranged as if in summer, with the crossings at the raised pole, that is, where the North Pole rises, and with those at the arctic, where the south [sic] is at the opposite. Those which on account of their lower melody are lower than the Dorian are arranged as if in winter, with the crossings at the invisible pole, that is, where the South Pole rises towards those at the arctic, where the North is at opposite" (translation by Solomon 1999, pp. 160–161; see also Barker 1989, pp. 386–387). The geocentric view we find elsewhere in the collection (see *OH* 4.3+n) might also have been influenced by Ptolemy. If there is a connection between him and the *Hymns*, this would provide a fairly secure terminus post quem of around 200 AD for their composition (see further the introduction to the translation). A mode in ancient times represented a collection of notes of certain pitches at fixed intervals out of which a melody might be composed, a kind of tonal palette. Aristides Quintilianus preserves six that he terms ancient ones, among them the Dorian (18.5–19.10; see Barker 1989, pp. 419–420, for translation and notes; see also the discussion in Barker 1984, pp. 165–166). The term Ptolemy employs, "tonos," can also be used to mean "mode," or it can signify what we would call a key (see Barker 1989, pp. 17–27, and West 1992, pp. 184–189). Traditionally, the Dorian mode had the characteristics of being steady, calm, and restrained (it was also considered to be the most manly and dignified; see West 1992, pp. 179–180). Ptolemy, as seen in the quote above, gives a similar valuation to the Dorian *tonos* as the means between extremes (see also *Harmonics* 3.7). The emphasis on the Dorian in our hymn might also have been facilitated by Apollon's prominence among Dorian areas such as Sparta and Krete (see introduction). One of the most famous dictums of the ancient world, "mēden agan" ("nothing in excess"), was inscribed on the temple of Apollon at Delphi. Sun in Proclus' first hymn is said to fill the cosmos with harmony (1.23; see further van den Berg 2001, pp. 169–170 and line 4 of that hymn), while his son Phoibos calms the strife of elements as he sings to the kithara (1.13–14 and 19–20; see van den Berg 2001, pp. 168–169).

24–25: For Pan and his "whistling winds" see *OH* 11.10–12+n. Sun is also associated with string and wind instruments (*OH* 8.11). All three divinities are called Paian in their hymns (see note to line 1). An identification of Pan and Apollon is not as far-fetched as it may seem at first blush. Besides their association with music, both are pastoral gods (see Euripides *Alkestis* 1–7 and Kallimakhos *Hymn to Apollon* 47–54). Pan is connected with Mount Lykaion ("wolf mountain") in Arkadia (see Larson 2007, p. 151) and Apollon is sometimes called "Lykeios" (which can mean "wolf-like, of a wolf"; Pan also bore this name at Tegea). Both Apollon and Pan, among other gods, were also worshipped on Mount Kotilion in Arkadia (see Larson 2007, p. 99). Apollodoros (1.4.1) tells us that Apollon learned prophecy from Pan, but this Pan is said to be the son of Zeus and Hybris and thus to be distinguished from the Pan whose father is Hermes (see *OH* 11i). Nevertheless, such a fine distinction might well be lost or misunderstood, and it is possible that our composer was influenced by an account that made the god Pan Apollon's teacher (a relationship perhaps even intentionally imitating the centaur Kheiron's traditional role in training mortal heroes, including in the arts of music).

35. To Leto

Leto is the daughter of the Titans Koios and Phoibe (Hesiod *Theogony* 404-408; see also line 2 of this hymn). Her importance in Greek myth is fully derived from that of her children, Apollon and Artemis. Hesiod emphasizes her gentle ways; compare also *Iliad* 21.497–504 and the folk-etymologies of her name at Plato *Cratylus* 406a–b. However, even she can be roused to anger, such as when Niobe boasts of her own children (Ovid *Metamorphoses* 6.146–312). She sometimes has her own cult (see Burkert 1985, pp. 171–172), but her role in cult is more often subordinate to one or both of her children, and she seems to have played no role in Orphic myth.

5 Ortygia, . . . Delos: Ortygia (from the Greek "ortux," meaning "quail"), is sometimes another name for Delos, e.g., in Kallimakhos *Hymn to Apollon* 2.59. Leto's sister Asteria, while fleeing the advances of Zeus, turns herself into a quail, dives into the ocean, and becomes the island Delos (Apollodoros 1.4.1). However, these two places are often distinguished from each other, as in Homeric *Hymn to Apollon* 3.16, which is identical to line 5 of this hymn. If Ortygia is to be understood as a separate place, one likely candidate is the small island Rheneia that lies opposite Delos and that, according to Strabo 10.5.5, once was called Ortygia. Thucydides reports that Polykrates, the tyrant of Samos in the middle of the sixth century BC, once chained the two islands together (3.104). Perhaps our composer sees them as two parts that form a unity, for he does refer to Apollon and Artemis as twins in line 1, which would be difficult to reconcile if their respective places of birth were significantly far apart. Nevertheless, calling them twins is conventional, and the "problem" might not have been felt as such; the gods, after all, are capable of many wonders. Of the other places known as Ortygia, the most likely alternate candidate would be the sacred grove near Ephesos, where a competing narrative of the birth of Apollon and Artemis was told (Strabo 14.1.20; for the importance of Ephesos for Artemis, see *OH* 36i). The more traditional account places the birth of Apollon (and sometimes Artemis) on Delos (see Homeric *Hymn to Apollon* 3.14–139, Kallimakhos *Hymn to Delos*, and Apollodoros 1.4.1). Note that Artemis is called Ortygia at Sophokles *Women of Trakhis* 213, and in the *Birds*, Aristophanes puns on a Greek word to call Leto "quail-mother" (870).

36. To Artemis

Artemis, like her brother Apollon, governs many different spheres, some contradictory. She loves to hunt wild animals with her bow and arrow, yet she also protects them. Artemis is called "Mistress of Animals" (e.g., *Iliad* 21.470) and often appears as such in early iconography, usually winged, with animals to her left and/or right that she holds in a firm grasp (e.g., Boardman 1991, pl. 46.2). The wilderness is her domain, particularly forests and mountains, far away from human settlements, but she is also a goddess who protects cities. As our hymn mentions in lines 3–5, she assists in childbirth (including that of her brother, Apollon, according to Apollodoros 1.4.1), even though, as a virgin goddess (Homeric *Hymn to Aphrodite* 5.16–20), she never experiences this process herself. Similarly, she is the one who protects and nurtures the young, while at other times she is blamed for the premature deaths of children. As with many Greek divinities, the ability to do one thing entails the capacity for its opposite, particularly expressed in terms of preservation versus destruction.

The dark side of the goddess is seen in her connection, at least in myth, with human sacrifice. While the Greek army is mustering at Aulis for the expedition to Troy, Agamemnon kills a deer sacred to Artemis. The goddess prevents the Greeks from sailing, and the seer Kalkhas reveals that the only way to propitiate her is for Agamemnon to sacrifice his daughter Iphigeneia as recompense for the slaying of Artemis' "daughter." The father grimly complies (see, e.g., Aeschylus *Agamemnon* 104–257). In some versions of the story, Artemis substitutes a deer for Iphigeneia at the last moment, unbeknownst to the men. This is the storyline adopted in Euripides' *Iphigeneia at Tauris*, but here, too, human sacrifice plays a role: Iphigeneia has been made Artemis' priestess in this barbarous land and now presides over the sacrifice of strangers (cf. Herodotos 4.103.1–2). Her brother Orestes comes to rescue her. They steal the statue of the goddess and bring it back to Athens, where a ritual is enacted that involves a worshipper slightly slitting his throat and letting the drops of blood fall on the altar. Artemis' belligerent nature appears in the great slugfest among the gods at *Iliad* 21.468–496, during which she chides her brother for refusing to fight Poseidon and then is soundly thrashed when confronted by her step-mother Hera.

Yet there is a joyous side to her as well. Nymphs typically attend her as she roams the countryside and hunts. She is also a leader of the dance and song, often as her brother Apollon provides the music (see, e.g., Homeric *Hymn to Artemis* 27.11–20 and Homeric *Hymn to Apollon* 3.186–206). In fact, dances of young girls, particularly those on the cusp of marriage, are a prevalent feature of her worship (for a possible example of which, see Alkman *PMGF* 1). Many of her cults, such as the famous one in the Attic deme of Brauron, are centered on the feminine spheres under her control, which include childbirth and protection of the young. Her most important cult site was in Asia Minor at Ephesos, where her sanctuary numbered among the ancient wonders of the world. According to Kallimakhos, it was the Amazons who instituted sacrifice for Artemis, by setting up a statue and dancing a war dance around it (*Hymn to Artemis* 237–258). For more on her worship, see Burkert 1985, pp. 149–152, and Larson 2007, pp. 101–113.

Artemis became assimilated with many divinities over time (cf. "of many names" in line 1). Her worship at Ephesos was a result of being identified with Kybele (see *OH* 27i), a connection perhaps facilitated through their shared association with mountains and lions (see *OH* 27.2+n; lions often appear in the "Mistress of the Animals"-iconography). The Thracian goddess Bendis, who is at times identified with Kybele, is also matched with Artemis (*Orphic fragment* 257). Very common is Artemis' merging with Moon, and thence with Hekate, as at *Orphic fragment* 356, where Tyche is also added (see further *OH* 1i, *OH* 9i, and *OH* 72.2n). Artemis' concern with childbirth and association with Moon also naturally link her with Eileithyia; see *OH* 2i. Thus the hymns to Hekate (*OH* 1) and Moon (*OH* 9) should also be read closely with this one. Compare further the two Homeric hymns to Artemis (nos. 9 and 27) and Kallimakhos' *Hymn to Artemis*. She plays very little role in Orphism, and consequently our hymn focuses on her traditional attributes.

2 Titanic: Apollon is also called a Titan; see *OH* 34.3+n.

2 Bacchic: Compare also "frenzy-loving" in line 5. Artemis and Dionysos share many traits: mountain haunts, blood-thirsty savagery, Eastern associations, and groups of female followers. Artemis joins a divine Dionysian *thiasos* in Pindar fragment 70b.19–21, and Timotheus (*PMG* 778(b)) might be describing her as a maenad. As "Bacchic" and "torch-bearing" (line 3), she might be so imagined here as well; see *OH* 1.3+n and *OH* 52i. For a possible identification of Apollon and Bacchos, see *OH* 34.7n.

3 torch-bearing goddess bringing light to all: This imagery evokes Artemis' identification with Moon and Hekate; see *OH* 9.3n. In *Orphic fragment* 400, Artemis appears in a list of alternate names for Persephone, which also include Torch-Bearer and Light-Bringer (see also *OH* 40.11+n). She is also called a bringer of light at Kallimakhos *Hymn to Artemis* 204.

3 Diktynna: This is a Kretan goddess, who is sometimes identified with Artemis (Euripides *Hippolytos* 145–147) or made into one of her companions (Pausanias 2.30.3). The maiden fled the amorous attentions of Minos by leaping into the sea (cf. the story of Ino; see *OH* 74i), where she was rescued in the nets of a fisherman (see Kallimakhos *Hymn to Artemis* 189–203). Hence she was called Diktynna, Lady of Nets (Greek "diktuon" means "net"). The name, however, in reality is probably to be connected with Mount Dikte, as in Kallimakhos' telling of the myth. The epithet "lady of Kydonia" in line 12 below refers to the Kretan town, where there was a temple to Diktynna (Herodotos 3.59.2; Strabo 10.4.13). For more on this goddess, see Larson 2007, pp. 177–178.

6 roam in the night: For Moon's movement at night, see *OH* 9.2. Hekate is also closely associated with night; see *OH* 1.5.

7 masculine: There are a number of goddesses who are called masculine in the collection; see *OH* 9.4n.

8 Orthia: This might refer to a temple of Artemis on Mount Lykone in Argos, which also contained cult statues of Apollon and Leto (Pausanias 2.24.5). However, it is more likely an alternate spelling of Ortheia, a Spartan goddess who comes to be identified with Artemis. Part of her worship included boys enduring lashes from their fellows at her altar in a test of endurance; see Pausanias 3.16.7–11, who also gives an account of the origin of the wooden cult statue of the goddess. It is perhaps of note that he says a sanctuary to Eileithyia is not far from the one to Ortheia (3.17.1).

37. To the Titans

The Titans in myth are a group of twelve beings born of Earth and Sky, along with the three Kyklopes and three Hundred-Handers. For the story of their birth and their problems with Sky, and later Zeus, see *OH* 4i and *OH* 13i. In Orphic mythology, the Titans, sometimes spurred by Hera, become jealous when Zeus places the infant Dionysos on his throne. They paint their faces and, with the help of toys and a mirror, lure the child away from the throne despite his being guarded by the Kouretes. They then kill him and eat his corpse. Zeus eventually finds out about this horrid crime and incinerates the Titans with his lightning bolts. The heart of Dionysos is saved by Athene, and this heart serves as the basis for the god's reconstitution. Out of the smoldering ashes of the Titans, charged with Zeus' lightning bolts, is born the human race. Our knowledge of this story comes from later sources, and it is not clear how far back it goes: see *Orphic fragment* 57–59 and 301–331, West 1983, pp. 74–75, Burkert 1985, pp. 297–298, and Graf/Johnston 2007, pp. 66–93. For the significance of this myth for Orphism, see the introduction to the translation. Our hymn obliquely refers to this origin of the human race in lines 2 and 4, and it is expanded to include all living things in line 5; see also *OH* 78.11–12+n, and cf. *OH* 10.14–16+n. The murder of Dionysos is tactfully left out.

3 Tartarean homes: After their defeat by Zeus, the Titans are cast down into Tartaros, a primeval being who had become a particularly gloomy part of the underworld; see *OH* 18.2n. There they are imprisoned, guarded by the monstrous Hundred-Handers (Hesiod *Theogony* 717–735). Despite being locked up in mythology's version of Alcatraz, they can still wreak harm on the upper world. They are among the gods Hera invokes when she strikes the earth with the palm of her hand in a request to give birth apart from Zeus to a powerful child; this results in Typhon, a great monster that threatens the gods and is eventually defeated by Zeus (Hesiod *Theogony* 820–880). She makes a similar, if less sinister, appeal at *Iliad* 14.271–279.

38. To the Kouretes

This is the second hymn in the collection addressed to the Kouretes; for more information on these figures, see *OH* 31i. That hymn concentrates on their more traditional associations with Krete and the Phrygian Kybele. This hymn integrates the Kouretes into a more wide-ranging grouping popular in late antiquity that brought together a number of originally independent bands of male divinities involved with soteriological mystery cults. Explicitly mentioned are the gods of the island Samothrace (lines 4 and 21) and the Dioskouroi (line 21). The cult on Samothrace seems to have had pre-Greek origins but later developed into a Greek mystery cult. It became very popular after the Classical period; one of the most famous statues from antiquity, the Nike of Samothrace, now in the Louvre, was dedicated to the gods of this cult for a naval victory (second century BC). They were in particular supposed to protect sailors from drowning at sea. After a friend had pointed out the dedications from rescued sailors at Samothrace as proof that the gods must exist, the notorious atheist Diagoras of Melos (late fifth century BC) is reputed to have quipped that dead men do not make dedications (Cicero *De natura deorum* 3.89). For more on this mystery cult, see Burkert 1985, pp. 281–285, and Larson 2007, p. 174. The brothers of Helen, Kastor and Polydeukes, were also called on to aid sailors in distress. The phenomenon now known as St. Elmo's fire was in antiquity considered to be their epiphany (see Alkaios fragment 34 and the Homeric *Hymn to the Dioskouroi* no. 33). In myth, they are the sons of Tyndareus, a king of Sparta. Homer in the *Iliad* considers them to be mortal (3.236–244), but later tradition holds Polydeukes, along with Helen, to be descended from Zeus, who surreptitiously mated with Tyndareus' wife Leda in the form of a swan. She gave birth to two pairs of twins, the male Kastor and Polydeukes and the female Klytemnestra and Helen, the first child in each pair descended from Tyndareus and the second from Zeus. Kastor was granted immortality at the request of his brother, but they alternate their time in the land of the living with their time in the kingdom of the dead (see *Odyssey* 11.298–304 and Pindar *Nemean Odes* 10.80–82). They thus can be construed, like Dionysos, as gods who die and are reborn, which may help explain their merging with the gods of Samothrace and the Kouretes here. In fact, the name Dioskouroi is a composite meaning "Zeus' [*dios*] young men [*kouroi*]," "kouroi" being linguistically related to the "kour-" in Kouretes (a word meaning "youths"; see *OH* 31i). Like the Kouretes, they also dance a *pyrrhikhē* (see Plato *Laws* 796d and *OH* 31.1–4n).

This hymn equates the Kouretes, the Dioskouroi, and the gods of Samothrace by associating these figures with the winds that are connected with fertility and the dangers of the sea; what binds these two ideas together, in turn, is the idea that certain winds come at certain seasons (cf. Hesiod's extended discourse on the topic at *Works and Days* 618–694). This hymn should be compared to those addressed to Leuokothea and Palaimon (*OH* 74–75), the winds Boreas, Zephyros, and Notos (*OH* 80–82), the other hymn to the Kouretes (*OH* 31), the one to Korybas (*OH* 39), and the two Homeric hymns to the Dioskouroi (nos. 17 and 33).

1–2: The hymn opens with traditional attributes of the Kouretes. The percussive sound of the beating of brazen arms is analogous to the bronze clappers and cymbals used in ecstatic cult, particularly that of Kybele (see *OH* 27.11n).

2 dwellers of heaven, of earth and sea: Compare also line 8. Numerous divinities in this collection are connected with these three realms; see *OH* 10.14–16n. There is a natural analogue to this, though, since the Kouretes are identified with the winds, which are physically present in all three.

3 life-giving breezes: The Kouretes are connected with fertility, as they are in Kretan cult (see *OH* 31i), but here, and in lines 22 and 24, they are identified with the winds that blow throughout the world. The association is perhaps facilitated by the connection of the Kouretes with Zeus, the storm and weather god. In our collection Hera, who is associated with air, sends "soft breezes" that "nourish the soul" (see *OH* 16.3+n).

6 first to set up sacred rites for mortals: The Kouretes, as in *OH* 31.5, are portrayed as mythical paradigms for actual cult practice; see further *OH* 76.7+n.

13–19: The typical Greek conception that what a god gives can also be taken away by the same god is found here. This is further strengthened by the identification with winds, which can be gentle and beneficial or powerful and destructive. As with many other hymns in the collection, the composer is aware of this contradictory dichotomy so essential to Greek religious thought. The negative side is acknowledged in these lines; the positive side is explicitly desiderated at the end (lines 24–25).

20–21 Kouretes, Korybantes, ... / masters of Samothrace, true Dioskouroi: The hymn reaches a crescendo with the aggregation of various appellations. The Kabeiroi in the opening address to Mousaios seem to be viewed as another name for the Dioskouroi; see *OH* O.20+20–22n and *OH* 39i.

39. To Korybas

Korybas is the singular form of Korybantes, the group of priests and adherents of Kybele who were known to practice rites designed to cure madness (see *OH* 27.13n) and who were often equated with the Kouretes (see *OH* 31i). In this regard, it is significant that Korybas is called Koures, the singular of Kouretes, in line 3 (and see below). Sometimes Korybas is said to be the son of Kybele and the eponymous father of the Korybantes (Diodorus Siculus 5.49). Hippolytos reports of a hymn to Attis, well-known in his time, which was understood by the Naassenes, a sect of Christianity, as expressing their own beliefs (*Refutation of All Heresies* 5.9.8; translation and discussion in Borgeaud 2004, pp. 106–107). In this hymn, Attis is said to have been called Adonis by the Assyrians, Osiris by the Egyptians, Adamna by the Samothracians, Korybas by the Haemonians, and Papas by the Phrygians. "Haemonians" is a synecdoche for Thessalians, a people infamous for its witches (see *OH* 1.1n).

Clement of Alexandria in his *Protrepticus* relates a foundational myth for the rites of the Korybantes (2.19). In this story, they are three brothers; two of the brothers kill the third; they then cover the body with a purple cloth and garlands, convey it on a bronze shield, and bury it on the foothills of Mount Olympos. Clement summarizes the mysteries succinctly as "murders and burials." This story is almost certainly alluded to in line 6 of this hymn. If so, we see that Korybas, thus foully murdered, becomes a restless spirit roaming the earth and potentially wreaking vengeance on any he encounters by driving them to madness; compare with the Erinyes and Melinoe (see *OH* 69i and *OH* 71.4–5+n). Like Melinoe, he is also called on to avert the horrid phantoms he is also capable of sending (see *OH* 71.11n).

Clement further identifies these brothers with the Kabeiroi, another group of divinities found in mystery cults. In fact, these gods are equated at times with those of Samothrace. They are mentioned in the opening address to Mousaios with the Kouretes and Korybantes (see *OH* O.20–22+n), and it seems likely that the association is lurking in the background here, more tightly connecting Korybas with the previous hymn to the Kouretes who are invoked as Samothracian gods (*OH* 38.4, 21; compare also the Attis hymn cited above). What is more, Clement says that the brothers as fugitives took a basket containing the genitals of their dead brother, now called Dionysos, to Etruria, where they established his worship (cf. *OH* 46i). He ends his account by acknowledging that some people with reason call Dionysos Attis. The connection is significant, because Attis castrates himself after suffering madness sent by Kybele (see *OH* 27i). A loose identification among Attis, Dionysos, and Korybas seems to lie at the heart of our hymn. It is probably as a doublet of Dionysos that Korybas is called "the greatest king of eternal earth" (line 1) and "warlike" (line 2 see note) and this identification helps explain why the hymn follows one dedicated to the Kouretes, who in Orphic accounts guard the enthroned infant Dionysos (see *OH* 31i).

The merging of identities is further underscored by the presence of Demeter in this hymn, called Deo in line 7. This goddess is sometimes equated with Rhea and Kybele (see *OH* 14i and *OH* 27i). Clement, in his discussion of the Korybantic rites, notes that the priests, called "Lords of the Rites" (Greek "Anaktotelestai"), do not allow celery to be placed on the altar, since they consider it to have been born from the blood of the murdered brother. He then compares this taboo with the worship of Demeter during the Thesmophoria festival, where pomegranate seeds that have fallen on the floor are forbidden to be consumed on the grounds that such seeds were born from the blood of Dionysos. Clement's discussion of the Eleusinian Mysteries frames his account of the rites of the Kabeiroi. Interestingly enough, Psellos at *Quaenam sunt graecorum Opiniones de daemonibus* 3 says that a Korybas and a Koures were mimetic forms of demons who were included in the initiation to the Eleusinian Mysteries. Prima facie, this indicates that the pair Korybas/Koures belonged to that part of Orphic/ Dionysiac demonology that became connected with Eleusis, at least in the minds of those who tried to unravel the mysteries. It is therefore no surprise that the block of four "Eleusinian" hymns in our collection immediately follow this one.

Korybas, then, as an analogue of the murdered Dionysos, ends the theme of this god's rebirth that is implicit in *OH* 31–38, which are addressed to figures who played a role in this endeavor (and divinities subordinate to them), and which transitions to the central section of the collection (see further *OH* 30i, *OH* 32i, *OH* 40i).

2 the warlike: This is an adjective used of Dionysos at *OH* 30.4 and of the Kouretes' weapons at *OH* 38.1 and 7.

8 into the shape of a savage, dark dragon: The significance of this is obscure. It is probably alluding to some myth now lost to us. Clement cites an anonymous poet referring to the birth of Dionysos from Persephone and Zeus: "A bull, father of a dragon [or: snake], and a father of a bull, a dragon [or: snake]; / in the mountain an oxherd carries his secret goad" (*Protrepticus* 2.16.3). Note that Demeter's chariot is drawn by dragons in the following hymn (see *OH* 40.14+n).

40. To Eleusinian Demeter

Demeter is the goddess of agriculture, specifically of cereals and their cultivation. She is one of the "original six" Olympians born from Kronos and Rhea. However, as one of the most important fertility goddesses in the Greek pantheon, she often is identified with Earth herself. In antiquity, her name was commonly analyzed as "dē" (believed to have been a variant of "gē," "earth") and "mētēr" ("mother"); *Orphic fragment* 399, for example, addresses her as "Earth mother of all, Demeter, giver of prosperity and wealth." This identification extends to other fertility goddesses as well, such as Rhea and Kybele (see *OH* 14i and *OH* 27i). It is reported that Orpheus himself supposedly claimed Rhea was known as Demeter after the birth of Zeus, etymologizing the "dē" element as related to the "di-" root in Zeus' name (*Orphic fragment* 206). Zeus mates with her, and she gives birth to a daughter, Persephone, with whom she is closely connected in cult. We find mention of this already in Hesiod *Theogony* 912–914. In Orphic accounts of this union, Demeter, here equated with her mother Rhea, attempts to flee the amorous attentions of her son Zeus by transforming herself into a snake. Undeterred, Zeus does likewise, and from this was born Persephone, who has monstrous features that frighten her mother away (see *OH* 14i). A similar story is found in Arkadia; here, Demeter turns herself into a horse to escape Poseidon, who follows suit. Their children are the Erinyes and the wonder horse Areion (see *OH* 69i). The ophidian rape by Zeus has been diplomatically omitted from this hymn.

The most important myth concerning Demeter is the abduction of Persephone by Hades, memorably told in the beautiful Homeric *Hymn to Demeter*. The story, however, is not mentioned at all in this hymn but in the following one to Mother Antaia, another name of Demeter, as well as in *OH* 18, *OH* 29 and *OH* 43. For details, see *OH* 41i. It is notable that again, just as in the case of Zeus' rape of Demeter, the unpleasantness of the abduction of Persephone is passed over in silence in this hymn.

The account of Persephone's abduction, Demeter's search for her, and their consequent reunion formed the foundation myth of the Eleusinian Mysteries, which were very old, perhaps performed in some form as far back as the bronze age. Eleusis is a village that was originally independent of Athens but eventually became part of its territory at some point before the seventh century. The cult was appropriated by the Athenians, who in later times worked hard to give these local mysteries Panhellenic importance, much like Delphi. In this they were quite successful. The mysteries were very popular and continued unabated until officially shut down by the emperor Theodosius in 392 AD, although they were by then already largely neglected. For details of the cult, see Burkert 1985, pp. 285–290, and Larson 2007, pp. 69–85, who also discusses other cults of Demeter and Persephone. The Eleusinian Mysteries were concerned with securing wealth and happiness in this life and a better fate in the hereafter—concerns which we find also in Dionysian/Orphic mysteries, among others, as well. Our hymn focuses exclusively on the material benefits of this life, and it radiates a joy in the wealth and abundance of the world, which may help to explain the omissions of the unsavory mythological elements as noted above. The Eleusinian Mysteries might also be specifically mentioned in our collection because they were felt to have special connection with the actual cult in which the *Hymns* were in use. It is notable that Mousaios had connections with the Mysteries; see *OH* Oi. Their prestige might also be a factor in their appearance throughout the collection; compare their possible influence on the early development of the Orphic myth of Dionysos in Graf/Johnston 2007, pp. 73–75. At any rate, the polytheistic nature of Greek religion made such associations possible. One may be a member of many mystery religions, to hedge one's bets as it were. On one of the Bacchic gold tablets, for example, the initiate claims to "have the rites of Bacchos and Demeter Chthonia and the Mountain Mother" (no. 28). Most likely some, if not all, of our initiates were members in other mystery cults, too.

This hymn is the first of a group of four with Eleusinian themes. It comes in the middle of the collection (in terms of number of lines), and it leads directly to the ritual complex involving Dionysos (see *OH* 44i), which probably was the high point of the rite during which these hymns were originally performed. It is perhaps not accidental that Eleusinian Demeter receives the most elaborate request at the end of her hymn: peace, law, wealth, and health. A number of hymns before this one mention three of these items in their closing appeals (see *OH* 15i), and the only hymns that mention even two of these afterward are *OH* 65 and *OH* 84.

1 **Deo**: This name of Demeter is usually understood by modern scholars to be a shortened form of "Demeter," although it is possible that it is just a by-form of the "dē" element. Ancient scholars saw it as such and tried to attach it to words that alluded to aspects of her mythology. For example, the author of the Derveni papyrus, in his interpretation of a poem by Orpheus, asserts that the "dē" is derived from a Greek verb meaning "to tear, to cut up" and explains that Zeus injured the goddess during intercourse, something which he reports that Orpheus "makes clear" later in the poem he was reading (see Betegh 2004, pp. 189–190; the Derveni author might be giving an allegorical meaning to an explicit mention of plowing).

2 nurturer of youths: This epithet is applied to other divinities in our collection: Hekate (*OH* 1.8), Artemis (*OH* 36.8), and Eirene (Peace) in the hymn to Ares (*OH* 65.9; cf. *OH* 12.8 and *OH* 19.22). As the hymn to Ares makes clear, peace and agriculture are closely linked, for when there is no war, men turn their swords to ploughshares; compare lines 4 and 19 of this hymn. Demeter may also be seen as a nurturer of youths insofar as she was nurse to Demophoön and tried to make him immortal (Homeric *Hymn to Demeter* 2.98–255). This same epithet recurs in line 13.

8–9: Those who were the first to do something were held in high regard by the ancient Greeks, who did not hesitate to invent such figures and/or give credit to the gods when no historical personage was at hand. Here Demeter is lauded as the first to create crops and the first to develop the technical means to harvest them. In respect to the latter, she fits the pattern of the culture hero, the one whose innovations pave the way for the development and improvement of human civilization; cf. *OH* 38.6+n and *OH* 76.7+n, where the Kouretes and the Muses respectively teach mortals the sacred rituals (as does Demeter in the Homeric *Hymn to Demeter* 2.473–482). The most famous divine culture hero in myth is probably Prometheus (see, for example, Aeschylus *Prometheus Bound* 436–506, and cf. *OH* 28i and *OH* 66i). Demeter is said to have taught the Eleusinian prince Triptolemos the secrets of agriculture, and he in turn traveled the world to teach his fellow man. We find Demeter linked to plowing in Hesiod's injunction to his brother to pray to Demeter and Chthonian Zeus right before beginning to plow (*Works and Days* 465–469). Another early connection between the goddess and agricultural technique is found in a Homeric simile where Demeter is shown separating grain from chaff (*Iliad* 5.499–502).

10 Bromios: Another name for Dionysos; the name means the "roarer" (cf. *OH* 30.1+n). This god becomes associated with Demeter at Eleusis through Iacchos, who seems to be a personified form of the cry the sacred procession would shout out on their way to Eleusis; see *OH* 42.4+n.

11 torch-bearing and pure: Torches are typical staples in the process of celebrating fertility divinities, who often have their festivities celebrated at night, including Dionysian revels (see *OH* 52i and *OH* 54.10). They were an important part of the Eleusinian cult, as might be deduced from the title of one of its highest functionaries, the Dadoukhos (a word meaning "torch-bearer"); see *OH* 42.4n. Demeter carries a torch while fasting and in search of her daughter (Homeric *Hymn to Demeter* 2.47–50, 59–63), and Artemis-Persephone is called Torch-Bearer" (see *OH* 36.3n). See further *OH* 9.3n. Purity is a general concern in Greek religion but especially in matters such as initiations. For example, potential initiates in the Eleusinian Mysteries needed to bathe themselves in the sea along with the pig they were to sacrifice. Both these adjectives, then, are as much descriptive of our initiates as they are of the goddess herself. See also *OH* 30.4+n.

14: A different kind of yoking than mentioned in line 8. Triptolemos is often portrayed in a winged chariot, bringing the knowledge of Demeter to all (see Boardman 1991, p. 219, Boardman 1975, p. 226, and Boardman 1989, p. 226). The dragons here are symbolic of Demeter's chthonic connection; compare line 12 where the goddess is addressed as appearing from beneath the earth. Demeter Chthonia (Demeter From Beneath the Earth) was in fact worshipped at Hermione (see Larson 2007, pp. 78–79). The dragons might also have a connection with Korybas, who in the previous hymn was said to have taken the form of a dragon in accordance with "Deo's thinking" (lines 7–8), an obscure allusion.

15: Demeter is here described in maenadic terms; see *OH* 1.3n. The throne might be referring to Kybele's throne (see *OH* 27.5+9n). The circular movement perhaps symbolizes the revolution of the celestial bodies around the earth (see *OH* 4.3n).

16 only daughter . . . many children: The contrasting juxtaposition is typical of our poet's style, but the reference here is somewhat puzzling. Persephone is usually her only child in myth, but Demeter sometimes is said to have children beside her. In an early myth, she has as a lover the mortal hero Iasion, with whom she lies in a thrice-plowed field. From this union she gives birth to Ploutos (Wealth; see *OH* 18i), but Iasion is killed by Zeus (Hesiod *Theogony* 969–974 and *Odyssey* 5.125–128; see also Homeric *Hymn to Demeter* 2.488–489). Herodotos mentions that Aeschylus (in a play now lost to us) made Artemis the daughter of Demeter on the basis of an Egyptian tale (2.156.5–6); the historian, however, is skeptical of this last detail. Kallimakhos says that Hekate was the daughter of Demeter (fragment 466; see *Orphic fragment* 400). Since Artemis and Hekate eventually are identified as the same goddess, it is possible that both births point to one original account, perhaps Orphic. They both might have already been identified with Persephone, too (see *OH* 29i). However, in our collection Persephone is explicitly said to be Demeter's only daughter (*OH* 29.1–2). It is difficult, though not impossible, to construe "many" to just mean Persephone-Artemis-Hekate and Ploutos. On the other hand, "many children" may be symbolic insofar as Demeter is viewed as a nurturer of children (see lines 2 and 13) or it may be used in the sense that the crops she sends up are "her children." The attribute "only daughter" is even more puzzling, as she has two sisters, Hestia and Hera, in conventional mythology. But Demeter was equated with Hestia and Hera in early Orphic thought (see *OH* 14i and Betegh 2004, p. 222), and our composer might have in mind Demeter as the personification of female fertility in these lines; this gains some support from the general description of her powers in line 17 and the "many children" in line 16, if we are to understand this attribute broadly.

18–20: The repetitions augment the sense of religious fervor and insistence as the hymn closes with a mighty crescendo. The theme running throughout the hymn, that Demeter is a goddess who brings benefits that contribute to the well-being of both the individual and society, is neatly summarized in these lines. The word "riches" is a translation of the Greek "ploutos," which alludes to her son Ploutos (see note to line 16 above). Peace and rule of law might be intended as personifications of two of the Seasons, Eirene and Eunomia respectively (see *OH* 43i), and perhaps health should be personified as well (Hygeia), the addressee of *OH* 68; see also *OH* 15.10–11n.

41. To Mother Antaia

Mother Antaia is here another name for Demeter. The mythological complex surrounding the abduction of Persephone, absent in the previous hymn, is the focus of this one. Indeed, one of the remarkable features about the hymn is that more than half of it is narrative, a departure from the usual aggregation of epithets, names, and description.

The Homeric *Hymn to Demeter* contains the most famous version of the myth. Demeter fasts in grief after her daughter's disappearance, although she does not know yet that Hades has abducted her. Hekate comes to assist her, and they find out from Sun what has happened. Depressed, Demeter wanders the world disguised as an old woman (cf. also *OH* 74i). She eventually reaches Eleusis and becomes a nurse to Demophoön, the newly born son of the king of Eleusis. The baby becomes a kind of surrogate child for the goddess. The mother one night sees the nurse putting her son in the fire and cries out, not knowing that Demeter had intended to make him immortal. In anger Demeter leaves but not before ordering that a temple be built in her honor and promising to introduce rites in Eleusis later. For now, she keeps apart from the gods and causes a great famine with the intent to wipe out the human race and thus deprive the gods of the sacrifices they so very much crave. Hades is willing to let Persephone return, but she has already tasted of the pomegranate seeds he had given to her. Therefore she cannot remain permanently in the land of the living. For the one part of the year she must remain in the underworld with her husband; during this time Demeter grieves over her daughter and nothing grows. However, during the other two parts of the year, she is reunited with her daughter, and in her joy life flourishes anew. Thus the myth explains the origins of the seasons, which the ancient Greeks generally numbered three (see *OH* 29i). At the end of the poem, Demeter returns to the plains of Rharion outside of Eleusis. She restores the crops and teaches her mysteries, as she had promised, to the princes of Eleusis. There are a number of allusions to this story that are sequentially spread over a number of hymns in the collection; see *OH* 43i. For a similar story involving Kybele, see *OH* 27i. The abduction of Persephone and the wanderings of Demeter were the subject of at least one poem attributed to Orpheus (collected under *Orphic fragment* 379–402; see Richardson 1974, pp. 77–86, for a discussion of the versions of Orpheus, Mousaios, and Eumolpos). Relevant details are in the notes passim.

1 **Antaia**: The word is properly an adjective with the base meaning of "opposite" and further specialized senses of "hostile" and "besought with prayers." As an adjective it is used of Kybele in Apollonios of Rhodes *Argonautika* 1.1141. Later grammarians say that it was also used as a proper name for Rhea and Hekate. It is therefore not surprising to see Demeter called by this name. Both the negative and positive connotations of the word are probably intended in this hymn. The goddess was once hostile to men; now they shower her with prayers, as this hymn does.

1–2 **mother / of immortal gods and of mortal men**: Similarly described are Rhea (*OH* 14.8–9), Earth (*OH* 26.1), and Kybele (*OH* 27.7); see also *OH* 10.1+n.

4: In the Homeric *Hymn to Demeter* 2.192–211, after the disguised Demeter agrees to be a nurse for Demophoön, she comes to Eleusis. She stands brooding in the palace until an old woman, Iambe, offers her a stool covered with a white fleece. Demeter sits but says nothing until Iambe tells her jokes that make her laugh. She refuses wine from the queen but asks instead that they make for her a drink made of water, barley-meal, and pennyroyal. It is with this that she breaks her fast. The drink, known as the *kukeon*, was also imbibed by initiates at the Eleusinian Mysteries. In the Orphic version(s), Iambe does not appear, but instead we find a woman named Baubo, a native Eleusinian, who gets the mourning mother to laugh by exposing her pudenda and who then offers her the *kukeon* that Demeter had earlier refused (Clement of Alexandria *Protrepticus* 2.20.3–21.1; *Orphic fragment* 394–395).

5–7: In the Homeric *Hymn to Demeter*, it is not the goddess but rather Hermes who goes into the underworld to fetch Persephone. Dysaules is the husband to Baubo (see the note to line 4 above). Pausanias reports that the Phliasians claim that he was the brother to Keleos (king of Eleusis in the Homeric *Hymn to Demeter*), that he came to them after being expelled by an Athenian, and that he taught them the mysteries (2.14.2). Pausanias is skeptical of the story, remarking that Dysaules is not mentioned among the group instructed by Demeter in her Homeric hymn and citing lines 2.474–476, but he admits that Dysaules might have arrived due to some other reason (2.14.3). In the Orphic version, Dysaules' sons Triptolemos and Eubouleus inform Demeter of the abduction of Persephone, and she teaches them the knowledge of agriculture as a reward (Pausanias 1.14.3). Clement of Alexandria tells us that Triptolemos was a cowherd and Eubouleus a swineherd and that the swine of Eubouleus fell into the earth during the abduction of Persephone (*Protrepticus* 2.20.2 and 2.17.1; see *Orphic fragment* 390–391). The latter is adduced to explain the custom in the Thesmophoria, a festival in honor of Demeter and Persephone, of women throwing pigs in a pit and later taking back the rotting corpse (see Larson 2007, p. 70), which would seem to be symbolic of Persephone's (and Demeter's?) journey. It is likely that Eubouleus is the one to whom the "innocent child of Dysaules" refers in this hymn. At Eleusis, there was a god named Eubouleus who was considered to have brought Persephone back up from the underworld, much like Hermes does in the Homeric *Hymn to Demeter*.

8: A problematic line. As it stands, Euboulos might be a vague reference to Ploutos, the son of Demeter and Iasion (see *OH* 40.16n), or to the Kretan grandfather of the goddess Diktynna (another name of Artemis; see note to *OH* 36.3n), whom Diodorus Siculus calls the son of Demeter (5.76.3). Elsewhere in the collection, Hades is called Euboulos (*OH* 18.12). The name might be an alternate form of Eubouleus, but it cannot refer to the one mentioned in the previous line. Eubouleus is also used of gods: Hades, Zeus, Dionysos, and Protogonos (see *OH* 6i). None would fit the context, however. This led Theiler to suggest changing the Greek verb "bore" to "made": the sense then would be that Demeter changed Eubouleus (who had helped her find and retrieve Persephone) into a god, and thus he was no longer bound by human needs. This would fit in neatly with the story of Demophoön in the Homeric *Hymn to Demeter* and with the fact that there was a god Eubouleus at Eleusis (see note to lines 5–7 above). Note, too, that on some Bacchic gold tablets it is claimed that the initiate will become a god (nos. 3, 5, 9; see *OH* 87.12n). A third possibility is that something has fallen out between lines 7 and 8. The "you" might then be someone else, such as Persephone.

42. To Mise

Mise is an obscure goddess who appears to be connected with Demeter and Eleusis. She is mentioned in a poem by Herodas, in which a character sees a girl at a "Descent of Mise," a cultic context that suggests a journey to the underworld (*Mimiamb* 1.56). In the lexicon of Hesykhios, she is connected with Meter and said to be invoked in oaths (entry M 1442). The name might appear in an account attributed to Asklepiades of Tragilos (fourth century BC) by Harpocration (see *Orphic fragment* 391), who says that the Eleusinian pair Dysaules and Baubo had two daughters, Protonoe and Nisa, the latter name possibly a corruption of "Misa," which would be another form of "Mise." Two inscriptions have been discovered bearing the name. One was found in the precinct of Demeter in Pergamon, the other on an altar dedicated by a priestess to "Mise Kore" near Pergamon. For a review of the evidence and interpretation, see Ricciardelli 2000, pp. 398–400 and Morand 2001, pp. 169–174. In this hymn, Mise is identified with Dionysos and seems to be a reflection of the female side of the god who elsewhere appears androgynous (see note to line 4). Whether they are considered distinct or the same is difficult to determine. The Eleusinian connection is strong in the beginning portion of the hymn: the epithet "law-giving" in line 1 is also a cultic title of Demeter and Persephone, Iacchos was the name of a god chanted by the sacred procession to Eleusis (see note to line 4), and Eleusis is the first place mentioned in the list found in lines 5–10. The three goddesses mentioned in lines 6–10 are all connected with a young boy who dies and is reborn: Meter and Attis (see *OH* 27i), Aphrodite and Adonis (see *OH* 56i), and Isis and Osiris, who already in the Classical period was identified with Dionysos (Herodotos 2.144; see also Diodorus Siculus 1.13.5 and 1.22.7–23.8 and Plutarch *De Iside et Osiride* 364e ff.). For the identification of Isis with Aphrodite, Meter, Demeter, and other goddesses, see *OH* 55.15–28n.

1 **fennel stalk**: A reference to the thyrsos; see *OH* 45.5n.

2 **unforgettable and many-named seed**: See also *OH* 50.2+n.

4 **Iacchos**: Participants in the Eleusinian Mysteries would walk from Athens to Eleusis at night by torchlight with song, dance, and bawdy banter; see *OH* 40.11n. The god invoked was Iacchos, who seems to be a personification of the cry "iakkhe!" This god was identified with Dionysos; see Sophokles *Antigone* 1146–1152. The chorus of initiates calls on Iacchos in their procession in Aristophanes *Frogs* 340–353 and 372–416, and a ghost procession is supposed to have materialized during the Persian Wars as a sign of the eventual disaster of the Persian campaign (Herodotos 8.65). The name Iacchos appears in the Eleusinian myth in which Baubo exposes her genitals to the mourning Demeter (*Orphic fragment* 395 and see *OH* 41.4n), where there probably was a pun on "iakkhos" ("female genitalia") and Iacchos, who sometimes is regarded as the child of Demeter; see Graf 1974, pp. 194–199. Iacchos also played a role in the Lenaia, an Athenian festival (see *OH* 50i). For the androgyny of Dionysos, see *OH* 30.2n; for a list of androgynous deities in the *Hymns*, see *OH* 9.4n.

6 **mystic rites in Phrygia**: Compare *OH* 49.2–3 where Hipta, a nurse of Dionysos, is said to take part in the mysteries of Sabos and the dances of Iacchos.

9–10 **your divine mother, / . . . black-robed Isis**: The epithet "black-robed" is used of the goddess in the third hymn to Isis by Isidoros (3.34); see Vanderlip 1972, p. 62. For Isis as the mother of Dionysos, see Plutarch *De Iside et Osiride* 365e–f.

10 **train of nurses**: A reference to the Nymphs who took the infant Dionysos after the death of Semele; see *OH* 46.2–3n.

11 **contests**: The Stars, too, are asked to come to the "learned contests of this sacred rite"; see *OH* 7.12+12–13n.

43. To the Seasons

The Seasons (Greek Horai), as their name suggests, are the personifications of the seasons. This hymn adopts the Hesiodic genealogy (*Theogony* 901–903) that makes them the daughters of Zeus and Themis ("established custom" or "law"), and, like their mother, they represent an aspect of the cosmic order (see further *OH* 79i). For Homer, these divinities are in charge of access to Olympos (*Iliad* 5.748–751) and in one scene take care of the horses of Hera and Athene when they return (*Iliad* 8.432–435). The Orphic *Rhapsodies* follow Hesiod with respect to the birth and names of the Seasons (*Orphic fragment* 252). Their names mean "law-abiding" ("eunomia"), "justice" ("dike"), and "peace" ("eirene"). Dike has her own hymn (*OH* 62), Eunomia is the mother of the Graces (*OH* 60.2), and both Eunomia and Eirene are summoned, though not personified, at the end of the hymn to Eleusinian Demeter (*OH* 40.19; but see *OH* 40.18–20n). According to Pausanias (9.35.2), however, at Athens there were only two Seasons worshipped, whose names were Karpo (Fruit) and Thallo (Blossom). The Seasons do not merely embody the seasons but also come to represent youthful feminine beauty as well. They clothe Aphrodite when she emerges from the sea and adorn her with numerous ornaments (Homeric *Hymn to Aphrodite* 6.5–18), and they crown the newly-fashioned Pandora with a garland of spring flowers (Hesiod *Works and Days* 74–75). This connection with spring and flowers is emphasized in this hymn, which fits the context of fertility introduced with Eleusinian Demeter (*OH* 40).

The Seasons are also linked with the myth of Persephone's abduction and return in our collection. The entire story is scattered over several hymns, but nevertheless the chronological order is maintained; in performing the hymns, the initiates recreate the myth piecemeal. The abduction portion appears in two earlier hymns: the one to Plouton, where there is brief narration (*OH* 18.12–15), and the one to Persephone (*OH* 29.14). The next part, Demeter's search and recovery of her daughter, again with short narration, is told in the hymn to Mother Antaia (*OH* 41.3–7). Now in this hymn, the cycle is completed. Every year, Persephone's reappearance in the land of the living heralds the beginning of spring, the season of growth. It is not surprising, then, to see the personifications of spring dancing with her in celebration of the return of life (see also *OH* 29.9–13); note in particular the "circling dances" and "come forth to the light" in line 8 and that their dancing pleases "Zeus and their mother, giver of fruits" in line 9. "Their mother" refers to Themis, who rejoices that the cosmic order, manifested in the cycle of seasons, is maintained. The idea of renewal is also important to Dionysos, the focus of the previous hymn, both because he is a fertility god himself and also because he was reborn, just like his mother Persephone (albeit metaphorically). In this context, the invocation at the end of the hymn that the goddesses appear to the new initiates has special point. They, too, are being "born again" into a new life (see *OH* 30i). It also segues into the theme of birth, which had appeared in the earlier hymns of the collection and which will dominate *OH* 44–55 (see *OH* 44i).

The Fates, too, join the festivities. They do so not only because they are the (half-)sisters of the Seasons (see *OH* 59i) but also because they have a natural interest in the cosmic order as well. The seasons recur as they are fated to do so. We find the Seasons and Fates linked in cultic contexts. In the precinct of Zeus at Athens, Pausanias saw an unfinished statue of the god with both groups above his head (1.40.4). On the altar at Amyklai they were depicted next to Demeter, Persephone, and Plouton, along with Aphrodite, Athene, and Artemis (Pausanias 3.19.4).

The Graces naturally take part in the dance as well. They are very similar to the Seasons in that they, too, are a plurality of three young women who are paradigmatic of feminine beauty and charm (see *OH* 60i). They join the Seasons in adorning Pandora (Hesiod *Works and Days* 73–74). In perhaps one of the most beautiful scenes from ancient Greek literature, both groups dance in a circle with Hebe, Harmonia, and Aphrodite. In their midst Artemis sings. Ares and Hermes play along with them. And all of this is in tune with the glorious music of

Apollon as he expertly plays the lyre (Homeric *Hymn to Apollon* 3.186–206). Our composer has skillfully captured the essence of this joie de vivre and grafted it to a genuine religious awe before the uncanny powers of fertility. It is a fitting coda to the block of four hymns with Eleusinian themes.

44. To Semele

Semele is one of the daughters of Kadmos, the founder of Thebes. Zeus falls in love with her, and they begin to have an affair. Eventually Semele, sometimes at the instigation of a disguised and jealous Hera, secures an oath from Zeus and then demands that he appear to her as he does to his wife. Thus constrained, Zeus reluctantly complies; he reveals himself to the mortal woman in his full stature as god of thunder and lightning. The resulting fireworks burn Semele to a crisp. Zeus notices that she was pregnant, and he decides to save the unborn child. He sews it up in his thigh, and, once it reaches full maturity, Zeus gives "birth" to his son, Dionysos; see Euripides *Bacchae* 1–42, Apollodoros 3.4.3, Ovid *Metamorphoses* 3.257–313, *Orphic fragment* 328, and *OH* 48.3+n and *OH* 50.3+n. Sometimes Dionysos is given to Semele's sister, Ino, to nurse, and she in turn is further pursued by Hera (see *OH* 74i); in other versions, baby Dionysos is given to his half-brother Hermes, who hands the child off to the Nymphs in the East to rear (see *OH* 51i), sometimes with Silenos (see *OH* 54.1+n). For the nurse Hipta, see *OH* 49i. Semele is already mentioned as the mother of Dionysos by Homer (*Iliad* 14.325), by Hesiod (*Theogony* 940–942), and in the three Homeric hymns to Dionysos (1.21, 7.1, 26.2). An alternate name for her is Thyone (Homeric *Hymn to Dionysos* 1.21, Sappho fragment 17, Apollodoros 3.5.3). The Orphics offered a different version, namely that Dionysos, sometimes called Zagreus, was the son of Zeus and Persephone (see *OH* 29i), but some accounts attempt to retain the traditional genealogy; for a reconstruction of how and why this was done, see Graf/Johnston 2007, pp. 74–80. In one of these versions, after Dionysos is killed by the Titans, Athene saves his heart and brings it to Zeus; he promptly cuts it up, makes a little soup out of it, and feeds it to Semele, who then is impregnated and gives birth to Dionysos; see *Orphic fragment* 314–316 and 327, Proclus *Hymn to Athene Polymetis* 7.7–15 (translation and commentary in van den Berg 2001, pp. 277 and 287–293), West 1983, pp. 162–163, and Graf/Johnston 2007, p. 78. In our collection, both Semele and Persephone are called the mother of Dionysos, but in one case it is implied that Persephone received Dionysos to rear after he was born (presumably by Semele; see *OH* 46.6–7+n, and cf. *OH* 30.2+n).

This hymn begins a series (through *OH* 54) whose focus is on Dionysos; in particular, these hymns are linked by the motif of (re)birth, a theme that is prevalent at the beginning of the collection (see *OH* 2i). A number of them refer to ritual contexts and, insofar as the hymns are performative acts (see *OH* 30i), probably reflect something of the actual activities of our cult during this particular rite, though details are vague; see lines 6–9 and note.

3 thyrsos-bearing: A typical attribute of Dionysos and his followers; see *OH* 45.5+n.

6–9: There is a tradition that Dionysos descended into the underworld to retrieve his mother and convey her to Olympos (Pausanias 2.37.5; cf. Pindar *Olympian Odes* 2.25–28 and the comic parody in Aristophanes *Frogs*, in which Dionysos goes to fetch the recently-departed playwright Euripides). Here, though, it seems that Persephone has received her kindly in the underworld. Semele might originally have been an earth goddess, and these lines might be an indirect remnant of this tradition. The "ritual of the table" is obscure. Perhaps it is related to the myth mentioned in the introduction to the hymn that has Zeus feeding Semele Dionysos-soup. Note the phrase "all mortal men reenact your travail," which of course suggests birth, and it would certainly be easier for a worshipper to drink soup in a ritual context than to be set on fire (see also *OH* 47.5n). The idea of ingesting the god is already bound together with his role as god of wine and the concept of *enthousiasmos* (see *OH* 30i). See also Graf/Johnston 2007, p. 156.

45. Hymn to Dionysos Bassareus and Triennial

Dionysos is already the addressee of *OH* 30, but this hymn is the first of a series dedicated to a specific cultic identity of Dionysos. Here he is invoked as Bassareus and Triennial; cf. *OH* 52, which is addressed to Triennial and which mentions Bassaros in line 12, a variant of Bassareus. This epithet is derived from the Thracian word "bassara," "fox" and, by extension, the fox-skin worn at times by the god and his maenads. Thracian maenads could be called Bassarids, and a lost play by Aeschylus bears their name as a title. In this play, it seems they tear apart Orpheus, who, incidentally, is their countryman. The violence mentioned in our hymn might very well have been influenced by this play, although by now the violent death of Orpheus had become a literary standard. In any case, it is possible that the Thracian connection induced our poet to include a hymn addressed to Dionysos Bassareus. Bassarids are first mentioned by Anakreon (*PMG* 411b), who also uses a related verb, "anabassareō," to indicate reveling at a symposium (*PMG* 356a). This hymn continues the birth theme (see *OH* 44i) and alludes to maenadic ritual in lines 3–5. It is not difficult to conceive a period of joyous shouting, dancing, and brandishing of thyrsi (perhaps limited to the female initiates, if there were any) that was intended to be symbolic at the rite when this hymn was performed; see also *OH* 52i and *OH* 54i.

1 bull-faced god conceived in fire: For Dionysos' relationship to bulls, see *OH* 30.3–4+n. "Conceived in fire" would appear to refer to his traditional birth from Semele (see *OH* 44i and *OH* 30.2n).

2 many-named: For a list of the names used of Dionysos in the collection, see *OH* 50.2n.

3 bloody swords: Not a weapon normally associated with Dionysos. Plutarch tells us of a rite in which women who represented the Minyads, the daughters of Minyas who had rejected Dionysos (see note to line 5, "wrathful in the extreme"), were pursued by a priest armed with a sword (*Quaestiones graecae* 299c–300a). There are a number of Attic vases from the first half of the fifth century BC that portray Orpheus being killed by Thracian women who wield all sorts of weapons, including swords (see Bundrick 2005, pp. 116–126). The violence of the god is further alluded to in line 5. See also *OH* 30.4+n ("warlike").

3 holy Maenads: See the introduction to this hymn.

4: For a picture of Olympians celebrating Bacchic frenzy, see Pindar fragment 70b.6–21. Loudness is a characteristic of Dionysos and his worship; see *OH* 30.1+n.

5 thyrsos: The thyrsos is a wand topped with a pine cone that is sometimes wrapped in ivy. The shaft can be made from the fennel stalk; see *OH* 42.1 and Euripides *Bacchae* 147. It is one of the most widespread attributes of Dionysian worship, frequently mentioned in literature and often depicted in iconography. In the context of discussing initiation, Plato gives a prose quotation vaguely attributed to "the followers of the mysteries" that "the fennel-stalk bearers [*narthēkophoroi*] are many, the *bacchoi* few" (*Phaedo* 69c =*Orphic fragment* 576), which seems to point to a distinction between general worship of Dionysos (maenadism?) and the more restricted mystery cults that require initiation, such as the Eleusinian Mysteries (see also Graf/Johnston 2007, p. 143). The thyrsos is sometimes used as a weapon, e.g., by Dionysos in the Gigantomachy or by a maenad repelling the licentious advances of a satyr in vase paintings (e.g., Boardman 1975, pl. 313). See also *OH* 44.3, *OH* 50.8, and *OH* 52.4.

5 wrathful in the extreme: Examples of Dionysos' wrath abound in mythology, particularly in a group of myths that involve the rejection of his worship. Some of the more famous victims include Lykourgos, the Thracian king who hounded Dionysos and his maenads (*Iliad* 6.130–140), Pentheus and the women of Thebes (Euripides *Bacchae*), the daughters of Minyas, who eschewed going to the mountains to worship the god (Ovid *Metamorphoses* 4.1–40 and 390–415; also see the Plutarch citation in note to line 3), and the daughters of Proitos, who in some versions of their story also refuse Dionysos (Apollodoros 2.2.2). Orpheus himself experienced the god's wrath after rejecting him, being ripped apart (*sparagmos*) by maenads and/or the Bassarids (see *OH* 52i). See also *OH* 30.4+n and *OH* 47i.

7 leaping god: Leaping, frolicking, gamboling, prancing—all these are typical expressions of abandon in ecstatic cult; Dionysos himself often leads the wild processionals (see, e.g., *OH* 52.3–4 and 7–8). Other related figures described in similar terms are Pan (*OH* 11.4), the Nereids (*OH* 24.7), the Kouretes (*OH* 31.1), and the Nymphs with Pan (*OH* 51.8). Note that all of these are groups, save Pan, who, like Dionysos, can function as chorus-leader. The leaping may have fertility connotations like the "leaping" in the Palaikastro hymn to Zeus does (see *OH* 31i). Dionysos is called the "dancer" at *OH* O.8, and his "feet quiver in the dance" at *OH* 46.4.

46. To Liknites

This hymn is addressed to Dionysos Liknites (Dionysos of the cradle), who is also mentioned in *OH* 52.3. The title "Liknites" comes from the Greek word "liknon," the primary meaning of which is "winnowing-fan." This was a common cult object in Dionysian mysteries, well-attested in vase paintings (e.g., Boardman 1989, pl. 233) and often containing a phallus; see Graf/Johnston 2007, p. 148, and compare the story of Korybas' murder (*OH* 39i). There are hints in later writers of a story in which the goddess Hipta places a winnowing fan on her head, wreathes it with a snake, and receives the infant Dionysos in it after he is born from Zeus' thigh (*Orphic fragment* 329); this coheres with her role as nurse of Dionysos in our collection (see *OH* 49.1). An enigmatic vase painting from the Classical period might be depicting a variant of this account (Boardman 1989, pl. 157; for discussion, see Loucas 1992); here, a woman (Hipta?) is bearing a covered winnowing-basket to two seated gods, who might be Sabazios and Kybele (see also *OH* 49i).

Dionysos was worshipped as Liknites at Delphi, and Plutarch tells us that it was believed his remains had been brought there (*De Iside et Osiride* 365a). This dovetails with one version of the Orphic myth of the Titans' dismemberment of Dionysos where it is Apollon who gathers the remains of his half-brother and buries them on Parnassos (*Orphic fragment* 322). Plutarch further says that the Holy Ones perform a secret sacrifice in Apollon's temple when Liknites is awakened by the Thyiads, a group of Attic women who performed maenadic rituals for Dionysos every other year on the slopes of Parnassos (see *OH* 52i and *OH* 53i; see further Plutarch *Mulierum virtutes* 249e–f and *De primo frigido* 953d). Dionysos was the most important deity at Delphi for three months in the winter, when Apollon was thought to be vacationing up north among the Hyperboreans. There is also some obscure testimony that Dionysos was at Delphi before Apollon, perhaps even identified with Python, the serpent Apollon kills (for Python, see *OH* 34.3n; for the identification of Dionysos and Python, see Fontenrose 1959, pp. 374–379). For more information on the worship of Dionysos at Delphi, see West 1983, pp. 150–152, and Larson 2007, pp. 137–138; cf. also *OH* 79.7–10n. Our hymn does not appear to refer explicitly to the Delphic Liknites, but for the sleeping Dionysos, see *OH* 53.2–3+i. The theme of birth continues in this hymn. It also adds the notion of vegetation ("blossoming" in line 2), which is further developed in some of the following hymns, thus highlighting Dionysos' connection with plant-life (see further *OH* 50i). There is no explicit mention of a ritual, but the name itself implies one, and it can easily be imagined that at this stage of the rite a winnowing-basket was brought in and/or its contents revealed (see *OH* 47i).

2–3: The Nymphs rear Dionysos already in Homer (*Iliad* 6.132) and are found throughout the collection in this capacity (see *OH* 30.8n). Apollonios of Rhodes recounts that a specific nymph, Makris, received the infant Dionysos (*Argonautika* 4.540 and 1131–1140). For other nurslings of nymphs, see *OH* 51.3n. Hipta, too, is called the "nurse of Bacchos" (*OH* 49.1), while sometimes it is his aunt Ino, among others, who rears the child after her sister perishes (see *OH* 44i). Nysa is the name of a number of mountains in Asia Minor, and it is where Dionysos is often said to have been reared by the Nymphs; see the two shorter Homeric hymns to Dionysos (1.6–9, where Nysa is situated in Egypt [cf. Herodotos 2.146.2]) and 26.3–9, as well as Apollodoros 3.4.3 and *OH* 51.15. Its appearance here stresses Dionysos' Eastern associations, as do Sabazios and Hipta, the addressees of the two hymns after the next, respectively; note, too, that a winnowing basket seems to have been a part of Sabazios' mysteries, at least in Athens (see *OH* 48i). In ancient etymologies Nysa was used to explain Dionysos' name (for a somewhat technical discussion, see West 1978, pp. 373–375, with further references). The Homeric *Hymn to Demeter* locates the abduction of Persephone in the Nysian field (2.17) but gives no indication where this field might be in the world. The mention of Aphrodite suggests an identification with Adonis; see further note to lines 6–7.

4 quiver in the dance: For Dionysos as a dancing god, see *OH* 45.7n and *OH* 52i.

5: Compare the short Homeric *Hymn to Dionysos* (no. 26) and see *OH* 51.15–16n.

6–7: Persephone is often the mother of Dionysos in Orphic mythology, but here she is the ultimate nurse of the child Dionysos, just as she is the nurse of Aprhodite's son Adonis (compare line 3 and see *OH* 56i). This would seem to contradict other hymns in the collection where she is explicitly the mother of Dionysos (e.g., *OH* 30.6–7), and it is possible that we have a vague reference to a tradition that retained Semele as the conventional mother of Dionysos and worked in Persephone as his most important nurse. For the problem of reconciling the birth of Dionysos from both Semele and Persephone in Orphism, see *OH* 30.2n and *OH* 44i.

7 loved by the deathless gods: The manuscripts have "feared" instead of "loved," which is odd since Dionysos quickly became an accepted member of the Olympic pantheon (e.g., for fetching Hephaistos; see *OH* 66i). If "feared" should be retained, perhaps comparable is Alexander's mother, Olympias, who scared men with tamed snakes coming out of winnowing-baskets (Plutarch *Alexander* 2.9); compare Pan's birth (*OH* 11i). On the other hand, this idea of fear might just be a generic reference to the kind of horror Dionysos can effect (as at the end of Euripides' *Bacchae*); compare the "bloody swords" and "wrathful to the extreme" in *OH* 45.3 and 5.

47. To Perikionios

This hymn, like the previous one, is addressed to Dionysos in one of his particular ritual manifestations, albeit one rather obscure to us. "Perikionios" means "twined round the pillar," and the only reference to this title comes from a scholiast to Euripides *Phoenician Women* 651, who cites the late third- or early second-century historian Mnaseas (fragment 18). The brief notice states that after the palace of Kadmos had been blasted by Zeus' lightning, ivy enveloped it to protect the infant therein; thus Dionysos was called Perikionios among the Thebans. Our poet might very well have had something like this in mind, especially if it is Dionysos who causes the ivy to cover the palace in the original myth (cf. line 2). It is possible that some confusion has occurred; our composer might have been influenced inadvertently by the story of Dionysos and the pirates, where as part of his epiphany ivy covers the sail and mast of their ship (Homeric *Hymn to Dionysos* 7.38–42). The far distance of our cult from Thebes could have facilitated such a misunderstanding. Perhaps related is Pausanias' account of the Thebans' claim that after Semele had been struck by the thunderbolt, a log fell down from heaven and that subsequently a certain Polydoros (Semele's brother in some sources) decked it out in bronze and called it Dionysos Kadmeios (9.12.3). This is Theban cult, but a number of Athenain vase paintings show a pole or column outdoors on which is affixed a mask of Dionysos (bearded) with other accoutrements (e.g., Boardman 1989, pl. 24). There are scenes of women around it handling wine or dancing wildly (sometimes with satyrs); see Larson 2007, p. 135. One in particular might have some (albeit indirect) relevance for our collection. On one side the mask of Dionysos lies in a *liknon* among ivy with two women standing around, one carrying a basket of fruit, the other a wine decanter (see Boardman 1989, pl. 233). This probably represents the stage before the mask is ritually affixed to the column. It is perhaps not a coincidence, then, that this hymn follows the one addressed to Dionysos Liknites and part of the rite performed by our initiates might have consisted of a mask of Dionysos being carried to a column, accompanied by the initiates' singing the previous hymn to Liknites, and then the incense offering being given as this hymn was sung. That is not to say that our cult had preserved a centuries-old form of worship unchanged. It is more likely that certain types of Dionysian worship were adopted and adapted in Orphic (and other) circles (compare the notion of the *bricoleur* in Graf/Johnston 2007, pp. 70–71 and passim; cf. also *OH* 4i). It is also a possibility that a rite might have been invented or an older one altered in later times on the basis of literary sources (see note to line 5) or under the influence of a local indigenous cult through an identification with a Hellenic divinity. Regardless of how the rite came to be and what exactly it entailed, it is difficult to see why a hymn to such an obscure figure as Dionysos Perikionios might have been composed for our collection unless it had some sort of immediate ritual significance for the cult.

1: For Dionysos as wine god, see *OH* 50i.

5: Who is "everyone" and why were they tied up? The hymn seems to refer to a single specific event, and up to this point the one that makes the most sense is the first "birth" of Dionysos at the death of Semele. Imprisonment, however, is not part of that story. Another possibility is suggested by a comparison to Euripides *Bacchae*. While there is no explicit connection in terms of language, and while Euripides mentions the palace of Pentheus and not Kadmos, nonetheless in the play Dionysos first causes an earthquake and then sets his mother's grave on fire with lightning bolts (576–603). The latter detail is certainly an explicit allusion to Dionysos' birth, the legitimacy of which is called in question at the outset of the play. Afterward we find out how Dionysos tricked Pentheus in order to escape his earlier imprisonment (604–641). Our poet seems to have grafted some literary antecedents to the particular ritual act that this hymn accompanies. The vivid details stir the imagination of the participants. In essence, the performance of this hymn recreates a mythic scenario, composed of the birth of Dionysos (compare the ritual of the table mentioned in *OH* 44.6–9+n) and aspects of his epiphanies found in previous literature. The "everyone" then would be the initiates, and the "bonds" a metaphor for their previous uninitiated life. Dionysos, a deity of transitional states (see *OH* 30i), is often connected with freedom and release (see *OH* 50i); indeed, the Romans called him Liber ("the free one").

48. To Sabazios

Sabazios was a Phrygian god. His worship is first attested to have reached Greece by the end of the fifth century. Aristophanes mentions him in a number of contexts. Two guards attribute their sleepiness to him, probably because of intoxication (*Wasps* 9–10). His mysteries are mentioned in the context of female ecstatic worship (*Lysistrata* 387–390), and he is mentioned alongside Kybele in a list of gods related to birds (*Birds* 873–875). One fragment, from the play *Seasons,* calls him Phrygian and a player of the *aulos* (fragment 578), an instrument particularly connected to Dionysian ecstatic worship. Demosthenes gives us some insight into the practice of his cult in fourth-century Athens, although we need to take his account with a grain of salt because he is trying to smear his rival Aeschines (18.259–260; see also *Orphic fragment* 577). While Sabazios is not explicitly named as the god of this cult, the latter is invoked with the cry "euoi, Saboi," and Strabo explicitly links the cult to Sabazios and Kybele (10.3.18). There are a number of Dionysian elements present: ivy, winnowing-basket (see *OH* 46.2–3n), fawn-skins, ecstatic dancing and singing. Initiations are mentioned, and one element that stands out is the handling of live snakes (also an element in some Dionysian cults; see also *OH* 46.7n). Sabazios' name appears in Orphic contexts, although he is not attested in any of the fragments attributed to Orpheus. He is identified with Dionysos as the son of Zeus and Persephone (Diodorus Siculus 4.4.1), and Clement of Alexandria mentions his mysteries in the context of Zeus mating with Persephone in the form of a snake (*Protrepticus* 2.16.2). For the possible influence of Sabazios' worship on this Orphic genealogy, see West, 1983, pp. 97 and 110. However, the importance of Sabazios in Asia Minor also allowed his identification with Zeus, as in our hymn, which retains the Dionysian connection by making Sabazios the father of Dionysos (but see *OH* 49.2n); interestingly enough, the historian Mnaseas called Sabazaios the son of Dionysos (fragment 36). Among the four inscriptions dedicated to "mother Hipta," Sabazios-Zeus is mentioned in three of them (see *OH* 49i). This hymn fits the birth theme that is prominent in this central Dionysian group (see *OH* 44i) and, with the following hymn, forms a male-female pairing, a familiar pattern in the collection (see *OH*

14.8–9n). That two divinities from Phrygia in Asia Minor are given such a prominent position is a strong indication that our cult was also located in this region.

3 Eiraphiotes: Dionysos is also called this name in the Homeric *Hymn to Dionysos* 1.17 and in some Orphic accounts of his birth from Zeus' thigh; see *Orphic fragment* 328. Of the etymological explanations for this name given in antiquity, most relevant is the one that derives it from the verb meaning "sew" and it thus might be rendered as "the one sewn up"; see *OH* 44i and *OH* 50.3n.

49. To Hipta

Hipta was an Asiatic mother goddess of whom very little is known. Proclus mentions her in connection with the Orphic version of Dionysos' birth from Zeus' thigh: she receives the child in a winnowing-basket wreathed with a snake and takes him to Kybele at Mount Ida (see *OH* 46i). This myth—or a similar one—might be behind Strabo's notice that Sabazios-Dionysos is "in some way the child of Mother" (10.3.15): the qualification "in some way" suggests something along the lines of a nurse or adopted mother. The only other certain instances of Hipta's name come from four inscriptions found in an area not too distant from Mount Tmolos in Lydia; see Morand 2001, pp. 177–181. On three of these inscriptions Sabazios-Zeus is also mentioned (see *OH* 48i). This pairing is mirrored in the placement of this hymn after the one to Sabazios. Hipta is addressed as "Mother" in all four, which strongly suggests an identification with Kybele; compare the vase painting mentioned in *OH* 46i. Such an identification might be intended in our hymn, since she is called "chthonic mother" (line 4) and connected with Mount Ida in Phrygia and Mount Tmolos (see *OH* 27i). That Proclus distinguishes between Hipta and Mother does not entail their separation in our collection; he might have had a different version of the story in mind, or tried to rationally reconcile two slightly different ones. Indeed, Strabo might have called Hipta by the more familiar "Mother" in his report.

2 Sabos: An alternate name to Sabazios. The mysteries mentioned here are coordinated with the "dances of Iacchos" in line 3. Since Iacchos can be another name for Dionysos (see *OH* 42.4n), it would seem that Sabos is being identified with Dionysos, contrary to *OH* 48.1–3. It is possible, of course, that our poet is distinguishing each name to refer to a different entity or at least taking advantage of the different names to intentionally blur lines. Mise is described as taking part in Phrygian mysteries with Mother; see *OH* 42.6.

50. To Lysios Lenaios

This hymn is dedicated to Dionysos under two epithets. The first one, "Lysios," means "he that frees, he that sets loose, the redeemer." The notion of freedom from restraint, whether this restraint be physical, social, or spiritual, was an essential part of the religious conception of Dionysos. Insofar as he is a god of transitions, he "loosens" the moorings that tie an individual to any particular fixity; see *OH* 30i. Myth reflects this particular trait: Dionysos cannot be bound (e.g., Homeric *Hymn to Dionysos* 7.13–15), and he can free others from their bonds (e.g., Euripides *Bacchae* 443–450); see also *OH* 47.5+n. Lysios was a cult title of Dionysos (see Pausanias 2.2.6–7, 2.7.5–6, and 9.16.6), found also at *OH* 52.2. It is used as an epithet at *OH* 42.4 ("redeeming") as well as in lines 2 and 8 of this hymn. In Orphic contexts, Dionysos is said to be able to release one from madness and other suffering (see *OH* 53i) and even free an initiate from the guilt inherited from his murder at the hands of the Titans (Bacchic gold tablets no. 26a and b; see also Graf/Johnston 2007, pp. 132 and 147). Dionysos, more so than any of the other divinities in the collection, is the god that saves. Our poet, however, has evidently opted for a more limited view of Lysios, the one joined with the idea of the freedom of restraint as induced by intoxication. The second epithet, Lenaios, makes this clear, as it functions to limit the preceding Lysios. The word means "of the wine-press" (Greek "lēnos"; see Diodorus Siculus 3.63.4). It was a cult title of Dionysos at Athens and connected with the Lenaia festival, which was a celebration that took place every January. The Lenaia became an official venue for the performance of comedy and then eventually tragedy in the second half of the fifth century, although it was not as prestigious as the Greater Dionysia. We know very little about this festival. Of particular relevance is that officials from the Eleusinian Mysteries were involved in the procession and that part of the ritual involved the worshippers calling on the god as "son of Semele, Iacchos, giver of wealth" (for Iacchos, see *OH* 42.4n). While the name itself would seem to suggest this festival revolved around wine, modern scholars have favored a different interpretation that sees the name Lenaia as being derived from "lēnai," another word for maenads (see *OH* 52i). And this etymology might very well have been on the mind of our initiates, for the name of the festival occurs at *OH* 54.9 in a clearly maenadic context (cf. line 8 of this hymn, which contains maenadic imagery). For more on the Lenaia, see Pickard-Cambridge 1988, pp. 25–42, and Larson 2007, pp. 134–135. Our hymn, however, focuses on Dionysos as the god of wine and its effects: the release from cares, the happiness it brings, and the ever-present danger of disorderly conduct. This ambiguity of the power of wine is seen in the story of Ikarios. When Dionysos comes to Attika, he is received hospitably by this man. In gratitude, Dionysos teaches him the secrets of making wine. Ikarios shares the fruits of his labor with some shepherds one night, who, later believing to have been poisoned, kill him (see Apollodoros 3.14.7). Normally, though, wine was seen as a beneficial gift the god gives to human beings as a temporary respite from their daily existence (e.g., Hesiod *Works and Days* 614 and Euripides *Bacchae* 280–282; see also *OH* 30i). Dionysos is often depicted in the iconography himself in the act of drinking or carrying the necessary accoutrements, usually accompanied by satyrs and/or maenads (e.g., Boardman 1975, pll. 6, 110, 256, and 343). He is intimately connected with the symposium and revelry. Wine can be thought of as the god himself (see Euripides *Bacchae* 284–285), who, when ingested, possesses the worshipper (*enthousiasmos*) and effects a state of *ekstasis* (see *OH* 30i).

This hymn continues the theme of Dionysos' birth (lines 1 and 3), and, as with previous hymns in this grouping (see *OH* 44i), contains a reference to a specific Dionysian cult. The connection with vegetation, introduced with *OH* 46.2, is understandably strong here (lines 2, 4, 6, 10), and Dionysos seems to be imagined as the grape-vine itself in line 5 (see also *OH* 30.4–5 and cf. *OH* 56i). There is much overlap with *OH* 52, both in linguistic and iconographic terms.

1 **two mothers**: For the convoluted references to Dionysos' births in the collection, see *OH* 30.2n.

2 **unforgettable seed, many-named**: Comparably invoked are Protogonos (*OH* 6.4), an Orphic figure that was sometimes identified with Dionysos (see *OH* 6.3n+i), and Mise (*OH*

42.2), who appears to be a female form of Dionysos and who also receives the epithet "many-named" alongside "unforgettable seed" in the same metrical position. Dionysos is again called "many-named" at *OH* 45.2 and *OH* 52.1 (and see note), and it is particularly apt in this grouping where he is invoked as Bacchos (*OH* 44–54 passim, i.e., the entire group), Bassareus/Bassaros (*OH* 45.2 and *OH* 52.2), Liknites (*OH* 46.1 and *OH* 52.3), Perikionios (*OH* 47.1), Eiraphiotes (*OH* 48.3), Iacchos (*OH* 49.3), Lysios and Lenaios (*OH* 50 and *OH* 52.2), the God of Trienneial Feasts (*OH* 45 and *OH* 52), Eubouleus (*OH* 52.4), Erikepaios (*OH* 52.6), the God of Annual Feasts (*OH* 53), and perhaps Sabos (see *OH* 49.2+n).

3 born of secrecy: This refers to Dionysos' birth from the thigh of Zeus (cf. Homeric *Hymn to Dionysos* 1.7); see *OH* 44i. He is the "secret offspring of Zeus" at *OH* 52.5; see also *Supplementum Hellenisticum* 276.9 (Kallimakhos). For secrecy in mystery cults, see *OH* 30.3n.

5 many-shaped god, you burst forth from the earth: Although many entities in the collection are described as having many shapes or forms, it is particularly apt of Dionysos, a god whose fluid nature resists any form of permanence (see *OH* 30i). In addition to adopting various mortal disguises (e.g., as his own priest in Euripides *Bacchae*), he can also appear as an animal, such as a bull (see *OH* 30.3–4+n), goat, and lion (Homeric *Hymn to Dionysos* 7.44). In this line he even seems to be identified with the grape-vine itself. Compare lines 4 and 10, where he is the one who yields the sweet fruit, and see further *OH* 30.5+n, *OH* 51.3n, and *OH* 53.8–10+i. The same effect of blending god and object is found in the hymn to Persephone (see *OH* 29.12–14+n); see further *OH* 56i and *OH* 67.5+n. For the many forms of Protogonos, see *OH* 6i.

8: For the thyrsos, see *OH* 45.5+n; for madness and the revel, see *OH* 52.7–8n.

51. To the Nymphs

The Greek word "numphē" generally refers to a young woman, either of marriageable age or newly-wed (see *OH* 71.1n), but it also signifies any of a variety of minor female deities of nature. Nymphs were connected with a number of geographical features: forests, trees, mountains, springs, and meadows (*Odyssey* 6.122–124, Homeric *Hymn to Aphrodite* 5.97–99). Groups often are called by specific names that reflect their topographical associations. Thus Dryads are nymphs of the trees (Greek "drus"), Oreads are nymphs of the mountains (Greek "oros"), Naiads are nymphs of the springs (from the Greek verb "naō," "I flow"), and so forth; see also notes to lines 12 and 14. Nymphs are referred to as the daughters of Zeus by early poets (e.g., *Iliad* 6.420, Hesiod fragment 304, Alkaios fragment 343). The Ash Tree Nymphs, on the other hand, are born from the blood that drips from the severed genitals of Sky (Hesiod *Theogony* 183–187). Hesiod also gives the mountain nymphs a different genealogy, making them the sisters of the Kouretes and satyrs (see *OH* 31i and *OH* 54i). The Nereids and Okeanids (see line 1 and note), both pluralities of young women connected with natural features, could also be construed as nymphs. Our hymn identifies them specifically with the Okeanids at first but subtly widens the scope to include their traditional venues of woods, mountains, and meadows while stressing their connection with water (see note to lines 15–16). Rustic and pastoral settings away from civilization are their domain. Caves and grottos are favorite haunts. They are found running with Artemis, frolicking with Hermes and Pan (see note to line 8), or sporting with Eros, Aphrodite, and Dionysos (see *OH* 58.3n). They also are part of the Dionysian *thiasos* (see *OH* 54.6), and in some accounts they are the ones who raise the infant Dionysos after the death of Semele, as here (see line 3 and note). This last detail integrates the hymn in the series that focuses on Dionysos' birth (see *OH* 44i). We capitalize "Nymphs" when they refer to this particular grouping.

Nymphs were widely worshipped in antiquity, almost always tied to a particular locale. Odysseus kisses the ground on his return to Ithaka and prays to the Naiads whose sacred cave is nearby (*Odyssey* 13.345–360). A famous cave to the nymphs and Pan on Mount Parnassos, the Korykian Cave, gained Panhellenic importance due to its proximity to Delphi. Any feature of the land could become a place to worship a nymph or group of nymphs. For more details on their cults, see Larson 2007, pp. 153–155. Nymphs were known to kidnap men that caught their fancy from time to time, such as Herakles' friend Hylas (Apollonios of Rhodes *Argonautika* 1.1207–1239) and Hermaphroditos (Ovid *Metamorphoses* 4.285–388), a belief that survives in modern-day Greek folklore.

1: The Okeanids are the daughters of Okeanos and Tethys; see *OH* 83i and *OH* 22i, respectively. They may have been identified with the Nereids with whom they are sometimes confused; see *OH* 24.9–11n.

3 nurses of Bacchos: See *OH* 30.8n and *OH* 46.2–3n. Nymphs often were viewed as nurturers of the young, similar to their mistress Artemis, and Dionysos is not the only baby they rear. Aphrodite announces that they will raise her child Aineias until he reaches adolescence (Homeric *Hymn to Aphrodite* 5.256–275); the chorus in Sophokles *Oedipus Tyrannus* fancifully speculate whether Oedipus was born from a nymph and either Pan, Apollon, Hermes, or Dionysos (1099–1109); and Zeus was nursed by nymphs (Kallimakhos *Hymn to Zeus* 32–48), as was Hermaphroditos (see the introduction to this hymn). That they are both the nurses of Dionysos and the ones who "nurture" the fruits (line 4) might indicate an identification between Dionysos and vegetation, as apparently at *OH* 50.5 (see note there and *OH* 53i).

4 you haunt meadows: When Persephone was abducted by Hades, she was picking flowers in a meadow with the Okeanids; see Homeric *Hymn to Demeter* 2.1–8 and 2.414–425. This meadow is sometimes located in Nysa (see *OH* 46.2–3n). For chthonic associations of meadows, see *OH* 18.2n.

8 Pan: The nymphs are often found in connection with Pan (e.g., Homeric *Hymn to Pan* 19.19–27). They are mentioned together at *OH* O.15. See also *OH* 11.9+n.

12 herds of goats: Compare *Odyssey* 9.154–155, where Odysseus believes that the nymphs have sent him and his men goats. Like Hermes, nymphs were believed capable of increasing the fertility of herds. This is presumably the reason why the faithful swineherd Eumaios offers a portion of pork to the nymphs and Hermes (*Odyssey* 14.435–436). The nymphs known as the Epimeliads (from Greek "mēlon," "sheep") probably were thought to increase flocks of sheep (Pausanias 8.4.2).

14 Hamadryad: A tree nymph (Dryad) whose life is coextensive with that of the tree in which she dwells (Greek "hama," "together with"). Their appearance in myth is particularly tied to stories of an impious woodsman cutting down the tree, thus killing the nymph as well. See Homeric *Hymn to Aphrodite* (cited in the note to line 3), Pindar fragment 165, Kallimakhos *Hymn to Delos* 79–85, Apollonios of Rhodes *Argonautika* 2.475–483, and Ovid *Metamorphoses* 8.738–878.

15–16: For Nysa, see note to line 4 above. By "frenzied," it is suggested that the Nymphs are maenads (see *OH* 52i), as at *OH* 53.2; cf. *Iliad* 6.130–137, Pindar fragment 70b.12–14, and the chorus to Euripides' *Bacchae*. Deo is another name for Demeter (see *OH* 40.1n). She and Dionysos are joined together here in their capacities as divinities of grain and vegetation respectively, both of which require water for growth. This involves the Nymphs, since they are explicitly and repeatedly connected with water in this hymn. They are Okeanids (line 1), "clothed in dew" (line 6), and "water-loving" (line 14), they "frequent springs" (line 6), and they are asked to "pour streams of pure rain" (line 18). They are chthonic (line 3) not only because of their fertility associations but also because the sources of rivers, springs, and lakes are underground (compare line 2). Their description in line 9 equally applies to mountain streams, and that they find pleasure in cold (line 13) probably refers to their love of fresh, cold bodies of water. In the *Lesser Krater*, attributed to Orpheus, nymphs are actually equated with water (*Orphic fragment* 413.2). Their liquid nature makes them fit companions of Dionysos (see *OH* 30i).

52. To the God of Triennial Feasts

This hymn is the first of a group of three that bring to a close the Dionysian, cultic section of the *Hymns*. The previous three hymns dedicated to Dionysos (*OH* 46, 47, 50) call on the god under specific cult titles. The titles of this hymn and the following two, in contrast, refer to general characteristics of cult rather than any specific one. "Triennial" refers to a celebration every two years (the ancient Greeks counted inclusively). While there were a number of festivals that occurred biennially (e.g., the Isthmian Games and Nemean Games), it appears that a large number of such celebrations were devoted to Dionysos, particularly maenadic ones, e.g., that of the Thyiads (Pausanias 10.4.3; see also Euripides *Bacchae* 133, Diodorus Siculus 4.3.2–3, Larson 2007, pp. 127–128, and further *OH* 46i). This hymn also follows the trend, as it primarily depicts the kind of processions that are typically performed by maenads (sometimes with satyrs; see *OH* 54i). While many of the traditional trappings of maenadic processions appear intermittently in the other Dionysian hymns of the collection, nearly all of them are mentioned here. The worshippers proceed at night, guided by torchlight (see *OH* 9.3n). They brandish thyrsi (see *OH* 45.5n) and wear fawn-skins. Madness seeps into them along with the god. Vigorous movement leading to wild dancing and singing creates a raucous revel (see note to lines 7–8). The ivy-wreathed group, the *thiasos*, heads to the mountains, where animals are ripped apart (*sparagmos*; see *OH* 11.9n, *OH* 30.5n, and *OH* 45.5n) and the raw flesh devoured (*ōmophagia*; see line 7 and note); other wondrous works, such as causing milk and wine to spring from the ground and the handling of snakes, are performed by the frenzied. To what extent this ideal reflects real practice and to what extent it is the result of the powerful images Euripides evokes in his *Bacchae* is something that is debated by scholars (see Larson 2007, pp. 136–137, with further references). Whatever the case may be, by the time our collection had been composed, such elements had become standard indications of ecstatic Dionysian worship and iconography, so much so that their appearance in the *Hymns* does not imply that the initiates were female, any more than the hymn to Eleusinian Demeter entails the group was located at Eleusis (and note that Kadmos and Teiresias dress up as maenads in Euripides *Bacchae* 169–214; cf. further Herodotos 4.79 and *OH* 54i). It is a routine rhetorical strategy in hymns to remind the gods of their favorite haunts and activities. This particular one focuses on Dionysos as the leader of processions. The god is often depicted in literature and art as participating in his own rituals among his worshippers (e.g., Euripides

Bacchae 135–167; see also *OH* 53.6). In the *Hymns,* a number of female divinities are portrayed as maenads or described with maenadic imagery (see *OH* 1.3n), and Themis in her hymn founds maenadic rites (see *OH* 79.7–10+n). Such participation on the part of the gods helps blur the line between worshipped and worshipper, bringing the initiates into a more intimate contact with the powers they invoke (see *OH* 30i). There may have been a(nother) torch-lit procession at this point of the ritual (albeit probably not to a mountain), and Dionysos and his *thiasos,* upon finding such kindred spirits engaged in mimetic performances, would be more disposed to join the initiates in the ceremony. Triennial celebrations are mentioned at *OH* 30.5, *OH* 44.7, *OH* 53.4–5, and *OH* 54.3; see also Homeric *Hymn to Dionysos* 1.11.

1 many-named: See *OH* 50.2n; as in that hymn, so, too, here Dionysos is addressed by many names.

2 bull-horned, . . . Lysios, Lenaios: For Dionysos and bulls, see *OH* 30.3–4n. The cult titles Lysios and Lenaios, the titles under which *OH* 50 is dedicated to Dionysos, are repeated here, as well as that of Liknites in line 3, to whom *OH* 46 is addressed.

2–3 Nysian . . . conceived in fire. / Nourished in the thigh: These lines reflect the traditional myth of Dionysos' birth, for which see *OH* 30.2n and *OH* 44i. "Nourished in the thigh" alludes to that part of the story when Zeus, having saved the fetus after the immolation of Semele, sews him into his thigh to hide him from Hera; hence, he is the "secret offspring of Zeus" in line 5 (see also *OH* 48.3n and *OH* 50.3n). For Nysa, see *OH* 46.2–3n.

4 thyrsos-shaking Eubouleus: For the thyrsos, see *OH* 45.5n; for Eubouleus, see *OH* 30.6n.

5 nature three-fold: It is not entirely clear what is meant by this. At *OH* 30.2, Dionysos is called "two-natured, thrice-born" (and see note). The three natures indicated here might refer to those births in that he has three different "mothers": Semele, Persephone, and the thigh of Zeus. On the other hand, since Dionysos was devoured by the Titans and thereby had contact with them, it is possible that his nature is threefold: human through Semele, Titanic through the Titans, and Olympian through Zeus (cf. the composite nature of human beings in Orphic anthropogonies, summarized and discussed in Graf/Johnston 2007, pp. 85–90). Another possibility is that Dionysos' nature can be seen to embody the bestial, the human, and the divine. As with the contradictory references to Dionysos' birth throughout the collection, the ambiguity might be intentional.

6: "Primeval" is the translation of "prōtogone," which naturally recalls the Orphic entity known as Protogonos, who also shares with Dionysos the sobriquets Erikepaios, Eubouleus, and Bromios; see *OH* 6.4n+i. Through this identity, Dionysos can rightly be called both the "father and son of the gods."

7 raw flesh: See the introduction to this hymn and *OH* 30.5+n.

7–8: Madness is a running motif throughout the collection, as many divinities are described as bringing it and/or being able to cure it, particularly those beings that are related to ecstatic cults, with the concomitant belief that the worshipper becomes possessed by the divinity in question (see *OH* 71.11n). Madness thus also finds expression in the wild abandon to song and dance in the revel; see *OH* 27.11n and *OH* 50.8. This is the state of *ekstasis* that results from *enthousiasmos* (see *OH* 30i), and something that is not limited to Dionysos alone (see *OH* 11i and *OH* 27i). Dionysos' connection with madness was probably facilitated by his connection with wine and intoxication (see *OH* 50i). As often with the case of this god, the normal order in the world is subverted (cf. its use to great effect as a running motif in Euripides *Bacchae*) and leads to paradox; here, madness is transformed into lucidity (see also *OH* 54.11). For Dionysos as a dancing god, see *OH* 45.7+n.

10 annual feasts: This looks ahead to the title of the next hymn, where the triennial celebration is reciprocally mentioned in line 5.

11 Paian: This is normally a name for Apollon; see *OH* 34.1n; for Dionysos' worship at Delphi, see *OH* 46i.

53. To the God of Annual Feasts

This is the last hymn to Dionysos in the collection, and it is closely related to the previous one (*OH* 52i). There, the emphasis is on maenadism. We find this theme here as well in lines 6–7, which serves as a bridge to the following hymn, but Dionysos is first and foremost presented as a god of vegetation, whose "awakening" in the spring heralds the return of plant-life after the winter; cf. the Thyiads at Delphi who wake Dionysos Liknites; see *OH* 46i. Plutarch reports a similar practice among the Phrygians and Paphlagonians, who believed a god was asleep in the winter, and he further says that the Phrygians awakened him in the summer by "Bacchizing" (*De Iside et Osiride* 378f). As our group of initiates might have been active in Phrygia, it is just possible that Plutarch is referring to the local rite that was made "Orphic" by the group (less likely the ritual itself). This is the only place in the collection where Dionysos is called "chthonic" (line 1), and his association with the underworld, where he "sleeps," is indicated by the "sacred halls of Persephone" (line 3). The initiates invoke him with "fruity" terms (lines 8–10), and elsewhere in the collection he appears to be identified with the fruit itself (see *OH* 50.5+n). He is therefore much like Adonis and Persephone (see *OH* 56i and *OH* 41i, respectively), whose time split between the upper and lower worlds was interpreted as the cause of the seasons (and cf. line 7 of this hymn). In *Orphic fragment* 350, someone is foretelling Dionysos of his future worship in annual rites and his ability to free mortals from suffering and madness; see West 1983, pp, 99–100, for translation and brief discussion, and further *OH* 71.11n.

4 pure: For the importance of ritual purity, see *OH* 30.4n.

4–5 every third year. / . . . triennial revel: See *OH* 52i, which also refers to annual feasts in line 10.

6 he sings a hymn: For Dionysos as participant in his own worship, see *OH* 30i and *OH* 50i.

8 horned: For the horned god, see *OH* 30.3–4+n.

54. To Silenos Satyros and the Bacchae

This is the last hymn of the group whose overriding theme is Dionysian cult. It addresses the figure Silenos and mentions the other traditional members of the mythical Dionysian *thiasos*, the silens/satyrs and the Bacchae (or maenads); for the Bacchae, see *OH* 52i. The silens and satyrs were probably originally distinct, but very early merged into one group and their names are used interchangeably. The first mention of silens is on the François Vase (see Boardman 1991, pp. 33–34 and pl. 46), and satyrs are first mentioned by Hesiod (fragment 123, preserved at Strabo 10.3.19; see *OH* 51i). As line 7 of this hymn tells us, they are half-man, half-beast. Specifically, they are for the most part human, with equine tales and ears, snub noses, and a receding hairline; their bodies can be covered with hair, and early vase paintings sometimes give them hooves instead of feet. They are often shown ithyphallic. Sometimes they are found with hircine features. These are creatures of the wild, and they pursue quite a hedonistic lifestyle, spending their days laughing, drinking, dancing, making music, and chasing after nymphs (see, e.g., Homeric *Hymn to Aphrodite* 5.262–263). While originally independent of Dionysos, they became part of his retinue at an early date. They were insanely popular on vase paintings; see, for example, Hedreen's 1992 book-length study (which only treats the Archaic period!). In myth, they play no significant role outside of being in the company of Dionysos (e.g., the story of the return of Hephaistos; see *OH* 66i). We find them as the chorus of a peculiar kind of drama, the satyr play, which was introduced with (or shortly after) Attic tragedy. In Classical times, a tragic poet would stage three tragedies followed by a satyr play at the Greater Dionysia. These performances were light-hearted affairs, aptly called "tragedy at play" by Demetrius (*On Style* 169). Despite the fact that the only extant satyr play is Euripides' *Kyklops*, on the basis of this and numerous fragments we have some idea of the nature of this genre. Lissarrague neatly sums it up thus: "The recipe is as follows: take one myth, add the satyrs, and observe the results" (1990, p. 236). The chorus in a satyr play is led by Papposilenos (Granddaddy Silenos!), who is distinguished from the rest by being costumed as an old satyr, covered with white hair (as depicted on the Pronomos vase, which shows the actors at a rehearsal; see Boardman 1989, pp. 167–168 and pl. 323); he is the leader of the *thiasos* here as well (see line 6). Silenos occasionally plays a role in myth as a distinct individual. His most famous "exploit" is being found drunk in the garden of Midas, king of Phrygia. The king returns the lost satyr to Dionysos, who grants him a boon that turns into the famous "golden touch" (Ovid *Metamorphoses* 1.85–145). Another satyr, Marsyas, either invents the reed instrument known as the *auloi* or picks them up after Athene discards them (see *OH* 32i). He then challenges Apollon to a music contest in Phrygia, loses, and is flayed alive by the god (see Ovid *Metamorphses* 11.146–193). In cult, too, the satyrs are completely dependent on their master, although Pausanias does mention a temple for Silenos at Elis and stresses it is completely independent from Dionysos (6.24.8). Male worshippers of Dionysian ecstatic rituals could apparently take the role of satyrs, as well as pans, as is attested by Plato (*Laws* 815c–d) and by early rituals involving masks (see Burkert 1985, pp. 103–104); see also *OH* 52i. Satyrs and Silenos himself seem to be entirely ignored in Orphism, maybe because their light-hearted nature did not fit well with the serious cosmic and eschatological themes found in the mysteries (but see note to line 10 below). Their appearance in our collection is due to their traditional association with Dionysos. As they are followers of Dionysos, so, too, their hymn follows his. It is possible that our initiates dressed up as satyrs and Bacchae (perhaps just for this part of the ritual); see also *OH* 45i and *OH* 52i.

1 **foster father**: On some vase paintings, Silenos receives the infant Dionysos from Hermes (see, e.g., Boardman 1989, p. 225 and pl. 126), and it seems that his rearing of Dionysos was mentioned in satyr play (alluded to in Euripides *Kyklops* 1–8; cf. Horace *Ars Poetica* 239 and the euhemerized account in Diodorus Siculus 4.4.3–4). In this respect, Silenos is similar to the centaur Kheiron, another horse-human hybrid, who often raises heroes.

3 **triennial feasts**: See note to line 9 and *OH* 52i.

5 **wakeful reveler**: This refers to the all-night character of ecstatic Dionysian worship. If the ritual in which the *Hymns* were performed took place at night, as it seems likely (see *OH* 3i

and *OH* 78i), then Silenos would be a model for our initiates, who might be getting a little sleepy at this point! See also *OH* 85.9–10n.

6 Naiads: For this particular type of nymph, see *OH* 51i.

9 Lenaian: *OH* 50 is addressed to Lysios Lenaios; see the introduction to that hymn.

10 revealing torch-lit rites: Silenos and the satyrs are sometimes portrayed as being among the first initiates in Dionysian mysteries (see, e.g., Euripides *Bacchae* 120–134). As in the opening address where Orpheus' initiation of Mousaios would have been felt to be paradigmatic of all future initiations, so, too, Silenos and company function as the mythic paradigm of passing down esoteric knowledge to new initiates; see further *OH* 76.7n. Despite their wild and unrestrained temperament, these creatures sometimes do display a divine wisdom. In some versions of the Midas story, Silenos is intentionally captured by the king who wishes to know his secrets (see Herodotos 8.138.3, who locates the story in Macedonia, and Pausanias 1.4.5; compare also Vergil's sixth eclogue). Alkibiades' long praise of Sokrates ironically plays on the satyrs' contradictory nature of surface chicanery and concealed knowledge (Plato *Symposium* 215a–222d), which fits well the context here of Silenos being a revealer of secret rites. The hybrid nature of these creatures in general, both physically and psychologically, makes them very suitable companions for their master Dionysos (see *OH* 30i).

11 finding calm in the revels: This paradoxical statement is very similar to what is expressed at *OH* 52.7–8 (and see note).

55. To Aphrodite

Aphrodite is the goddess of love, beauty, and sexual relations. For Homer, she was the daughter of Zeus and Dione (*Iliad* 5.370–417), a goddess sometimes considered a Titan, sometimes a nymph (see *OH* O.19n); her name is a feminine variation of Zeus. Hesiod gives another account, in which she is born after Kronos castrates his father Sky and tosses the severed genitals into the sea. They undergo a sort of foamy chemical reaction out of which Aphrodite is born (*Theogony* 188–206). Hesiod's story teems with etymological explanations. Aphrodite is so called because she was born from foam (Greek "aphros"). She bears the names Kythereia because she came to the island Kythera; and the name Kyprogenes because she first came out of the sea on Kypros and so was "born on Kypros." She also took on the epithet "fond of genitals" because of their role in her birth. When she rises out of the sea, the Seasons are there to clothe her and deck her out with all sorts of finery, a scene memorably portrayed in Botticelli's painting *The Birth of Venus* (compare also the sixth Homeric hymn). In Hesiod's version, then, Aphrodite is thus a cosmic power that antedates Zeus and the other Olympian gods. Orphic mythology accepted the Hesiodic version, although in at least one variant it is Zelos (Envy) and Apate (Deception), not the Seasons, that welcome the goddess out of the sea (*Orphic fragment* 189; see also *OH* 3.2n). The Orphics, however, also maintained that she (or a second Aphrodite) was the daughter of Zeus but that Zeus created her by ejaculating into the sea (*Orphic fragment* 260).

Aphrodite was connected with both the carnal and spiritual sides of love, and accordingly literature portrays many sides of her. The Homeric *Hymn to Aphrodite* (no. 5) opens with a grand description of her powers: even Zeus is under her sway, and only three goddesses—Artemis, Athene, and Hestia—are immune to her charms (5.1–44). When Hera seeks to seduce Zeus to distraction during the Trojan War, she borrows a magical piece of clothing from Aphrodite, a concrete manifestation of the love goddess' abilities (*Iliad* 14.197–223). Aphrodite is raised to a cosmic principle of procreation, much like in our hymn, in Lucretius' opening address to her (*On the Nature of Things* 1.1–49), and she is endowed with further philosophical embellishment in the Neoplatonist Proclus' second hymn. Yet there is a comical side to this goddess as well. She is caught having an affair with Ares by her husband, Hephaistos, and the entangled lovers are displayed to the male gods, whereupon Apollon and Hermes engage in some playful banter (*Odyssey* 8.266–366). It should be kept in mind that the bard in the story who sings this tale does so to cheer up the sorrowing Odysseus. Apollonios of Rhodes shows her as a frustrated mother at wit's end on how to handle her unruly child Eros (*Argonautika* 3.1–166). There is a nasty side to this divinity, too. Helen meekly acquiesces to Aphrodite's demand to go to bed with Paris after the goddess ominously warns her not to disobey (*Iliad* 3.383–420). She unceasingly victimizes the mortal Psyche, first by asking Eros to make her fall in love with a monster; then, after Eros saves Psyche only to be betrayed by her, Aphrodite imposes a series of impossibly difficult tasks that eventually lead to Eros rescuing Psyche and a reconciliation with Aphrodite (Apuleius *Metamorphoses* or *The Golden Ass* 4.28–6.24). There is also something sinister lurking in Sappho's depiction of the goddess, who can cause someone to fall in love even if they are unwilling (fragment 1.21–24). Love can be pleasant, wonderful, charming, exhilarating, frightening, and brutal—often all at the same time—and the stories of Aphrodite provide firm evidence that the Greeks were acutely aware of this complexity.

At *Symposium* 180d–181c, Plato sharply distinguishes two cult manifestations of the goddess, Aphrodite Ourania (Aphrodite the Heavenly or Born from Sky) and Aphrodite Pandemos (Aphrodite of All the People). The former, for him, represents the spiritual side of love, while the latter the physical. However, in actual cult practice this distinction is not observed. Indeed, Aphrodite Pandemos is found worshipped as a deity promoting civic harmony, the power of love to soothe civil discord and bring opposing sides together (see note to line 9). Her daughter, Harmonia, may be seen as a reflection of this (see *OH* 65i). Not surprisingly, Aphrodite is also worshipped in connection with marriage, particularly the producing of children. She also protects sailors. For more on Aphrodite and her role in cult, see Burkert 1985, pp. 152–156, and Larson 2007, pp. 114–125. She is found connected with other male gods in both myth and cult, in particular Hermes, Ares, and Hephaistos; see *OH* 57.3–5n, *OH* 65i, *OH* 66i, respectively. The significance of these pairings seems largely to consist of a harmonious unison of opposites (male/female, life/death, war/peace, beauty/ugliness). We also find her connected with Dionysos in cult (Pausanias 7.25.9) and in our hymn (lines 2 and 7; compare "maddening" in line 13, and also see *OH* 56i). As a goddess of beauty, she often consorts with other beautiful goddesses, such as the Seasons and Graces (see *OH* 43i and *OH* 60i, respectively).

The placement of this hymn resumes the series of major Olympian gods that had been interrupted by a long digression on divinities associated with Dionysos, and the resumption is facilitated by Aphrodite's connection to him (see further *OH* 69i). The hymns to Adonis (*OH* 56), Eros (*OH* 58), and the Graces (*OH* 60) are grouped with her for obvious reasons. Chthonic Hermes (*OH* 57) is said to be her son in his hymn, while the Fates (*OH* 59) also appear to have been conceived as connected with Aphrodite, perhaps as her daughters (see note to line 3 and *OH* 59i), thus forming a triplet with Chthonic Hermes and Eros. *OH* 61–68 may also be considered part of the "Aphrodite" group; see *OH* 61i, *OH* 65i, and *OH* 68i.

1 heavenly, smiling Aphrodite, praised in many hymns: The first word of the hymn, "heavenly," is one of the main cult titles of the goddess (Aphrodite Ourania). "Smiling" is a translation of the Greek "philommeidēs," which literally means "fond of smiles." The word, like the similar "philommēdēs" ("fond of genitals"), is a common epithet of the goddess, who is often portrayed as smiling. Aphrodite is indeed "praised in many hymns": there are three Homeric hymns dedicated to her (nos. 5, 6, 10), two hymns by Proclus (nos. 2, 5), and literary pieces in the hymnic style, including Sappho fragments 1 and 2 and the opening of Lucretius' *On the Nature of Things*. The reference to "many hymns" probably is first and foremost to the ubiquity of her worship through the identification with similar goddesses in other traditions and thus anticipates lines 17–19. This hymn, then, is imagined as following worthy precedents.

3 mother of Necessity: Necessity (Greek Anankē) is a divinity who plays a role in Orphic theogony. She mates with Time in the form of a winged serpent, and their children are Ether and Khaos (*Orphic fragment* 77, 110–113; see West 1983, pp. 70, 194–197, and 231 for more details). If "necessity" in the hymn to the Fates should be personified, then our poet would appear to have conceived them to be the daughters of Aphrodite (see *OH* 59.18n). Necessity is identified with Adrasteia in Orphism. As Adrasteia can sometimes be identified with Nemesis, the inevitability of Nemesis might also explain the position of *OH* 61–64 in the collection (see *OH* 61i). The idea of compulsion appears in the imagery of yoking (lines 4, 13, 14); compare also Homeric *Hymn to Aphrodite* 5.33–43, Sappho fragment 1.21–24, and *PGM* 4.2934.

4–7: Aphrodite's wide-ranging powers are expressed through their geographical extent over the sky, earth, and sea, a rhetorical strategy employed in describing the powers of other gods as well; of particular relevance here are the hymns to Rhea (*OH* 14.9–10) and the Mother of the Gods (*OH* 27.4–8); see further *OH* 10.14–16n. Eros is similarly described in his hymn, although his powers extend beneath the earth as well (*OH* 58.5–7). See also Homeric *Hymn to Aphrodite* 5.2–6, Euripides *Hippolytos* 447–451, and Lucretius *On the Nature of Things* 1.1–27.

8 Erotes: A divinity may sometimes be conceived as a plurality, as for example Pan and Eileithyia (see *OH* 2i and Burkert 1985, pp. 170–171). Pindar also makes Aphrodite the mother of Erotes (fragment 122.4), and Proclus gives the group a Neoplatonic interpretation in his second hymn at line 3 (see van den Berg 2001, pp. 199–200).

9 Persuasion: Sometimes Persuasion is conceived as a separate goddess. She was worshipped together with Aphrodite at Athens (Pausanias 1.22.3). Sappho makes her the daughter of Aphrodite (fragment 200). In the decking out of Pandora, Persuasion joins the Graces in placing necklaces around her neck, while the Seasons crown her with a garland of spring flowers (Hesiod *Works and Days* 73–75). She is thus conceived as part of the traditional retinue of Aphrodite. One of the Okeanids is named Persuasion (Hesiod *Theogony* 349), and this might be the same Persuasion in the Pandora episode. In Orphic theogony, Eros and Persuasion are the parents of Hygeia (see *OH* 68i). Aphrodite's connection with persuasion is a function both of its utility in amatory pursuits as well as its benefits in forging a consensus in public affairs.

15–28: The second half of this poem, equal in length to the first half, is an extended invocation to the goddess to appear, and it includes a list of places where the goddess might be. It is typical of the hymnic style to attract the attention of the addressee by calling to mind their favored locales, which often have specific cultic importance. This is the significance of the mention of Kypros, one of her most important cult sites and traditionally the place where she first stepped onto land after she was born. The other locations broaden her associations. Olympos is mentioned first, as she is naturally conceived above all as a Greek goddess. This also places her in the sky, and the further mention of land and sea recalls the three realms over which Aphrodite was earlier said to have dominion (lines 4–7). Syria points to her connection with the Semitic goddess Astarte, already identified with Aphrodite by Herodotos (1.150), while Egypt alludes to Isis. Aphrodite is included in a long list of deities identified with Moon/Isis in Apuleius *Metamorphoses* or *The Golden Ass* 11.2 and 11.5, as well as an even longer list in the first hymn to Isis by Isidoros (line 24, and note that the Syrian Astarte appears in line 18).

20: Sappho imagines that the golden chariot of the goddess is pulled by sparrows (fragment 1.8–10), birds that were considered in antiquity to be particularly promiscuous.

56. To Adonis

Adonis is an old Near Eastern divinity of vegetation and fertility. His name is derived from the Semitic "adon" ("lord"), and he is a counterpart to the Babylonian Tammuz, who is loved by a fertility goddess (Ishtar), dies an untimely death, and is ritually lamented. Another similar figure is Attis, who is a lover of the great mother goddess Kybele; see *OH* 27i. The worship of Adonis seems to have come first to Kypros and from there to have spread to Greece. Therefore, not only his nature but also his earlier sojourn to Kypros explains his special connection with Aphrodite (see *OH* 55i; for her similarity with Ishtar, see Burkert 1985, p. 155). However, it appears that the Greeks, as they often did with foreign imports, adapted Adonis and his worship to their own mythological and religious framework. His Eastern connection is made clear by the various genealogies given by Apollodoros (3.13.3–4): his father is either Phoinix, Kinyras (a refugee from the East who became king of Kypros), or Theias, king of Assyria. He is the product of an incestuous union between a father and his daughter, named Myrrh or Smyrna, who is transformed into a myrrh tree out of which Adonis is born (see also Antoninus Liberalis 34 and Ovid *Metamorphoses* 10.298–518; note that the story in Ovid is narrated by Orpheus). Endowed with exquisite beauty, he catches the eye of Aphrodite herself and becomes her paramour. In one account, Aphrodite is already in love with Adonis as an infant. She places him in a chest and hands him over to Persephone for safekeeping. Persephone also becomes enamored of the child and later refuses to give him back to Aphrodite. They appeal to Zeus for a resolution. He decrees that Adonis must spend one third of the year with Persephone, another third with Aphrodite, and the remaining third with the goddess of his choice; he opts to spend this third with Aphrodite. Thus Adonis, like Persephone, spends part of his time in the land of death and the other part in the land of living, and, insofar as he is a god of vegetation, this tale corroborates the dying of plant life in the sweltering heat of the summer (see also *OH* 53i). The story is also reminiscent of the dispute between Hermes and Apollon in the longer Homeric *Hymn to Hermes* (no. 4): the younger half-sibling appropriating the property of the older one, their squabble, and the appeal to their father, Zeus. As a young man, Adonis becomes quite fond of hunting, which eventually leads to his death at the tusks of a wild boar. This boar is sometimes said to have been sent by a jealous Ares (or is Ares himself disguised) or Artemis.

Adonis was worshipped by women throughout the Greek world, who would ritually lament his death every year. Our earliest reference to the practice comes from Sappho (fragment 140), but we know about it chiefly as it was practiced at Athens in the Classical period. In the summer, seeds were sown in broken pots and taken to the roofs of homes after the plants sprouted. There these "Gardens of Adonis" were left to wither and die. The women loudly and expressively mourned the death of the god. They then laid out figures representing Adonis in a symbolic burial and afterward disposed of the "body" and the pots into the sea. For references and details of this practice, see Burkert 1985, pp. 176–177, and Larson 2007, p. 124. Theokritos devotes an entire idyll to an elaborate festival at Alexandria (*Idyll* 15), and Lucian mentions the worship of Adonis at Byblos, where the women at first mourn the dead Adonis and then celebrate his rebirth (*On the Syrian Goddess* 6–7). The bucolic poet Bion (ca. 100 BC) wrote a *Lament for Adonis* that blends myth with ritual content.

Our hymn alludes to this practice of lamenting Adonis in lines 2 and 6, and many of the traditional features of the myth of Adonis are incorporated. He is a hunter (line 7), and splits his time between life and death (lines 5, 10–11). He is repeatedly connected with vegetation: his hair is emphasized (lines 2 and 7), he is an "unwithering bloom" (line 4), the "spirit of growth" (line 6), and a "sweet blossom" (line 8). The emphasis, though, is not on his death but on his rebirth (line 10–11), as it seems to have been at Byblos. The similarities between Adonis and Dionysos have led to the identification of the two gods in this hymn. Just like Dionysos, Adonis has the epithet "many-named" (cf. *OH* 42.2, *OH* 45.2, *OH* 50.2+n, *OH* 52.1), is called Eubouleus (cf. *OH* 29.8, *OH* 30.6+n, *OH* 42.2, *OH* 52.4), is both male and female (cf. *OH* 30.2+n, *OH* 42.4), and wears horns (cf. *OH* 30.3+n). They are both conceived as vegetation (see *OH* 50i+5n and compare to lines 6 and 11 of this hymn). Furthermore, Dionysos is the "nursling" of the Nymphs and Aphrodite elsewhere in the collection (see *OH* 46.2–3+n), while Adonis in this hymn is the son of Aphrodite (see note to lines 8–9). He is also the son of Persephone, just as Dionysos is (cf. *OH* 30.6–7 and *OH* 30.2–3n), although Dionysos is also said to be reared by Persephone (see *OH* 46.6–7+n), just as Adonis is. This identification is also attested by Plutarch, who mentions that some people consider Adonis to be Dionysos (*Quaestiones conviviales* 671b).

4 you vanish and then shine again: Very similar phrasing is used of Sun at *OH* 8.15. It is perhaps worth noting that Proclus in his hymn to Sun says that some people identified this divinity with Adonis (1.26, and see van den Berg 2001, pp. 173–174). Interestingly enough, Phaethon, who is usually the child of Sun, is made the son of Kephalos and Dawn by Hesiod and then is snatched away by Aphrodite to be an official in her temple (*Theogony* 986–991). Hesiod describes Phaethon as "a man of god-like beauty" and "still in the tender blossom of luxuriant youth," and it is not hard to see how in later times the myths of Phaethon and Adonis might have blended. Indeed, Apollodoros lists Phaethon as the great-great-grandfather of Adonis, and the full patrilineal genealogy runs Kephalos, Tithonos, Phaethon, Astynous, Sandokos, Kinyras, and Adonis (3.14.3; granted, he cites Hesiod as a source that Phoinix is the father of Adonis). It is therefore possible that our poet (and Proclus) is alluding to an identification that was made in a work now lost to us.

6 spirit of growth: Asklepios is also described as such; see *OH* 67.5+n.

8–9: An interesting twist to the usual genealogy—one, however, that keeps the theme of incest, insofar as Eros is the son of Aphrodite (see *OH* 55.8). That Persephone is also the mother of Adonis is probably intended as a metaphor based on the return of Adonis from the underworld every year, as well as allowing Adonis to be equated with Dionysos.

57. To Chthonic Hermes

The first hymn to Hermes already hinted at the god's connection with the dead (*OH* 28.2), but this function has apparently taken a life of its own and achieved the status of a (quasi-)separate divinity in this hymn. Much like Hades can be called Chthonic Zeus, so here Chthonic Hermes is distinguished from Hermes, even though the two divinities are not kept entirely independent of one another (cf. also *OH* 73i). The role of Hermes as *psukhopompos* (guide of the souls) is well attested in the earliest Greek literature and is punned in the Greek on line 6 ("*psukh*ais pomp*os*," translated as "the souls you bring"). In the *Odyssey*, the god shepherds the souls of the dead suitors to the underworld (24.1–14), and in the Homeric *Hymn to Hermes*, guiding the dead is listed among the god's various functions (4.572). Hermes can also, when occasion calls for it, lead out from the land of the dead, as he does Persephone in the Homeric *Hymn to Demeter* (2.375–386). Hermes was also *psukhopompos* in Orphism (*Orphic fragment* 339), but it is curious that he is hardly mentioned in the extant sources and does not appear at all on the Bacchic gold tablets. The silence might very well be because his role is simply assumed. Perhaps, though, at least in some cases such as the gold tablets, the middleman might have been purposely left out in favor of the initiate's soul proactively (with the help of the instructions) taking matters into its own hands (thus further differentiating the initiate from the uninitiated). Outside of Orphic cult, we find Hermes worshiped as Chthonic Hermes in connection with pouring libations to the dead; for details, see Burkert 1985, pp. 157–158, and Larson 2007, pp. 149–150. The hymn seems oddly placed, but the explicit mention of Tartaros, Aphrodite, and Dionysos (merged with Adonis in the previous hymn) appear to have been sufficient grounds for its inclusion among the Aphrodite group.

1 **the road of no return**: This is normally true, but mythology is replete with heroic and divine exceptions, one being Adonis as seen in the previous hymn. The sentiment that one cannot return from Hades is a commonplace in Greek literature; see, e.g., Anakreon *PMG* 395.

1 **Kokytos**: One of the rivers of the underworld, and where Melinoe was born; see *OH* 71.2+n.

3–5: The genealogy given here is unique in literature and quite different from the conventional one as expressed at *OH* 28.1 (Zeus and Maia). It is also curious to find Dionysos in particular as the father of Chthonic Hermes, since in literature and art Hermes is at times depicted as bringing the newly-born infant Dionysos to the nymphs of Nysa and/ or Silenos (e.g., Apollodoros 3.4.3, Boardman 1989, pl. 126). Hermes and Aphrodite are often linked in cult (see Burkert 1985, pp. 220–221), but not as mother and son. The source and significance of this parentage of Chthonic Hermes remains a puzzle. In any event, this makes Persephone, who gives him his "high office" (line 9–10), his grandmother.

4 **Paphian maiden**: Paphos, a city on the island of Kypros, had one of the oldest and most famous cult centers of Aphrodite.

6 **destined harbor**: Maybe a reference to Kharon, the one who conveys the dead across a river to the underworld proper, if not a general metaphor for the land of the dead.

7–8: The wand of Hermes is one of his most prominent attributes. Its ability to lull to sleep and to awaken are already mentioned in Homer; in particular note *Odyssey* 24.2–5, where, after describing the powers of this wand, the poet shows Hermes leading the souls of the dead with it. In our text the powers of sleep merge with the powers of death; for the close connection of the two concepts in Greek thought, see *OH* 85i. It is not clear what is intended in these lines. It may refer to the Orphic belief that souls are reborn. Another possibility is that they refer to the initiate's expectations in the afterlife—that it is in fact the prerogative of Chthonic Hermes, as the agent of Persephone, to "awaken" those souls who have been put to "sleep" so that they may find their way to their special place in the underworld, as the Bacchic gold tablets describe.

58. To Eros

Eros, better known under his Latin name Cupid, has become a familiar figure in the Western literary and iconographical tradition. He is the playful winged and cherubic child, flitting around with his little bow and arrows, capriciously shooting the unwitting and causing them to fall desperately in love—ofttimes, alas, with tragic effect. The fanciful juxtaposition of great power with the even greater irresponsibility of a child betrays a profound psychological insight in the experience of love that first takes root in the earliest of the lyric poets; see the references in the note to line 3. Our hymn elects not to ignore this poetic conceit but having paid sufficient homage to it, quickly passes over to the other side of Eros, the cosmic force of love and attraction that is essential to the chain of copulations that underlies the anthropomorphizing tales of creation. This Eros is among the oldest divinities in Hesiod, coming after Khaos and coeval with Earth and Tartaros (*Theogony* 116–122), and Sappho offers a similarly ancient pedigree by making him the son of Earth and Sky (fragment 198). In Orphism, Eros is identified with Protogonos, another primeval figure; see *OH* 6i+5–7n, and compare the mock theogony in Aristophanes' *Birds*, where Eros' role is analogous to that of Protogonos in Orphism (see *OH* 6.2n). It is perhaps a different Eros that becomes the companion to Aphrodite after her birth (*Orphic fragment* 261; compare Hesiod *Theogony* 201–202), and the father of Hygeia (with Persuasion her mother; see *Orphic fragment* 262 and further *OH* 68i). However, in more conventional genealogies he is the son of Aphrodite, as he is in our collection (*OH* 55.8), while the father is variously said to be Zeus, Hermes, or Ares (if a father is even mentioned, which often is not the case). Another account, attributed to the semi-legendary Olen, claims that Eros was the son of Eileithyia, the goddess of childbirth (see *OH* 2i). This is mentioned by Pausanias in his brief description of the worship of Eros at Thespiai, and he notes a few other cult centers (9.27.1–4). There is perhaps an allusion to Orphic myth in Simias' (early third century BC) pattern poem *Wings*, where the winged child Eros is bearded and explains this anomaly by referring to his great antiquity, claiming to have been born in the earliest times when Necessity was in charge and denying to be the child of Aphrodite and Ares. Ether and Khaos are also mentioned, although textual corruption makes it difficult to know in what capacity. The poem ends with Eros describing his powers: he rules with gentleness (implicitly contrasting himself favorably to Necessity) and the earth, sea, and sky all yield to him. This assertion of wide-ranging power and the fusion of the cosmic with the literary are quite similar to what we find in this hymn.

2 who runs swiftly on a path of fire: The Greek word used here, "puridromos," is also used of the Stars (*OH* 7.9), Sun (*OH* 8.11), and Astrapaios Zeus (*OH* 20.2). It gives Eros a celestial coloring, anticipating the transition from the chubby archer boy to sublime cosmic power.

3 **who plays together with gods and mortal men:** The description of the power of love as "play" occurs in early Greek lyric; see for example Alkman *PMGF* 58 and Anakreon *PMG* 358. Anakreon *PMG* 357 is a mock prayer to Dionysos asking the god to be a "good counselor" to Kleoboulos (with a pun on this name, which means "famous for counsel"—and possibly also a play on Eubouleus, an alternate name of Dionysos; see *OH* 41.8n). In this poem, Dionysos is described as playing with Eros, nymphs, and Aphrodite. The poem was composed for a symposiastic setting, a situation where wine and love frequently mingled. The setting is the same for Plato's aptly named *Symposium,* where the nature of Eros is discussed (see also Plato's *Phaedrus*). A natural link between Eros and Dionysos is their ability to cause madness. Indeed, another fragment of Anakreon calls the dice of Eros "madness and battle" (*PMG* 398); the word "battle" is Homeric, and Anakreon is probably suggesting the Trojan War, whose immediate cause was passion. Apollonios of Rhodes portrays Eros cheating at dice against Ganymede (*Argonautika* 3.111–130).

4 **two-natured:** Other divinities in the collection are two-natured (which probably refers to their androgyny), the most relevant being Protogonos (*OH* 6.1+n), who is equated with (the cosmic) Eros in Orphism (see the introduction to this hymn). Antagoras of Rhodes (see the note to lines 5–7 below) employs a synonymous epithet. For other androgynous divinities in the collection, see *OH* 9.4n.

5–7: Compare the geographical extent with Aphrodite's at *OH* 55.4–7; for this theme elsewhere in the collection, see *OH* 10.14–16n. The reference to the underworld ("of all that lies in Tartaros") perhaps is intended to recall Orpheus' charming of Hades and Persephone when he descended to their realm in order to bring back his beloved Eurydike; see *OH* 87.9n and cf. Ovid *Metamorphoses* 5.359–384 and 10.25–29. The "goddess of grass and grain" is probably either Demeter or Persephone—more likely the latter, if our poet had in mind Kleanthes' play on the name Persephone as warm air (see *OH* 29.15–16n). The mention of winds is interesting. In Aristophanes' account of the birth of Eros from an egg in the *Birds,* the egg is a wind-egg (line 695) and Eros is described as being like the swift whirlwinds (line 697). The choice of a wind-egg may just be a joke on Aristophanes' part, playing off the incongruity of one thing being born out of another that is unproductive by nature. However, in at least one version of Orphic myth, the parents of Eros are Time and all the winds (*Orphic fragment* 360), and Sappho's younger contemporary Alkaios said that Eros was the son of Iris (Rainbow) and Zephyros, the west wind (see *OH* 81i). A later poet, Antagoras of Rhodes (early third century BC) in a literary hymn to Eros frankly expresses his puzzlement as to the god's parentage. He lists four possibilities: (1) Erebos and Night (alluding to Aristophanes' comic account), (2) Aphrodite, (3) Earth, and (4) the winds. See further the discussion at West 1983, pp. 200–201.

59. To the Fates

The Fates (Greek Moirai) are three sisters who were thought to be responsible for certain immutable facts about the cosmos. Sometimes they are merged into the notion of a singular personified abstraction Fate. The word "moira" means "lot, portion." When the early Greeks felt the need to explain why things happened to them the way they did, they cast their questions in terms of a personal "who is giving this" rather than an abstract "what is causing this," and the Fates are an answer to the question of who is doing the giving; compare the concept of a *daimōn* (*OH* 73i). They thus represent what is allotted in life, the portion of life one receives. That this does not necessarily entail "preordained destiny" can be seen in the *Iliad,* where Akhilleus has a choice whether to return home, where he will live to a ripe old age but die unknown, or to return to battle, where he will die young but earn immortal glory (9.410–416). Euchenor, son of the seer Polyidos, had a somewhat similar choice: to stay home and die of sickness or to go to Troy and be killed by the Trojans (*Iliad* 13.663–670). In Plato's "Myth of Er," the souls about to be reborn are able to choose their next life, which is ratified by the Fates only after the choice is made (*Republic* 617d–621a). The idea that the Fates apportion destinies is a specific instance of the more general idea of apportioning limits on a cosmic level. The Fates also are the limits of the physical universe, and, since for the Greeks very often the physical structure of the world is also an ethical one, the Fates also delimit moral boundaries (see note to lines 8–10). In this connection, their role is sometimes expanded to being the protectors of these limits, punishing those who transgress the established boundaries, i.e., those who commit hubris. They are thus aligned with other divinities in our collection who are also concerned with maintenance of the cosmic order, such as Nemesis (*OH* 61), Justice (*OH* 63), Nomos (*OH* 64), and the Eumenides (*OH* 70). Most of all, though, they overlap with the Erinyes (*OH* 69), who in their hymn are actually called the Fates (translated "goddesses of fate" in line 16; see note).

In Hesiod, the Fates are the daughters of Zeus and Themis (*Theogony* 904–906), and this relationship symbolically marks them as part of the divine order, just as it does with their sisters, the Seasons (see *OH* 43i). Of course, the divine order existed before Themis became a wife of Zeus, and Hesiod gives the alternate account that Night bore the Fates parthenogentically (*Theogony* 217–222; see also *OH* 61i). In this genealogy, the order they represent is an essential part of the development of the world. Orphic accounts also make the Fates the daughters of earlier generations. They are born from the "first gods" (*Orphic fragment* 176) or, along with the Hundred-Handers and the Kyklopes, are the children of Earth and Sky (*Orphic fragment* 82). The Kretan seer Epimenides makes them the daughters of Kronos and says their sisters are the Erinyes and Aphrodite (fragment 51). This last detail is interesting, not only because of the close relationship between the Erinyes and Fates already described but also in light of the fact that our hymn seems to be part of a grouping of divinities explicitly linked to Aphrodite (*OH* 55–60). We find the Fates and Aphrodite connected elsewhere. Pausanias reports an inscription he saw in Athens which claimed that Aphrodite was the oldest of the Fates (1.19.2).

Our composer seems to have followed the Hesiodic version making Night the mother of the Fates. However, elsewhere in the collection, Night is called Kypris, another name of Aphrodite (see *OH* 3.2+n). This would further explain why the hymn to the Fates has been included among other figures connected with this goddess (see also *OH* 55i). Moreover, the "necessity" in line 18 of this hymn could possibly be understood as a personification. In this case, Aphrodite as "mother of Necessity" (see *OH* 55.3+n) would then be the mother of the Fates, thus reinforcing the equivalence between herself and Night.

3–4: The imagery used here is obscure. Those who dwell in caves near bodies of water are usually beings with definite chthonic connections, as, for example, the Erinyes in *OH* 69.3–4. Furthermore, the Fates themselves, called "daughters of Night" in line 1, are explicitly given chthonic coloring in this hymn. Here, however, it is clear that the location is celestial (see also *OH* 7.9n). The lake and the cave may have been imagined to be on Mount Olympos. Another possibility, though, is that the Fates are here being connected with the moon. This would certainly resolve the apparent contradiction, for the moon, while clearly a celestial body, nevertheless had strong chthonic ties. It was associated with Persephone, and indeed was sometimes thought to be the Isle of the Blest (for example, by Pythagoras; see Iamblichus *Life of Pythagoras* 82) or where souls went after death (see Plutarch *De facie quae in orbe lunae apparet* 942d–945d). The stars, too, could also be linked with souls (see *OH* 7.9n). In the lost poem *Peplos* (*Robe*), attributed to Orpheus, our source says that the Fates were allegorized as parts of the moon (with a wordplay here on the meaning of "moira," "portion"). Furthermore, the Fates are said to be "clothed in white" insofar as they are parts of the moon's light (*Orphic fragment* 407). It should be noted that the word here translated as "frozen" (Greek "leukos") literally means "white," a color that is sometimes used to describe moonlight. In the magical papyri, Moon is identified with the threads of the Fates (*PGM* 4.2795) and the singular being Fate (*PGM* 4.2861). It is true that celestial bodies were often thought to be composed of fire, but the moon was sometimes considered to be a mixture of fire and air—a view held by, among others, the Stoics (Plutarch *De facie quae in orbe lunae apparet* 921f), who thought that air froze water (Plutarch *De primo frigido* 949b–c)—and for Empedokles the moon was frozen air that had been separated from fire (Plutarch *De facie quae in orbe lunae apparet* 922c). It is possible then that our poet is allusively conveying the notion that the Fates dwell on the moon, and perhaps there is an intentional playing on the idea found in "Peplos" that the Fates are the moon.

5–6: Similarly, Nomos is imagined as having descended from the heavens to bring laws to the human race (*OH* 64.5).

6–7: The idea being expressed here seems to be that even the best-laid plans are worthless if the Fates do not grant fulfillment. In Aeschylus' *Agamemnon*, Kassandra's last words before she goes offstage to her death are: "Ah, the fortunes of men. If all is going well, / a mere shadow may darken them all. But if they already fare poorly, / a wet sponge wipes the writing away, / and this I find to be the more pitiful" (1327–1330). The idea of personal destiny and personal fortune are closely related; see *OH* 72i.

8–10: These lines represent the idea that the Fates are antecedent to such abstractions as justice, hope, law, and order. These concepts are thus derivative of the physical and moral structure of the cosmos which the Fates embody and are thus responsible for maintaining (see also *OH* 8.16n and *OH* 64i). However, the Greek word "doxa," here translated as "glory," may also have the meaning "(fallible) opinion, fancy." Under this reading, the word would have the connotation of self-delusion, with the chariot thus symbolizing the human drive to believe oneself capable of transgressing certain fixed limits (i.e., it would be symbolic of what the Greeks called "atē," "blind infatuation, ruin," which leads to hubris). The Fates' "march toward men" in line 6 would then be with punitive intent, and the following lines would pick up the idea that unjust acts can never go unnoticed. See also *OH* 61.6–7+n. Of course, our composer could be playing on both meanings of the word.

11–14: For the eye of Zeus, see *OH* 62.1+n. The Fates, in addition to sometimes being the daughters of Zeus, are found together with him in cultic contexts. In Thebes, a sanctuary of the Fates was in close proximity to one of Zeus and another of Themis (Pausanias 9.25.4), thus recalling one of the Hesiodic genealogies. Zeus is sometimes worshipped as Moiragetes (Leader of Fates). He appears with the Fates in a relief on an altar to Persephone (Pausanias 8.37.1), and an altar probably belonging to him is near an altar to the Fates at Elis

(Pausanias 5.15.5). The "Zeus' mind [*noos*]" is comparable to the Stoic Khrysippos' equation of the reason [*logos*] of Zeus with that which has been fated (Plutarch *De Stoicorum repugnantiis* 1056c), and, according to the author of the Derveni Papyrus, Orpheus called Fate "phronēsis," which might mean "thought" or "prudence" (see Betegh 2004, p. 39, for translation and pp. 200–202 for discussion).

16: These names are already in Hesiod (*Theogony* 905) and are standard in Greek myth. Klotho is the Spinner, Lakhesis the Alotter, and Atropos the Irreversible. They reflect the notion that every life is like a thread that Klotho provides, Lakhesis measures out (see also *OH* 61i), and Atropos cuts at the moment of death. This metaphor of the "thread of life" persisted throughout antiquity and indeed has continued into our own times.

17 airy, invisible: The Erinyes are also described this way (*OH* 69.9).

18 necessity: For the figure of Necessity in Orphic thought, see *OH* 55.3n. An important quality of the Fates is their inevitably (compare "inexorable" in line 17 and the meaning of the name Atropos), and thus they are often associated with Necessity who shares the same fixity. The Stoic Khrysippos equated Atropos with Pepromene (Destiny), Necessity, and Adrasteia (Plutarch *De Stoicorum repugnantiis* 1056c). Adrasteia is sometimes identified with Necessity, and sometimes with Nemesis, a divinity who overlaps somewhat with the Fates (see *OH* 61i). In Plato's "Myth of Er," the Fates are daughters of Necessity, and they turn the spindle that Plato portrays as the framework of the cosmos (*Republic* 616c–617d).

In the manuscripts, the last line of this hymn reads: "This is the end of the song of the Fates, which Orpheus composed." It is a dactylic hexameter line, the same meter used in all of the hymns in the collection. It is possible that it was part of the original composition, although it is difficult to see why only this hymn asserts its Orphic authorship. The explicit mention of Orpheus perhaps is meant to distinguish it from another hymn to the Fates, now lost to us, which was not by Orpheus (or even mistakenly attributed to him). On the other hand, it might be that this hymn was separate from the collection and was later added, due to its similarity to the other hymns; the line could have been part of the original and simply retained. Then again, it might simply be the work of a playful scribe engaging in a little poetic license. In this scenario, the line would have been a marginal note that eventually was misunderstood to have been part of the hymn and appended to its end. The word translated "composed" literally means "wove." While the metaphor of weaving a song is very old in Greek literature (Bacchylides 5.9), it is perhaps more than a coincidence that it was chosen for a hymn dedicated to divinities who are also closely connected with the metaphor of weaving (see note to line 16).

60. To the Graces

The Graces (Greek Kharites) are a plurality of female divinities concerned with beauty, merriment, and good cheer. Aglaia is Splendor, Thalia Festivity, and Euphrosyne Joy, and their names are indicative of their function. They are frequently connected, and even confused, with the Seasons (see *OH* 43i). There is also some linguistic and conceptual overlap between this hymn and the one to the Seasons. Like the latter, the Graces are "ever-blooming," the third one listed is "(thrice-)blessed," flowers are used to describe their physical beauty, and both groups are called on to bring fertility. The affinity between these two groups is made even more concrete since the mother of the Graces is Eunomia, one of the Seasons. This differs from the Hesiodic account, where they are also daughters of Zeus, but their mother is Eurynome, one of the daughters of Okeanos (*Theogony* 907–911). The Orphic *Rhapsodies*, however, agree with our hymn (*Orphic fragment* 254). For other variations of their names and genealogy, see Pausanias 9.35.1–7. Of particular interest is his mention of mysteries that were performed near their statue at the entrance of the Athenian acropolis (9.35.3). Euripides recounts that they were sent by Zeus along with the Muses to mollify Kybele-Demeter, who was angry at the abduction of her daughter Persephone (*Helen* 1338–1345; see *OH* 27i). The Graces are especially associated with Aphrodite. In the Homeric *Hymn to Aphrodite* 5.60–64 they are the goddess' attendants. In the *Iliad* Diomedes pierces Aphrodite's robe, which was the handiwork of the Graces (5.337–338). Zeus orders Aphrodite to "pour grace around [Pandora's] head," and in the actual decking out of Pandora, the Graces themselves with the goddess Persuasion hang golden necklaces around her neck, while the Seasons crown her with a garland of spring flowers (Hesiod *Works and Days* 65 and 73–75). According to Pausanias, there was a sanctuary of the Graces at Elea where there were images of the goddesses—one holding a rose, another a die, the third a sprig of myrtle—and a statue of Eros next to them (6.24.6–7). Pausanias interprets this group by noting the symbolism of the rose and myrtle for Aphrodite and pointing out that young people, who are not yet marred by the ugliness of age, often play at dice.

The Graces' close association with Aphrodite helps to explain why their hymn follows on the heels of hymns dedicated to this goddess (*OH* 55) and to those explicitly connected with her: Adonis, Chthonic Hermes, and Eros (*OH* 56–58). For the connection of the Fates with Aphrodite, see *OH* 59i. The Fates and the Graces are further bound together by way of their mother Eunomia, whose name means "law-abiding." As her daughters, the Graces are part of that divine order in which their mother partakes (see *OH* 43i) and that is exemplified by the Fates (see *OH* 59i) and those goddesses to whom the subsequent hymns are dedicated: Nemesis, Dike (another Season, and so one of their aunts!), Justice, and Nomos (*OH* 61–64).

61. Hymn to Nemesis

Nemesis is another personified abstraction that became deified. Her name comes from the verb "nemō," "I deal out, distribute." She is the goddess of righteous indignation, who punishes those who transgress customs and laws. Hesiod makes her the daughter of Night (born from no father) and describes her as a "woe for mortals" (*Theogony* 223–234). A more positive portrayal of this goddess appears in the conclusion to his account of the Iron Race of men. There is so much wickedness in the world that Nemesis apparently gives the human race up and leaves with Aidos (Shame) to Olympos (*Works and Days* 197–201). Both indignation and shame were important forces in early society that helped prevent unjust deeds and consequently contributed to constructing a stable community. Hesiod subtly links Nemesis and Dike in the *Works and Days*, since Dike, too, leaves the earth in the face of wicked acts; she rushes to her father, Zeus, to demand punishment against those who have mistreated her (*Works and Days* 256–262; see also *OH* 62i and *OH* 69.9n).

Nemesis is connected with the Trojan War in an interesting variant. Zeus falls in love with her, but she flees his advances, out of shame and indignation (the words "aidos" and "nemesis" are used), since Zeus is her father. With the god in hot pursuit, she keeps changing herself into different animals, desperate to escape. Zeus catches up to her when she is in the form of a goose, and he mates with her in the form of a swan. Nemesis lays an egg, which is given to Leda, queen of Sparta, and out of the egg hatches Helen. The death and destruction that result in the war for her sake are thus connected with the righteous anger of Nemesis at the abuse of her father. For versions of this story, see *Kypria* fragment 7 (= Athenaios 8.334b–d), Apollodoros 3.10.7, and Pausanias 1.33.7; see also *OH* 79i. Other goddesses also become wrathful at such forced unions, e.g., Demeter at Poseidon (see *OH* 69i), and Persephone at Zeus (see *OH* 29i and *OH* 71.4–5+n).

This myth is reflected in the cult of Nemesis at Rhamnous, a town in Attika. Pausanias describes a statue by the famous sculptor Pheidias (modern scholars prefer to attribute it to his pupil Agorakritos) depicting Leda leading Helen to her mother Nemesis; also depicted is Leda's husband, Tyndareus, with their children, as well as Agamemnon, Menelaos, Neoptolemos and Hermione, the daughter of Helen (1.33.8). The statue was built from marble that the Persians had arrogantly brought with them in their invasion of Attika, with the intent to build a trophy for the victory they felt inevitable; thus the goddess became explicitly connected with their defeat (Pausanias 1.33.2). The statue held an apple branch in its left hand and a libation bowl in its right (engraved with Ethiopians); on its head was a deer and images of Nike. The symbolism of Nike is clearly connected with the defeat of the Persians. The apple branch suggests fertility connections, maybe even a connection with Aphrodite, while the deer perhaps hints at Artemis or some other similar ancient mistress of animals; see Larson 2007, pp. 179–180. Themis had a shrine in Nemesis' sanctuary (see *OH* 79i). Nemesis was also worshipped at Smyrna, where the abstraction becomes a plurality of three Nemeses (Pausanias 7.5.3).

It is interesting that the Fates are placed before Nemesis in Hesiod's list of Night's progeny and that they are the ones who he says look over the deeds of mortals and gods and punish transgressions (*Theogony* 220–222). This is normally the purview of Nemesis. However, for the Greeks the ideas of justice and fate were intertwined in the cosmic order, so it is not surprising that at times divinities concerned with one of these should be concerned with the other as well (see *OH* 59i). Nemesis was sometimes called Adrasteia (Ineluctable) and invoked apotropaically before one would say something that could be construed as boasting or otherwise overbold (see, e.g., Aeschylus *Prometheus Bound* 936 and Plato *Republic* 451a). Adrasteia can function like Fate, too, and later is equated with Necessity; see West 1983, pp. 194–196. Nemesis became associated also with Tyche; compare lines 7–8 of the second century AD hymn to Nemesis by Mesomedes: "Beneath your wheel that neither ceases nor remains on the beaten track / there rolls the bright Tyche of men" and *OH* 72. Mesomedes further develops the idea of Nemesis as Fate through the image of scales (line 1, "O Nemesis, winged scales of life," and line 13, "with scales in hand") and the symbolism of measuring (line 11, "you measure out livelihood"; cf. Lakhesis the "allotter" at *OH* 59.16+n). This close relation probably influenced the placement of this hymn near the one dedicated to the Fates, and, insofar as Aphrodite is called "mother of Necessity" (*OH* 55.3), Nemesis could very well have been imagined as part of the Aphrodite block of hymns. The intimate bond between justice and the indignation that arises against those who transgress it further explains the grouping of this hymn with the three that follow it. The importance of acting in accordance to justice is thus emphasized. The first and last of the four (*OH* 64, to Nomos) are marked by their lack of offering, and it is likely that the initiates paused in their sacrifices and merely sang to these divinities. There is further a possible male/female pairing implied between Nemesis and Nomos (see *OH* 14.8–9n), whose names, incidentally, are etymologically related. The other two hymns sandwiched in between address the closely related pair of Dike and Justice.

The themes of the blessings of justice and the inevitable punishment of the unjust unite all four and connect these figures with similar deities, namely, the Fates (*OH* 59), the Erinyes (*OH* 69), and the Eumenides (*OH* 70).

2 all-seeing eye: Similarly in line 8. A number of addressees in the collection are described in this way. The most relevant parallel is Dike (*OH* 62.1); see further *OH* 8.1n.

4: This line does not mean that Nemesis is herself inconsistent, arbitrary, or fickle. It is the wickedness of men that is so varied, and this entails that the principle embodied by Nemesis must appear differently in her various concrete manifestations. Compare the story of her flight from Zeus, where she is a shapeshifter. The line also fits in with the theme of deities who are multiform and ever-changing.

5: Fear as a motivation to act justly was recognized early on by the Greeks. An astounding witness to the fact is the fragment from the late fifth-century tragedy (or satyr play) *Sisyphos*, sometimes attributed to Euripides. In the fragment, the lead character baldly states that gods were invented merely as a means to frighten people into behaving themselves; cf. *OH* 69.15n.

6–7 the arrogant soul, / the reckless one: Transgression is properly a going beyond the bounds of what is allowed and/or appropriate, and the Greeks were very concerned about respecting boundaries and maintaining proper limits; see *OH* 63.7n and cf. *OH* 30i. This idea lies at the heart of the concept of hubris, a word not used in our hymn but found in Mesomedes' (line 5: "hating destructive hubris of mortals"). See also *OH* 59.8–10+n.

8 you arbitrate all: Compare line 14 of Mesomedes' hymn, where Nemesis is invoked as a judge, and the idea of Nemesis as Fate as noted in the introduction to this hymn.

62. To Dike

Dike (Right) is not really different from Justice in the next hymn, whose name in Greek (Dikaiosunē) is derived from Dike's (see *OH* 63i). For Hesiod, she is one of the three Seasons and a daughter of Zeus and Themis (*Theogony* 901–903). She receives special attention in the *Works and Days* where she is represented as a maiden who takes vengeance on the unjust, particularly in juridical matters, whether she takes punishment into her own hands (220–224) or complains to her father, Zeus (256–262; see also *OH* 61i and *OH* 69.9n). Note that the word "dikē" in Greek can also mean "punishment." Orphism adopts the Hesiodic genealogy (*Orphic fragment* 252) but adds a second one, making Dike the daughter of Nomos (Law; to whom *OH* 64 is addressed) and Eusebeia (Piety); see also *OH* 63i. Mesomedes in his hymn to Nemesis makes her the daughter of Dike; here genealogy reflects function. Finally, Dike is equated with Moon in the magical papyri (*PGM* 4.2785 and 2860), in the same context as the Fates and the Erinyes, both of whom also have as their function the punishment of malefactors; see also *OH* 69.15n.

1 all-seeing eye: So, too, Nemesis in the previous hymn (*OH* 61.2). The idea of the "eye of Dike" goes as far back at least to Sophokles (fragment 12). The imagery occurs in our collection again at *OH* 69.15, where the Erinyes are said to "gaze as the eye of Dike." Two gods who are traditionally watchers in the sky are also so described in the collection. Sun is addressed as the "eternal eye that sees all" (*OH* 8.1+n), as well as Apollon in his identity as the sun god (*OH* 34.8). Sometimes, the eye of the sun is limited to just the physical entity, though, as at *OH* 11.17. Zeus, too, possesses an all-seeing eye. In the hymn to the Fates, the poet says that they alone of the gods watch over mortals "except for Zeus' perfect eye" (*OH* 59.13). In the *Works and Days*, Zeus has an eye that sees all (267); this comes shortly after Hesiod describes how Dike runs to tell him of the injustice of the world. Note, too, that in an Orphic hymn to Zeus, the sun and moon are said to be his eyes (*Orphic fragment* 243.16). The imagery of a celestial sky god who perceives all is very ancient and its appearance in Greek poetry seems to have roots in its Indo-European heritage (see West 1978, pp. 223–224). Dike, too, can be construed as a celestial goddess. Aratos tells us that the constellation known as the Maiden is either the daughter of Astraios or is Dike herself. He then relates the story of how Dike had dwelt among men during the innocence of the Golden Age and urged them to righteousness; in the Silver Age, disgusted with the wickedness she found in the people, she retreated from society and warned men of their evil ways; and finally in the Bronze Age she could no longer bear to remain on the earth, so she retired to the sky where she became a constellation (*Phainomena* 96–136). This story appears to have been influenced by Hesiod's account of Dike leaving the earth to complain to her father.

2: For the concept of Dike sharing the throne of Zeus, compare Hesiod *Works and Days* 256–262, Sophokles *Oedipus at Kolonos* 1382, and the introduction to the translation. She is described as a companion and follower of Zeus in Orphic literature (*Orphic fragment* 32–33, 233, and 247–248). Her daughter Nemesis is said to sit by her in Mesomedes' hymn to Nemesis (line 18).

6–7: The concern for verdicts is reminiscent of the Hesiod passages in the *Works and Days*, cited in the introduction to this hymn. The word "dikē" can also have the sense of "judgment, trial, suit."

9: Depicted on the chest of Kypselos, as described by Pausanias (5.18.2), is Dike, in the form of a beautiful woman, both choking and whacking with a staff an ugly woman, who is Adikia (Wrong). The idea that Dike is nice to her friends and nasty to her enemies reflects an ethic that goes back to Archaic times. A similar sentiment is found in *OH* 10.15, right after Physis is identified with Dike; cf. also *OH* 63.10.

63. To Justice

Justice (Dikaiosunē) was one of the most important, if not the most important, virtues in Greek ethical thought, often discussed by poets and philosophers. There is a certain amount of overlap between this word and "dikē," and the two words may function as synonyms. One distinction between Dike and Justice in their portrayals here is that the former has a somewhat more concrete personalization while the latter is presented more as an abstract entity (but cf. *OH* 8.18, where Sun is called the "eye of justice," and *OH* 62.1n). Justice also seems to be more broadly construed; see note to lines 14–15. We do find Justice personified and worshipped, although it is rare. Euripides is our earliest source for the personification. He mentions the "golden countenance of Justice" in his lost play *Melanippe* (fragment 486). An inscription on Delos from 115/114 BC identifies Isis with Justice as well as Tyche, Protogoneia (a feminine form of Protogonos, First-Born), Thalia (the name of one of the Graces that means "joy"), and Aphrodite the Righteous. Another inscription from Epidauros in the second century AD confirms that Justice received worship there. In Orphic theogony, Nomos (Law) and Eusebeia (Piety) are said to have given birth to Justice (*Orphic fragment* 248), and it is therefore notable that in the opening address to Mousaios both Justice and Piety are mentioned together (*OH* O.14). However, Hermias, the source for this genealogy, in the same work also says it is Dike who is their daughter. Whether he thought they were two distinct entities or he is using the names interchangeably is hard to determine. To make matters more complicated, Hermias again in the same work says that there are three Nights in Orphic mythology and that the third one gave birth to Justice (*Orphic fragment* 246). And another source says that, for Orpheus, Dike was a daughter of Zeus and Themis and that she was one of the Seasons (see *OH* 43i). These might represent different variants that developed independently over time and that are being indiscriminately used by later authors. However, as the multiple Nights show, it is possible that a single entity could be duplicated in Orphic mythopoetics. Clearly the notion of justice was as important to the Orphics as it was to the wider Greek world.

7 **the balance of your mighty scales**: Balance, equality, and fairness are important themes in this hymn; they also recur in the other three of the group. An important component in the Greek view of justice was that each person receives what they deserve; injustice occurs when the undeserving take more than their fair share (a form of hubris) and the deserving are short-changed. In section 29 of *The Theology of Arithmetic* (see *OH* 12.3n), the author says that the Pythagoreans considered the tetrad (i.e., the number four) to be Justice, because a square that had sides the length of four would have its area (length times width: 4 x 4 = 16) and its perimeter (four sides of 4 = 16) equal (Waterfield 1988, p. 63). In the Pythagorean saying "Do not step over the beam," the "beam" was sometimes construed as the beam of a balance, and the dictum was interpreted as meaning that one should not transgress against justice (see Iamblichus *Life of Pythagoras* 186 and *The Theology of Arithmetic* 40 in Waterfield 1988, p. 72).

8 **a lover of revel**: This would seem to refer to Dionysian ecstatic worship and to suggest that it receives Justice's stamp of approval.

14–15: It is interesting that the hymn now includes living creatures in addition to human beings. Hitherto this hymn, as well as the previous two, has been exclusively concerned with human conduct; see further *OH* 64i. It is perhaps relevant to recall in this context that Hesiod tells Perses to "obey the voice of Dike and always refrain from violence" and then continues, "This is the law [*nomos*] Zeus laid down for men, / but fish and wild beasts and winged birds / know not of justice [*dikē*] and so eat one another. / Justice [*dikē*], the best thing there is, he gave to men" (*Works and Days* 276–279).

15 **sea-dwelling Zeus**: A circumlocution for Poseidon; compare Hades being called "Chthonic Zeus" (see *OH* 18.3+n).

64. Hymn to Nomos

This ends a sequence of four tightly integrated hymns. As with *OH* 61, there is no indication of incense, which suggests this was perhaps sung without being accompanied by any other ritual activity; together they mark the beginning and end of the series. A crescendo effect is achieved by the scope of each hymn. The first two, the hymns to Nemesis and Dike, are limited to the various races of men (cf. *OH* 61.2 and *OH* 62.3). The third hymn to Justice also is concerned with human justice, but at the very end expands to include all living creatures (*OH* 63.14–15+n). All three divinities are female, and their concern is with things that are alive. In this hymn, the male Nomos (Law) has been raised to a cosmic principle that sees to it that both the inanimate elements of nature and the creatures that live among them keep to their proper limits. This connects the hymn conceptually to the previous three, as respecting boundaries is a core component of Greek ethical thought (see *OH* 61.6–7n and *OH* 63.7n). The hymn is structured to reflect the cosmos-human duality. The first part expresses Nomos as the physical order of the universe (lines 1–4). A transitional bridge brings Nomos down to earth—literally (lines 5–6). The focus is then on Nomos as a foundational ethical force for living beings in general and the individual in particular (lines 7–11). This notion that the underlying structure of the cosmos is as ethical as it is physical and that this universal ethic is connected to moral action in the human sphere returns to a theme found in the earlier hymns (see *OH* 8.16n) and appears again near the end (see *OH* 86i); see also *OH* 59.8–10n and *OH* 69.15n.

The earliest evidence for the personification of Nomos is Pindar fragment 169a.1–4, which is cited by Plato (*Gorgias* 484b). Nomos as a divinity seems to have been appealing to the philosophers. A fragment of Herakleitos says that "all human laws [*nomoi*] are nourished by the one that is divine" (Kirk, Raven, and Schofield 1983, no. 250), which might imply that for him Nomos was a divinity. The Stoics, who were influenced greatly by Herakleitos, do explicitly recognize him as such. Philodemus tells us that the Stoic philosopher Khrysippos recognized "the sun, the moon, and the other stars as gods ... as well as law (*nomos*)" (*On Piety* 11); compare lines 2–4 of this hymn. Philodemus also tells us that Khrysippos said Zeus was Nomos (*On Piety* 14). Kleanthes, an earlier Stoic philosopher, in his hymn to Zeus describes him as "steering everything with Nomos" (line 2); the same metaphor (albeit with different wording) is found in line 8 of this hymn. In Orphic thought, Nomos was also considered a god. He is the father to Dike and/or Justice (*Orphic fragment* 248; see *OH* 63i), and he sits next to the enthroned Zeus, who has Dike as a companion (*Orphic fragment* 247). This last idea is very similar to that expressed by Kleanthes.

1 holy lord of men and gods: This is very similar to the opening of Pindar fragment 169a: "Nomos, the king of all men and gods" (lines 1–2).

2–4: Compare this to Pan, who is conceived as the force that keeps the four elements separate (*OH* 11.13–18); see also *OH* 10.14–16n.

4 nature's balance: The sense of balance here has the connotation of stability; cf. *OH* 63.7+n and 9.

6 he drives out malicious envy: We find the same phrasing in Mesomedes' hymn to Nemesis (line 6).

65. To Ares

Ares, the god of war, is the son of Hera and Zeus (Hesiod *Theogony* 921–923). Although Athene is also concerned with war (see *OH* 32i), she represents the strategic, intellectual side, while Ares portrays the blood-and-guts aspect. In literature, the two are sometimes brought together in sharp contrast. They fight against each other in epic poetry, whether directly (*Iliad* 21.391–414) or through a heroic proxy. Athene gives direct assistance to Diomedes when he attacks Ares (*Iliad* 5.755–863), and she helps Herakles in his battle against Kyknos (the son of Ares) and Ares himself (Hesiod *Shield* 433–466). Athene employs reason in trying to restrain Ares' anger at the death of one of his mortal sons on two occasions, further emphasizing the gulf between intelligence and pure battle rage (*Iliad* 15.100–142 and Hesiod *Shield* 446–449). The ancient Greeks in general had a strong distaste for the violence of war, and the negative treatment of Ares in myth is a reflection of this. The sons of Aloeus, Otos and Ephialtes, capture him, place him in chains, and keep him in a cauldron for thirteen months; Hermes eventually has to rescue him (*Iliad* 5.385–391). Zeus himself harshly rebukes him when he returns to Olympos fresh after being wounded by Diomedes (*Iliad* 5.888–898). Ares is often associated with aggressive figures who are threats to civilization, such as the Amazons. However, there is a positive side to Ares as well. In the *Iliad*, being called a "servant of Ares" (2.110), a "scion of Ares" (2.540), and the like is a mark of approval and praise. Ares is also a figure of masculine beauty; for example, Sappho praises a bridegroom as being as handsome as Ares (fragment 111). When the gods sing and dance, Ares also takes part (Homeric *Hymn to Apollon* 3.186–206). The ambiguity of his position in the Greek pantheon may be seen symbolically in his children with Aphrodite (Hesiod *Theogony* 933–937). Their two sons are Fear and Panic. They are often portrayed as driving the chariot of their father, and they rescue him from Herakles after Kyknos is slain. Their daughter, on the other hand, is Harmonia, the embodiment of civil concord (see also *OH* 55i). The legendary foundation of Thebes also reflects Ares' ambiguity. Kadmos slays a dragon who is either an offspring or favorite of Ares. The teeth of the dragon are sown, and immediately armed warriors sprout out of the earth and commence fighting. Only five survive the savage fray, and these five become the forefathers of the five noble houses of Thebes. After this, though, Kadmos marries Ares' daughter Harmonia, and the city is founded. Cults involving Ares are few; see Larson 2007, pp. 156–157, for details. Another war god, Enyalios, who interestingly had a female counterpart named Enyo, was eventually merged with Ares, although traces of independent cult still survived; see *OH* 76i.

As Ares is a god who controls war, he also can perforce control peace in the sense that he can prevent war from breaking out in the world (compare line 6). Our hymn is divided into two parts that clearly play on these two sides. The violent and bloody nature of the god is given adequate expression in the first five lines; the hymn does not shirk from admitting this aspect of the god. Yet he is asked to transform himself into an agent of peace in the final four lines. This follows the pattern found in many of the other hymns in the collection: a divinity who has the potential to wreak great harm is asked propitiously to manifest themselves in their beneficial guise. This hymn should be read in conjunction with the Homeric *Hymn to Ares*, which most likely dates from the Hellenistic period or later, possibly even composed by Proclus; see West 1970. For the placement of this hymn with the following one to Hephaistos, compare line 10 of the address to Mousaios. After the digression from the hymn to Aphrodite to four abstractions concerned with order and law (*OH* 61–64), we return to two major Olympian deities who are both sons of Zeus and who both have associations with Aphrodite. The relationship between peace and justice connects this particular hymn with the previous four and eases the transition.

5 rude clash: The word for rude, "amouson," literally means "without the Muses." The activities of these goddesses are intricately bound up with peace (see *OH* 76i), although Ares, as mentioned in the introduction to this hymn, is not unfamiliar with their charms. The opposition between war and the arts is powerfully portrayed by Homer when he shows us the great warrior Akhilleus, who in anger has withdrawn from the fighting at Troy, in his tent, singing the deeds of the great men of the past (*Iliad* 9.185–194). In the Greek text, this word significantly is the last one before the composer asks Ares to leave off from his war-like nature in the following line.

7 **Kypris**: Another name for Aphrodite (see *OH* 22.7+n). Ares is often portrayed as a lover of Aphrodite, as in the somewhat risqué story of how Hephaistos captures the adulterous pair in flagrante, sung by the bard Demodokos as part of the entertainment for Odysseus at Scheria; see *OH* 66i. There seems to have been an Orphic version of their relationship in which Ares rapes Aphrodite (*Orphic fragment* 275). In one fragment from the *Shorter Krater*, a work attributed to Orpheus, the gods are interpreted allegorically, and Ares, who is equivalent to war, is explicitly contrasted with Aphrodite, who is made equivalent to peace (*Orphic fragment* 413.4).

7 **Lyaios**: Another name for Dionysos; it means the "one who loosens/sets free" (see *OH* 50i). For the connection of music and peace, see note to line 5. The ecstatic worship of Dionysos represents a kind of madness that is kindred to the battle rage of Ares; compare the martial prowess of the possessed Bacchantes in Euripides *Bacchae* 714–768. It should be noted that, like Ares, Dionysos and Orpheus are said to have come from Thrace. Athene and Pan also are associated with madness and battle (see *OH* 32.6n).

8–9: Agricultural works often suffer in times of war, both due to the fact that the farmer leaves his homestead to fight and that marauding armies might ravage the land as they pass through. As with music and celebration, agriculture is a mark of civilization and thus incompatible with the savagery of war. Peace nurtures the young for obvious reasons. It is illustrative to compare Tyrtaios' admonition to the young that it is noble to die on the front lines (fragment 10) with the words of the defeated Kroisos to Kyros, the king of Persia: "No one is so foolish as to choose war over peace; for in peace sons bury their fathers, but in war fathers bury their sons" (Herodotos 1.87.4). See also *OH* 40.2n.

66. To Hephaistos

Hephaistos, the famed blacksmith of the gods, is the son of Zeus and Hera or in some accounts just Hera, who bore him apart from Zeus in retaliation for the latter's fathering of Athene without (direct) feminine aid (Hesiod *Theogony* 927–929). According to Homer, Hephaistos was cast down out of Olympos on two occasions. Once Zeus threw him out when he tried to take up the cause of his mother. All day he hurtled through the sky until he landed at the island Lemnos near sundown, where the Sinties succored the god (*Iliad* 1.590–594). Another time was at his very birth by Hera because she despised the fact that her son was born lame; Thetis and Eurynome kept him safe and cared for him in secret (*Iliad* 18.394–405 and Homeric *Hymn to Apollon* 3.311–325). Hephaistos eventually joins the Olympians. He takes vengeance on his mother by artfully constructing a chair that binds her fast when she sits on it. Hephaistos then conveniently skips town and thereafter refuses to return when entreated by the gods. In one version, Ares tries to free his mother but is frightened off by fires. Dionysos is dispatched. He gets the dour Hephaistos drunk, brings the wayward son home, and a reconciliation is finally reached (cf. Alkaios fragment 349, Pausanias 1.20.3, and Hyginus 166). Thus two outsiders are integrated into the society of the gods. The story was very popular in Archaic times as evidenced by the numerous vase paintings depicting the return. Perhaps the most famous one, found on the François vase, comically shows Hephaistos riding a mule amid reveling satyrs and nymphs as Dionysos leads the party to the seated Olympian gods (Boardman 1991, pl. 46.7). A tale with a somewhat similar pattern appears in Homer. In the *Odyssey*, the bard Demodokos sings of the adulterous affair between Ares and Aphrodite, Hephaistos' wife. Sun acts as informant, and Hephaistos forges a net with strands so fine, that they are practically invisible. The net entraps Ares and Aphrodite the next time they make love. Hephaistos bursts on the scene and calls the gods to witness; the goddesses, we are told, stay home out of modesty. Here it is Poseidon, not Dionysos, who barely mollifies the enraged god (*Odyssey* 8.266–366; see also *OH* 65.7n). Although Aphrodite is Hephaistos' wife in the *Odyssey*, it is Kharis, one of the Graces, in the *Iliad* and Aglaia, another one of the Graces, in Hesiod (*Theogony* 945–946) and an Orphic account (*Orphic fragment* 272). In all of these cases, there is an intended contrast, perhaps humorous, between beauty and ugliness. Even in antiquity, sometimes the geek gets the girl.

A characteristic emphasized in the literature is the cleverness and inventiveness of Hephaistos. As a divine artisan, he creates wondrous things, e.g., exquisite jewelry, self-moving tripods, self-blowing bellows, android women of gold, watchdogs made of gold and silver (*Iliad* 18.372–377, 417–421, 470–473; *Odyssey* 7.91–94). He forges weapons and armor for Herakles (Hesiod *Shield* 122–140) and Akhilleus (*Iliad* 18.478–614); in both cases, the poet focuses on the elaborate imagery Hephaistos puts on the shield. Along with Athene, Aphrodite, and others, he fashions Pandora (Hesiod *Works and Days* 59–82). The mirror that the Titans use to lure Dionysos is also a product of Hephaistos (*Orphic fragment* 309). In the Homeric *Hymn to Hephaistos* he is praised as a teacher of fine crafts and skills to man, whom he thereby elevated from savagery to civilization. In this, he is similar to other trickster gods associated with fire, such as Prometheus (cf. Aeschylus *Prometheus Bound* 436–506) and Loki in Norse mythology; see further *OH* 40.8–9n. Indeed, Hephaistos was so closely associated with fire, his very name could be used as a metonymy for the element, as already in Homer (*Iliad* 2.426); note, too, that he is addressed as "unwearying fire" in our hymn (line 1). He is invoked by Hera to fight off the river Skamandros from Akhilleus, a battle of the elements fire and water (*Iliad* 21.328–382). Hephaistos also has similarities with the clever, inventive, and magical blacksmith figures in myth: the Telkhines, Idaian Dactyls, and Kabeiroi (see *OH* O.20–22). These last are sometimes considered to be the sons or grandsons of Hephaistos at Lemnos (cf. Herodotos 3.37).

It is on this island that Hephaistos had significant cultic importance. Lemnos had an ancient non-Greek population. The name Hephaistos is not of Greek origin, and it is a non-Greek people, the Sinties, who Homer claimed were hospitable to the god when he fell from Olympos. We do not know much about his worship there. Philostratus, who was from Lemnos, gives a description of one ritual (*Heroicus* 53.5–7). It seems that every year, the hearths—and especially the smiths' forges—were rekindled with fire brought from Delos. For nine days all fires were extinguished on the island and offerings to the dead were made, during which the ship from Delos could not land. The new fires are expressly said to start the new life of the community. The only other place in antiquity where Hephaistos had significant worship was at Athens, where the god was closely connected with that other divinity of skills and crafts—Athene; for details, see Plato *Critias* 109c–d and 112b, Burkert 1985, pp. 167–168, 220, and Larson 2007, pp. 159–160. These two divinities are joined outside Athenian cult as well, e.g., in *Odyssey* 6.233, Plato *Protagoras* 321d–322a, and *Laws* 920d. In one of the poems ascribed to Orpheus, it is said that the (cosmic) Kyklopes were the first artisans and they were the ones who taught Hephaistos and Athene the arts (*Orphic fragment* 269).

4–5: The element fire is one of the four basic elements postulated by Empedokles, a thesis accepted by many later philosophers (see *OH* 5.4n and *OH* 15i). Fire appears to have had a central role in Herakleitos' philosophy (cf. Kirk, Raven, and Schofield 1983, nos. 217–220). The Stoics, influenced by Herakleitos, held that fire was the basic substance in the world and thought that the universe periodically returned to its original state in a great conflagration (see Long and Sedley 1987, pp. 274–279; see also the "ever-living fire" of Zeus' thunderbolt in Kleanthes' *Hymn To Zeus* 9–13). Ovid hints at this in passing only to playfully give an idea of what such conflagration might be like in his description of Phaethon's failure to control the chariot of Sun (*Metamorphoses* 1.253–261, 2.161–313; cf. Hesiod *Theogony* 687–710 and 853–868). The belief that the world would end in fire is of course not limited to the Greeks; compare Ragnarök in Norse mythology and, to a more limited extent, the destruction of Sodom and Gomorrah in Genesis 18:20ff. The author of the Derveni papyrus also seems to consider fire to be a constitutive element of the original state of the cosmos, and, according to him, the initial separation of fire into the sun is what precipitates the creation of the universe. Elsewhere in the collection, Ether, conceived as fire, is called the "best cosmic element" (*OH* 5.4).

6–7: In describing the shield of Akhilleus, Homer mentions first and foremost that it is bounded by the ocean and that in its center are the sun, moon, and stars. Hephaistos forged the heaven in some Orphic accounts (*Orphic fragment* 274), and there might be some connection between this and the Homeric shield. The Demiurge who creates the world in Plato's *Timaeus* is also an artisan and perhaps ultimately lurks behind this characterization of Hephaistos. The Greek word "dēmiourgos" literally means "worker for the people" (formed from "dēmos," "people," and "ergon," "work"). It does not appear in this poem, but it could not, since the word cannot be fitted into the hexameter rhythm; the closely related word "ergastēr," "worker," does appear in line 4, however. There may be Stoic influence in these lines as well. The fire that was the base substance of the world was referred to them as a "designing fire" ("tekhnikon pur"), which is what initiated and sustained creation as a rational whole, as opposed to "undesigning fire" ("atekhnon pur"), which had no such generative potential (see Long and Sedley 1987, fragments 46A–D, G, and 47A, C, F, and pp. 277–278). Naturally, the ether, stars, sun, and moon, believed to be composed of the fiery element, have such associations in their respective hymns (*OH* 5, 7, 8, 9; and note the different order in this hymn, probably again due to metrical considerations).

8: This line probably is referring to the central role of fire in civilization; see the introduction to this hymn. Fire was exceedingly important for everyday life; e.g., it provided light and was used in cooking and sacrifices. Compare also the hymn to Hestia, where the goddess is addressed as "mistress of ever-burning fire" (*OH* 84.2).

9 you dwell in human bodies: The hymn moves in a top-down fashion: cosmic fire, cultural fire, and now individual fire. There was a belief in antiquity that the soul was composed of fire, or at least a hot element. The Stoics, for example, equated the soul with fire, and thus composed out of the same element as the cosmos. In light of lines 12–13, however, a more biological fire might be meant. Fire, heat, and warmth play a role in ancient theories of life. Among the Stoics, Kleanthes argued by analogy from the fire that constituted the life of a living being to the fire that sustained the entire cosmos, which was conceived as a living being; Khrysippos opted for the term "pneuma," here meaning something like "hot air" (see Long and Sedley 1987 fragments 46B, G, J, 47C, O, 53X, Y, and pp. 286–287, 319). In both cases, that which constitutes celestial phenomena and the individual life is the same element, merely differing in scope. It is perhaps worth remembering in this context that human beings in the Orphic cosmogony are created from the Titans who were incinerated by Zeus' lightning bolt (see *OH* 37i), and Dionysos, too, can be said to have been "conceived in fire" (*OH* 45.1, *OH* 52.2). Fire and heat also are used by poets to describe emotional effects: love can burn or melt, and Sappho's famous catalogue of the physical effects of jealousy include a "subtle fire [coursing] under the skin" (fragment 31). See also *OH* 5.3, *OH* 10.27+n, and *OH* 18.9n.

12: Fire brings many benefits to man, yet it is also destructive (cf. "all-eating" in line 5), as in the case of the thunderbolt that kills Semele but leads to Dionysos' birth. Hephaistos, too, has two sides to his personality. He can play the role of jester, as when he hobbles around to excite laughter from the gods and defuse a tense situation between Zeus and Hera (*Iliad* 1.595–600); on the other hand, as mentioned in the introduction to this hymn, he is also susceptible to anger. As often in the collection, an ambiguous deity is asked to come in his beneficial guise while putting aside his deleterious nature.

67. To Asklepios

Asklepios seems to have originally been a hero-physician from Thessaly. He is first mentioned in Homer as the father of the "good doctors" Makhaon and Podaleirios (*Iliad* 2.731–732). In myth, he is usually the son of Koronis and Apollon (see Homeric *Hymn to Asklepios* 16.2–3). Before he was born, though, Koronis marries or has an affair with a mortal. Apollon learns about this and sends his sister Artemis to kill the pregnant Koronis. However, when the corpse of Koronis is on the pyre, Apollon takes pity on his unborn son and rescues him. The boy is entrusted to the wise centaur Kheiron, who instructs him in the arts of medicine. Asklepios becomes the world's greatest physician, but he runs afoul of Zeus by bringing a dead man back to life. Zeus punishes this transgression by kerblasting Asklepios with a lightning bolt. For the story, see Pindar *Pythian Odes* 3, Ovid *Metamorphoses* 2.600–634, and Apollodoros 3.10.3. Apollodoros lists a number of individuals claimed by various sources to be the person Asklepios resurrects, including Hymenaios by the "Orphics" (see further *Orphic fragment* 365).

Asklepios later came to be regarded as divine, and he might originally have been a god who was "demoted" to a hero by the time of Homer. He had important cults at Epidauros and Kos, and people would come to his temples for healing. One notable (though not exclusive) feature of Asklepian cult is incubation. Here the worshippers would spend the night in the god's temple in the hopes of receiving a dream vision that would be accompanied by healing (see also *OH* 86i). Examples in literature include Aristophanes' comedy *Wealth*, where the eponymous figure is cured of his proverbial blindness by undergoing such a ritual, and the fourth mimiambus of Herodas. The last words of Sokrates are to Krito, asking him to offer a rooster to Asklepios, a fitting gesture for one who cheerfully looked on death as a release of the soul from the prison of the body (Plato *Phaedo* 118a). The tragic poet Sophokles is said to have played a role in bringing Asklepios' cult from Epidauros to Athens (ca. 420 BC). For more on the cult of Asklepios, see Burkert 1985, pp. 267–268, and Larson 2007, pp. 192–195. See also *OH* 9i.

Our hymn has very little connection with the mythological account or traditional cultic worship. Instead, it focuses on the soteriological aspect of the one who brings healing in a world filled with pain and suffering. Health is one of the material benefits that are a recurring concern in the collection (see *OH* 68i). For the placement of this hymn in the collection, see *OH* 69i.

1 Paian: For this name/title of Apollon, see *OH* 34.1n. The alternate form Paion is used of Herakles, who is also portrayed as a healer in his hymn (see *OH* 12.10+n). It is possible that just as Herakles' divine portion in myth is transferred to Olympos upon the immolation of his physical body and then deified (see *OH* 12i), so, too, perhaps there was an account now lost to us where Asklepios, immolated by Zeus' lightning, undergoes a similar process. Semele, the mother of Dionysos, was also deified after being struck by Zeus' lightning (see *OH* 44i). See also note to line 5.

2 charm away the pains: Asklepios is similarly described in his Homeric hymn (16.4) and in Pindar *Pythian Odes* 3.51–52. Musical incantations were used in healing (see West 1992, pp. 32–33), and it is a commonplace in Greek literature that music brings temporary relief to cares and worries (e.g., Hesiod *Theogony* 55). It might be that Apollon's role as musician led to his being associated with the healing arts; see *OH* 34i.

4: For the collocation of sickness and the inevitability of death, see Sophokles *Antigone* 361–364 ("for death alone / he [man] will not find an escape, / but escapes from invincible diseases / he has contrived"); also see Euripides *Alkestis* 963–972, which mentions the inability of Orpheus (or his poetry) and the "sons of Asklepios" (i.e., the Hippocratics) to ward off Necessity (i.e., death). One could interpret this line in a provisionary sense; insofar as Asklepios can heal fatal diseases, he consequently "puts an end to death," albeit temporarily. Another possibility is to understand "harsh" as being emphasized. The end of this hymn asks the divinity to "bring life to a good end," which might be construed as requesting a painless one at a ripe old age (cf. *OH* 87.12+n); a similar idea is to be found in the following hymn (*OH* 68.9+n). Thus, the "harsh fate of death" would refer to death by disease. Given the last line of the hymn, it probably does not allude to the rewards in the afterlife the initiates might have expected to receive.

5 spirit of . . . growth: The Greek word translated here is used elsewhere of Earth (*OH* 26.3), Eleusinian Demeter (*OH* 40.10), and, most notably, Adonis (*OH* 56.6), who also is killed and reborn (albeit as a flower). Dionysos, too, is closely tied to vegetation; see *OH* 30i and *OH* 50.5n. Indeed, there is some overlap in the stories of his and Asklepios' birth. Both have a mother killed by a jealous divinity, both are pulled out of fire by their father before being born, and both are given to wise hybrid creatures to be raised (Kheiron the centaur in the case of Asklepios, Silenos in the case of Dionysos; see *OH* 54.1+n). This affinity further enhances Asklepios' soteriological appeal. See also note to line 1 and *OH* 68.1n.

6 son of Phoibos Apollon: This accords with the accounts of Asklepios, and it is the only explicit mythical detail in this brief hymn. On the other hand, there are a number of instances in this hymn where a word is reminiscent of a cult epithet of Apollon in his capacity as healer. First, Asklepios is called Paian (line 1) and "savior" (line 8), as is the Apollon of cult. The phrase "you ward off evil" (line 5) is a translation of a single word, "apalexikakos," which is a compound form of the word "alexikakos," another cult epithet of Apollon. Similarly, "helper" ("epikouros") at line 5 is closely related to the cult title "epikourios." Both of these words appear only here in the collection.

68. To Hygeia

Hygeia, also spelled Hygieia (e.g., *OH* 67.7), is the Greek word for "health," and, as with many other abstractions, has been vaguely personified as a goddess. She is usually conceived as the daughter of Asklepios, but she exceptionally is said to be his wife in the previous hymn. In *Orphic fragment* 262, she is the child of Eros (Love) and Persuasion; both of these deities are usually connected with Aphrodite (see *OH* 55.9n), and it is possible that the placement of the Asklepios/Hygeia pair of hymns was due to this association (see *OH* 69i; note, too, the overlap between Asklepios and Adonis, for which see *OH* 67.5n). We have the opening of a poem by Likymnios, a late fifth-century poet, addressing her as "glistening-eyed mother most high, / desired queen of the august seats of Apollon, / soft-smiling Hygieia" (*PMG* 769). Her worship was closely tied to that of Asklepios, but she was not always subordinate to him; at Sikyon (Pausanias 2.11.6), for example, women dedicated their hair and scraps of clothing to her cult statue. It is notable that a native of Sikyon, the poet Ariphron (late fifth or early fourth century BC), wrote a paian to Hygieia (*PMG* 813); he calls her the "most revered of the blessed ones" and avers that all human happiness requires her. Asklepios does not appear in it, although it is possible that the poem as we have it is only a fragment. In Athens, Hygieia could be invoked along with Zeus and Agathos Daimon (Good Divinity; see *OH* 73i) in libations poured after the washing of the hands and before the drinking in the symposium. Athene was also worshipped as Health at Athens (see *OH* 32.16n). In the Hippocratic oath, her name follows that of Asklepios. It is also possible that the placement of this hymn intentionally echoes the Hippocratic order, but more likely it just follows the usual practice of our composer to place hymns to subordinate divinities (here a male/female pair) after the more important member (see further *OH* 14.8–9n).

1 **blooming**: Health is naturally described as blooming, and her gift is described in similar terms (cf. "every house blossoms" in line 4). The bulk of Ariphron's fragment cited in the introduction is a conditional sentence that runs as follows: if there is any pleasure for men, "then with you, blessed Hygieia, it is in full bloom and shines with the gentle talk of the Graces." The theme of vegetation is found in the previous hymn, where Asklepios is called a "blessed spirit of joyful growth" (*OH* 67.5+n). It appears in Persephone's hymn (*OH* 29.18–19), and it is a prominent motif in the hymns to Dionysos (see *OH* 50i+5n).

2 **mother of all**: Compare the Likymnios fragment, cited in the introduction to this hymn, and see also *OH* 10.1n.

6 **loathed by Hades**: Hygieia, in her capacity as a healer of disease and consequently a goddess who keeps living things alive, perforce delays Hades from increasing his kingdom.

7 **apart from you**: The same sentiment is found in Ariphon's poem; see note to line 1.

8 **wealth**: Some combination of wealth, riches, and prosperity are desired along with health throughout the collection; see *OH* 15.10–11n.

9 **the many pains of old age**: The idea here is not that Hygieia keeps young men healthy so

NOTES | 69. TO THE ERINYES 189

that they survive to experience the suffering connected with old age. Rather, the wish is to reach old age without pains, i.e., in good health; cf. *OH* 29.19, *OH* 67.4n and *OH* 87.12+n.

69. To the Erinyes

The Erinyes (often translated as "Furies," after the Latin Furiae, but the etymology is uncertain) are a group of female divinities who take vengeance for criminal acts; they are particularly concerned with the slaughtering of kin and the breaking of one's oath. We find different origins in the mythological record. Hesiod tells us that they were born from the blood that fecundated Earth after Kronos castrated his father Sky (*Theogony* 183–187). Although the violent Giants were also born from this act, it is especially appropriate for the Erinyes in light of their role as instruments of vengeance. Later in the poem (469–473), Rhea asks her parents Earth and Sky "to contrive such a plan that the birth of her dear child [Zeus]/would go unnoticed and her father's Erinys would take revenge." Sometimes, though, the Erinyes are said to be daughters of Night (e.g., Aeschylus *Eumenides* 321–323). In either case, their origin is from a primeval, chthonic entity. Sophokles ingeniously combines both traditions by describing the Eumenides (who here are equivalent to the Erinyes; see below) as "daughters of Earth and Darkness" (*Oedipus at Kolonos* 40). Darkness is a male figure (Greek Skotos) and thus an appropriate masculine analogue to the feminine Night.

The Erinyes also have fertility associations, and this might have been their original domain. This connection with fertility is suggested by the fact that Earth is sometimes their mother. It is also evidenced by their close relation with the Eumenides. The two groups were originally distinct but later were usually identified with one another—the Erinyes representing the negative, punitive aspect of transgressing boundaries and the Eumenides the positive, beneficial result of maintaining such. A process of transformation is described in Aeschylus' *Eumenides*, where he connects the mythical Erinyes, who form the chorus to this play, with the cult of the Eumenides (called Semnai Theai, the August Goddesses, at Athens). At the end of the play, the Erinyes, having been denied their prerogative to mete out punishment to Orestes for his matricide, threaten to afflict Athens with disease that would make the land "leafless" and "childless"; after Athene assuages their anger by offering them honors in Athens, the Erinyes in turn promise benedictions for a prosperous land. This ability to destroy or nurture life hints at their powers of fertility. Furthermore, we find Demeter worshipped as Demeter Erinys (sometimes called just Erinys). According to Pausanias (8.25.4–10), Demeter, while searching for Persephone, turns herself into a horse in order to escape the unwanted attentions of Poseidon. Upon recognizing the ruse, he transforms himself into a horse as well. The result of their union is a mysterious daughter (whose name is not given) and the wonder horse Areion, who is sometimes said to have Earth as his mother. Demeter was given the name Erinys due to her initial anger over the encounter; compare the anger of Nemesis (*OH* 61i) and Melinoe (*OH* 71.4–5+n). The name Erinys is also found among other divinities in a Linear B tablet from Knossos, but nothing about this goddess is known. It may be that she was a completely independent fertility goddess who eventually became identified with Demeter, and, in a separate development, was expanded into a plurality representing different aspects of the original goddess, whatever they were (cf. note to line 1).

In cult, the Erinyes do not appear to have been directly worshipped. Aside from the cult of Demeter Erinys, who might not be connected with the group, there was a temple to the

Erinyes of Laios and Oedipus in Sparta and its colony Thera (Herodotos 4.149.2); it is interesting to note that we have evidence for the close proximity between a tomb of Oedipus and the Eumenides' cult both in Athens and the Attic deme Kolonos. The Spartan cult, though, was founded by a particular clan in an effort to ward off continued infanticide (compare the threats made by the Erinyes in the *Eumenides*, which are another sign of their connection with fertility), but the nature of worship is unclear. In general, however, it is likely that in many cases the cults to the Eumenides are, in fact, to the Erinyes, albeit in their capacity to bring blessings. One approaches divinities for favors, and the invocation of the deity by means of a euphemistic name was felt to increase the chance that the divinity would appear in its friendlier guise. To call on the Erinyes by this name would increase the risk that the goddesses would appear in their unpleasant aspect (cf. *OH* O.12+n and *OH* 71.11n). By the same token, it is the Erinyes (alongside other chthonic powers)—and not the Eumenides—who are invoked in curse tablets, where their violent and deadly powers are deliberately sought for deleterious effect. For a similar reason, they also at times appear in magical spells, e.g., to help bring back a lover or catch a thief. The Erinyes are sometimes portrayed in the literature as physical manifestations of curses, and in fact are called Curses (Greek Arai) from time to time. They can also be found rationalized as a perpetrator's guilty conscience. Both the Erinyes and Eumenides are mentioned in the first few columns of the Derveni papyrus; see further *OH* 70i. Very little of the text can be read, let alone understood, and addressing the various possible interpretations is beyond the scope of this commentary; see Betegh 2004, pp. 74–91, 218–219.

The close connection between the Erinyes and Eumenides is maintained in our collection. The hymns to these goddesses form a contiguous pair (cf. *OH* 14.8–9n), and there are many correspondences in language and imagery. Some of these are pointed out in the notes below, as well as in the following hymn. Yet, despite these similarities, the two groups are not identified with one another but rather are kept distinct. The Eumenides are given a genealogy, for example. Even more surprising, in view of the tradition, is that they are described in demonic terms—more so than the Erinyes. Further differences are that each group is summoned for somewhat different reasons and given different offerings. Since the *Hymns* were composed for a specific, pragmatic purpose, such a material distinction implies a conceptual one. The negative/positive polarity of the Erinyes/Eumenides found in earlier times has been effaced; instead we have two very similar sets of divinities, invoked in a slightly different, but related, manner. This allows for a certain consistency with the often conflicting literary and religious traditions. A similar explanation applies to the close relationship of the Erinyes with the Fates (see *OH* 59i) and Nemesis (see *OH* 61i).

This hymn begins a series (*OH* 69–77) whose placement within the collection is curious. The other hymns show evidence of having been deliberately positioned (see in particular *OH* 15i, *OH* 30i, *OH* 55i, *OH* 61i, *OH* 79i, and *OH* 87i), but these hymns seem out of place, a mere listing of pairs (except for the hymn to Melinoe, which is nevertheless closely related to the Eryines/Eumenides pair and clearly belongs with them; see *OH* 71i). Now, it may very well be that our composer did not know how to integrate these entities and so just tossed them together in a sort of random miscellany near the end of the collection. On the other hand, one thread that ties them together is that all of the addressees are much more bound up with cult worship than with literary mythology. The exception to this proves the rule: both the Muses and Mnemosyne are explicitly connected with cult practice in their hymns (*OH* 76.7 and *OH* 77.9–10), and note that memory plays an important role in the eschatology of some of the

Bacchic gold tablets. Here, though, Mnemosyne is invoked right before Dawn to help the initiates, who have probably been worshipping the entire night, to remember the rest of the hymns and the ritual (see *OH* 77i). The block of *OH* 69–77 may further be connected with the Dionysian hymns (*OH* 45–54) through their cultic, mythological, and linguistic associations (e.g., the maenadic imagery in *OH* 69, Leukothea the addressee of *OH* 72, the Muses and Mnemosyne as founders of mystic rites). There might also be ring composition with the final group of hymns, as they end with death (literally) and the *OH* 69–77 group begins with death figures (Erinyes, Eumenides, and Melinoe).

1 Tisiphone, Allekto, noble Megaira: We have only sparse attestations for the names, one of which is Apollodoros (1.1.4), whose source seems ultimately to have been derived from an Orphic theogony (West 1983, pp. 121–126). Therefore, it is possible that they are Orphic in origin. The names are significant. "Tisiphone" means "vengeance for murder," Allekto (sometimes Alekto) "unceasing," and Megaira "grudge." Taken together, they represent in particular the Erinyes' role as punishers of murderers. The dead victim bears a "grudge" that requires "vengeance for the murder," and this grudge is "unceasing" until the murderer is punished. The same exact line appears in the *Orphic Argonautika* (968), and these are the only places where all three Erinyes are named together in extant poetry. Persephone appears in place of Tisiphone in a prayer to Moon found in a magical handbook, but it is possible that this was a lapse by the writer; Persephone's name appears again a few lines later in the text; see note to line 16.

2 Bacchic cries: Throughout this hymn, the Erinyes are described through Dionysian and particularly maenadic imagery (see *OH* 1.3n and *OH* 52i). Like the maenads, they raise Bacchic cries, they are active at night (line 3), they are rabid (line 6), they howl (line 6), they wear animal skins (line 7), and snakes adorn their hair (line 16; see note below). This association already appears in Greek tragedy; for references and an interpretation, see Johnston 1999, pp. 253–256. For loud noise in Dionysian worship, see *OH* 30.1n.

4 Styx: A river in the underworld. Its name means "hate." The Olympian gods, when making an oath, swear by its waters (Hesiod *Theogony* 775–806). Hesiod tells us that the Erinyes assisted in the birth of Oath, whose mother was Strife (*Works and Days* 803–804). The water of the Styx is described as splendid in Orpheus' address to Mousaios (*OH* O.29), and this is the only other mention of the river in our collection. Styx is a daughter of Okeanos; see *OH* 83.3n.

9 phantoms airy, invisible: Two closely related passages in Hesiod seem relevant to this description. First, Dike, whenever wronged in a court of law, visits ruin on the city clothed in airy mist (*Works and Days* 222–224). A little later in the same poem, Hesiod addresses the kings and reminds them that "upon this earth that nurtures many Zeus can levy / thirty thousand deathless guardians of mortal men, / who keep a watchful eye over verdicts and cruel acts / as they rove the whole earth, clothed in mist" (252–255). Thereupon Dike is represented as a girl who runs to daddy Zeus whenever men make false charges in order that vengeance be taken on them (the verb used, "apoteisei" (260), is cognate with the "tisi" in Tisiphone; see note to line 1). See also *OH* 61i and *OH* 62i. The Erinyes as described in our hymn have a similar function, and it is very suggestive that a fragment attributed to Orpheus (*Orphic fragment* 851) implies that the Erinyes are the agents of Zeus' indignation at those who do not respect the ordinances of their "ancestors." A forged letter attributed to Herakleitos explicitly connects the Erinyes with the Hesiodic guardians: "Many are the Erinyes of justice [*dikē*], the watchers of moral failings. Hesiod lied when he said there were thirty thousand. They are few and not sufficient for the evil in the world. There is much wickedness" (9.3.1). For the Erinyes' connection with Dike, see note to line 15 below. Homer twice uses the epithet "mist-roving" (*Iliad* 9.571, 19.87) to describe an Erinys; the same word is used to describe Moon (*OH* 9.2), but there the word does not have the connotation of invisibility. Words denoting "air(y)" or "mist(y)" appear with some frequency in the *Hymns*. Usually they merely refer to the element "air" and are not used descriptively of a phantasmal appearance. Both ideas, however, are combined, when Zephyros is called "airy, . . . invisible" (*OH* 81.6), just as the Erinyes are here. For more information on airy phantoms, see *OH* 71i.

15 **you gaze as the eye of Dike**: For the eye of Dike, see *OH* 62.1+n. The Erinyes are often connected with Dike in literature. The chorus of Erinyes in Aeschylus' *Eumenides* declare that fear of their punishment makes a man obey Dike (490–565); compare the *Sisyphos* fragment mentioned in *OH* 61.5n. Their role in the social order of man also finds curious reflection in a fragment of the Pre-Socratic philosopher Herakleitos (Kirk, Raven, and Schofield 1983, no. 226), which happens also to be cited in the Derveni papyrus. Herakleitos says that the sun will not overstep its proper measure; otherwise the Erinyes, "assistants of Dike," will find him out (see also note to line 9). A similar portrayal of the Erinyes is found in an enigmatic saying attributed to Pythagoras by Hippolytos: "If you travel abroad from your own [land?], do not turn back; otherwise the Erinyes, helpers of Dike, will come after you" (*Refutation of All Heresies* 6.26.1). Perhaps the mention of the "speedy flames of the sun and the moon's glow" (line 10) is a remnant of such philosophical speculation. Our hymn certainly portrays the Erinyes as part of divine order: they "howl over Necessity's dictates" (line 6) and are called "goddesses of fate" (line 16; see note below). Their connection with Dike reinforces the idea that not only is there order in the world but that it also possesses an ethical dimension; see further *OH* 64i.

16 **snake-haired**: A traditional characteristic in literature and art. Aeschylus is the first extant writer to describe the Erinyes thus (*Libation Bearers* 1048–1050), and, if Pausanias (1.28.6) is to be believed, he was the first one to do so. The same word appears in line 10 of the next hymn in the same metrical position (and see *OH* 70.9–10+n).

16 **many-shaped goddesses of fate**: Compare "of the thousand faces" (line 8; the two words both end in "-morph," "shape"). Their connection with "Necessity's dictates" (line 6) is consistent with their equivalence to the Fates. In Vergil's *Aeneid*, the Erinys Allekto is described as having "a thousand [= many, countless] names" (7.337), and Servius in his comment on this line reports that Euripides in one of his tragedies (now lost) has Allekto claim that she was not born to fulfill a single function (implied are her traditional roles, as described above) but that she is Fortune (probably Tyche in the original), Nemesis, Fate, and Necessity (fragment 1022). This probably is what Herakleitos and Pythagoras had in mind (see note to line 15), and, indeed, Euripides might have been directly influenced by one or both of them. A prayer to Moon in a magical handbook also calls the Erinyes "many-shaped." Even more pertinent, at the beginning of this prayer Moon is equated with them (they are named here, with Persephone in place of Tisiphone; see note to line 1), Dike, and the Fates, while at the end she is equated with Necessity, Fate, Erinys, and Dike (*PGM* 4.2795–2799; 2858–2860; see also note to line 9). This shows how easily the Erinyes could be seen as a different manifestation of similar divinities, not just of the

Eumenides. Usually, though, the Fates and Erinyes are kept separate. Both are, in some accounts, daughters of Night, and so could be considered sisters (see the introduction to this hymn). Agamemnon blames Zeus, Fate, and the Erinys for his ruinous dispute with Akhilleus (*Iliad* 19.86–90). In the *Eumenides*, Fate is said to have conferred on the Erinyes their prerogatives (334–339). In our collection the two groups are kept distinct, despite the number of verbal and conceptual correspondences between their hymns (as with the Eumenides; see *OH* 70i). They are both concerned with the moral order of the cosmos (see *OH* 59i), albeit from different perspectives. The Fates work from above—while still maintaining chthonic associations (see *OH* 59.3–4n)—and the Erinyes from below, with us hapless mortals caught in between.

70. To the Eumenides

The Eumenides, the "kindly-disposed ones," are a group of female divinities similar to, and usually identified with, the Erinyes. In Athens, they were called the August Goddesses (Semnai Theai). In *Oedipus at Kolonos* 461–492, Sophokles gives a literary description of a rite of atonement to the Eumenides, and their worship has a significant role in this play. For more information about the Eumenides, and their relation to the Erinyes, see the introduction and notes to the previous hymn. They are usually considered beneficial goddesses, as their name would suggest. Unlike the Erinyes, they are not invoked in spells or curses. In our hymn, however, they are given a more Stygian and infernal character that is usually reserved for the Erinyes. The Eumenides were in fact originally fertility goddesses with definite chthonic associations. This can be seen in Aeschylus *Eumenides* 903–967, where the transformed Erinyes promise first and foremost bountiful production. The Orphic tradition seems to have recognized their primeval function as well, for in *Orphic fragment* 293, they are called "flower-producers." See also the note to lines 2–3. The Derveni papyrus enigmatically equates the Eumenides with souls.

2–3: Chthonic Zeus is another name for Hades; see *OH* 18.3+n. Persephone is also called the mother of the Erinyes at *OH* 29.6. The parentage given in the *Hymns* differs from the one found in the mainstream tradition (see *OH* 69i). However, two fragments ascribed to Orpheus (*Orphic fragment* 292–293) also present Hades and Persephone as the parents of "the Eumenides under the earth." This chthonic connection is not exclusively Orphic; for example, the Athenian Semnai Theai dwelt in a cave beneath the earth (cf. Aeschylus *Eumenides* 1004ff.; also *OH* 69.3–4 and 8). Orpheus is also supposed to have written that Demeter prophesied to her daughter that she would "mount the blooming bed of Apollon / and give birth to splendid children, their faces burning with fire" (*Orphic fragment* 284). These children are the Eumenides, who are also described as "bright-faced" in *Orphic fragment* 293. It would seem, then, that the Orphic tradition had two different fathers for the Eumenides. However, the name Apollon was often connected with the verb "apollumi," "I destroy," and it is possible that Apollon here is used as an oracular periphrasis for Hades, "the destroyer" (just as he is called "Chthonic Zeus" in our hymn); another possibility is that the different fathers represent two alternate versions that were considered Orphic in antiquity. These two interpretations are discussed by West 1983, pp. 95–98, 243–244.

4–5: The Erinyes also watch over human beings "as the eye of Dike, ever in charge of justice"

(*OH* 69.15), and they "howl over Necessity's dictates" (*OH* 69.6). Both groups are described by the adjective "timōroi" (translated "retribution" at *OH* 69.7 and "punish" here), which is used in the same metrical position. These goddesses, then, are described as having more or less the same function. One interesting difference, though, is that the Eumenides are said to be concerned with "impious mortals," whereas the Erinyes, like the Fates, watch over all mortals, just and unjust alike.

6 black-skinned queens: The color black is often associated with the underworld and its denizens. The Eumenides are also "nocturnal" (line 9) and "of the night" (line 10, and see note to line 10). The word translated as "black-skinned" is also used of Sky (*OH* 4.7, there translated "dark blue"), and Aphrodite is called on to join the company of the "dark-faced nymphs" (*OH* 55.22). The Eumenides are similarly called "sable-skinned" at Euripides *Orestes* 321.

6–7 your awesome eyes . . . / . . . darts of light: Compare the description of the Eumenides mentioned in *Orphic fragment* 284 and 293, cited in the note to lines 2–3. In a hymn to Moon found in the magical papyri, she is called "flesh devourer" (*PGM* 4.2866) in a context where she is equated with the Erinyes and others (see *OH* 69.16n "many-shaped"), and there are a number of close verbal correspondences between this passage and our hymn (see further note to line 10). Moon is also said to be seen eating human flesh in other parts of the same spell book. A curse spell calls on "the flesh-devouring gods," among others, for its fulfillment.

8 frightful: The same word recurs at line 10, where it is rendered "terrible." It is a noun in ancient Greek, and its adjectival form is used once of the monster Ekhidna (*Orphic fragment* 81.2) and once of Ares (*Oracula Sibyllina* 13.78). These are the only appearances of the word and its cognates in ancient Greek. A closely related adjective is used of the Erinyes at *OH* 69.8 ("dreaded maidens").

9 paralyzing the limbs with madness: Insanity is typical of how the Erinyes lay low their victims, as they themselves mention in their binding spell over Orestes at Aeschylus *Eumenides* 329–330 and 342–343. It is again notable that the Eumenides are attributed with a negative function normally associated with the Erinyes. Deliverance from madness or frenzy appears elsewhere in the *Hymns*: see *OH* 71.11n.

10 snake-haired, terrible maidens of the night: The Erinyes are also described as "snake-haired" (*OH* 69.16; same metrical position), and there are only two other appearances of this word in ancient Greek. It is again used of the Eumenides by the first-century AD philosopher Annaeus Cornutus, and it is one of the many epithets lavished upon Moon in her hymn in the magical papyri (*PGM* 4.2863). This hymn bears many striking verbal similarities to ours: in addition to this word, both goddesses are dark (line 6 ~ 4.2863), eat flesh (see note to lines 6–7), inflict madness (line 8 ~ 4.2868; see also *OH* 71i), and are "nocturnal" (line 9 ~ 4.2855). The Eumenides' connection with the night is established in this line as well, and the word translated here as "of the night" is the same one translated as "nocturnal" in the hymn to the Erinyes in the same metrical position (*OH* 69.3); for other close similarities between these two hymns, see the notes to lines 4–5 and 8.

71. To Melinoe

Melinoe is an obscure figure. This hymn is the sole literary testimony of her existence, and the only other appearance of her name is found inscribed on a magical device, which was presumably used for divination (see Morand 2001, pp. 185–88). On this device, the name appears with others (including Persephone) in an invocation to Hekate. An affinity of Melinoe to Hekate is found in the *Hymns*. Both are "saffron-cloaked" (line 1 ~ *OH* 1.2), called "nymph" (line 1 ~ *OH* 1.8), and are invoked to come in good spirits. They also are active at night (line 9 ~ *OH* 1.5). Hekate is elsewhere associated with driving mortals mad (see note to line 11 and *OH* 1i). However, the two are not quite the same in the collection, as they do not share the same father. Melinoe is represented more as an infernal, psychic force—a spectral embodiment of Persephone's anger that irrationally lashes out at mortals—and hence the need to appease her. Hekate, too, was commonly believed to be capable of inflicting insanity by means of such spooks. Melinoe's ability to cause madness or insanity here is reminiscent of the Eumenides' similar capability described in the previous hymn. There are other explicit connections between the two, which explains why the hymn to Melinoe follows that of the Eumenides (see *OH* 69i). It is particularly significant that they are born from Persephone, especially since she is not the traditional mother of the Eumenides. Melinoe is asked to "show to the initiates a kindly . . . face" (line 12), and the word for "kindly" ("eumenes") is the root from which the name Eumenides is derived. Moreover, the name Melinoe might provide a further clue. One possible meaning of this word is "gentle-minded," which would be quite analogous to the euphemistic name Eumenides (see *OH* 70i). However, the name may also be derived from a Greek word meaning "yellow" and thus be a euphemism for Hekate in her role as a moon goddess (see Ricciardelli 2000, p. 495). Moon is described as "amber-colored" (*OH* 9.6), and both goddesses receive the same offering (aromatic herbs). Madness was also associated with the moon in antiquity, as can be seen in the etymology of the English word "lunatic," which is derived from Latin "luna" ("moon"); see also *OH* 1i and *OH* 70.10n. Nevertheless, given the lack of evidence, we should probably not pedantically press for a meaning. The name Melinoe could very well have had both connotations, the color and the mood, for the initiates, however her name was generally understood. In any event, Melinoe should be considered to belong to the cluster of goddesses that include Hekate, Moon, Artemis, and Persephone, here assimilated to a degree (by genealogy and function) to the Erinyes/Eumenides pair.

1 **saffron-cloaked**: The epithet occurs in the same metrical position in Hekate's hymn as well as in Hesiod's description of Enyo (one of the Graiai) and the Okeanid Telesto (*Theogony* 273 and 358, respectively). Homer uses it of Dawn, and Alkman of the Muses (*PMGF* 46). "Saffron-cloaked" here might just be a decorative epithet, or it could be a play on the color implied by Melinoe's name (see the introduction to this hymn). If Melinoe is another name for Hekate in her capacity as moon goddess, then the choice of the word might be a conscious play on Homeric usage, connecting diurnal and nocturnal light.

1 **nymph**: This does not designate Melinoe as a member of a group of lesser divinities, but rather a young woman of marriageable age; see *OH* 51i. The singular is also used of Hekate (*OH* 1.8) and Tethys (*OH* 22.1; here it means "bride").

2–3: Very similar phrasing is found in the hymn to Adonis (*OH* 56.9), who is also born from Persephone.

2 Kokytos: A river in the underworld; its name means "wailing." It is mentioned once more in the collection as the location of the dwelling of Chthonic Hermes (*OH* 57.1), just as the Styx marks the home of the Erinyes (*OH* 69.4) and Acheron is the throne of Hades (*OH* 18.10). According to *Orphic fragment* 340, the souls of those who committed injustices in their lives come to Tartaros by way of Kokytos (see *OH* 18.2n).

3 Kronion: A common epithet of Zeus, meaning "son of Kronos."

4–5: The story is obscure, and interpretation is made more difficult by the fact that the original Greek is problematic, perhaps corrupt. The "wily plots" are necessary since Persephone is probably already the bride of Hades. Most likely they indicate that Zeus had disguised himself, as he often does in his amorous pursuits. In Orphic mythology, he took the form of a snake when he fathered Dionysos by Persephone. Since Dionysos has the same parentage in the *Hymns* (*OH* 30.6–7), it is possible that this act was understood by the initiates to have also produced Melinoe; see *OH* 29i. The snake, as symbol of chthonic powers, would be an appropriate form to produce such an infernal creature, and both Dionysos and Melinoe are connected with madness. Compare *Odyssey* 11.633–635, where Odysseus is afraid that Persephone might send a ghost or a monster after him during his stay in the land of the dead.

8–9 shining in darkness— / . . . gloom of night: Melinoe's activity at night belies her chthonic nature. Line 8 has been interpreted to allude to different phases of the moon (Ricciardelli 2000, p. 498). Compared with the rest of the hymn, though, it seems more likely that the various stages of visibility are more naturally understood as a concrete extension of how Melinoe vexes mortals. Shining (or gleaming) in darkness is found also in the hymn to Night, describing both her (*OH* 3.7) and the fears she is asked to disperse (*OH* 3.14).

10 O queen of those below: Almost the same exact phrase is used of Melinoe's mother, Persephone, in *OH* 29.6 ("queen of the netherworld").

11: A very similar request is made of Pan (*OH* 11.23+7n). For the madness caused by Pan ("panic"), see *OH* 11i. It is typical that a divinity has the power to cure what lies in its power to cause. Dionysos is able to remove madness as well as bring it (see *OH* 53i). Rituals to cure madness are attested for the Korybantes, Kybele, and, possibly, Hekate; see Dodds 1951, pp. 75–80 (particularly pp. 77–78.). Rhea is often identified with Kybele, and so it is not surprising to find that she, like Melinoe, has a connection to madness in the *Hymns* (see *OH* 14.3+n), although she is invoked at the end of her hymn to banish "death and the filth of pollution," not madness. The Korybantes were connected with Rhea-Kybele, and it might be the case that their rituals to alleviate madness were not distinct from but rather part of Kybele's. Their namesake Korybas bears some affinity to Melinoe in this regard; he is summoned to avert fantasies (the Greek word is related to that of "apparitions" in line 6) from the soul (*OH* 39.4 and 10), as well as fear (*OH* 39.3) and anger (*OH* 39.9). The collection's concern with madness is probably to be understood in light of the overall strategy in summoning divinities. Encountering the divine is always a risky endeavor; one can never be certain how one stands in the eyes of such beings. Contact with the more-than-human carries with it the danger of losing one's speech, one's senses, even one's sanity. This concern is reflected throughout the collection in that many of the hymns either explicitly ask that madness be driven away or implicitly do so by requesting the divinity addressed to come with a peaceful disposition; see *OH* 30i and *OH* 69i and further Graf/Johnston 2007, pp. 146–148, 155–156. Comparable is the petition at the end of the hymn to Dream that requests "do not through weird apparitions show me evil signs" (see *OH* 86.18+n); note that the shapes of Melinoe are also described as "weird" (line 7).

72. To Tyche

Tyche, which is the Greek word for "fortune" or "chance," is the personification of a concept that became very prominent in Hellenistic and especially in Roman times. She is not found in Homer but Hesiod counts her among the Okeanids (*Theogony* 360). Similarly, we find a Tyche among the nymphs who were picking flowers with Persephone before she was abducted by Hades (Homeric *Hymn to Demeter* 2.420; see also *Orphic fragment* 387, from a similarly themed poem attributed to Orpheus). It is not clear whether they were conceived as individual personifications of the concept *tyche* or if the name is merely a "speaking name." We do find Tyche personified outside of epic. Alkman calls her the daughter of Forethought and sister of Eunomia and Persuasion (*PMGF* 64). Pindar addresses her as "Tyche the Savior" at *Olympian Odes* 12.2 and elsewhere numbers her among the Fates as their mightiest member (fragment 41, preserved by Pausanias 7.26.8; see also below). The tragedians of the fifth century occasionally mention a personified Tyche. In Euripides' *Kyklops*, Odysseus utters a short prayer to Hephaistos and Sleep for help in blinding the Kyklops, and at the end of the prayer he claims that if the gods fail to heed his request, it will be necessary to regard "tychē" as a "divinity" and one more powerful than the gods (606–607). The concept, even in its personified aspect, has been tenacious and one that still survives in Greece.

Tyche as an actual goddess instead of a mere personification of an abstract idea does not seem to occur until the fourth century BC, when what we might call a folk religious attitude emerges, as is evidenced by the picture gleaned from the orators and the poets of New Comedy. Tyche becomes a sort of "Lady Luck," who may bring unexpected fortune (or disaster) to enterprises. A parallel development is the concept of a personal Tyche that attends an individual from birth and is "responsible" for that person's fortunes in life. This is a concept akin to the Fates "weaving" each person's destiny; see *OH* 59.15n, and compare the stars' role in personal destiny (*OH* 7i). Pindar, as mentioned above, included Tyche among the Fates and the plural Tychai are personified and mentioned alongside the Fates in the magical papyri. Mesomedes identified both Tyche and Fate with Nemesis in his hymn to that goddess (see *OH* 61i). For a brief summary of this transformation of Tyche in the fourth century, see Mikalson 1998, pp. 62–63. In terms of cult, there is no evidence of any before the fourth century BC, unless Pausanias' description of a statue of Tyche in Smyrna carved by Boupalos, who was active in the sixth century BC, was used as a cult figure (4.30.6). According to Pausanias, this was the first depiction of Tyche with a heavenly sphere above her head and of her holding in one hand the horn of Amaltheia (later known as the cornucopia, or "horn of plenty"), the wonder-goat who suckled the infant Zeus (see also Pausanias 7.26.8). The horn is common in the iconography of Tyche in later times. Pausanias also mentions a statue of Tyche holding the infant Wealth in her hands in her sanctuary at Thebes from the early fourth century (9.16.1–2). Tyche became particularly associated with the protection and foundation of cities, and it is interesting to note that already Pindar, according to Pausanias, is said to have called her "pherepolis" ("she who supports the city"; Pausanias 4.30.6 = Pindar fragment 39).

An anonymous poetic fragment in hymnic style addressed to Tyche is preserved by Stobaeus (1.6.13 = *PMG* 1019). This fragment emphasizes the blessings she may bring, and notable is the light imagery that, as often in Greek poetry, is symbolic of deliverance from ills (compare the Pindar *Olympian Odes* 12). In our hymn, Tyche is just as capable of granting wealth as poverty. Furthermore, as is appropriate for this collection, she takes on a more chthonic coloring than elsewhere (except, perhaps, in the Homeric *Hymn to Demeter* and the related lost Orphic work). She has been ostensibly integrated into the Dionysian-Orphic scheme. For the position of this hymn and the next in the collection, see *OH* 69i.

2 **goddess of the roads**: Hekate is normally associated with roads, particularly intersections (see *OH* 1.1). It seems that Tyche is here being assimilated to Hekate (see *OH* 36.2), and it is perhaps not a coincidence that this hymn follows after the one to Melinoe, who also has similar associations (see *OH* 71i). In Hesiod's *Theogony*, Hekate is similarly represented as being capable of granting numerous kinds of blessings to those she favors but also of withholding such gifts when she so chooses (see *OH* 1i, and compare with lines 6–8 in this hymn). The identification with "Artemis the guide" in the following line reinforces this supposition, as Artemis is but another aspect of Hekate (see *OH* 36i). We also find mention of Moon in this connection, and it is interesting to note that Tyche is invoked as another name for Moon in the magical papyri—in fact, right after the name "Selene" (*PGM* 4.2665). Tyche is not one of the divinities mentioned in Orpheus' address to Mousaios, which perhaps speaks for her identification with Hekate-Artemis-Moon in the collection.

4 **Eubouleus**: In our hymns, this is another name for Dionysos, Zeus, and Adonis. In Orphic cosmogony, it is also another name of Protogonos (see *OH* 6i). Here it seems to be used of Zeus, who is the father of Artemis. See *OH* 41.8n.

73. To Daimon

In Greek, the word "daimōn" denotes a vague appellation of divine force, sometimes personified, but more often not. All divinities can be called a *daimōn*, and so can human beings after they have died. The Golden Race in Hesiod's myth of the five races become such figures after their extinction (*Works and Days* 121–126); in later times, it was common to refer to the deceased as a *daimōn* in grave inscriptions. The modern idea of a demon, that is, a malevolent supernatural entity, is first attested for Xenokrates, one of Plato's students. For the overlap and distinction between daimōn and god, see Burkert 1985, pp. 179–181. The ancient Greeks did not like unexplained phenomena and often cast about for something to firmly ground their understanding of the source of their experiences (see also *OH* 59i). Desire in early Greek poets, for example, is not an emotion welling from within, but an external force that emanates from the eyes of the beloved. Sokrates attributed the premonition he felt before engaging in an action to be somehow "*daimōn*-like." Indeed, in speaking of divine activity, the ancient Greeks often took such careful precautions. An unknown cause of an event can be expressed by saying "a god" or "some god" willed it to be thus, and the efficacy of divine power might be qualified by, e.g., statements that the gods "somehow" or "in some way" accomplish such and such. The concept of *daimōn* coheres to a large extent with this sentiment and provided a sort of a blank check, as it were, for causal explanations. It was particularly linked to individual fortunes, both good and bad.

It is specifically in this capacity that we find *daimōn* worshipped as a household god, where the concept is personified to a degree and the entity so produced called Agathos Daimon (Good Daimon). Libations poured before the drinking of wine could be accompanied with an invocation to this divinity, and at symposia he would be invoked along with Zeus Soter (the "savior") and Hygieia (see *OH* 68i). The connection with personal fortune brings Agathos Daimon in contact with (Agathe) Tyche (Good Fortune), and they are often found together. In Isidoros' hymns (first century BC) Isis is associated with Agathe Tyche and another Egyptian goddess, Renenutet, who was connected with individual fortunes. This figure has a male consort, Sokonopis, who corresponds to Renenutet's consort Shay and whom Isidoros identifies with Agathos Daimon (see Vanderlip 1972, p. 6). (Agathe) Tyche and (Agathos) Daimon are also sometimes invoked together in the magical papyri.

Our author seems to be intentionally incorporating elements of Agathos Daimon in this hymn, particularly the concern for material blessings and his connection with Tyche (subtly expressed thematically and linguistically). That the addressee is twice called Zeus, however, indicates something more. The wealth discussed in this hymn primarily refers to agricultural wealth (cf. "livelihood" in line 2). It is not surprising, then, that there are a number of points of contact between this hymn and others in the collection addressed to chthonic deities connected with agriculture, particularly Hades. This god is sometimes addressed as "Chthonic Zeus," as we find in the hymn to Plouton (see *OH* 18.3+n). Thus Daimon might represent a particular aspect of Hades. However, it is much more likely that it is Zeus himself that is being addressed. Despite being a celestial god, Zeus was also intimately involved in fertility. Rain is necessary for the crops to grow, and, as the god who sends the rain, Zeus may legitimately be called the one "who gives livelihood to mortals" (line 2). Moreover, worship of Zeus had a chthonic aspect as well, particularly as a tutelary household god. In this, he bears a close affinity to Agathos Daimon, and it would be quite natural to refer to Zeus as Daimon. Two particular incarnations of Zeus that seem relevant to this hymn are Zeus Ktesios (Zeus of Wealth) and Zeus Meilikhios (Zeus the Gentle); see the notes to lines 2 and 4. It should also be mentioned that the other hymns addressed to Zeus focus on the celestial side of this god, particularly as the great weather god (*OH* 15 and *OH* 19–20). It would be very strange if the chthonic side, one that was quite prevalent in actual religious practice and that is particularly germane to our cult, would be neglected in the collection. Comparable, perhaps, is the separate treatment of Hermes and Chthonic Hermes (see *OH* 57i). When calling on the gods, the Greeks preferred to err on the side of inclusiveness.

Three different *daimōn* figures are mentioned in Orpheus' address to Mousaios. There we find a bifurcation into a "holy" *daimōn* opposed to a *daimōn* responsible for the ills that befall mortal men (line 31); the holy *daimōn* is presumably responsible for the beneficial events and might actually have been considered to be Agathos Daimon by the cult. The next line speaks of divinities (*daimones*) who inhabit every nook and cranny of the cosmos. Consistency might be imagined by postulating a hierarchy of *daimones*: a Zeus-*daimōn* at the head, followed by a personification of two aspects of Daimon—one good, one bad—and finally an acknowledgment of the plurality of *daimones* that are connected with the various individual fortunes. But perhaps we should not overly press for a systematic theology; the notion of a *daimōn* is very fluid, encompassing many senses and fulfilling different functions. The hymns capture both the idea of a race of guardian spirits, already found in Hesiod (see *OH* 69.9n) and the personified abstraction of such an idea, as seen in the person of the Agathos Daimon. The hymn to Tyche would naturally suggest one for an individualized *daimōn*, a female-male pairing that is repeated in the subsequent hymns to Leukothea and Palaimon as well as throughout the collection (see *OH* 14.8–9n). The identification of Daimon with Zeus in his chthonic aspect is natural and another example of the complex web of associations that form the tissue of our collection.

2 gentle: This same adjective is used of Tyche in the same exact place in the previous hymn. The *daimones* mentioned by Orpheus in his opening address are included among divinities referred to as "gentle." The Greek word, "meilikhios," is also a cult title of Zeus. Under this name, he was worshipped both as a household and polis divinity. The power to grant good or bad fortune was his, and sacrifices were made as a way to stay in this god's good graces. An overview of Zeus Meilikhios (and other similar incarnations) may be found in Larson 2007, pp. 21–23.

2 who gives birth to all: Zeus is often considered the father of gods and men, and the epithet "who gives birth to all" is also used in the hymn of Astrapaios Zeus (*OH* 20.5, translated there as "begetter of all"). See also *OH* 15.3–5+n. A very similar epithet is used of the sky gods Sky (*OH* 4.1) and Kronos (*OH* 13.5), as well as Zeus' son Herakles (*OH* 12.6). This also speaks against interpreting Daimon as Hades in this hymn.

4 giver of wealth: Cognates of the epithet translated here as "giver of wealth" ("ploutodotēn") are used to describe Demeter ("giver of all," *OH* 40.3) and Hades ("you give the wealth of the year's fruits," *OH* 18.5). We also find it used to characterize one of the functions the Golden Race possesses after they die out and become *daimones* (Hesiod *Works and Days* 126). Isidoros applies this epithet to both Isis-Renenutet-Tyche (1.1) and Sokonopis-Agathos Daimon (2.10). At the end of a spell in the magical papyri that details the construction of a phylactery to bring success, the god addressed is invoked as Aion, giver of wealth, and Agathos Daimon (*PGM* 4.3165–3166; for Aion, see *OH* O.28–29n). Zeus Ktesios (Zeus of Wealth) is also called "ploutodotēs." This is another aspect of Zeus, similar in function to that of Zeus Meilikhios (see Larson 2007, p. 21). Very relevant for our hymn is that Zeus Ktesios is found with Tyche and Asklepios as a trinity of household divinities capping a list of gods in a late dedicatory inscription found in Stratonicea (Asia Minor). Pausanias reports that Zeus Plousios (Zeus of Wealth) had a temple in Sparta (3.19.7).

74. To Leukothea

Leukothea, the "white goddess," is represented in literature as a sea divinity. Her first appearance is in the *Odyssey*, where she attempts to aid the foundering Odysseus (5.333–353). She was once the mortal named Ino, one of the daughters of Kadmos and a sister of Semele, Dionysos' mother (Hesiod *Theogony* 975–976). Both names are mentioned together at *OH* O.34. Ino became the nurse of Dionysos after Semele had been incinerated by Zeus' magnificence (see *OH* 44i). A jealous Hera drives Ino's husband, Athamas, insane, and he kills their older son, Learkhos. A terrified Ino scoops up the younger son, Melikertes, and is chased by the raving Athamas until she reaches a precipice overlooking the sea. Cornered, she plunges herself and her son into the sea. The sea divinities take pity on her and transform her into one of their own. She receives a new name, Leukothea. Melikertes, too, is transformed and becomes the god Palaimon (see further *OH* 75i). See Ovid's *Metamorphoses* 4.416–542, and for a somewhat different account, Apollodoros 3.4.3. In other versions of the myth, Ino kills or attempts to kill the children of a previous wife of Athamas, Nephele (Apollodoros 1.9.1), or of a later one, Themisto (Hyginus *Fabula* 4, based on the lost *Ino* of Euripides; cf. *Fabula* 1 for a different account). The significance of the name White Goddess is obscure. The white may refer to the foam of the sea and/or the complexion of her skin; compare the names of the sea-nymphs Galatea ("gala" = "milk") and Tyro ("turos" = "cheese").

Leukothea played an important role in cult. Aristotle reports that the Eleans asked Xenophanes (later sixth century BC) whether they should sacrifice and sing dirges to Leukothea;
he answered that if they thought she was a goddess, they should sacrifice but not lament, but if
they thought she was human, then they should lament but not sacrifice (*Rhetoric* 1400b5–8).
Cicero, writing in the first century BC, mentions that Leukothea was worshipped throughout
Greece (*De natura deorum* 3.15). The Megarians believed that the corpse of Ino had washed
up on their land, and they claimed that they were the first to call her Leukothea (Pausanias
1.42.7); they also thought the rock from which she jumped was in their territory (Pausanias
1.44.8). Ino was worshipped in a few places in Lakonia. At Epidauros Limera, people would
throw barley cakes into a lake. If the cake sunk, it was a sign of the goddess' acceptance; if it
floated, it indicated her rejection (Pausanias 3.23.8). There was also a dream oracle on the road
to Thalamai; the sanctuary had bronze statues of Sun and Pasiphae, who Pausanias claims
was not a native goddess and whose name was a title for Moon (3.26.1). For more on dream
oracles, see *OH* 86i. Leukothea is invoked along with Hermes, Hekate, Ploutos, Persephone,
Artemis, Demeter, and anonymous heroes to protect a grave in an inscription found in Pantikapaion (modern day Kerch); all of the deities have the epithet "chthonian." A cultic connection with Dionysos is perhaps to be read in an inscription on an altar found in Syria. It reads
"the vineyard of the goddess Leukothea and Melikertes. Asklas, son of Thaddaios, dedicated
the altar at his own expense out of piety" (Sartre 1993, p. 52). The context is unclear, but in the
mention of a vineyard belonging to Leukothea and Melikertes it is tempting to read a Dionysian association, perhaps in a cultic context (also see the collection of inscriptions in Sartre's article for more Leukothea inscriptions from Syria). Pausanias reports that in Lakonian
Brasiai the inhabitants claimed that the wandering Ino arrived and consented to be nurse
to Dionysos, who had washed up on shore (cf. Melikertes); he also saw the grotto where
she brought up the infant, and he learned that the plain was called the Garden of Dionysos
(3.24.3–4). The grotto might have housed a cult, but Pausanias gives no indication of one.
The theme of a wandering goddess bereft of her child and nursing another's as a surrogate is
found in the story of Demeter, who after the abduction of her daughter Persephone wanders
the world in disguise and eventually becomes a nurse to the infant Demophoön at Eleusis
(see *OH* 41i).

The connections with Dionysos and indications of chthonian character make it unsurpris-
ing to find her addressed in our collection. In addition, the rebirth of a mortal into a god
(cf. the question of the Eleans to Xenophanes) is consonant with the hopes of initiates in
such cults, as the Bacchic gold tablets attest. Furthermore, another inscription found in Syria
(also in Sartre's article) mentions the apotheosis of the dedicatee's son in a cauldron used in a
ritual for Leukothea of Segeira. It begins with the Greek version of the Latin formula "for the
welfare of the Emperor," and the emperor mentioned is Trajan (98–117 AD). What exactly is
meant by "apotheosis" (literally or figuratively understood?) is unclear, but there is perhaps
some relation to the versions of the myth where Ino places Melikertes in a cauldron (e.g.,
Apollodoros 3.4.3) and might be trying to revive her son, as suggested by Farnell 1921, pp.
43–44.

It is interesting, though, that this hymn focuses almost exclusively on the maritime associations, particularly the soteriological aspect already found in the *Odyssey*. Only the brief
mention of Dionysos in line 2 serves to connect her with the mythological record. The placement of this hymn and the following hymn to her son is also puzzling. One would expect,
perhaps, a contiguous location to the second one addressed to the Kouretes, who, in their

connection with Samothrace and the Dioskouroi, are associated with the sea and succoring sailors (see *OH* 38i). Indeed, an epigrammatic parody of dedications by Loukillios (first century AD) connects Leukothea and Palaimon (under their mortal names!) with the Samothracian gods: "To Glaukos and Nereus and Ino and Melikertes / and to Zeus of the Depths [= Poseidon] and the Samothracian gods / I Loukillios, for being saved from the sea, have shorn / the hairs of my head—for I possess nothing else!" Both this hymn and that to the Kouretes look toward the deities to provide beneficial weather, and, as a nurse of Dionysos, Leukothea would fit with the series of addressees involved in the life of the infant Dionysos (*OH* 31–39). However, Leukothea seems to be considered chiefly as a cult figure and thus is included in the more congenial group (see *OH* 69i). For the female/male pair of Leukothea/ Palaimon, see *OH* 14.8–9n.

75. To Palaimon

For the story of how Melikertes, the son of Leukothea, is transformed into the sea-god Palaimon, see the introduction to the previous hymn. The mortal remains of the boy are usually described as being conveyed to Corinth on a dolphin. Games were then instituted in his honor (sometimes by the hero Sisyphos), and these became later known as the Isthmian Games (see Pausanias 1.44.8, 2.1.8), which, alongside the Olympian Games, were one of the four main national contests in ancient Greece. The games, though, are sometimes attributed to Theseus (Plutarch *Theseus* 25.5). The name Palaimon means "wrestler," and this name is generally assumed to be due to Palaimon's association with athletic competitions, since the baby Melikertes could hardly be labeled a wrestler; it is possible that Palaimon was a separate entity, a divine youth, who later became merged with Melikertes. Be that as it may, Pausanias reports that the body was kept in an underground cave (2.2.1), which suggests chthonian rites. In describing a painting of the reception of Melikertes, Philostratus mentions mysteries (*orgia*) for Palaimon instituted by Sisyphos (*Imagines* 2.16); earlier Aristides (a contemporary of Pausanias), at the end of his prose hymn to Poseidon (*Orations* 46.40), similarly alludes to rites (*teletai*) and mysteries (*orgiasmoi*). An inscription containing the laws of a Dionysian cult at Athens (inscribed before 178 AD) mentions Palaimon (Dittenberger 1920, no. 1109), along with Dionysos, Kore (= Persephone), Aphrodite, and Proteurythmos, after a series of priestly offices in the context of a sacrifice.

Palaimon, like his mother Leukothea, has connections with Dionysos. They are relatives (see note to line 1), and in myth their stories are sometimes connected (e.g., Apollodoros 3.4.3). As already mentioned, Melikertes/Palaimon seems to have had chthonic associations and his own mystery cults, and it is also possible he was part of a Dionysian one at Athens in the time of the Roman Empire. Furthermore, the "rebirth" of Melikertes as Palaimon, along with the transformation of Ino, his mother, into the sea goddess Leukothea, bears some affinity to the dual birth of Dionysos, and such a transformation is a typical concern of Dionysian and Orphic mystery cults. See further Seelinger 1998. The focus of this hymn, however, just as in his mother's, is almost exclusively on the nautical, soteriological element, and there is no explicit mention of the mythological trappings and cultic associations found elsewhere in Greek literature regarding this figure.

1 **comrade of joyous Dionysos**: Dionysos is technically a cousin to Melikertes, as their mothers were sisters. Moreover, Ino is often portrayed as the nurse of Dionysos, as in our

collection (*OH* 74.2+i), and so it is not that much of a stretch to imagine a closer relation between the two aside from the mere fact of blood relation. In our hymn, Palaimon is explicitly made part of the Dionysian *thiasos,* as are others in the collection; see *OH* 1.3n and *OH* 54i. The Nereids are said to "revel in the waves" (see *OH* 24.2–3).

6–8: For Palaimon as a savior of sailors, see Euripides *Iphigenia at Tauris* 270–271: "O child of lady Leukothea, you who watch over ships, / master Palaimon, be gracious to us." The prayer is somewhat humorous, in that the god in his role of saving sailors is invoked in very different circumstances. Here a barbarian herdsman, someone tied to the land, calls on Palaimon at the sight of two men on land (Orestes and Pylades) mistakenly assumed to be gods; the incongruity is further emphasized when the herdsman asks : "whether in fact these two are the Dioskouroi who sit atop mountain peaks / or the delights of Nereus, he who the well-born / chorus of fifty Nereids sired." The Dioskouroi are Kastor and Polydeukes, who are usually the ones associated with the protection of seamen in literature. *The Hymns* mention them in connection with the Kouretes (see *OH* 38.21+i).

76. To the Muses

One of the most enduring and endearing creations of Hellenic imagination, the Muses are the goddesses of artistic and intellectual inspiration. In the epic tradition, they are represented as the nine daughters of Zeus and Mnemosyne (*Odyssey* 24.60, Hesiod *Theogony* 53–62), and their holy voices, often accompanied by Apollon's lyre, delight the assembled gods and set various young divinities dancing (e.g., *Iliad* 1.601–604, Homeric *Hymn to Apollon* 3.186–206, Homeric *Hymn to Hermes* 4.450–452). For the Greeks, the activities the Muses inspire were intimately bound up with religious festivity and peace. The embassy sent by Agamemnon to attempt a reconciliation with Akhilleus finds the great hero, this man of violent passions, singing of the famed deeds of the heroes of old (*Iliad* 9.185–194). His attention to the peacetime activity of epic poetry dramatically underscores his refusal to participate in the Trojan War. The dichotomy of music and battle is expressed in the first fragment of Arkhilokhos: "I am the servant of Lord Enyalios [= Ares] / and the Muses, knowing their lovely gift." See also *OH* 65.5n+i. Early poets often began their song with an appeal to the Muses. It is not clear whether the "goddess" Homer addresses at the beginning of the *Iliad* is a Muse, but he explicitly addresses one at the beginning of the *Odyssey* (see also *OH* 77i). Hesiod begins his *Works and Days* with the Muses, and in the *Theogony* we find a more expansive address in what amounts to a "Hymn to the Muses" (1–114). The convention is not just limited to the opening of a poem; before launching into the imposing "Catalog of Ships," Homer calls on them for their aid (*Iliad* 2.484–493). *Orphic fragment* 361 mentions that "not even in any way do mortals forget the Muses. For they are / the rulers for whom the dance and lovely festivities are a concern." West speculates this fragment (and perhaps *Orphic fragment* 362, cited below in the note to lines 8–10, which comes from the same source) might have been part of a hymn to the Muses, which perhaps in turn was the opening part of a larger composition, possibly a theogony (West 1983, pp. 265–266).

This earliest picture of the Muses as graceful and benevolent deities who inspire artists and especially poets and who frequently sing as Apollon plays the lyre is the one that became standard and that was developed in the succeeding centuries. However, there are alternate traditions. For one thing, their number and names are not entirely fixed. Pausanias 9.29.2 reports that there was an account of three Muses, named Melete (Practice), Mneme (Memory), and Aoide (Song). Pausanias subsequently mentions that the Archaic poet Mimnermos had distinguished between two generations of Muses: an older one, daughters of Sky, and a younger one, daughters of Zeus (9.29.4). Similarly, Alkman records two different genealogies in different poems, with one group descended from Earth and Sky (Diodorus Siculus 4.7.1 = PMGF 67). Mousaios is also supposed to have mentioned two generations, an older one born in the time of Kronos, and a younger one born of Zeus and Mnemosyne. What we seem to have here is myth's propensity for doublets, as in the succession myths involving Sky/Kronos and Kronos/Zeus or the two wars known as the Titanomachy and Gigantomachy.

The Muses were worshipped privately and in public cult. Hesiod's astounding encounter with the Muses while tending his flocks at the foothills of Mount Helikon (*Theogony* 22–34) led him to dedicate a tripod he had won in a poetic contest (*Works and Days* 654–659). The special connection between poet and Muse is affirmed by Homer in the person of the bard Demodokos (*Odyssey* 8.62–73 and 486–500) and, negatively, in the story of Thamyris, who boasted that he could outdo the Muses in song (*Iliad* 2.594–600). A legend of the poet Arkhilokhos has him meeting the Muses, disguised as mortal women on the way back from work, in the early morning hours as he was leading a cow to the market. They asked if the cow was for sale, and when he replied that it was, they promised him a good price for it. Thereupon women and cow disappeared, and a lyre lay at the feet of the awestruck future poet.

The most important cult site was probably in the Vale of the Muses at Helikon. The cult might have already been in existence in Hesiod's time. However, there is scant evidence for it until the beginning of the fourth century BC, when the town Thespiai was in control of the cult and strove to increase its importance from a restricted, local affair. In this the town was successful. During its history, the cult attracted the support from Greek cities and organizations and in particular from rulers of Pergamon, Egypt, and Rome. Numerous dedications are described by Pausanias (9.29.1–31.3). The place evidently became a popular tourist destination. Connected with the site was a festival called the Mouseia that comprised both musical (at first primarily theatrical it seems) and athletic events. There are cults to the Muses sprinkled throughout Greece, notably at Delphi (in connection with Apollon) and Athens. In addition to such traditional religious expressions, worship of the Muses became connected with private institutions of learning. Perhaps the most famous is the Mouseion at Alexandria, where the scholars were supported by the kings of Egypt. (The word "Mouseion" means "place of the Muses," and, via Latin, is the source of our "museum.") Almost a century before Alexandria, however, Plato established a Mouseion and a private cult to the Muses in the district of Akademos (whence English "academy"), where his school was located. Aristotle's Lyceum had one as well, and the phenomenon of dedicating an institution of higher learning to the Muses and calling it a Mouseion was widespread.

Orpheus as a poet is naturally connected to the Muses through his avocation. The relationship might have been deeper. Plato suggests that some claimed he was directly descended from the Muses (*Republic* 364e), and Pausanias mentions his descent from Kalliope as one of the falsehoods believed by the Greeks (9.30.4). See also *Orphic fragment* 896, 898, 902–906, and *OH* 24.9–11n; for other Muses, see *Orphic fragment* 907–908. Orpheus was from Thrace, and the Muses as well at times are connected with this country and its people. Strabo reports that the Macedonians in his time inhabited places once occupied by the Thracians where the Muses were especially worshipped and that the Thracians were the ones to bring the Muses to Helikon (9.2.25, 10.3.17; cf. Pausanias 9.29.3). Thamyris was Thracian, and in the tragedy *Rhesos* attributed to Euripides, the title character, a Thracian, is made the son of a Muse and river god.

This hymn forms a pair with the following one dedicated to Mnemosyne (cf. *OH* 14.8–9n). For their position in the *Hymns*, see *OH* 69l.

1: Our hymn follows the more widespread tradition of the Muses' genealogy, and there seems to be no sign of the older generation mentioned by some Archaic poets.

2 Pierian Muses: Pieria is a mountain to the north of Mount Olympos in Macedonia, and it is the traditional birth place of the Muses. Of course, the Muses come to live on Olympos, where they entertain the gods. As mentioned in the introduction to this hymn, they are also associated with Helikon, and they are sometimes referred to as the "Helikonian Muses" (e.g., Hesiod *Theogony* 1).

4 in every discipline: The Muses are the catalysts of all artistic and intellectual activity. The association of one specific Muse with one particular branch of art (e.g., Kalliope with epic poetry) is a later development. See also Murray 2004.

7: The Muses are usually not directly linked with mystic rites. However, the widespread pedagogical function of the Muses in addition to the role music and dance played in mystery cults makes it quite easy to attribute to them the revelation of such matters. The role of their mother, Mnemosyne, in Orphic cult (see *OH* 77i), as well as the fact that one of their number, Kalliope, is sometimes claimed to be Orpheus' mother, also facilitate such a connection; see further *OH* 24.9–11+n, where the Nereids are said to have been the first to establish Bacchic rites. It might be suggested in these lines that the Muses were the source of the rite Orpheus teaches to Mousaios in the beginning of the collection (see *OH* Oi); compare the revelatory nature of the Muses and their epiphany to the poet Hesiod (*Theogony* 22, 26–28). See Hardie 2004 for further discussion. In addition to the Nereids, we find elsewhere in the collection that the Kouretes are credited with being the "first to set up sacred rites for mortals" (*OH* 38.6+n), the Dionysian *thiasos* is said to reveal "torch-lit rites" (*OH* 54.10+n), and Themis is suggested to be the one who introduced maenadism (*OH* 79.7–10n). See also *OH* 40i. Diodorus Siculus gives a euhemerized account of Dionysos' *thiasos*, among whom are a group of extraordinarily talented and educated women called the Muses who provide entertainment (4.4.3, 4.5.4).

8–10: Lines 8–9 are probably quoted directly from Hesiod *Theogony* 77–79, who may have been the first to name these divinities. Our poet deviates from Hesiod's words in his elaboration on Kalliope, who nevertheless was the preeminent Muse for Hesiod as well. "Mother" might refer to the tradition that she was Orpheus' mother (see the introduction to this hymn), and this might further explain the pride of place given to her. Since the opening address to Mousaios tells us there are nine Muses (*OH* O.17–18), Hagne (meaning "holy") here would either be another name for Kalliope (as we have translated it) or refer to some other goddess, perhaps Mnemosyne. The Greek word "hagnos" is used of the Muses in Orpheus' opening address. According to Pausanias, Persephone was called Hagne in Messene, where there was a sacred grove containing her statue along with one of Apollon and Hermes carrying a ram; he then piously declines to discuss the mysteries practiced there in honor of Hagne and Demeter, which he considers second in rank to Eleusis (4.33.4–5). It is interesting to note that a river close by is linked to the blinding of Thamyris (4.33.3). The names of the Muses are significant in that they are in some way connected with their musical endeavors. The one exception is Ourania (Heavenly); her name might be a remnant of the older generation descended from Sky, as discussed in the introduction to this hymn. The meanings of the names of the others are as follows: Kleio, "celebrator"; Euterpe, "well-pleasing"; Thaleia, "abundance"; Melpomene, "singer"; Terpsichore, "joy in dance"; Erato, "lovely"; Polymnia, "many hymns"; Kalliope, "pretty voice." *Orphic fragment* 362 is from a scholiast to Apollonios of Rhodes *Argonautika* (3.1–5c), who discusses a scholarly debate over the mention of Erato in that poem; one side claimed that, according to the "Orphics," she was traditionally the inventor of dancing.

12 **glory and emulation**: This might have the connotation of rivalry, albeit the positive sort that pushes one to reach or surpass the level that another has attained. Compare the use of the related verb by Hesiod to describe the effects of Good Strife: "One neighbor emulates the other / who hastens to wealth" (*Works and Days* 23–24). There may be an allusion to the "learned contests" mentioned at the end of the hymn to the Stars (see *OH* 7.12–13n and *OH* 33i).

12 **lovely and sung by many**: The Muses' mother Mnemosyne is also described as "lovely" in *OH* O.17, and this word is a play on the name Erato. Likewise, "sung by many" (Greek "poluumnon") is a play on the name Polymnia.

77. To Mnemosyne

Traditionally, Mnemosyne was one of Zeus' lovers and gave birth to the Muses (Hesiod *Theogony* 53–54 and 915–917). This seems to be the extent of her importance in traditional myth. According to Hesiod, she herself is the daughter of Sky and Earth (*Theogony* 135; cf. *Orphic fragment* 179) and so one of the original Titans. Her name means "memory," and this is a quality that is of utmost importance in an oral culture and especially for the oral poet. Of course, it continued to be important even as the Greeks increasingly became a literate society, just as it is still considered advantageous for someone to possess in our day and age. As mentioned in *OH* 76i, one tradition claimed there were only three Muses, one of whom was called Mneme (Memory). Plutarch tells us that the Muses were also known as Mneiai, i.e., the Memories (*Quaestiones conviviales* 743d). Poets traditionally start with the Muses or at least invoke them before embarking on a difficult stretch, and Plato, about to recount to Krito a conversation in which he recently engaged, somewhat ironically states "as for the rest of it, Krito, how might I properly relate it to you? For it is no small matter to be able to recover through narrating such incredible wisdom as I heard. So that I for my part, just like the poets, need to call upon the Muses and Mnemosyne at the beginning of my narration" (*Euthydemus* 275c–d). Hermes in his eponymous Homeric hymn calls upon Mnemosyne at the start of his song (4.429–430). See further *OH* 76i. It is quite possible that the goddess of *Iliad* 1.1 and the Muse of *Odyssey* 1.1 is none other than Mnemosyne herself; the same might be said of the Muse invoked at the beginning of the Homeric *Hymn to Aphrodite* (no. 5).

There is very little evidence of cult activity for Mnemosyne. One of the lives of Aesop reports that he set up a temple to the Muses and placed Mnemosyne among them instead of Apollon, which incensed the god. In his visit to Athens, Pausanias describes a private home where Dionysos was worshipped (1.2.5). The god was called Melpomenos (Singer, and cf. the name of the Muse Melpomene), and Pausanias reports that he found a statue or picture of Mnemosyne along with Athene, Zeus, and the Muses. It is unclear if the goddess was worshipped here. However, two writers on Athenian history, Philokhoros (fourth/third century BC) and Polemon (third/second century BC), mention that wineless libations were poured to Mnemosyne at Athens, as well as to Dawn, Sun, Moon, the nymphs, and Aphrodite Ourania.

The Erinyes also received such libations (Sophokles *Oedipus at Kolonos* 100), and the practice implies chthonian rites.

In Orphic eschatology Mnemosyne—or rather her lake—played a significant role. A number of the Bacchic gold tablets mention this geographical feature in the instructions that are intended to remind the soul of the initiate what to do once in the underworld. Indeed, the first line of the first one states "this is the work of Mnemosyne," and near the beginning of the eighth it seems that the initiate is called "hero who remembers" (but the text is somewhat corrupt). While there are some divergences in detail, the general procedure has the initiate's thirsty soul avoiding the first body of water it perceives in the gloom, marked by a white cypress tree. All the other souls take their drink from there, but the initiate's soul is directed to go further along to the Lake of Mnemosyne (nos. 1, 2, 8, 25). This lake is guarded (by whom or what, we are not told), and the guards ask the purpose of the soul's visit. The answer to be given is to state that one is dying of thirst, to ask for a drink and to claim descent from Earth and starry Sky. The guards then grant a drink, and the soul, after drinking, proceeds to some special blessed area in the underworld reserved for initiates and/or that holds special distinction among the dead. For Johnston's identification of the dangerous waters to avoid as the Spring of Forgetfulness, see *OH* 85.8n. Our hymn, too, shows a concern for combating oblivion. The first reference speaks to this in general terms (line 3); at the end, the prayer is particularized to the "sacred rite." It might refer to some aspect of the ritual in which these hymns were presumably employed, perhaps the "learned contests" found in the hymn to the Stars (see *OH* 7.12–13n and *OH* 76.12n). In any case, as the ritual was drawing to a close, our initiates would certainly have need to invoke memory to remember the last remaining hymns and ritual acts (see van den Berg 2001, p. 215, and Graf/Johnston 2007, p. 155). If they had been active the entire night, they were probably growing weary as dawn approached (see further *OH* 78i). The contrast between remembering and forgetting also appears in *Orphic fragment* 415, from the *Little Krater* ascribed to Orpheus. In this fragment the "harmony of the Muses" and all human endeavors granted by Mnemosyne are said to have been hidden through forgetfulness by time (perhaps Time?) and are preserved for humans by memory. Finally, of interest, though not directly connected with our hymn, is that Pausanias explains that before one goes to consult the oracle of the hero Trophonios, he is first required to drink from the fountain of Lethe (Oblivion) to clear his mind of all things before encountering the god and then from the fountain of Mnemosyne to remember what the oracle states (9.39.8); after the oracle is given, the person is put on the seat of Mnemosyne and asked what he learned from the god (9.39.13). This use of liquid to induce psychological states is reminiscent of the transformation the consumption of wine effects; see *OH* 50i.

78. To Dawn

Dawn (Greek Eos) is the lovely goddess on whom Homer lavishes some of his most beautiful epithets (e.g., "rosy-fingered," "saffron-cloaked"). We find variants in her genealogy. Hesiod makes her the daughter of the Titans Hyperion and Theia and the sister of Sun and Moon, two other divinities with a notable connection to light (*Theogony* 371–374); she then gives birth with the obscure Astraios to the winds Zephyros, Boreas, and Notos, as well as to the Morning Star (Eosphoros, "dawn-bringer") and all the stars (*Theogony* 378–382; see also *OH* 7.3n). In myth, Dawn is primarily portrayed as a goddess with a fondness for plucking mortal men off the face of the earth to be her lover, usually with unhappy results. Most famous of all is perhaps Tithonos. She loved him so much that she asked Zeus to grant him immortality, forgetting to ask for eternal youth as well. Eventually she tosses the aged Tithonos into a closet, where he withers away to a mere plaintive voice and eventually is turned into a cicada. See Homeric *Hymn to Aphrodite* 5.218–238. They had two sons, Emathion, who was killed by Herakles during this hero's western wanderings, and Memnon, king of the Ethiopians, who was killed by Akhilleus at Troy. Ovid tells in detail the story of her abduction of Kephalos and his eventual rejection of the goddess in favor of his true love, the mortal Prokris (*Metamorphoses* 7.690–862). The hunter Orion was also an interest of Dawn's, and according to Homer he was killed by Artemis for this relationship (*Odyssey* 5.121–124). Homer also briefly mentions a fourth lover, Kleitos (*Odyssey* 15.250–251). This pattern of behavior was noticed in antiquity, and one reason offered for it was that Aphrodite had cursed Dawn for having an affair with Ares (Apollodoros 1.4.4). Our hymn takes no notice of such charming tales.

Dawn seems to have had no role in cult practice, although there is a brief hint in Ovid that she was worshipped somewhere (*Metamorphoses* 13.588: "For I possess the scantiest amount of temples throughout the wide world."); however, this might just be an understated way of saying that there were no temples to Dawn. It is possible that the goddess is addressed as Orthria and Aotis in Alkman *PMGF* 1. This is hotly debated, but, if true, it would indicate worship of Dawn at Sparta in the Archaic period. The placement of this hymn in the collection might seem odd at first glance; one would expect it to be grouped with the hymn to Night (*OH* 3). However, if the hymns were intended to be performed in the order transmitted and if the proceedings took place at night, then the position of this hymn might indicate that it was sung right before or at the break of dawn (as opposed to the hymn to Night, who is requested to come to the initiates in the hymn dedicated to her, which is positioned right at the beginning of the collection; see *OH* 3i and *OH* 77i, and cf. *OH* 54.5+n). While many hymns describe a divinity in terms of light, this is the only hymn that calls on an entity to provide light to the initiates. Comparable, perhaps, might be Alkman *PMGF* 1.60–63, which has been interpreted to refer to the closing of a nightly ritual at the approach of dawn (see also *OH* 7.12–13n). This functional interpretation would also explain our hymn's emphasis on Dawn in her capacity as harbinger of the day as well as the complete lack of mythological dressing, with even genealogical details lacking. Note, too, the close proximity of the hymns to the three winds (*OH* 80–82), the same ones Hesiod designates as Dawn's progeny (see also *OH* 80.5–6n). Cynical minds recalling the story of Tithonos will find significance in the fact that it follows the hymn to Mnemosyne.

3 the illustrious Titan: A reference to Sun, son of the Titan Hyperion; see *OH* 8.2+n and *OH* 34.3+n.

4–5: Compare *Theogony* 744–761, where Hesiod tells us of the house of Night and Day located in the underworld; see *OH* 3i. The one greets the other on the threshold after discharging her daily obligation, and the house is always occupied by one and not the other.

6–10: Dawn and her light sending men and beasts off to work is a literary trope, first attested in Hesiod *Works and Days* 578–581: "The dawn claims the third portion of a day's work, / the dawn gives a headstart for journeys and jobs, / the dawn's arrival sends many men on their way / and puts the yoke on the necks of many oxen." Alkman might have expressed similar sentiments in the poem from which the fragment cited in the following note derives. Ovid *Amores* 1.13 is a witty "anti-hymn" to Dawn, in which Dawn is criticized for causing men and beasts to work. The speaker in Ovid's poem harangues the goddess for, among other things, her spurring the traveler to resume his journey, for the various activities her light heralds (agricultural, domestic, military, judicial, and scholastic), and especially for her ending of the sweet nocturnal trysts of lovers. Sappho fragment 104 is largely corrupt in the second line but also seems to view the coming of Dawn in a negative light: "Evening, you who bring all that light-giving Dawn disperses, / †you bring the lamb, you bring the kid, you bring away to its† mother the child."

11–12: The comprehensive listing of creatures of the sky, sea, and earth to denote the powers of a divinity is also a literary device. For this, compare the Homeric *Hymn to Aphrodite* 5.2–6, particularly 3–5, where this goddess "subdues the races of mortal men as well as / the birds that swoop from the sky and all the beasts / that are nurtured in their multitudes on both land and sea," and the one to Earth, Mother of All (30.34) whose "beauty nurtures all creatures that walk upon the land, / and all that move in the deep of fly in the air." In a similar vein, the Titans are the ancestors of "the brood of the sea and of the land, then the brood of the birds" at *OH* 37.5. It is a variation on the technique of listing domains to indicate the wide-spread power of a divinity; see *OH* 10.14–16n. Alkman *PMGF* 89.3–5 gives a splendid picture of quietude in a mountain landscape; the whole world sleeps, including "all creeping things the black earth nourishes / and beasts bred in the mountains and the race of bees / and the creatures in the depths of the deep blue sea; / there sleep the tribes of long-winged birds." It is possible that the original poem contrasted this restfulness with the hustle and bustle of human activity (another literary trope) that the light of dawn awakens (see previous note). It has also been suggested that this fragment might be referring to religious silence and so have been originally performed at a nocturnal ritual. If this is true, it is certainly possible that the light of dawn, which would signal the end of the proceedings, was mentioned elsewhere in the original, thus corresponding to our hymn's possible function, and was perhaps related to the ritual during which the first fragment of Alkman was performed (see the introduction to this hymn).

14 more sacred light: The light here probably has multiple layers of meaning. In the first instance, as mentioned in the introduction to this hymn, it could refer to the light of the coming dawn that would signal the end of the nocturnal ritual context in which these hymns were originally performed. The qualification "more" perhaps refers to the torches that would still have been in use for illumination and possibly in ritual acts. "Light" here might also have soteriological connotations.

79. To Themis

The name Themis means "established custom or law." She belongs to that class of deities who are personified abstractions. In myth, she is usually one of the original Titans, a daughter of Earth and Sky (Hesiod *Theogony* 135), as in our hymn; sometimes she is identified with Earth herself (Aeschylus *Prometheus Bound* 209–210). Hesiod makes her the second wife of Zeus (after Metis) and says that she bore to him the Seasons as well as the Fates (*Theogony* 901–906). Orphic theogony seems to have agreed with this progeny (*Orphic fragment* 252–253). In the *Hymns*, Themis and Zeus are again the parents of the Seasons (*OH* 43.1), but Night is the mother of the Fates (*OH* 59.1). It should also be noted that there might have been two sets of Fates in Orphic teaching (*Orphic fragment* 176), which would perhaps correspond to the duality found in Hesiod, who makes the Fates daughters of Night earlier in the *Theogony* (217–222; see *OH* 59i). Themis' children reflect her function as an embodiment of the established cosmic order, and this explains the possible identification of Themis with Necessity in Orphism (*Orphic fragment* 250). We also find Themis associated with prophecy and oracles, particularly as Apollon's predecessor at Delphi; see note to lines 3–6. Pindar makes it Themis who warns Zeus (and Poseidon) about the danger in pursuing Thetis, who was destined to give birth to a son who would overthrow his father (*Isthmian Odes* 8.31–45a). This story is taken up by Aeschylus in *Prometheus Bound*, where he also has Themis tell Prometheus (here her son) that the coming war between the Titans and gods would be won by trickery (201–218). In the lost epic *Kypria*, Themis and Zeus plot the Trojan War in order to reduce the population of the earth (fragment 1); see also *OH* 61i. Themis might have been involved in this plan as a daughter of Earth, and it should be noted that Pindar has Themis counsel that Thetis be married off to Peleus—a subject treated in the *Kypria* and that eventually leads to the Trojan War. Despite Themis' connections with Delphi, however, it seems that she played no role in cult there. Indeed, there is scant evidence for her worship in the ancient world. At Rhamnous in Attika, she was worshipped in conjunction with Nemesis (see *OH* 61i). Pausanias also reports a temple to Themis near the acropolis at Athens (1.22). For more on her cult, see Larson 2007, p. 179.

This hymn starts a group that seems to recall the ordering according to elements found in *OH* 15–29 (see *OH* 15i). Themis, as daughter of Earth, would represent the element earth; the next hymns to the winds, air; the one to Okeanos, water; and the one to Hestia, fire. This would make for a ring composition that would signal that the ritual was coming to a close. Perhaps reinforcing this notion is that the sequence at *OH* 15–29, repeated twice, starts each time with fire and ends with earth, while here it begins with earth and ends with fire. Given the association between earth and night (chthonic) and light and day (celestial), this might also reflect the coming day that heralded the end of the ritual.

3–6: Apollon is associated with the Delphic oracle, but there are a number of instances where he is the last of a line of divinities connected with this institution and Themis often appears in this group. Aeschylus says that the Delphic oracle originally belonged to Earth, who then gave it to her daughter Themis, who in turn passed it to the Titaness Phoibe, and finally Apollon received it as a birthday gift (*Eumenides* 1–8). Similarly, Pausanias relates that Earth and Poseidon shared the oracle then Earth passed her share on to her daughter Themis, who then ceded it to Apollon as a gift, and finally Apollon bartered for Poseidon's share (10.5.6). This peaceful relationship between Themis and Apollon might also have its origins in the goddess' having provided the infant Apollon with nectar and ambrosia at his birth (Homeric *Hymn to Apollon* 3.124–125). The transference of the oracle is not always so civilized, however. Euripides tells a version in which the oracle originally belonged to Earth, who wished her daughter Themis to possess it, but had it taken from her after Apollon slew the dragon Python; Earth then took vengeance on the young usurper, who appealed to his father, Zeus (*Iphigeneia in Tauris* 1234–1283). See also *OH* 86i. In the Homeric *Hymn to Apollon* (no. 3), it is the god himself who establishes the oracle.

4–6 as prophetess . . . the art of giving laws: Both of these phrases are translations of Greek words that pun on the name Themis ("themisteuousa" and "themistosunas," respectively).

4 Delphic hideaway: A reference to the chamber where the Pythia was supposed to have inhaled the vapors that brought her to a state of ecstasy. Modern doubt as to the veracity of the ancient tradition has been challenged; see Spiller, Hale, and de Boer 2002, along with their bibliography.

5 Pythian. . . Python: A similar close mention of location and figure is found at *OH* 34.3–4. For the story of Apollon slaying the dragon Python, see *OH* 34.3n. There are a number of variants of this myth, and sometimes the dragon is made into a human brigand (see Fontenrose 1959, pp. 13–27). The reference here to Python as king suggests he is conceived as human as well.

7–10: Just as Themis is represented as the first to institute oracles, so here she is represented as the inventor of Bacchic rites (cf. *OH* 76.7+n), particularly maenadism (see *OH* 52i). Other goddesses are also integrated into Dionysian rites (see *OH* 1.3n). This also further links Dionysian worship and Delphi; see *OH* 46i.

80–82. To Boreas, To Zephyros, To Notos

The winds in the ancient world, like other natural phenomena, were objects of worship and veneration. Tied to the seasons and often associated with specific meteorological conditions, they were important for agricultural and nautical activities. Already in bronze-age Knossos there was a "priestess of the winds." The winds could be viewed as an aggregate—winds in general, bad winds, etc.—or distinguished by the direction from which they originated and thus individualized and personified. The two notions can be found in the same author. Homer speaks of the winds feasting in the home of Zephyros, the west wind (*Iliad* 23.198–201), but also has the winds controlled by the mortal Aiolos (see *OH* 23.5–7n). Hesiod says that three winds, Boreas (north), Notos (south), and Zephyros (west), were born from Astraios and Dawn (*Theogony* 378–382), along with the stars (see *OH* 78i); the other, "evil" winds arose from Zeus' defeat of Typhon, who seems to have originally been a wind *daimōn* (*Theogony* 869–880; see further *OH* 15i). A similar dichotomy is found in actual worship. Pausanias tells of an altar for the winds at Titane, where one night out of the year sacrifice is made; of interest to us is that Pausanias also reports that mystery rites were performed over four pits (one for each wind?) and that spells supposedly from Medeia were incanted (2.12.1). Akhilleus prays to Boreas and Zephyros to keep Patroklos' pyre burning all night long; he performs libations, and at dawn the winds return to Thrace (*Iliad* 23.194–230). The summoning of favorable winds and the banning of unfavorable ones is often accomplished by magic, and Herodotos reports that the Persian Magi used spells to quell stormy winds (7.191; cf. 7.189, where the Athenians call on Boreas to blow against the Persians). The individual winds also received worship (e.g., for Boreas, see Pausanias 8.36.6; for Zephyros, see Pausanias 1.37.2). They, too, are called on to provide or hold back their force. The request for Boreas, Zephyros, and Notos to be beneficial in their respective hymns here is a reflex of this old tradition.

There are other personified winds from other directions. Homer knows of the personified east wind, Euros (*Odyssey* 5.295), for whom there survives a fragment of a paian composed at Sparta by an anonymous poet (*PMG* 858, where he is addressed as "savior" at the end, an epithet that frequently occurs in the *Hymns*). At Methana, to stay the Lips, a southwest wind, from ruining vine blossoms, a white rooster was cut in half; each half was carried by a man, who would run around the vines in opposite directions, and, when they returned to the starting place, the pieces were buried (Pausanias 2.34.2–3). However, aside from the mention of all the winds in the opening address to Mousaios (*OH* O.37), only Boreas, Zephyros, and Notos merit attention from our author. Note, however, that the second hymn addressed to the Kouretes (*OH* 38), where they are identified as both the Samothracian gods and Dioskouroi, portrays them as winds in general. This seems to reflect Hesiod's influence. For the position of these three hymns in this collection, see the *OH* 79i and 83i. They were probably intentionally arranged in alphabetical order (Greek "zeta" precedes "nu").

80. To Boreas

Boreas is the north wind, traditionally associated with cold and winter. He is a blustery sort and is represented as powerful and violent. Vivid descriptions of his frosty might may be found in Hesiod *Works and Days* 504–558 and Ibykos *PMGF* 286.8–13 (see also note to line 2). In myth, he is perhaps most famous for his abduction of the Athenian princess Oreithyia; their children, Kalais and Zetes, participated in Jason's quest for the Golden Fleece (see Apollonios of Rhodes *Argonautika* 1.211ff. and Ovid *Metamorphoses* 6.675–721). It is in this role as "son-in-law" that the Athenians called on him to harass the Persian fleet during the battle of Artemision, and for his help they later built him an altar by the river Ilissos (Herodotos 7.189, and compare 7.178 and 7.191; see also Plato *Phaedrus* 229c). The sons of Boreas had winged feet that conferred on them the power of flight; see also *OH* 81.6. Pausanias claims that he read in a poem (now lost to us) that Mousaios was given the ability to fly by Boreas; the poem seems to have been attributed to Mousaios himself, a claim Pausanias disputes (1.22.7).

2 come from snowy Thrace: Boreas is imagined as originating from Thrace, and thus is Orpheus' countryman. The Greeks in general considered the Thracians a wild and uncouth people, and the personified Boreas often takes on the same rude characteristics. In Aesop's eighteenth fable, Boreas and Sun try to determine who is more powerful by seeing who can force a man to take off his cloak. Boreas huffs and puffs with all his might, which only makes the man wrap himself tighter; Sun merely turns up the heat which forces the man to disrobe. The moral of the story is that persuasion is better than force. Ovid seems to be playfully alluding to this tale by having his Boreas first ask nicely for the hand of Oreithyia and resorting to violence only when he is rebuked. It is interesting that Homer at times considers Zephyros a similarly wild wind from Thrace as well (*Iliad* 9.4–7).

3–4: Compare Lucian *True History* 2.14, where on the Isle of the Blest the clouds draw up moisture from rivers of myrrh and then gently release that moisture on the symposiasts after being squeezed by the winds. For clouds as the carriers of rain, see *OH* 82.4.

5–6: Since Boreas can bring rough weather, he can perforce bring fair weather (cf. *OH* 38.14–25). The breaking up of the storm clouds leads to the appearance of the sun. These lines perhaps indicate the coming dawn and the imminent end of the ritual during which the *Hymns* were performed (see *OH* 78i). See also *OH* 5.6+n.

81. To Zephyros

Zephyros, originally any westerly wind, came to be thought of as the west wind proper. He is regarded as a warm, gentle breeze (see, e.g., Hesiod *Works and Days* 594). Homer sometimes represents him as a storm wind from Thrace (see *OH* 80.2n), but Zephyros also appears as the pleasant wind sent by Okeanos to refresh the dead heroes in the Elysian Fields (*Odyssey* 4.561–569). Akhilleus' horses are Zephyros' sons by way of the harpy Podarge (*Iliad* 16.148–151); this is not as strange as a union as it may appear, since the Harpies (Snatchers) were originally storm *daimones*. Their sister is Iris, and she also had relations with Zephyros, begetting none other than Eros (Alkaios fragment 327). Note that *Orphic fragment* 360 gives another genealogy for Eros, saying that this god was produced by Time and all the winds; see further *OH* 58.5–7n. Some versions of the myth of Apollon and Hyakinthos portray Zephyros as a rival to Apollon for the lad. In this case, the discus that kills Hyakinthos is blown off course by the wind as opposed to accidentally hitting him (Pausanias 3.19.5). A later epigram attributed to Bacchylides describes the dedication of a temple to Zephyros by one Eudemos of Rhodes in thanks for the god's assistance in winnowing (*AP* 6.53); the altar to Zephyros in Attika, found near a shrine to Demeter and Persephone on the way to Eleusis, may also have had agricultural significance (Pausanias 1.37.2).

3–4 loved by harbors / . . . gentle passage: In the *Odyssey,* Aiolos ties up all the winds except the west wind in a magic bag so that Odysseus may have safe passage home. The premature release of the winds blows the ship back to the island of Aiolos (10.19–55; see also *OH* 23.5–7n). Zephyros, however, is not the only wind associated with aiding ships; see *OH* 82i.

6 O light-winged ones: Winds are conventionally represented as winged; compare *OH* 82.2 and the winged feet of Boreas' sons (see *OH* 80i). The wings are indicative of the winds' speed.

82. To Notos

Notos is the south wind and as such opposite to Boreas; compare Bacchylides 13.124–132, an extended metaphor where Boreas rages throughout the night until dawn while during the day Notos safely guides the ship to dry land (cf. *OH* 81.3–4).

4: The Clouds' hymn has the same last line as this one (*OH* 21.7). Both hymns are followed by ones addressed to water deities, namely, Tethys (*OH* 22) and Okeanos (*OH* 83). It is a natural placement, since rain was thought to come from the moisture drawn up by the clouds from bodies of water; Herodotos explicitly says this about Notos (2.25.2). For philosophical speculation on such metereological phenomena, see *OH* 21i and *OH* 22.7n. The Clouds are "filled with water" (*OH* 21.3) and wear "dewy cloaks" (*OH* 21.6), and Tethys is said to be the "mother of dark [= rain] clouds" (*OH* 22.7).

83. To Okeanos

Okeanos was conceived in myth as a fresh-water river flowing counterclockwise (i.e., from west to east; see Mimnermos fragment 12 and Stesikhoros *PMGF* S17) around the land masses of the world. His wife is Tethys (*OH* 22.1), and their daughters are the Okeanids (*OH* 51.1+n). There are different accounts of his place in the divine hierarchy. Hesiod considers him to be one of the original Titans, a son of Sky and Earth (*Theogony* 133). Homer, on the other hand, has Sleep call Okeanos the "begetter of all" (*Iliad* 14.246); it is unclear whether Homer thought him to be the oldest god or the first god to initiate procreation; see also *OH* 3i. This hymn reflects Homeric belief. We find similar variations in different Orphic theogonies, with Okeanos being counted in the generation of Titans (*Orphic fragment* 179) and either among an earlier generation or as the progenitor of all (*Orphic fragment* 21–22; cf. West

1983, pp. 117–121; 183–190). Okeanos might have been rationalized as the sea in the theogony sung by Orpheus in Apollonios of Rhodes *Argonautika* 1.495–512; his daughter Eurynome is paired with Ophion, and they are called the first rulers of Olympos. Water divinities as the first existing beings are found in Sumerian (Nammu), Babylonian (Apsu and Tiamat), and Egyptian (Nun, the Ogdoad) traditions, among others. It seems quite likely that such stories influenced the Greeks. It is also notable that Thales, the earliest Pre-Socratic philosopher and one who came from Asia Minor, theorized that water was the first principle, and already in antiquity he was thought to have been influenced by the ancient tradition; see Aristotle *Metaphysics* 983b27–984a3, who also mentions that the earliest theologians (including Orpheus?) thought Okeanos and Tethys were the "parents of begetting." In our collection Proteus, another sea god, is endowed with demiurgic powers; see *OH* 25.2–3+i. Okeanos played no role in cult. For the placement of this hymn, see *OH* 79i. An explanation for why Okeanos would have been chosen to represent water in this group of hymns as opposed to some other water deity might be his connection with death (see note to line 3 and *OH* 87i). Just as this hymn follows those addressed to the winds, so too does the hymn to Sea (*OH* 22) follow the one to the airy Clouds (see also *OH* 82.4n). The author of the Derveni papyrus equates Zeus, Okeanos, and air, but this is introduced as an interpretation that goes against what the "multitude" believe (see Betegh 2004, pp. 193–200), and nothing in our hymn suggests any awareness of this doctrine.

3 **boundaries of the earth**: See *OH* 11.15. Hephaistos makes Okeanos the outer rim on the shields of Akhilleus (*Iliad* 18.607–608) and of Herakles (Hesiod *Shield* 314–315). It is not, however, the absolute limits of the world, at least not the world of the living. Odysseus must cross Okeanos to reach Hades (*Odyssey* 10.508–512), and Hesiod places a number of monsters beyond its stream such as the Hesperides, the Gorgons, and Geryon (*Theogony* 215, 274–275, 289–292). All of these creatures are thus death figures. The Isles of the Blest are located near Okeanos (Hesiod *Works and Days* 171; cf. *Odyssey* 4.561–569). Okeanos' association with death is strengthened by the fact that the river Styx is his eldest daughter (see *OH* 69.4n). It might be that the placement of this hymn, coming near the end of the collection and shortly before the hymn to Death, is supposed to symbolize the crossing of Okeanos for the initiate (cf. *OH* 87.12n). The stars are sometimes described as rising from and setting into Okeanos.

4–5: Okeanos is naturally seen as the source of all other watery bodies (see also *Iliad* 21.195–197; line 196 is exactly the same as line 4 in this hymn). This is expressed genealogically by Hesiod, who reports that Okeanos and Tethys are the parents of three thousand daughters and an equal number of (male) rivers (*Theogony* 363–368). However, Hesiod does not make him the father of the salty seas, as there are older water deities for this poet to represent them (e.g., Pontos).

8: Okeanos appears as a laid-back individual in myth. He does not fight with Kronos against their father Sky (*Orphic fragment* 186) nor does he battle against Zeus in the Titanomachy (Hesiod *Theogony* 398; compare the role of his daughter Styx at 389–403). According to Homer, he and his wife protect Hera during this war (*Iliad* 14.200–204, and cf. Thetis and Eurynome, an Okeanid, taking in Hephaistos after he had been thrown out of Olympos by Hera at *Iliad* 18.394–405 and also Thetis succoring Dionysos in his flight from Lykourgos at *Iliad* 6.135–137). In the *Prometheus Bound*, Aeschylus portrays Okeanos as sympathetic to the plight of the rebel Prometheus, although unwilling to challenge Zeus.

84. To Hestia

Hestia, meaning "hearth," is, unsurprisingly, the goddess of the hearth. Despite being a full-blooded Olympian divinity, she never really becomes fully anthropomorphized. Consequently, she rarely makes an appearance in literature and art. Homer does not mention her at all. She was the first child born to Kronos and Rhea, and, because she was the oldest, she was the first to be swallowed by Kronos and the last to be disgorged (Hesiod *Theogony* 454, 497). While Orphism seems to have had a similar genealogy (see *Orphic fragment* 202), the author of the Derveni papyrus appears to cite from a poem where Orpheus equated her with Demeter, Deio, Rhea, Earth, and Mother (see *OH* 14i). The hymn to the Mother of the Gods in our collection says that this goddess is also known as Hestia (*OH* 27.9+n). There are two short Homeric hymns to her (nos. 24 and 29) that briefly touch on her capacity as household goddess (the latter hymn also invokes Hermes in this role), and they seem to have been composed for the occasion of the consecration of a new house. She also makes an appearance in the Homeric *Hymn to Aphrodite* where she spurns the courting of Poseidon and Apollon; she swears that she will remain a virgin, and in place of marriage she receives the honor of being the goddess of homes, including temples (5.21–32). This turned out to be quite an honor indeed. As goddess of every private domicile's hearth, much of domestic piety was lavished on her. She received daily offerings, and she was also invoked on special occasions, e.g., the introduction of new members into the household. Since the temple of a god was considered a "home" for that god, it is not surprising to find Hestia worshipped there as well, e.g., Apollon's temple at Delphi (see Homeric *Hymn to Hestia* no. 24). As the hearth was a central point unifying the household and temple, so, too, did communities have a public hearth that promoted the polity's well-being, and thus Hestia also received state cult honors. The cult of her famous counterpart in Rome, Vesta, included a college of women whose function was to keep the sacred flame of the city's hearth continually burning. We find similar instances of the maintenance of an eternal, pure flame in Greek civic hearths. She was the first and the last deity to whom libations were poured at a public feast (see Homeric *Hymn to Hestia* 29.3–6). That she was the first to be swallowed and the last to be disgorged by Kronos is perhaps a mythological reflection of this; our hymn's position near the end of the collection might also have been influenced by this practice (see further *OH* 79i). In general, though, it was customary to give her offerings before other gods. Sokrates, about to embark on a discussion on the etymology of gods' names, asks his interlocutor if they should start with Hestia, as is the custom, and later notes that Hestia is the first divinity invoked at sacrifices (Plato *Cratylus* 401b2 and d1–2). It is not hyperbole to state that she was the most worshipped divinity in the ancient world as well as the most important divinity in the daily lives of the majority of people. For more information on the cult of Hestia, see Larson 2007, pp. 160–62.

2 center of the house: This probably originated in the plan of the bronze-age *megaron*, which had its hearth in the center; early temples, too, seemed to have been planned around a hearth. The hearth by its nature is a central element in any house, regardless of its exact physical location.

4 purity: Fire is an element that by its very nature is pure, and this concept of purity was extended to the hearth fire and, naturally, to the conception of Hestia herself. She was a virgin goddess, and the women who tended Vesta's flame in Rome were virgins on pain of death. Hesiod admonishes his brother "not [to] sit by the hearth / with your genitals exposed and bespattered with semen" (*Works and Days* 733–734). For the role of purity in cult, see *OH* 30.4n.

5 home of the blessed gods: So, too, Sky (*OH* 4.4); see also *OH* 5.1n.

8 prosperity . . . health: Hestia was imagined to be both benefactress and protectress of the home; compare the end of the Homeric *Hymn to Hestia* 29 as well as *OH* 27.9+n.

85. To Sleep

Sleep, along with the race of Dreams and Death, is a child of Night, who bore this brood alone (Hesiod *Theogony* 211–212; cf. *OH* 3.5, 7). Thus, the last three hymns in the collection form a natural triplet. In the Homeric epic, too, he is the personified brother of Death, and Hera enlists his services to put Zeus to sleep (*Iliad* 14.224–279). The Greeks felt a close affinity between sleep and death, probably inferring it from the close resemblance between a body asleep and a body dead. Hesiod says that for the Golden Race of men, "a sleeplike death subdued them" (*Works and Days* 116) instead of death, and both Sleep and Death do honor to Sarpedon, a son of Zeus, by carrying his corpse from the field of battle to his home in Lykia for a proper burial (*Iliad* 16.671–673 and 681–883). Pausanias reports that on the chest of Kypselos, Night holds two infants, one white, who is Sleep, the other black, who is Death (5.18.1). Hesiod describes a similar scene, although Night only holds Sleep; the poet further contrasts the gentle nature of Sleep with the hated figure of Death (*Theogony* 755–766). This fraternal relationship between Sleep and Death is emphasized in our collection, as can be seen in a number of conceptual and linguistic parallels in their hymns: they hold power over all mortals (*OH* 85.1–3 ~ *OH* 87.1–2), they have a liberating function (*OH* 85.5 ~ *OH* 87.3–4), and sleep is a kind of practice death (*OH* 85.7), while death is a kind of permanent sleep (*OH* 87.3, 5). Sleep played a negligible role in cult. However, according to Pausanias, the people of Troizen sacrificed on an ancient altar dedicated to the Muses and Sleep, claiming that the latter was most cherished by the former (2.31.3). This probably is a reflection of both divinities' ability to release, albeit temporarily, the minds of men from the worries and cares of their dreary daily existence (see note to line 8).

1–4: The idea that Sleep binds all is found in the epic epithet "pandamatōr" ("all-subduer, all-binder"), which occurs in Homer and *Orphic fragment* 223; in the latter it appears in the context of Zeus' overthrowing of his father, Kronos. The beginning of book 24 of the *Iliad* is a beautiful illustration of what happens to those whom this "all-taming lord" does not visit—the oldest description of the torments of insomnia (24.1–21).

8 Death and Oblivion . . . a true brother: For this relationship to Death, see the introduction to this hymn. The relationship with Oblivion requires some explanation. Hesiod makes Oblivion a granddaughter of Night and so a niece of Death and Sleep (*Theogony* 227). Oblivion (Greek Lethe) has close connections with Death. It is one of the rivers in the underworld, whose waters cause the drinker to forget their previous life. Johnston has argued that in the eschatology found on some of the Bacchic gold tablets, the body of water the soul of the initiate is instructed to avoid is the Spring of Forgetfulness (Graf/Johnston 2007, pp. 94–136, passim, especially pp. 116–120; this is opposed to the Lake of Mnemosyne, whither the soul is directed; see *OH* 77i). It may be that Oblivion is mentioned here because of Death, and the relation to Sleep is merely a function of his relation to Death. However, forgetfulness also has relevance to the living. In the hymn to Mnemosyne, "evil oblivion" is said to be "alien to her" (*OH* 77.3), and the goddess is asked to "ward off oblivion" so that the rite might not be forgotten (*OH* 77.9–10). On the other hand, oblivion may have positive connotations. In the hymn to Night, the goddess is said to "free us from cares" (see *OH* 3.6), which is a translation of a Greek word that literally means "causing to forget cares." This is comparable to the "free us of cares" in line 5 (a more literal translation of a different Greek word), and it is notable that the "sweet respite from toil" in this line is almost exactly parallel to the "you offer us welcome respite from toil" in the hymn to Night (*OH* 3.6). The sacrifice to the Muses and Sleep mentioned in the introductory note is also relevant here. Sleep is probably therefore imagined here as "a true brother" of Oblivion based on this affinity of function. (Presumably Oblivion is considered the daughter of Night, contra the Hesiodic genealogy, thus inheriting some of the powers of her mother.) Ovid portrays Sleep dwelling in a cave whence the river Lethe originates (*Metamorphoses* 11.602–604).

9–10: If the hymns were sung in order at an all-night ritual (see *OH* 3i and *OH* 78i), the position of this one dedicated to Sleep is quite understandable. The initiates would literally be calling on the god, of whose favor they would acutely feel the need; see further *OH* 54.5+n.

86. To Dream

For the genealogy of the race of Dreams, see Hesiod *Theogony* 211–212 and *OH* 85i. Ovid makes Dreams the sons of Sleep, and furthermore "modernizes" them by distinguishing certain specialists who, however, only appear to distinguished persons: Morpheus can take on any human form, Phobetor (aka Ikelos) any animal, and Phantasos any natural object (*Metamorphoses* 11.633–643). We find a personified Dream in the second book of the *Iliad*, where Zeus wishes to deceive Agamemnon and so dispatches "baneful Dream" (cf. line 1 of this hymn) to suggest that Troy will fall if promptly attacked, when in reality Zeus is planning woes for the Greeks (2.1–40). Homer compares Akhilleus' chasing of Hektor around the walls of Troy to a dream where the pursuer never catches the pursued, who nevertheless cannot wholly escape the pursuer (*Iliad* 22.199–201). In the *Odyssey*, Penelope tells her disguised husband that there are dreams that issue forth from one of two gates; false ones come through gates of ivory, while true ones through gates of horn (19.559–567; cf. Vergil *Aeneid* 6.893–896, where Aeneas returns from the underworld through the gates of ivory). This dichotomy between true and false revelation is paralleled in Hesiod's epiphany of the Muses, where the goddesses claim "we know how to tell many lies that pass for truth, / and when we wish, we know to tell the truth itself" (*Theogony* 27–28). Euripides gives an interesting etiology of dreams in his play *Iphigeneia at Tauris*. Earth, in anger at Apollon for his taking over the oracle at Delphi from her daughter Themis, sends prophetic dreams to men as they lie on the ground; the young Apollon complains to daddy Zeus about the competition, and Zeus simply causes the dreams to stop (1259–1282; see also *OH* 79.3–6n). The interpretation of dreams must be one of the oldest forms of divination; both in cult and literature, there were numerous dream oracles (for an example, see *OH* 74i) and more informal dream visions (see, e.g., *OH* 12.10; note, too, that the title character of *Iphigeneia at Tauris* misinterprets one at the beginning of the play, 42–58). Akhilleus, worn out from dragging Hektor's corpse, falls asleep on the shore and is visited by the dream-image of Patroklos, who, among other things, briefly foretells Akhilleus' death at Troy (*Iliad* 23.54–107). Over two thousand years before

Freud, we find books written to explain the significance of dreams; unfortunately, all but one, the *Oneirokritika* of Artemidoros (middle to late second century AD), survives. We also possess the *Sacred Tales* (= *Orations* 47–52) of Aristides (middle second century AD) that records revelatory dreams sent to him by Asklepios, whose worship had a connection with dreams through the visions that arose through incubation (see *OH* 67i).

Our hymn is particularly concerned with dream divinations, but it introduces an ethical criterion on the basis of which one may receive dreams that signify the future. Similar ethical criteria are found in the fate of the soul in Orphic eschatology (see *OH* 13i) and as a constitutive underpinning of the cosmos' structure (see *OH* 64i). With physical sleep probably imminent for the initiates, assuming an all-night ritual (see *OH* 3i), sweet dreams would naturally be a concern.

18 weird apparitions: Similarly described are the "weird shapes" by which Melinoe appears to mortals (see *OH* 71.6–9+11n). And, as is also the case with Melinoe and other threatening powers, "baneful Dream" is asked to come in his beneficial, not harmful, guise.

87. To Death

For the genealogy of the personified figure of Death (Greek Thanatos), see *OH* 85i. Death is to be distinguished from Hades, although Euripides imaginatively calls Death a "winged Hades" in his tragicomedy *Alkestis* 252. Thanatos appears on stage in this play which treats the story of Herakles wrestling Death for the soul of Alkestis (837–860, 1140). We are told by Pherekydes of Athens that Sisyphos kept Death tied up, until he was freed by Ares, who consequently served up Sisyphos to him. For obvious reasons Death and the boatman of the dead, Kharon, sometimes confused even in antiquity, have totally merged in the modern Greek figure of Charos with whom Digenes and other epic figures wrestle in "the marble threshing floors" of folk poetry. The personification of Death is rather weak in this hymn. Its appearance at the end of the collection is symbolic, forming a ring composition with the theme of birth that occurs at the beginning with the hymns to Hekate and Prothyraia (see *OH* 2i, and cf. *OH* 15i); birth and rebirth are motifs in the central Dionysian section as well (see *OH* 44i).

3–4: The idea that the body is a kind of prison for the soul is found in Plato *Cratylus* 400b–c, where Sokrates discusses three different etymologies for the Greek word for body, "sōma." Two of them involve a play on the Greek word "sēma": the body is the "tomb" ("sēma") of the soul or the body is the "marker" or "token" ("sēma") of the soul. A third possibility, the one which Sokrates claims seems the best to him, he attributes to the "Orphics," who assert that the body is a prison for the soul that keeps it safe until it "pays the penalty" ("sōma" being derived in this context from the verb "sōizo," "I keep safe, preserve"; compare also Plato *Phaedo* 62b). Plato does not mention what the penalty is, but presumably he has in mind the Orphic conception that human beings participate in the Titans' guilt for slaying Dionysos (see further *OH* 37i). Mention of retribution for a crime is found on two of the Bacchic gold tablets (nos. 6 and 7). See also the introduction to the translation.

8: There are a number of mythological figures who take on the role of judge of the dead, such as Minos, Rhadamanthys, and Aiakos; see *OH* 18.16+n. The punishments of such luminaries as Tantalos and Sisyphos imply such a judging. Here, however, the end of life itself is presented as a juridical sentence, a case of an ethical viewpoint being grafted onto a natural process (see *OH* 86i). It is "common to all" (see also lines 1 and 6), because all human beings share in the blood guilt of the Titans (see previous note).

9: There are, however, exceptions, most notably Orpheus himself, who descends to the underworld after his wife Eurydike has died. He charms Hades and Persephone with his music, and they allow him to bring Eurydike back to the land of the living, provided he does not look back at her until they reach the light. Tragically, Orpheus is unable to comply and thus loses Eurydike for good. See Vergil *Georgics* 4.453–506 and Ovid *Metamorphoses* 10.1–71; for a possible allusion to this story elsewhere in the *Hymns*, see *OH* 58.5–7n. Sisyphos, too, is said to have convinced Persephone to allow him to return to life (Theognis 701–712). The descent to and return from the land of the dead (called a katabasis, "descent"), either literally or figuratively, is one of the crowning achievements for heroes in mythology (e.g., Herakles, Theseus, Odysseus, Aineias), as well as for modern figures (e.g., Dante, Faust), and even for gods (e.g., Dionysos, Demeter, Persephone, Adonis, Hermes). In Aristophanes *Frogs* 1392, Aeschylus quotes a line from his *Niobe* (not extant) that "alone of the gods, Death does not desire gifts."

12 **old age**: There is a play on words involving "old age" ("gēras") and "prize" ("geras"). The notion of a prize is very interesting in light of the intimations of competition elsewhere in the collection (see *OH* 7.12–13n). One of the Bacchic gold tablets (Graf/Johnston 2007, no. 5) speaks of the initiate "reaching the desired garland by [her] swift feet." The imagery of winning a foot race is used metaphorically to describe the final prize sought by the initiate through participation in the cult, namely, remaining in the underworld with the heroes or becoming a god (see *OH* 20i, *OH* 29i, *OH* 33i, and *OH* 41.8n). This idea might be present in the hymn to the Stars, too. Athletics and struggle were closely connected in the minds of the ancients. Indeed, the Greek word "athlētēs" (whence English "athlete") literally means "the one who struggles/contends for the prize" and is particularly used for athletic contests; the Greek word "agōn" may denote a place for athletic competitions, the competition itself, or any struggle (cf. English "agony"). Just like an athlete, so, too, must the initiate struggle and practice discipline in performing the lengthy ritual. Toil and relief from toil are found elsewhere in the collection (cf., e.g., *OH* 3.6, *OH* 85.5+8n), and these are probably not mere literary arabesques but reflect to some degree the attitude of the initiates to their practices, especially if they shared the view found among the Bacchic gold tablets that life was an atonement for the crimes of the Titans (see *OH* 37i). This might lead one to expect a pessimistic and dismissive attitude to the world of the living, and there is much precedence for such in the annals of Greek literature. For example, Theognis says that "of all things, it is best for earth-bound men not to be born, / nor even to gaze upon the piercing rays of the sun / but if one is born, then it is best to reach the gates of Hades as quickly as possible / and to lie under a mass of dirt piled high" (425–28). This is a species of Greek pessimism in general, but the attitude was not universal. The shade of Akhilleus could say that he would prefer to be a slave to a poor farmer on earth rather than a king among the dead (*Odyssey* 11.489–491), and the Athenian lawgiver Solon has kind things to say about old age in his poems (fragments 18, 20, 27). The *Hymns* evince a positive valuation of life, too (see, e.g., *OH* 40i+18–20 and *OH* 68.9+n). They unabashedly focus on the material blessings of the here and now, e.g., health, prosperity, peace, and show, interestingly enough, no interest in the fate of the soul, at least explicitly. Whatever the eschatological views of the initiates, and whatever the rest of the ritual involved, the performance

of the *Hymns* functions in a way similar to the story that Akhilleus tells Priam in order to console him (*Iliad* 24.525–533). Zeus possesses two jars, one filled with good things, the other with evils. For a human life, Zeus apportions either a little from each jar or all from the one of evils. It is thus our fate to suffer, and all one can do is cope. The *Hymns* are likewise a coping mechanism. They present a world full of uncanny powers that have the potential to threaten and benefit, and they give the initiate a means of taking an active role to secure the latter. The means to do so—the performance of the *Hymns* (and whatever "contests" the ritual involved)—were perceived as arduous. Like Herakles performing his Labors, the initiates struggle and suffer. And when they finish the hymn to Death, which could very well have coincided with the morning light, they, like Herakles, in a sense have overcome death. The references to sailing and favorable winds in the collection might be understood metaphorically in this sense (see *OH* 83.3n). The experience would have been felt to have changed their lives, and the new day as symbolic of the transformation. The *Hymns* offer much for those interested in various aspects of antiquity: mystery cults and Orphism, mythology and folklore, literature and literary reception, philosophical and cosmological speculation. It is easy to lose sight that they were performed by real people, with real hopes and real fears. While their means of addressing these concerns might seem strange, even bizarre, to the modern reader, the goal is something with which anyone can readily sympathize. The *Orphic Hymns* speak to human fundamentals. And therein lies our ultimate fascination with them, and antiquity in general.

SELECT BIBLIOGRAPHY

English translations for most of the primary sources may be found online at the Perseus Project (http://www.perseus.tufts.edu).

Alexander, Christine. 1933. "Abstract of the Articles on the Bacchic Inscription in the Metropolitan Museum." *American Journal of Archaeology* 37 (2): 264–270.

Arnim, Hans von. 1903–1921. *Stoicorum veterum fragmenta*. Leipzig: Teubner.

Barker, Andrew. 1984. *Greek Musical Writings*. Vol. 1. Cambridge: Cambridge University Press
———. 1989. *Greek Musical Writings*. Vol. 2. Cambridge: Cambridge University Press

Bernabé, Alberto. 2004–2007. *Orphicorum et Orphicis similium testimonia et fragmenta*. Vol. 2 of *Poetae epici graeci, testimonia et fragmenta*. Munich: Teubner.

Betegh, Gábor. 2004. *The Derveni Papyrus: Cosmology, Theology and Interpretation*. Cambridge: Cambridge University Press.

Betz, Hans D. 1986. *The Greek Magical Papyri in Translation, Including the Demotic Spells*. Vol. 1. Chicago: University of Chicago Press.

Boardman, John. 1975. *Athenian Red Figure Vases: The Archaic Period*. London: Thames and Hudson.
———. 1989. *Athenian Red Figure Vases: The Classical Period*. London: Thames and Hudson.
———. 1991 *Athenian Black Figure Vases*. Corr. ed. London: Thames and Hudson.

Borgeaud, Philippe. 2004. *Mother of the Gods: From Cybele to the Virgin Mary*. Baltimore, MD: Johns Hopkins University Press.

Bundrick, Sheramy D. 2005. *Music and Image in Classical Athens*. Cambridge: Cambridge University Press.

Burkert, Walter. 1972. *Lore and Science in Ancient Pythagoreanism*. Cambridge, MA: Harvard University Press.
———. 1985. *Greek Religion*. Malden, MA: Blackwell.
———. 1987. *Ancient Mystery Cults*. Cambridge, MA: Harvard University Press.

Ceccarelli, Paola. 2004. "Dancing the *Pyrrichē* in Athens." In *Music and the Muses: The Culture of 'Mousikē' in the Classical Athenian City*, ed. Penelope Murray and Peter Wilson, 91–117. Oxford: Oxford University Press.

Davies, Malcolm. 1991. *Poetarum melicorum graecorum fragmenta*. Vol. 1. Oxford: Oxford University Press.

Diels, Hermann, and Walther Kranz. 1951–1952. *Die Fragmente der Vorsokratiker*. Berlin: Weidmann.

Dittenberger, Wilhelm. 1920. *Sylloge inscriptionum graecarum*. Vol. 3. Leipzig: Hirzel.

Dodds, Eric R. 1951. *The Greeks and the Irrational*. Berkeley: University of California Press.

Farnell, Lewis R. 1921. *Greek Hero Cults and Ideas of Immortality*. Oxford, UK: Clarendon Press.

Fontenrose, Joseph E. 1959. *Python: A Study of Delphic Myth and Its Origins*. Berkeley: University of California Press.

Furley, William D. 1995. "Praise and Persuasion in Greek Hymns." *Journal of Hellenic Studies* 115: 29–46.

Furley, William D., and Jan M. Bremer. 2001. *Greek Hymns*. Tübingen: Siebeck.

Graf, Fritz. 1974. *Eleusis und die orphische Dichtung Athens in vorhellenistischer Zeit*. Berlin: De Gruyter.

Graf, Fritz, and Sarah Iles Johnston. 2007. *Ritual Texts for the Afterlife: Orpheus and the Bacchic Gold Tablets*. London: Routledge.

Green, Peter. 2007. *The Argonautika*. Berkeley: University of California Press.

Guthrie, William Keith Chambers. 1952. *Orpheus and Greek Religion*. London: Methuen.

———. 1954. *The Greeks and Their Gods*. Boston: Beacon Press.

Hardie, Alex. 2004. "Muses and Mysteries." In *Music and the Muses: The Culture of 'Mousikē' in the Classical Athenian City*, ed. Penelope Murray and Peter Wilson, 11–37. Oxford: Oxford University Press.

Hedreen, Guy M. 1992. *Silens in Attic Black-figure Vase-painting*. Ann Arbor: University of Michigan Press.

Hermann, Gottfried. 1805. *Orphica*. Leipzig: Fritsch.

Holford-Strevens, Leofranc. 2005. *The History of Time: A Very Short Introduction*. Oxford: Oxford University Press.

Johnston, Sarah Iles. 1999. *Restless Dead: Encounters between the Living and the Dead in Ancient Greece*. Berkeley: University of California Press.

Kahn, Charles. 1975. *The Art and Thought of Heraclitus*. Cambridge: Cambridge University Press.

Kern, Otto. 1911. "Das Demeterheiligtum von Pergamon und die orphischen Hymnen." *Hermes* 46 (3): 431–436.

Kirk, Geoffrey S., John E. Raven, and Malcolm Schofield. 1983. *The Presocratic Philosophers: A Critical History with a Selection of Texts*. Cambridge: Cambridge University Press.

Kouremenos, Theokritos, George Parássoglou, and Kyriakos Tsantsanoglou. 2006. *The Derveni Papyrus*. Florence: Olschki.

Larson, Jennifer. 2007. *Ancient Greek Cults: A Guide*. New York: Routledge.

Levy, G. Rachel. 1934. "The Oriental Origin of Herakles." *Journal of Hellenic Studies* 54 (1): 40–53.

Linforth, Ivan M. 1941. *The Arts of Orpheus*. Berkeley: University of California Press.

Lissarrague, François. 1992. "Why Satyrs Are Good to Represent." In *Nothing to Do with Dionysos?*, ed. John Winkler and Froma I. Zeitlin, 228–236. Princeton, NJ: Princeton University Press.

Lobeck, Christian A. 1829. *Aglaophamus; sive De theologiae mysticae graecorum causis.* Königs-berg: Bornträger.

Long, A. A., and D. N. Sedley. 1987. *The Hellenistic Philosophers.* Vol. 1. Cambridge: Cambridge University Press.

Loucas, Ioannis. 1992. "Meaning and Place of the Cult Scene on the Ferrara Krater T128." In *The Iconography of Greek Cult in the Archaic and Classical Periods,* ed. Robin Hägg, 73–83. Athens: Centre d'étude de la religion grecque antique.

Maass, Ernst. 1895. *Orpheus: Untersuchungen zur griechischen, römischen, altchristlichen Jenseits-dichtungen.* Munich: Beck.

Macdonell, Arthur A. 1917. *A Vedic Reader for Students.* Oxford, UK: Clarendon Press.

Mikalson, Jon D. 1998. *Religion in Hellenistic Athens.* Berkeley: University of California Press.

Morand, Anne-France. 2001. *Études sur les "Hymnes Orphiques."* Leiden: Brill.

Murray, Penelope. 2004. "The Muses and Their Arts." In *Music and the Muses: The Culture of 'Mousikē' in the Classical Athenian City,* ed. Penelope Murray and Peter Wilson, 365–389. Oxford: Oxford University Press.

Mylonas, George. 1972. *Eleusis and the Eleusinian Mysteries.* Princeton, NJ: Princeton University Press.

Nilsson, Martin P. 1961. *Geschichte der griechischen Religion.* Vol. 2. Munich: Beck.

Nisetich, Frank J. 1980. *Pindar's Victory Songs.* Baltimore, MD: Johns Hopkins University Press.

———. 2001. *The Poems of Callimachus.* Oxford: Oxford University Press.

Nock, Arthur Darby. 1934. "A Vision of Mandulis Aion." *Harvard Theological Review* 27 (1): 53–104.

Page, Denys L. 1962. *Poetae melici graeci.* Oxford: Oxford University Press.

Pentikäinen, Juha. 2006. "Arctic Primitivism in the European Mind." In *In the Footsteps of the Bear,* ed. Clive Tolley. Pori, Finland: University of Turku and Satakunta Museum.

———. 2007. *Golden King of the Forest: The Lore of the Golden Bear.* Helsinki: Etnika.

Pickard-Cambridge, Arthur W. 1988. *The Dramatic Festivals of Athens.* Rev. John Gould and D. M. Lewis. Oxford: Oxford University Press.

Quandt, Wilhelm. 1955. *Orphei hymni.* Berlin: Weidmann.

Ricciardelli, Gabriella. 2000. *Inni orfici.* Milan: Mondadori.

Richardson, Nicholas J. 1974. *The Homeric "Hymn to Demeter."* Oxford: Oxford University Press.

Rudhardt, Jean. 1991. "Quelques réflexions sur les hymnes orphiques." In *Orphisme et Orphée,* ed. Philippe Borgeaud, 263–283. Geneva: Droz.

Rutherford, Ian. 2001. *Pindar's Paeans: A Reading of the Fragments with a Survey of the Genre.* Oxford: Oxford University Press.

Samuel, Alan E. 1972. *Greek and Roman Chronology: Calendars and Years in Classical Antiquity.* Munich: Beck.

Sargeant, Winthrop. 2009. *The Bhagavad Gītā.* Albany: State University Press of New York.

Sartre, Maurice. 1993. "Du fait divers à l'histoire des mentalités: À propos de quelques noyés et de trois petits cochons." *Syria* 70 (1–2): 51–67.

Seelinger, Robert A. 1998. "The Dionysiac Context of the Cult of Melikertes/Palaimon at the Isthmian Sanctuary of Poseidon." *Maia* 50: 271–280.

Segal, Charles. 1989. *Orpheus: The Myth of the Poet.* Baltimore, MD: Johns Hopkins University Press.

Siddiqi, Muhammad I. 1990. *Ninety-Nine Names of Allah*. Delhi: Kazi Publications.

Solomon, Jon. 1999. *Ptolemy: "Harmonics."* Leiden: Brill.

Spiller, Henry, John R. Hale, and Jelle Zellinga de Boer. 2002. "The Delphic Oracle: A Multidisciplinary Defense of the Gaseous Vent Theory." *Clinical Toxicology* 40 (2): 189–196.

Thom, Johan C. 1995. *The Pythagorean "Golden Verses."* Leiden: Brill.

———. 2005. *Cleanthes' "Hymn to Zeus."* Tübingen: Siebeck.

van den Berg, Rudolphus M. 2001. *Proclus' Hymns*. Leiden: Brill.

Vanderlip, Vera F. 1972. *The Four Greek Hymns of Isidorus and the Cult of Isis*. Toronto: Hakkert.

Vermaseren, Maarten J. 1977. *Cybele and Attis: The Myth and the Cult*. London: Thames and Hudson.

Waterfield, Robin. 1988. *The Theology of Arithmetic: On the Mystical, Mathematical and Cosmological Symbolism of the First Ten Numbers, Attributed to Iamblichus*. Foreword by Keith Critchlow. Grand Rapids, MI: Phanes Press.

Watkins, Calvert. 1995. *How to Kill a Dragon: Aspects of Indo-European Poetics*. Oxford: Oxford University Press.

West, Martin L. 1968. "Notes on the Orphic Hymns." *Classics Quarterly* 18 (2): 288–296.

———. 1970. "The Eighth Homeric Hymn and Proclus." *Classics Quarterly* 20 (2): 300–304.

———. 1971. *Hesiod: Theogony*. Oxford: Oxford University Press.

———. 1972. *Iambi et elegi graeci*. 2 vols. Oxford: Oxford University Press.

———. 1978. *Hesiod: Works and Days*. Oxford: Oxford University Press.

———. 1983. *The Orphic Poems*. Oxford: Oxford University Press.

———. 1992. *Ancient Greek Music*. Oxford: Oxford University Press.

Wilamowitz-Moellendorff, Ulrich von. 1959. *Der Glaube der Hellenen*. Darmstadt: Wissenschaftliche Buchgesellschaft.

Wolkow, Benjamin M. 2007. "The Mind of a Bitch: Pandora's Motive and Intent in the *Erga*." *Hermes* 135 (3): 247–62.

Redundant references (e.g., the occurrence of "Hekate" in the hymn to Hekate) are generally not included. Geographical and ethnic designations are combined under one heading where both occur in the notes (e.g., Egyptians under Egypt). If an author is indirectly cited or not given a reference in the notes, the author's name appears in this list, not the Index Locorum. Numbers in parentheses after a deity's name indicate the number of the hymn that is dedicated to that deity, and the entry is in bold font. Individuals belonging to a group are referred to that group, unless they are significant independent figures in their own right (e.g., Styx is listed separately from the Okeanids) and/or the sources offer contradictory accounts (e.g., Dione).

ODYSSEUS, *notes:* 11i, 12i, 18.9, 19i, 23.5–7,
 25.4–8, 28.10, 29i, 32i, 32.11, 51i, 51.12, 55i,
 65.7, 71.4–5, 72i, 74i, 81.3–4, 83.3, 87.9
OGDOAD, *notes:* 11i, 83i
OINOE, see Nymphs
OKEANIDS, *notes:* 22i, 24.9–11, 30i, 51i,
 51.1, 51.4, 51.15–16, 55.9; see also Dione,
 Nymphs, Persuasion, Styx, Tyche
 Doris, *notes:* 24i, 24.9–11
  Eurynome, *notes:* 22.8, 60i, 66i, 83i, 83.8
  Telesto, *note:* 71.1
OKEANOS (83), *hymns:* O, 11, 22, 38, 51;
 notes: 3i, 4i, 6.3, 8.16, 10.21–24, 12.3, 22i,
 22.7, 22.8, 24.9–11, 51.1, 60i, 69.4, 79i, 81i,
 82.4
OLD MAN OF THE SEA, *notes:* 23i, 25i; see
 also Nereus, Proteus
OLEN, *notes:* 2i, 58i
OLYMPIA, *notes:* 12i, 15i, 16i, 19i, 32.12, 33i
OLYMPIAN GAMES, *notes:* 12i, 15i, 34.3, 75i
OLYMPIAS, *note:* 46.7
OLYMPOS, *hymns:* 14, 25, 38, 45, 55, 56, 59;
 notes: O.19, O.25, 2i, 11i, 12i, 14.9–10, 16i,
 22.8, 39i, 43i, 44.6–9, 55.15–28, 59.3–4, 61i,
 65i, 66i, 76.2, 83i, 83.8
ONOMAKRITOS, *note:* 12i
OPHION, *notes:* 22.8, 83i
OREADS, see Nymphs
OREITHYIA, *notes:* 80i, 80.2
ORESTES, *notes:* 36i, 69i, 70.9, 75.6–8
ORION, *note:* 78i
ORPHEUS, *hymn:* O; *notes:* Oi, O.18, 1i, 2i,
 3i, 4.5, 6.8, 8i, 8.9, 10i, 10.14–16, 11i, 11.9,
 12i, 14i, 16i, 17i, 18.16, 22.8, 24.9–11, 25.4–8,
 34i, 34.8, 40i, 40.1, 41i, 45i, 45.3, 45.5, 48i,
 51.15–16, 54.10, 56i, 58.5–7, 59.3–4, 59.11–14,
 59.end, 63i, 65.7, 66i, 67.4, 76i, 76.7,
 76.8–10, 80.2, 83i, 84i, 87.9; see also Index
 Locorum
 works
  Enthronements of the Mother, note: 27i
  Korybantic Rite, note: 27i
  Lesser Krater, notes: 17i, 51.15–16
  Lyre, note: 11i
  Rhapsodies, notes: O.19, 3i, 4i, 6i, 6.1,
   6.3, 10.26, 13.3, 15.3–5, 19.16–17, 21i, 34.8,
   43i, 60i
  Thuēpolikon, note: Oi

ORTHEIA, *note:* 36.8
ORTHRIA, *note:* 78i
ORTYGIA, *hymn:* 35; *note:* 35.5
OSIRIS, *notes:* 34.7, 42i; see also Attis

PAIAN/PAION, *hymns:* 8, 11, 12, 34, 52, 67;
 notes: 8.11, 8.12, 10i, 11.10–12, 12.3, 12.10,
 34.1, 34.7, 34.24–25, 52.11, 67.1, 67.6; see
 also Apollon, Asklepios, Pan, Sun
PALAIKASTRO, *notes:* 15i, 31i, 45.7
PALAIMON/MELIKERTES (75), *hymn:* O;
 notes: 1.3, 14.8–9, 17.9–10, 73i, 74i
PALLADION, *note:* 32i
PALLAS, see Athene, Giants
PAN (11), *hymns:* O, 34, 51; *notes:* 6.3, 6.9,
 8.11, 10i, 10.14–16, 12i, 12.6, 12.10, 15.3–5,
 24.9–11, 25i, 27.8, 32.6, 34i, 34.1, 34.24–25,
 45.7, 46.7, 51i, 51.3, 51.8, 55.8, 64.2–4, 65.7,
 71.11; see also Zeus
 Paian, *hymn:* 11; *note:* 11.10–12
PANATHENAIA, *note:* 32i
PANDORA, *notes:* O.25, 13.1, 23.5–7, 28.10, 43i,
 55.9, 60i, 66i
PANIC, *note:* 65i
PANTIKAPAION, *note:* 74i
PAPAS, see Attis
PAPHLAGONIANS, *note:* 53i
PAPHOS, *note:* 57.4
PAPPOSILENOS, see Satyrs
PARIS, *note:* 55i
 Judgment of, *note:* Oi
PARMENIDES, *note:* 8i
PARNASSOS, *notes:* 34.1, 46i, 51i
PAROS, *note:* 11i
PARTHENON, *note:* 33i
PASIPHAE, see Moon
PATROKLOS, *notes:* 80–82i, 86i
PEGASOS, *notes:* 17i, 32.12
PEIRITHOÖS, *note:* 12.16
PELEUS, *notes:* 25.4–8, 79i
PENELOPE, *notes:* 11i, 86i
PENTHEUS, *notes:* 14.6, 30.3–4, 45.5, 47.5
PEPROMENE, *note:* 59.18
PERGAMON, *notes:* O.25, 3i, 32.13, 42i, 76i
PERIKIONIOS (47), see Dionysos
PERSEPHONE (29), *hymns:* O, 24, 30, 41,
 43, 44, 46, 53, 56, 57, 70, 71; *notes:* 1i, 1.4,
 8i, 8.1, 9.3, 12.16, 13.6, 14i, 14.8–9, 15i, 17i,

PYLADES, *note:* 75.6–8

PYLOS, *note:* 17i

PYTHAGORAS, *notes:* 4.3, 5.4, 8.9, 10i, 12i, 31i, 59.3–4, 63.7, 69.15, 69.16; see also Index Locorum

PYTHIA, *note:* 79.4

PYTHO, see Delphi

PYTHON, *hymns:* 34, 79; *notes:* 34.3, 46i, 79.3–6, 79.5

RAGNARÖK, *note:* 66.4–5

RENENUTET, *notes:* 73i, 73.4

RHADAMANTHYS, *notes:* 18.16, 87.8

RHAMNOUS, *notes:* 61i, 79i

RHARION, *note:* 41i

RHEA (14), *hymns:* O, 13; *notes:* 10.1, 10.14–16, 13i, 13.1, 13.7, 14i, 14.1, 14.3, 14.8, 14.9–10, 15i, 15.10–11, 16i, 17i, 18i, 22.8, 26i, 27i, 27.12, 29i, 30.2, 31i, 32i, 39i, 40i, 41.1–2, 55.4–7, 69i, 71.11, 84i; see also Kybele
    Antaia, *note:* 41.1
    Demeter, *note:* 40i

RHENEIA, *note:* 35.5

RHESOS, *note:* 76i

RHODES, *notes:* 8i, 8.19, 9i

RITES, *note:* 3i

ROME, *notes:* 29i, 31.1–4, 47.5, 76i, 84i, 84.4

SABAZIOS (48), *notes:* 14.8–9, 46i, 46.2–3, 49i
    Sabos, *hymn:* 49; *notes:* 42.6, 49.2, 50.2

SAKADAS, *note:* 34.3

SALII, *note:* 31.1–4

SAMOS, *note:* 35.5

SAMOTHRACE, *hymn:* 38; *notes:* O.20–22, 33i, 38i, 74i

SAMOTHRACIAN GODS, *notes:* O.20–22, 38i, 39i, 74i, 80–82i

SANDOKOS, *note:* 56.4

SAPPHO, *note:* 9i, 58.5–7; see also Index Locorum

SARPEDON, *note:* 85i

SATURN (planet), *note:* 7.8

SATURNALIA, *note:* 13i

SATYRS (54), *notes:* 12i, 14.3, 31i, 31.1–4, 47i, 50i, 51i, 52i, 66i; see also Silenos
    Marsyas, *note:* 54i
    Papposilenos, *note:* 54i

SCHERIA, *note:* 65.7

SEA (22), *note:* 83i; see also Pontos, Tethys

SEASONS (43), *hymns:* O, 11, 26, 29; *notes:* 8.11, 15.10–11, 29.9, 40.18–20, 55i, 55.9, 59i, 60i, 62i, 63i, 79i; see also Dike
    Eirene, *hymn:* 43; *notes:* 15.10–11, 40.2, 40.18–20, 43i
    Eunomia, *hymns:* 43, 60; *notes:* 40.18–20, 43i, 60i, 72i
    Karpo, *note:* 43i
    Thallo, *note:* 43i

SELENE, see Moon

SEMELE (44), *notes:* 12i, 15i, 16i, 19i, 30.2, 42.10, 45.1, 46.6–7, 47i, 47.5, 50i, 51i, 52.2–3, 52.5, 66.12, 67.1, 74i
    Thyone, *note:* 44i

SEXUAL PASSION, *note:* 3.2

SHAME, *notes:* O.25, 61i

SHAY, *note:* 73i

SIKYON, *note:* 68i

SILENOS (54), *notes:* 10.14–16, 11i, 44i, 57.3–5, 67.5; see also Satyrs

SINTIES, *note:* 66i

SIRENS, *note:* 8.9

SISYPHOS, *notes:* 69.15, 75i, 87i, 87.8, 87.9

SKAMANDROS, *notes:* 9.1–2, 66i

SKY (4), *hymns:* 27, 37, 79; *notes:* 3i, 3.1, 5i, 5.1, 6.2, 7.9, 8i, 8.1, 8.7, 10.18, 10.21–24, 10.26, 13i, 13.3, 13.6, 14i, 14.1, 14.8–9, 15i, 15.7, 16i, 26i, 26.2, 32i, 37i, 51i, 55i, 58i, 59i, 69i, 70.6, 73.2, 76i, 76.8–10, 77i, 79i, 83i, 83.8, 84.5

SKYTHINOS OF TEOS, *note:* 8.9

SLEEP (85), *notes:* 3i, 3.6, 5i, 72i, 83i, 86i

SMYRNA (person), see Myrrh

SMYRNA (place), *notes:* 61i, 72i

SOKONOPIS, *notes:* 73i, 73.4

SOKRATES, *notes:* 8.16, 18.16, 21i, 54.10, 67i, 73i, 84i, 87.3–4

SOPHOKLES, *note:* 67i; see also Index Locorum

SPARTA, *notes:* 11i, 31i, 34i, 34.16–23, 36.8, 38i, 61i, 69i, 73.4, 78i, 80–82i

SPRING OF FORGETFULNESS, *notes:* 77i, 85.8

STARS (7), *hymn:* O; *notes:* 5i, 6i, 9i, 10.21–24, 33i, 42.11, 58.2

STEROPES, see Kyklopes

STOICISM, 5.2, 5.4, 8.16, 10i, 12i, 21i, 25.2–3,

INDEX LOCORUM

See also Index Nominum for general references to authors.

AELIAN (fragments)
  19: O.18
AELIUS ARISTIDES, *Orations*
  40.12: 12.10
  46.40: 75i
  47–52: 86i
AESCHYLUS
  Agamemnon
    104–257: 36i
    1327–1330: 59.6–7
  Bassarai or *Bassarides*: 8i, 45i
  Eumenides: 69i
    1–8: 79.3–6
    292–294: 32.13
    321–323: 69i
    329–330: 70.9
    334–339: 69.16
    342–343: 70.9
    490–565: 69.15
    736–738: 32.10
    903–967: 70i
    1004ff.: 70.2–3
  Libation Bearers
    1048–1050: 69.16
  Prometheus Bound: 83.8
    88–92: 8.1

  90: 10.1
  201–218: 79i
  209–210: 79i
  436–506: 40.8–9, 66i
  936: 61i
  Suppliant Women
    674–677: 2i
AESOP, *Fables*
  18: 80.2
ALKAIOS (fragments)
  34: 38i
  129: 16i, 16.4, 30.5
  327: 58.5–7, 81i
  343: 51i
  349: 66i
ALKMAN (fragments, *PMGF*)
  1: 7.12–13, 36i, 78i
  1.60–63: 78i
  5 fr. 2 col. iii: O.41
  46: 71.1
  58: 58.3
  64: 72i
  67: 76i
  89.3–5: 78.6–10, 78.11–12
ANAKREON (fragments, *PMG*)
  356a: 45i

to Hermes (no. 4): 28i, 56i
 4.1–19: 28.1
 4.429–430: 77i
 4.450–452: 76i
 4.533–566: 28i
 4.567–568: 28i
 4.572: 57i
to Aphrodite (no. 5): 55.1
 5.1–44: 55i
 5.1: 77i
 5.2–6: 55.4–7, 78.11–12
 5.8–15: 32.8
 5.16–20: 36i
 5.21–32: 84i
 5.33–43: 55.3
 5.60–64: 60i
 5.97–99: 51i
 5.218–238: 78i
 5.256–275: 51.3, 51.14
 5.262–263: 54i
to Aphrodite (no. 6): 55i, 55.1
 6.5–18: 43i
to Dionysos (no. 7): 30i
 7.1: 44i
 7.13–15: 50i
 7.38–42: 47i
 7.44: 50.5
to Ares (no. 8): 7.8, 65i
to Artemis (no. 9): 36i
to Aphrodite (no. 10): 55.1
to Athene (no. 11): 32i
to Hera (no. 12): 16i
to the Mother of the Gods (no. 14):
14i, 27i
 14.1: 26.1
 14.3: 27.11
 14.4: 27.2
to Herakles (no. 15): 12i
to Asklepios (no. 16)
 16.2–3: 67i
 16.4: 67.2
to the Dioskouroi (no. 17): 38i
to Hermes (no. 18): 28.1
to Pan (no. 19): 11i, 14i
 19.19–27: 51.8
 19.21: 11.9
 19.27–47: 11i
 19.47: 11i

to Hephaistos (no. 20): 66i
to Apollon (no. 21): 34i
to Poseidon (no. 22)
 22.6: 17.1
to Zeus (no. 23): 15i
to Hestia (no. 24): 84i
to the Muses and Apollon (no. 25):
34i, 34.6
to Dionysos (no. 26): 30i, 46.5
 26.2: 44i
 26.3–9: 46.2–3
to Artemis (no. 27): 36i
 27.11–20: 36i
to Athene (no. 28): 32i
to Hestia (no. 29): 84i, 84.8
 29.3–6: 84i
to Earth, Mother of All (no. 30): 14i
 30.1: 26.1
 30.3–4: 14.9–10
 30.5–7: 26.2
 30.17: 26.1
 30.34: 78.11–12
to the Sun (no. 31): 8i
to the Moon (no. 32): 9i
to the Dioskouroi (no. 33): 38i
HORACE, Ars poetica
 239: 54.1
HYGINUS, Fables
 1: 74i
 4: 74i
 166: 66i
IAMBLICHUS, Life of Pythagoras
 82: 59.3–4
 155: 12i
 186: 63.7
IBYKOS (fragments, PMGF)
 286.8–13: 80i
ISIDOROS, Hymns, 73i
 1.1: 73.4
 1.18: 55.15–28
 1.24: 55.15–28
 2.10: 73.4
 3.34: 42.9–10
KALLIMAKHOS
 Hymns
 to Zeus (no. 1): 15i
 1.32–48: 51.3
 1.52–54: 31i